EPISTEMIC

JUSTIFICATION

OTHER WORKS OF WILLIAM P. ALSTON

Philosophy of Language

Divine Nature and Human Language:
  Essays in Philosophical Theology

Religious Belief and Philosophical Thought:
  Readings in the Philosophy of Religion (editor)

Readings in Twentieth-Century Philosophy
  (coeditor with George Nakhnikian)

The Problems of Philosophy: Introductory Readings
  (coeditor with Richard B. Brandt)

Epistemic Justification

ESSAYS IN
the Theory of Knowledge

William P. Alston

Cornell University Press

ITHACA AND LONDON

Copyright © 1989 by Cornell University Press

All rights reserved. Except for brief quotations in a review, this book, or parts thereof, must not be reproduced in any form without permission in writing from the publisher. For information, address Cornell University Press, 124 Roberts Place, Ithaca, New York 14850.

First published 1989 by Cornell University Press.

International Standard Book Number 0-8014-2257-4 (cloth)
International Standard Book Number 0-8014-9544-X (paper)
Library of Congress Catalog Card Number 89-42865
Printed in the United States of America
Librarians: Library of Congress cataloging information
appears on the last page of the book.

The paper in this book is acid-free and meets the guidelines for permanence
and durability of the Committee on Production Guidelines for Book
Longevity of the Council on Library Resources.

To the memory of Paul Henle

Contents

Preface

I am a late bloomer in epistemology. Though I began my career in 1949, my first unambiguously epistemological publication was in 1971, Essay 10 in this volume. Of course, like any other philosopher I could hardly avoid being concerned with problems about knowledge and the justification of belief, but my focus was on other matters until the late 1960s, when a concern with what is distinctive about the mental led me into a serious investigation of privileged epistemic access. This investigation eventuated in Essay 10 and, in the longer run, in a concentration on epistemology in the 1970s and 80s. I chose a fortunate time for this venture. Stimulated by Edmund Gettier's "Is Justified True Belief Knowledge?", the shortest article to be heard round the world, and by the development of causal and reliability accounts of knowledge, the field has been undergoing a remarkable burst of creativity, typified by the publication between 1985 and 1987 of Laurence Bonjour's *The Structure of Empirical Knowledge,* Alvin Goldman's *Epistemology and Cognition,* and Richard Foley's *The Theory of Epistemic Rationality.* It is exciting to be a part of this current ferment in epistemology; it offers one an opportunity of a sort that is, unfortunately, not so common in philosophy: being part of a genuinely cooperative and progressive enterprise.

When I first became a card-carrying epistemologist, my dominant idea was that one could be a foundationalist on the first level, at the price of being a contextualist about epistemic principles. The distinction of levels, which is prominent in these essays, was already at work. In the ensuing years, however, I have come to think that one might be a foundationalist on all levels, basing epistemic principles and other epistemic beliefs on first level foundations of a nonepistemic sort. That possibility, which is broached in Essay 1, is given some substance in Essay 12. The thinking, teaching, and writing on which I was launched by these initial concerns have led me into a variety of problems, some of which are addressed in these essays.

I should like to express gratitude first of all to the people from whom I got my start in epistemology. From the writings of Bertrand Russell, C. I. Lewis, Wilfrid Sellars, and Roderick Firth, I learned much about the problems of epistemology, and about how to think about the subject. In the case of the last named, a year at Harvard in 1955–56 provided the opportunity for extended discussion. Like practically all contemporary American epistemologists, I am greatly in the debt of Roderick Chisholm for his contributions to the field, for his example, and for his encouragement. In the early 1970s I was led by Chisholm to a study of Thomas Reid, and his has been perhaps the most powerful influence on my epistemology, though that is not adequately shown in this volume (see the end of the Introduction). In the late 1960s when I was beginning to move into epistemology, I received a great deal of help and stimulation from Richard Brandt.

As intimated above, the current "epistemological community" is a lively and active one. American Philosophical Association symposia and colloquia, and other gatherings such as the 1986 National Endowment for the Humanities Institute in Theory of Knowledge, provide occasions for discussion and criticism. Among those from whom I have learned much, both in these interchanges and from their writings, I think especially of Robert Audi, Laurence Bonjour, James Cornman, Carl Ginet, Alvin Goldman, Peter Klein, Keith Lehrer, Paul Moser, George Pappas, John Pollock, Ernest Sosa, Marshall Swain, and Frederick Will. Special thanks go to the participants in the 1979–80 sessions of the Center for Christian Studies at Calvin College, particularly George Mavrodes, Alvin Plantinga, and Nicholas Wolterstorff. Interactions with these people made a tremendous difference to my work in epistemology. Among philosophers who are not primarily working on epistemology I would particularly like to thank my chairman, Stewart Thau, for providing an academic environment maximally conducive to philosophical creativity, and my colleague Jonathan Bennett for more hours spent on critical and constructive reactions to my writings than any mortal should be asked to bear.

I would also like to express appreciation to the students in my epistemology courses and seminars over the years, who have provided a constant flow of feedback on my ideas and my work, as well as invigorating this older thinker with fresh infusions of energy and enthusiasm. Special thanks go to the office staff at the Syracuse University Philosophy Department, and especially to Sue McDougal and Lisa Mowins, for their unfailing readiness to type, photocopy, and do whatever else is needed for the greater advancement of epistemology. My thanks go also to the original publishers of these essays for granting me permission to reprint them in this volume. Jonathan Bennett and Robert Audi provided valuable comments on the Introduction.

Last, and therefore most, my everlasting love and gratitude go to my wife, Valerie, for her unfailing love and support, for her inexhaustible willingness to put up with the crochets of a frequently baffled epistemologist, and for providing me with the very model of a mature intelligent cognitive subject, uncorrupted by philosophical biases.

WILLIAM P. ALSTON

Syracuse, New York

Introduction

As the title indicates, the chief focus of this book is *epistemic justification*. But just what is epistemic justification and what is its place in the total scheme of epistemology? That is not a simple question. Let me bring out some of the complexities.

I

But first a word about epistemology. Etymologically epistemology is concerned with knowledge. Well and good. But with what kinds of issues about knowledge does it deal? The issues most prominently displayed differ considerably from one period to another, but some relatively general comments can be made. First of all, like any philosophical scrutiny of anything, it seeks the most basic kind of understanding of its subject matter; it seeks to determine what knowledge is, what it is to know something, what conditions must be satisfied if we are to have one or another kind of knowledge. This inquiry will lead us into similar investigations of what is involved in knowledge: truth, for example. And if being justified in believing that p is part of what it is to know that p (see Essay 7 for a discussion of this), we will be led into a discussion of justification. However, justification will find a place on the agenda quite apart from whether it figures in the analysis of knowledge. In thinking critically about human cognition, we will inevitably be led to reflect on our beliefs and on the conditions under which they are *justified, rational,* or *warranted.*

Implicit in the above is a distinction between what we may term *substantive epistemology* and *meta-epistemology.* Meta-epistemology is concerned with the basic concepts we employ in epistemology, concepts of *knowledge, truth, belief, justification, rationality,* and so on, and with the methods, procedures, and criteria to be employed in determining how to apply those concepts. Substantive epistemology, on the other hand, consists in our endeavors to use these concepts to arrive at results on such matters as the conditions under which we have knowledge or justified belief of one kind or another, and on what knowledge or justified belief we have. This volume is largely devoted to meta-epistemology, though substantive concerns are prominent in Parts I and IV, and in Essay 9.

So far I have been talking as if epistemology were a dispassionate investigation of a subject matter that is admitted on all hands to be sitting there, waiting to be studied. But anyone with even a passing familiarity with the history of philosophy will realize that this is not the case. On the contrary, the most powerful stimulus to reflection about knowledge has been the doubt as to whether there really is any. Skepticism about knowledge, and even about justified or rational belief, has had many powerful spokesmen in ancient Greece, in the Renaissance and early modern period, and today. It has largely been the attempt to answer skeptical doubts and show that we really do have knowledge or justified belief that has given rise to the most probing critical reflection on human cognition. Indeed, some philosophers take it that epistemology just *is* the attempt to answer skepticism, and that no other inquiry deserves that title. However, in opposition to this obsession with skepticism various twentieth-century thinkers who otherwise vary widely in the epistemological orientation—including philosophers as diverse as Chisholm and Quine—have bucked this trend and insisted that human knowledge and justified belief is a subject matter that, like others, we can study without first having to show that it is there to be studied. These essays are written in the spirit of this latter approach. Little will be heard about skepticism. I do not deny that skepticism is worthy of serious and prolonged consideration, but I do deny that it must find a place on every worthwhile epistemological agenda.

II

Now back to the notion of epistemological justification. I could give a simple answer to the question "What is this book about?" if it were the case that epistemologists who say they are dealing with "justification" were, at least for the most part, agreed on a pretheoretical account of what this is, an account that would enable us to unambiguously locate the target about which they are spinning their several theories. But such is far from being the case. Aside from the point that justification is a positive evaluative status of belief, there is no general agreement on what it is we are trying to understand when we investigate justification. And more agreement than that is needed, for it *is* clear that there are positive evaluative statuses of beliefs that are distinct from justification, for example, psychological certainty (the confidence with which a belief is held), and consonance with social consensus. Even if we rule out the above by ruling they are not positively evaluated from the "epistemic point of view", defined by the aim at believing what is true and not believing what is false, this will still not suffice to pick out our quarry. Truth is obviously a desideratum from the epistemic point of view. What more? And yet one might say that the whole point of talking about justification is that a belief may be justified whether or not it is in fact true.

Typically, when epistemologists do the most to tell us what justification *is*, they give us accounts that are far from theoretically neutral. Most explicit accounts are in deontological terms. For example:

> One is *justified* in being confident that p if and only if it is not the case that one ought not to be confident that p; one could not be justly reproached for being confident that p.[1]

But this is by no means theoretically neutral. Many accounts of justification, including my own, do not represent it as freedom from blame, or from having violated one's obligations, or anything else of the sort. Moreover, as is brought out in Essays 4 and 5, there are strong reasons for not taking any such deontological concept of justification as epistemologically viable. The same stricture of theoretical partiality, or worse, will have to be brought against characterizations of justification as "what you can defend against all comers",[2] or, in more elevated terms, what will survive dialectical challenges. Again, some theorists will locate justification on the epistemic map by saying that it is a matter of one's having sufficient reasons for one's belief. But that rules out of court without a hearing any form of immediate justification, such as justification by experience or intuitive obviousness (see Essay 3).

But then how can we specify what various theories of justification are all theories of? Perhaps we can't. Perhaps we will have to conclude that

---

[1]Carl Ginet, *Knowledge, Perception, and Memory* (Dordrecht: D. Reidel, 1975), p. 28.
[2]Richard Rorty, *Philosophy and the Mirror of Nature* (Princeton: Princeton University Press, 1979), p. 308.

the different theories (or a few groups thereof) are really elucidating different sorts of epistemic desiderata and that the only issue between them concerns which of these are more important for one or another purpose. Well, I don't think it's that bad. I will now suggest a way of picking out justification that will accommodate most theories that employ the term, though it will exclude some.

Let's look at another inadequate formulation and then seek to make it adequate. A few paragraphs back we noted that by just saying that justification is a desideratum for belief, from the epistemic point of view, we fail to distinguish it from truth. Of course, we could add "and it isn't truth" to the account, but that would be as desperately ad hoc as the famous definition of a plant as "a living thing that isn't an animal or a mushroom". The adhocness could be reduced by trading on a famous definition of knowledge as *true justified belief*. With that in mind we can say that justification is what must be added to true belief to get knowledge. But there are two difficulties with this. The most well advertised and most widely accepted one stems from Edmund Gettier's famous counterexamples to this definition.[3] His examples, and many others that have been added in the mountainous literature on this issue, make it clear that one can have a true belief that is justified by widely accepted standards, but that does not count as knowledge. For example, one can have a true belief about the weather based on the reading of a barometer that one knows to have been extremely reliable in the past; this true belief would obviously be justified. And yet if the barometer is not functioning at this moment and its reading is just accidentally correct, one could hardly be said to know that a storm is approaching. Again, one could beef up the account to "what has to be added to true belief to get knowledge, in addition to what is needed to deal with Gettier counterexamples", but then adhocness threatens again, especially since the boundaries of the term 'Gettier counterexample' are by no means clear. Here is the second difficulty. As is brought out in Essay 7, there are reasons for denying that justification is even necessary for knowledge. If it is not, then there would be additions to true belief other than justification that would, together with anti-Gettier moves, yield knowledge; and so justification cannot be uniquely identified as what fills that slot.

I don't see any way of remedying these defects other than by introducing an "internalist" constraint. What confers justification must be "internal" to the subject in that she has a specially direct cognitive

---

[3]Edmund L. Gettier, "Is Justified True Belief Knowledge?", *Analysis*, 23 (1963), 121–23.

access to it.[4] It must consist of something like a belief or an experience, something that the subject can typically spot just by turning her attention to the matter. With that further constraint in place we can say that "justification is a *directly cognitively accessible* item that will contribute to making true belief into knowledge". This will solve the Gettier-problem problem, since what has to be there in addition to true justified belief in Gettier cases is, on none of the competing accounts, "internal" in this way. And the formulation doesn't presuppose that justification is *necessary* for knowledge; on the contrary, it leaves open the possibility that other sorts of additions could have the same effect. It only requires that justification be the only efficacious *internal* addition, and there would seem to be no worry on this score. We've already noted that what is introduced to handle Gettier problems is not directly accessible. And what might substitute for justification would be something like reliability of belief formation, which again could hardly be supposed to be ascertainable just on reflection. Note that we have just arrived by a different route at one of the major conclusions of Essay 9: that the justifying ground of a belief must be the sort of thing that is typically directly cognitively accessible.

We have provided directions for picking out justification by relying on an unexamined and unexplicated concept of knowledge, and some might find this unsatisfactory. "After all," one might say, "if you are going to make such a fuss over how to say what justification is, how can you just take it for granted what knowledge is?" That's a fair question, but it has an answer. Whenever we seek to dig into one concept, we have to employ other concepts that are not currently being explicated. It's a matter of using the less obscure or problematic to elucidate the more obscure or problematic. And it seems clear to me that our pre-theoretical grasp of the concept of knowledge is much firmer than that of justification. 'Know' and its cognates are on the lips of Everyman and are employed with considerable consistency; while 'justification' is a term of art in epistemology, though it no doubt finds a place in the vernacular in application to actions. Hence I take it to be quite proper to use our prereflective mastery of the concept of knowledge to provide directions for locating justification.

Here is still another route to our way of picking out justification, one that more closely mirrors the historical development of epistemology. We typically turn our attention to justification and the like when we fall prey to doubts about the possibility of knowledge, about our capacity to get beyond our own thoughts and experiences to the real objective

---

[4]This is one of the modes of internality explored in Essay 8 and made use of in Essay 9.

truth about the world outside our minds. When in the grip of such pessimism it seems that we can at least determine whether it is justified or reasonable for us to hold certain beliefs, whether we have in our possession a sufficient basis for those beliefs. This line of thought leads to the idea that what can serve to justify a belief is something that is directly cognitively accessible to one. For nothing else would lend a belief some rational credibility when we are radically questioning our access to anything beyond our own consciousness. I don't however, wish to rely primarily on this route to an internalist constraint, because I don't want the investigation of justification to *depend* on the cogency of these skeptical doubts about knowledge. Even if they have some force, I deny that the epistemological project depends on that cogency being sufficient to force us into the egocentric position just described.

Unfortunately, our way of identifying justification is not completely theoretically neutral. It will, obviously, not accommodate those theorists who deny that a justifier must be internal in this way. These include Alvin Goldman,[5] who takes reliability of belief formation to be sufficient for justification whether or not the belief is supported by anything to which the subject normally has direct access, and Alvin Plantinga,[6] who takes this line with respect to a belief's resulting from the proper functioning of a cognitive faculty. Sorry about that, fellows, but I see no alternative to saying that you are just not dealing with the same epistemic desideratum as other thinkers when all of us are using the term 'justification'. Apart from an internalist constraint I see no way of differentiating justification from other epistemic desiderata such as truth. That is not to say that what these thinkers have identified is not of epistemic importance; it is only that it must be distinguished from what is properly called 'justification'. Note that Plantinga recognizes this, using the terms 'positive epistemic status' and 'warrant' for what he is focusing on, and reserving 'justification' (much too narrowly in my opinion) for a deontological conception.

III

Now that we have a pretheoretical way of identifying our target we can consider the various options for a theoretical account of its essential nature. But first we must attend to some basic distinctions

[5]"What Is Justified Belief?", in *Justification and Knowledge,* ed. G. S. Pappas (Dordrecht: D. Reidel, 1979); *Epistemology and Cognition* (Cambridge: Harvard University Press, 1986), chaps. 4, 5.
[6]"Positive Epistemic Status and Proper Function," *Philosophical Perspectives,* 2 (1988).

within this ball park. One that is frequently sloughed over, to the detriment of the discussion, is the distinction between the *state* of *being justified* in believing that *p,* and the *activity* of *justifying* the belief that *p,* establishing its truth or showing it to *be justified.* (See Essays 1, 3, and 9 for some examples of the unfortunate consequences of neglecting this distinction.) As is implicit in what was just said, the *state* concept is the more basic one, since the activity of justifying is an activity directed to showing that a belief is in the *state* of being justified. In any event, it is the state or condition of being justified that is the primary focus of discussion in this book. Second, there is the rather mysterious relationship between justification and rationality. Contemporary epistemologists are far from agreed on how to distinguish and interrelate these concepts. This is dramatically brought home by the fact that in two recent works Alvin Goldman chooses to concentrate on justification of the grounds that 'rationality' "is so vague in ordinary usage, and so disparately employed by different philosophers and social scientists",[7] while Richard Foley makes the opposite choice.[8] I won't try to straighten this out here; I suspect it is a tangled web.

As I argue in Essay 4, which is the central essay of this collection, the major distinction between accounts of justification has to do with whether being justified in a belief is taken to be a deontological status: having fulfilled one's intellectual obligations, not having violated such obligations, or something of the sort. In that essay, and in much greater detail in Essay 5, I contend that no form of a deontological conception gives us what we want. Either it makes an unrealistic assumption of the voluntary control of belief or the range of its applications fails to match the class of justified beliefs. The other side of the major divide delineated in Essay 4 is what is there called an "evaluative" conception, evaluative from the "epistemic point of view". More specifically, for one's belief to be a good thing from the epistemic point of view is for it to have been formed or maintained in such a way as to be likely to be true. In other words, it is for the belief to have been formed or maintained in such a way that one is thereby in a *strong position* to get the truth; hence in Essays 7 and 8 it is termed a "strong position" conception. In Essay 4 I fill this out with the further stipulation that the strong position consists in being based on adequate grounds, for prima facie justification, to which we must add "in the absence of sufficient overriding reasons" to get unqualified or "ultima facie" justification. It is argued in Essay 4 that, in the absence of any viable deontological concept, the concept

---

[7]*Epistemology and Cognition,* p. 27.
[8]*The Theory of Epistemic Rationality* (Cambridge: Harvard University Press, 1987).

just specified is the concept of justification we need for epistemology. (I indicate there and elsewhere that I agree that 'justification' is the wrong word for a nondeontological concept, but we seem to be stuck with it in contemporary theory of knowledge.) This way of thinking of justification is further developed in Essay 9, which is largely devoted to making explicit the ways in which justification, on this view, is internalist and the ways in which it is externalist.

In Essay 4, I include, with some reservations, the "based on adequate grounds" component as part of the *concept* of justification, while in Essay 9 this is merely presented as an account of what it takes for justification or as the right way of thinking of justification. So is it part of the concept (part of the meaning of the term) or isn't it? I am not convinced that there is a uniquely right answer to this question. I don't find the distinction between what is part of the concept (meaning) and what belongs to contingent facts about what the concept (term) applies to, to be a sharp one; though I by no means agree with Quine and others that there is no such useful distinction at all. So far as I can see, the distinction between *deontological* and *evaluative* is unambiguously a difference of concepts. If you take being justified to be a matter of being free of violation of obligations in believing that p, and I take it to be a matter of being in a strong position to get the truth in believing that p, I don't see how we could be credited with the same concept, differing only over what is true of that to which the concept applies. On the other hand, if you hold that the justification of perceptual beliefs requires support from the subject's total set of beliefs and I hold that it only requires support by experience, that is no reason for saying that we must be using different concepts of justification, though, of course, we might be. We might both be using a deontological concept, differing as to what intellectual obligations we have. Or we might both be using a strong position conception, differing as to what it takes to be in a strong position to get the truth. But whether being justified in believing that p is a matter of the belief's being based on an adequate ground seems to me to fall into a borderline area. It is not clear to me whether we could be using the same concept and differ about that. Hence I don't feel constrained to choose between Essays 4 and 9 on this point, but if forced to make a choice I will take the less stringent position of Essay 9 and allow the issue to be a factual one.

I can easily lay out the main options for a theory of justification by starting from the account in Essay 9 and considering variations. First of all, there is an internalist-externalist distinction. (For a general discussion of differing forms of this distinction, see Essay 8.) I have already ruled out a total externalism by stipulating that in order to count as a justifier, X must be the sort of thing that is typically directly cognitively accessible to the subject of the belief. This, however, only rules out externalism with respect to grounds; there is also an internalist-externalist distinction with respect to the adequacy of grounds. Is it necessary, and/or sufficient, for being justified in believing that *p,* that the belief be based on a ground that is in fact adequate (externalism); or is it also necessary, and/or sufficient, that the ground be *justifiably believed by the subject to be adequate* (internalism)?[9] In Essay 9 the internalist position is criticized, both on the ground that it is too sophisticated a requirement to be generally applicable to cognitive subjects, and on the ground that it implies that one must have an infinite hierarchy of justified beliefs in order to have even one; but many contemporary epistemologists take the internalist position.[10] The issue is complicated by differences over what it takes for a ground to be adequate; but given a certain view on that point we still have the question as to the respective role of that being the case, and of its being the case according to the subject's best judgment. It should be noted that the decision between a deontological and a strong position conception has an important bearing on this issue. As is pointed out in Essay 8, on a deontological conception, at least on one that takes the formation of beliefs and other propositional attitudes to be subject to obligations, one cannot be credited with a justified belief unless one adopted that belief on the basis of what, according to the best of one's knowledge, is an adequate ground. For if I come to believe that *p* on the basis of what, so far as I can tell, is not an adequate ground, I have violated intellectual obligations in so doing, even if that ground were, unbeknownst to me, an adequate one. Thus from the standpoint of a deontological conception it is the way adequacy is judged from within the subject's perspective on the world, not actual adequacy, that is crucial. And the reverse side of this coin is that on a strong position conception it is actual adequacy that is crucial, for that is what is needed to be in a strong position to get the truth.

It is argued in Essay 6 that "higher level" requirements, like the requirement that *one be justified in believing that the ground of one's belief is an adequate one,* have been greatly encouraged by "level confusions",

[9]In Essay 4 the externalist version of such requirements is called "objective", and the internalist version identified here is called "cognitive". The latter is in contrast to a more subjective requirement that only calls for the subject to believe that the ground is adequate. Richard Foley, *Theory of Epistemic Rationality,* supports a requirement that is intermediate between the "cognitive" requirement that calls for an objective justification for the subject's belief in the adequacy of the ground, and the radically subjective requirement that only calls for the belief.

[10]See the references to Wilfrid Sellars and Laurence Bonjour in Essay 3.

like the confusion between being justified in believing that p and being justified in believing that *one is justified in believing that p*. For it is clear that one must be justified in believing that the ground of one's belief that p is adequate if one is to be justified in believing that *one is justified in believing that p*. And so if that higher level belief is not clearly distinguished from the lower level belief that p, one may be led to suppose that the requirements for the former are also requirements for the latter. In Essay 6 various unfortunate results of this confusion are chronicled, and the confusion is also held responsible for important errors in Essays 1, 8, and 11.

The other major distinction I will mention here concerns whether it is enough for justification that the subject *have* an adequate ground or whether it must also be the case that the belief be based on that ground. Is it enough for me to be justified in believing that the butler did it, that I have enough evidence in my possession to support that judgment adequately, or must it also be the case that I come to believe this *because of* that evidence? In Essays 4 and 9 I argue that the "source relevant" concept that requires the right basis for the belief is a more complete concept of what it takes for one's belief to be epistemically desirable, and that the concept that requires mere possession of the adequate ground can be seen as only part of the whole picture. After all, even if I have adequate evidence for pinning it on the butler, if I come to believe this just because I don't like the butler's looks, I have not formed the belief in a way that is well calculated to lead to the truth. Nevertheless, it cannot be denied that the "possession" concept identifies an important epistemic desideratum and identifies a state we can be in vis-à-vis many possible beliefs that are not actually formed, beliefs with respect to which the question of a basis does not arise.

Thus the account of epistemic justification that emerges from these essays, most explicitly in Essays 4 and 9, is the following. To be justified in believing that p is for that belief to be based on an adequate ground. The ground must be of a sort that is typically directly cognitively accessible to normal human subjects; and the adequacy is a matter of the ground's being sufficiently indicative of the truth of the belief. To be in this condition is to hold the belief in such a way as to be in a strong position to get the truth, whether or not the belief is in fact true. It is clear that justification on this understanding makes an important contribution toward making a true belief into knowledge, and that, more generally, it is a highly desirable condition vis-à-vis the basic aim at attaining the true and avoiding the false. Moreover, it avoids implausible assumptions of voluntary control of doxastic attitudes, and it avoids infinite regresses that plague accounts that require a cognitive grasp by the subject of the fact that the grounds are adequate or that other conditions for justification are satisfied. Much more remains to be done to develop this account and to defend it against its competitors, but the outlines are provided in Essays 4 and 9.[11]

IV

So much for the most general meta-epistemological considerations concerning epistemic justification. Let's turn to more substantive matters. One issue much discussed by epistemologists concerns the general structure of knowledge or justified belief. To get into this, let's first distinguish between *mediate (indirect)* and *immediate (direct)* justification. A belief is *mediately* justified if and only if what justifies it is its relation to some other justified beliefs of the same subject, as when I am justified in supposing that Jones is having a party because I base that belief on my justified belief that there are a lot of cars parked in front of his house. Whereas a belief is *immediately* justified if and only if it is justified in some other way: by experience, by self-evidence, or whatever. Thus if I am justified in believing that my watch is on the desk because of my visual experience, or if I am justified in believing that $2 + 3 = 5$ because it is obvious to me that this is the case, these are examples of immediate justification.

Discussions of the general structure of knowledge or justified belief (from here on we will focus on justified belief) have been dominated by the contrast between *foundationalism* and *coherence theory*. Let's confine this discussion to the structure of an individual person's set of justified beliefs. According to foundationalism (1) each person has a set of immediately justified beliefs, and (2) the justification of each mediately justified belief can be traced back to one or more members of that initial set (the *foundations*).[12] Coherence theory denies (1) and hence denies (2). It holds that any justified belief has this status because and only because of the way it fits into the person's total set of beliefs (or some other large system of beliefs).

The above represents the core of foundationalism, but in the most historically prominent forms of the doctrine this core has been obscured by other elements that are not at all required for their being cases of foundationalism. These include constraints on the foundations

[11]The account is defended vis-à-vis Alvin Goldman's reliabilism in "Goldman on Epistemic Justification," *Philosophia* (Israel), 19 (1989), and against Richard Foley's more subjectivist account in "Foley's Theory of Epistemic Rationality," *Philosophy and Phenomenological Research*, 50 (1989).

[12]For more detailed formulations see Essays 1 and 2.

in addition to their being immediately justified: that they be infallible, incorrigible, or indubitable (see Essay 10 on these terms), or that the individual be immediately justified in holding the higher level belief that a particular foundation is immediately justified (Essay 1). There are also special requirements on the way in which the superstructure is derived from the foundations, for instance, that it be by deductive inference. Moreover, most of the attacks on foundationalism have concentrated on these peripheral, inessential elements and hence have failed to provide any general arguments against foundationalism as such.[13] See Essay 2 for documentation of this charge. One sort of criticism that really does strike at the heart of foundationalism is the attack on the possibility of immediately justified beliefs. To be sure, the commitment to immediate justification is not equivalent to a commitment to foundationalism, for there could be immediately justified beliefs without all other justification being based on them. Nevertheless, immediate justification is obviously necessary for foundationalism, and anything that strikes at the former automatically strikes at the latter. In Essay 3 I consider the most prominent current objections to immediate justification and conclude that they are without force.

Thus what emerges from Essays 1–3 is that foundationalism can by no means be counted out of the competition. The frequent obituaries, insofar as they are justified at all, concern one or another special form of the doctrine, not its most distinctive claims. But I do not wish to deny that serious problems remain to be surmounted before we have a completely adequate form of the doctrine. First, there are issues concerning the conditions under which a belief is immediately justified. Some of the possibilities for immediate justification are briefly canvassed and discussed in Essay 11; and the matter is touched on in Essays 2, 3, and 10. It is unfortunate that in most discussions, both pro and con, only one mode of immediate justification is in the picture. When the fate of foundationalism is made to rest on only one possibility for immediate justification, its prospects are not exhibited in the strongest light. But the most serious issue concerns what it takes to get the superstructure from the foundations. The seventeenth- and eighteenth-century foundationalists put themselves in a bind by restricting the foundations to the self-evident and to what one knows about one's own conscious states. This made it impossible to derive what we know or are justified in believing about the physical and social world without performing a

---

[13]In these latter days the term 'foundationalism' has come to be used with disreputable looseness in more literary circles. I won't venture into that swamp.

phenomenological reduction of this latter. In recent decades various proposals have been made to enlarge the foundational base to include (some) perceptual beliefs about the physical environment, beliefs about other people, and even beliefs about God. But even when the foundations are expanded to the limits of plausibility, there are still difficult questions as to what kinds of relationship to the foundations will render a nonfoundation justified. These sorts of questions are familiar not only from general epistemology, but also from attempts in the philosophy of science to determine how scientific hypotheses and theories can be based on observations. In both cases it seems that deductive inference and commonly recognized modes of inductive inference will not suffice to do the trick. Other modes of derivation will be required, but on what basis do we decide what other modes to allow? Chisholm attempts to cut the Gordian knot by, in effect, holding that we can allow whatever derivations are needed to get from the foundations to whatever else we recognize to be justified. But this move can be criticized as unfairly stacking the cards in favor of foundationalism. I don't mean to suggest that this problem is insoluble, only that it still needs a lot of work.

However incompletely developed foundationalism may be, it is in excellent shape compared with coherentism. Coherentism continues to be faced with the stubborn fact that, however the notion of coherence is spelled out, it seems clear that there is an indefinitely large multiplicity of equally coherent systems of belief, with no way provided by coherence theory for choosing between them. Furthermore, it just seems obvious that many beliefs, for example, simple perceptual or introspective beliefs, are justified regardless of how they fit into some larger system of belief. These criticisms, however, apply only to pure coherentism, the foil to the pure foundationalism we have been discussing. One useful point that has emerged from recent discussions is that there can be mixed views. A simple mix would be a structure with a foundation of purely immediately justified beliefs but with coherence consideration coming into the conditions for mediate justification. A more even-handed mix would be one in which the foundations as well are not so pure; each foundation is only partly immediately justified; it also requires support from other parts of the system to bring it up to a level of justification required for acceptability. In this version there is still a distinction between foundations and the rest of the system in that only foundations are partly immediately justified. The predominance would be tilted in the coherentist direction by a version in which every belief is partly immediately justified and partly mediately justified, though I find such a system quite implausible. In any event, I hope and expect that such mixed systems will be extensively explored in the coming years.

Essays 10 and 11 are primarily concerned with the epistemic status of beliefs about one's own current conscious states, though in Essay 11 there is a general epistemological background for this investigation. Essay 10 is specifically concerned with elucidating and interrelating various ways in which a person might be thought to have "privileged access" to her own states of consciousness. Actually much of this paper could be usefully embodied in an essay entitled "Epistemic Immunities", since a great deal of the essay is concerned with distinguishing and discussing one or another way in which we or our beliefs are sometimes thought to be immune from one or another epistemic disability: mistake, ignorance, doubt, or refutation. Essay 11 is centrally concerned with developing and defending a particular view as to what renders beliefs about one's own current conscious states justified: the idea that they are "self-warranted", justified just by being the kinds of beliefs they are. Unfortunately this view is incompatible with the view defended in Essays 4 and 9 that any justified belief has that status only because it is based on an adequate ground. If that is what makes even these beliefs justified, they are definitely not self-warranted. In the last paragraph of section V, Essay 4, I suggest that the beliefs discussed in Essay 11 can be viewed as limiting cases of beliefs based on an adequate ground, cases in which the ground is not distinguishable from the fact that makes the belief true. This would, however, assimilate these beliefs to what in Essay 11 is called "truth-warrant" rather than to self-warrant. Moreover, there are independent reasons for abandoning the self-warrant thesis. Although it still seems clear to me that beliefs about one's own current conscious states are, as I argued in Essay 11, either always or almost always true, I now think that this is best accounted for not by regarding them as self-warranted, but by the supposition that they are normally formed by a certain maximally reliable belief-forming mechanism, maximally reliable just because the state in question is, so to say, "self-luminous", or "self-presenting", and so serves as an adequate ground for a belief that it itself obtains. For if one should be so abnormal as to just guess at what conscious states one is in currently, the beliefs so formed should not count as justified, as they would if such beliefs are self-warranted. I include Essay 11 in the collection, despite my apostasy from its central thesis, partly because of the general framework in which that thesis is set, and partly because I think that the case for the self-warrant thesis set out there is worth preserving.

V

Essay 12 stands apart from the rest in being concerned with fundamental issues concerning the epistemology of epistemology, that is, with the epistemic status of epistemic principles, with how we determine what is required for the justification of various sorts of belief. The account of justification set out in Essays 4 and 9 represent principles of justification as making claims about the reliability of one or another *source* of belief, or, otherwise put, claims about the reliability of one or another belief-producing *mechanism*. And quite apart from how we analyze *justification,* questions about the reliability of the sources of our beliefs are of great interest to us. Where we are dealing with what we might naturally call "basic sources", sources the reliability of which we cannot investigate on the basis of information we get from other sources (i.e., sources whose reliability only shows itself when we use those very sources), the attempt to show that such a source is reliable falls into what is naturally called "epistemic circularity". In Essay 12 I argue that, despite appearances to the contrary, epistemic circularity does not prevent us from being able to justify, or from being justified in holding, the thesis that, for example, sense perception is a reliable source of belief, although it does interfere with the attainment of a traditional philosophical goal of "fully reflective justification". Nevertheless, the conclusion of the essay is only that epistemic circularity will not prevent us from showing that, for instance, sense perception is reliable *if sense perception is in fact reliable.* And one might well want to get rid of that *if,* especially since the above conditional holds of any belief-forming procedure, however outrageous. How can we find a basis for distinguishing between basic sources that it is rational to use and those it is not? This more radical question is not confronted in these essays, though it is in a forthcoming programmatic essay, "A 'Doxastic Practice' Approach to Epistemology".[14] There, building on work by Wittgenstein and, more especially, Reid, I argue that the most reasonable approach to take to this matter is to regard any socially established belief-forming practice as rationally engaged in unless we have sufficient reason to regard it as unreliable, and especially if the practice displays an appropriate kind of "self-support". I have begun to apply this idea to the "perceptual" justification of beliefs about God.[15] But this is largely work for the future.

[14]In *Knowledge and Scepticism,* ed. Marjorie Clay and Keith Lehrer (Boulder, Colo.: Westview Press, 1989).

[15]See, e.g., "Perceiving God," *Journal of Philosophy,* 83 (November 1986), 655–65; "Christian Experience and Christian Belief," in *Faith and Rationality,* ed. A. Plantinga and N. Wolterstorff (Notre Dame, Ind.: University of Notre Dame Press, 1983).

Introduction

A word of explanation about the distinction between footnotes and endnotes. Footnotes appear as they were in the original articles with very minor modifications, mostly updating of references. Endnotes have been added for this book. They are designed for current reflections on certain points in the essays and for interrelating the essays.

PART I

FOUNDATIONALISM

Two Types of Foundationalism

Foundationalism is often stated as the doctrine that knowledge constitutes a structure the foundations of which support all the rest but themselves need no support. To make this less metaphorical we need to specify the mode of support involved. In contemporary discussions of foundationalism knowledge is thought of in terms of true justified belief (with or without further conditions); thus the mode of support involved is justification, and what gets supported a belief.[1] The sense in which a foundation needs no support is that it is not justified by its relation to other justified beliefs; in that sense it does not "rest on" on other beliefs. Thus we may formulate foundationalism as follows:

(I) Our justified beliefs form a structure, in that some beliefs (the foundations) are justified by something other than their relation to other justified beliefs; beliefs that *are* justified by their relation to other beliefs all depend for their justification on the foundations.

Notice that nothing is said about *knowledge* in this formulation. Since the structure alleged by foundationalism is a structure of the justification of belief, the doctrine can be stated in terms of that component of knowledge alone. Indeed, one who thinks that knowledge has nothing to do with justified belief is still faced with the question of whether

From *The Journal of Philosophy*, 73, no. 7 (1976), 165–85. Reprinted by permission of the editors.

[1]Contemporary writers on foundationalism do not seem to notice that Descartes and Locke have a quite different view of knowledge and, hence, that, if they hold that knowledge rests on foundations, this will mean something rather different. See below, p. 35, for a translation of a bit of Descartes into current foundationalist idiom.

foundationalism is a correct view about the structure of epistemic justification.

Two emendations will render this formulation more perspicuous. First, a useful bit of terminology. Where what justifies a belief includes[2] the believer's having certain other justified beliefs, so related to the first belief as to embody reasons or grounds for it, we may speak of *indirectly (mediately) justified belief.* And, where what justifies a belief does not include any such constituent, we may speak of *directly (immediately) justified belief.* Correspondingly, a case of knowledge in which the justification requirement is satisfied by indirect (mediate) justification will be called *indirect (mediate) knowledge;* and a case in which the justification requirement is satisfied by direct (immediate) justification will be called *direct (immediate) knowledge.*

Second, we should make more explicit how mediate justification is thought to rest on immediately justified belief. The idea is that, although the other beliefs involved in the mediate justification of a given belief may themselves be mediately justified, if we continue determining at each stage how the supporting beliefs are justified, we will arrive, sooner, or later, at directly justified beliefs. This will not, in general, be a single line of descent; typically the belief with which we start will rest on several beliefs, each of which in turn will rest on several beliefs. So the general picture is that of multiple branching from the original belief.

With this background we may reformulate foundationalism as follows (turning the "foundation" metaphor on its head):

(II) Every mediately justified belief stands at the origin of a (more or less) multiply branching tree structure at the tip of each branch of which is an immediately justified belief.

(II) can be read as purely hypothetical (*if* there are any mediately justified beliefs, then . . .) or with existential import (There are mediately justified beliefs, and . . .). Foundationalists typically make the latter claim, and I shall understand the doctrine to carry existential import.

(II) can usefully be divided into two claims:

(A) There are directly justified beliefs.
(B) A given person has a stock of directly justified beliefs sufficient to

[2]Only 'includes', because other requirements are also commonly imposed for mediate justification, e.g., that the first belief be "based" on the others, and, by some epistemologists, that the believer realize that the other beliefs do constitute adequate grounds for the first.

generate chains of justification that terminate in whatever indirectly
justified beliefs he has.

In other words, (A) there are foundations, and (B) they suffice to hold
up the building.

In this essay we shall restrict our attention to (A). More specifically,
we shall be concerned with a certain issue over what it takes for a belief
to serve as a foundation.

I. The Second Level Argument

Let's approach this issue by confronting foundationalism with a
certain criticism, a recent version of which can be found in Bruce
Aune.[3]

> The line of reasoning behind the empiricist's assumption is, again, that
> while intra-language rules may validly take us from premise to conclu-
> sion, they cannot themselves establish empirical truth. If the premises
> you start with are false, you will have no guarantee that the conclusions
> you reach are not false either. Hence, to attain knowledge of the actual
> world, you must ultimately have premises whose truth is acceptable inde-
> pendently of any inference and whose status is accordingly indubitable.
> Only by having such premises can you gain a starting point that would
> make inference worthwhile. For convenience, these indispensable basic
> premises may be called "intrinsically acceptable." The possibility of em-
> pirical knowledge may then be said to depend on the availability of
> intrinsically acceptable premises.
>   If this line of thought is sound, it follows that utter scepticism can be
> ruled out only if one can locate basic empirical premises that are intrin-
> sically acceptable. Although philosophers who attack scepticism in accor-
> dance with this approach generally think they are defending common
> sense, it is crucial to observe that they cannot actually be doing so. The
> reason for this is that, from the point of view of common experience,
> there is no plausibility at all in the idea that intrinsically acceptable prem-
> ises, as so defined, ever exist. Philosophers defending such premises fail
> to see this because they always ignore the complexity of the situation in
> which an empirical claim is evaluated.
>   I have already given arguments to show that introspective claims are
> not, in themselves, intrinsically infallible, they may be regarded as vir-
> tually certain if produced by a reliable (sane, clear-headed) observer, but
> their truth is not a consequence of the mere fact that they are confidently

[3]*Knowledge, Mind and Nature* (New York: Random House, 1967).

made. To establish a similar conclusion regarding the observation claims of everyday life only the sketchiest arguments are needed. Obviously the mere fact that such a claim is made does not assure us of its truth. If we know that the observer is reliable, made his observation in good light, was reasonably close to the object, and so on, then we may immediately regard it as acceptable. But its acceptability is not intrinsic to the claim itself. ... I would venture to say that any spontaneous claim, observational or introspective, carries almost no presumption of truth, when considered entirely by itself. If we accept such a claim as true, it is only because of our confidence that a complex body of background assumptions—concerning observers, standing conditions, the kind of object in question—and, often, a complex mass of further observations all point to the conclusion that it is true.

Given these prosaic considerations, it is not necessary to cite experimental evidence illustrating the delusions easily brought about by, for example, hypnosis to see that no spontaneous claim is acceptable wholly on its own merits. On the contrary, common experience is entirely adequate to show that clear-headed men never accept a claim merely because it is made, without regard to the peculiarities of the agent and of the conditions under which it is produced. For such men, the acceptability of every claim is always determined by inference. If we are prepared to take these standards of acceptability seriously, we must accordingly admit that the traditional search for intrinsically acceptable empirical premises is completely misguided. (pp. 41–43)

Now the target of Aune's critique differs in several important respects from the foundationalism defined above. First and most obviously, Aune supposes that any "intrinsically acceptable premises" will be infallible and indubitable, and some of his arguments are directed specifically against these features.[4] Second, there is an ambiguity in the term 'intrinsically acceptable'. Aune introduces it to mean "whose truth is acceptable independently of any inference"; this looks roughly equivalent to our 'directly justified'. However, in arguing against the supposition that the "observation claims of everyday life" are intrinsically acceptable, he says that "the mere fact that such a claim is made does not assure us of its truth", thereby implying that to be intrinsically acceptable a claim would have to be justified just by virtue of being made. Now it is clear that a belief (claim) of which this is true is directly justified, but the converse does not hold. A perceptual belief will also be directly justified, as that term was explained above, if what justifies it is the fact that the perceiver "is reliable, made his observation in good light, was reasonably

---

[4]See the distinctions between infallibility, indubitability, and immediacy in Essay 10.

close to the object, and so on", *provided it is not also required that he be justified in believing that these conditions are satisfied.* Thus this argument of Aune's has no tendency to show that perceptual beliefs cannot be directly justified, but only that they cannot enjoy that special sort of direct justification which we may term "self-justification".[5]

Some of Aune's arguments, however, would seem to be directed against any immediate justification, and a consideration of these will reveal a third and more subtle discrepancy between Aune's target(s) and my version of foundationalism. Near the end of the passage Aune says:

> If we accept such a claim [observational or introspective] as true, it is only because of our confidence that a complex of background assumptions . . . all point to the conclusion that it is true.

And again:

> For such men [clear-headed men], the acceptability of every claim is always determined by inference.

It certainly looks as if Aune is arguing that whenever a claim (belief) is justified, it is justified by inference (by relation to other justified beliefs); and that would be the denial of 'There are directly justified beliefs'. But look more closely. Aune is discussing not what would justify the issuer of an introspective or observational claim in his belief, but rather what it would take to justify "us" in accepting his claim; he is arguing from a third-person perspective. Now it does seem clear that *I* cannot be immediately justified in accepting *your* introspective or observational claim as true. If I am so justified, it is because I am justified in supposing that you issued a claim of that sort, that you are in a normal condition and know the language, and (if it is an observational claim) that conditions were favorable for your accurately perceiving that sort of thing. But that is only because *I*, in contrast to you, am justified in believing that p (where what you claimed is that p, and where I have no independent access to p) only if I am justified in supposing that you are justified in believing that p. My access to p is through your access. It is just because *my* justification in believing that p presupposes my being justified in believing that you are justified, that my justification has to be indirect. That is why I have to look into such matters as conditions of observation and your normality. Thus what

---

[5]In Essays 10 and 11, I use the term 'self-warrant' for a belief that is justified by virtue of being a belief of a certain sort.

Aune is really pointing to is the necessity for "inferential" backing for any higher level belief to the effect that someone is justified in believing that *p*. (I shall call such higher level beliefs *epistemic beliefs*). His argument, if it shows anything, shows that no epistemic belief can be immediately justified. But it does nothing to show that the original observer's or introspector's belief that *p* was not immediately justified. Hence his argument is quite compatible with the view that an introspective belief is self-justified and with the view that an observational belief is justified just by being formed in favorable circumstances.

As a basis for further discussion I should like to present my own version of an argument against the possibility of immediate justification for epistemic beliefs—what I shall call the *second level argument:*

> (A1) Where S's belief that *p* is mediately justified, any justification for the belief that S is *justified in believing that p* is obviously mediate. For one could not be justified in this latter belief unless it were based on a justified belief that S is justified in accepting the grounds on which his belief that *p* is based. But even where S is immediately justified in believing that *p*, the higher level belief will still be mediately justified, if at all. For in taking a belief to be justified, we are evaluating it in a certain way.[6] And, like any evaluative property, epistemic justification is a supervenient property, the application of which is based on more fundamental properties. A belief is justified because it possesses what Roderick Firth has called "warrant-increasing properties".[7] Hence in order for me to be justified in believing that S's belief that *p* is justified, I must be justified in certain other beliefs, viz., that S's *belief that p* possesses a certain property, Q, and that Q renders its possessor justified. (Another way of formulating this last belief is: a belief that there is a valid epistemic principle to the effect that any belief that is Q is justified.) Hence in no case can an epistemic belief that S is justified in believing that *p*, itself be immediately justified.

Before proceeding I shall make two comments on this argument and its conclusion.

(1) It may appear that the conclusion of the argument is incompatible with the thesis that one cannot be justified in believing that *p* without also being justified in believing that one is justified in believing that *p*. For if being immediately justified in believing that *p* necessarily

---

[6]For one attempt to explain the distinctively epistemic dimension of evaluation, see R. M. Chisholm, "On the Nature of Empirical Evidence," in *Empirical Knowledge,* ed. Chisholm and R. J. Swartz (Englewood Cliffs, N.J.: Prentice-Hall, 1973), pp. 225–30.

[7]In "Coherence, Certainty, and Epistemic Priority," *Journal of Philosophy,* 41 (October 15, 1964), 545–57.

carried with it being justified in believing that I am justified in believing that *p*, it would seem that this latter justification would be equally immediate. I would not shirk from such an incompatibility, since I feel confident in rejecting that thesis. It is not clear, however, that there is any such incompatibility. It all depends on how we construe the necessity. If, for example, it is that my being justified in believing that *p* necessarily puts me into possession of the *grounds* I need for being justified in the higher level belief, then that is quite compatible with our conclusion that the latter can only be mediately justified.

(2) The conclusion should not be taken to imply that one must perform any conscious inference to be justified in an epistemic belief, or even that one must be explicitly aware that the lower level belief has an appropriate warrant-increasing property. Here, as in other areas, one's grounds can be possessed more or less implicitly. Otherwise we would have precious little mediate knowledge.

I have already suggested that the second level argument is not really directed against (II). To be vulnerable to this argument, a foundationalist thesis would have to require of foundations not only that *they* be immediately justified, but also that the believer be immediately justified in believing that they are immediately justified. A position that does require this we may call *iterative foundationalism*, and we may distinguish it from the earlier form (*simple foundationalism*) as follows (so far as concerns the status of the foundations):

> Simple Foundationalism: For any epistemic subject, S, there are *p*'s such that S is immediately justified in believing that *p*.

> Iterative Foundationalism: For any epistemic subject, S, there are *p*'s such that S is immediately justified in believing that *p* and S is immediately justified in believing that he is immediately justified in believing that *p*.[8]

It would not take much historical research to show that both positions have been taken. What I want to investigate here is which of them there is most reason to take. Since the classic support for foundationalism has

---

[8]One should not confuse the respect in which *iterative* is stronger than *simple foundationalism* with other ways in which one version of the position may be stronger than another. These include at least the following: (1) whether it is required of foundations that they be infallible, indubitable, or incorrigible; (2) whether foundations have to be self-justified, or whether some weaker form of direct justification is sufficient; (3) how strongly the foundations support various portions of the superstructure. I am convinced that none of these modes of strength requires any of the others, but I will not have time to argue that here. Note too that our version of the regress argument (to be presented in a moment) does nothing to support the demand for foundations that are strong in any of these respects.

been the regress argument, I shall concentrate on determining which form emerges from that line of reasoning.

II. The Regress Argument

The regress argument seeks to show that the only alternatives to admitting epistemic foundations are circularity of justification or an equally unpalatable infinite regress of justification. It may be formulated as follows:

(A2) Suppose we are trying to determine whether S is mediately justified in believing that *p*. To be so justified he has to be justified in believing certain other propositions, *q, r, . . .* that are suitably related to *p* (so as to constitute adequate grounds for *p*). Let's say we have identified a set of such propositions each of which S believes. Then he is justified in believing that *p* only if he is justified in believing each of those propositions.[9] And, for each of these propositions *q, r, . . .* that he is not immediately justified in believing, he is justified in believing it only if he is justified in believing some other propositions that are suitably related to it. And for each of these latter propositions . . .

Thus in attempting to give a definitive answer to the original question we are led to construct a more or less extensive true structure, in which the original belief and every other putatively mediately justified belief form nodes from which one or more branches issue, in such a way that every branch is a part of some branch that issues from the original belief. Now the question is: what form must be assumed by the structure in order that S be mediately justified in believing that *p*? There are the following conceivable forms for a given branch:

(*a*) It terminates in an immediately justified belief.
(*b*) It terminates in an unjustified belief.
(*c*) The belief that *p* occurs at some point (past the origin), so that the branch forms a loop.
(*d*) The branch continues infinitely.
Of course some branches might assume one form and others another.

The argument is that the original belief will be mediately justified only if every branch assumes form (*a*.) Positively, it is argued that on this condition the originally mentioned neces-

---

[9]I am adopting the simplifying assumption that for each mediately justified belief, there is only one set of adequate grounds that S justifiably believes. The argument can be formulated so as to allow for "overjustification", but at the price of further complexity.

sary condition for the original belief's being mediately justified is satisfied, and, negatively, it is argued that if any branch assumes any of the other forms, it is not.

(1) Where every branch has form (*a*), this necessary condition is satisfied for every belief in the structure. Since each branch terminates in an immediately justified belief that is justified without necessity for further justified beliefs, the regress is ended along each branch. Hence justification is transferred along each branch right back to the original belief.

(2) For any branch that exhibits form (*b*), no element, even the origin, is justified, at least by this structure. Since the terminus is not justified, the prior element, which is justified only if the terminus is, is not justified. And, since it is not justified, its predecessor, which is justified only if it is, is not justified either. And so on, right back to the origin, which therefore itself fails to be justified.

(3) Where we have a branch that forms a closed loop, again nothing on that branch, even the origin, is justified, so far as its justification depends on this tree structure. For what the branch "says" is that the belief that p is justified only if the belief that r is justified, and that belief is justified only if . . . , and the belief that z is justified only if the belief that p is justified. So what this chain of necessary conditions tells us is that the belief that p is justified only if the belief that p is justified. True enough, but that still leaves it completely open whether the belief that p is justified.

(4) If there is a branch with no terminus, that means that no matter how far we extend the branch, the last element is still a belief that is mediately justified if at all. Thus, as far as this structure goes, wherever we stop adding elements, we have still not shown that the relevant necessary condition for the mediate justification of the original belief is satisfied. Thus the structure does not exhibit the original belief as mediately justified.

Hence the original belief is mediately justified only if every branch in the tree structure terminates in an immediately justified belief. Hence every mediately justified belief stands at the origin of a tree structure at the tip of each branch of which is an immediately justified belief.[10]

---

[10]The weakest link in this argument is the rejection of *d*. So far as I am aware, this alternative is never adequately explained, and much less is adequate reason given for its rejection. Usually, I fear, *being justified* is confused with exhibiting one's justification, and it is argued (irrelevantly) that one cannot do the latter for an infinite sequence of propositions. It is interesting in this connection that in two very recent attacks on foundationalism the infinite regress rejected by the regress argument is construed as a regress of *showing justification,* and in different ways the critics argue that the impossibility of completing an infinite sequence of such showings does not imply that there may not *be* an infinite sequence of mediate justification. See Keith Lehrer, *Knowledge* (Oxford: Clarendon Press, 1974), pp. 15–16; and Frederick L. Will, *Induction and Justification* (Ithaca: Cornell University Press, 1974), pp. 176–85.

Now this version of the argument, analogues of which occur frequently in the literature,[11] supports only simple foundationalism. It has no tendency to show that there is immediately justified epistemic belief. So long as S is directly justified in believing some *t* for each branch of the tree, that will be quite enough to stop the regress; all that is needed is that he *be* justified in believing *t* without thereby incurring the need to be justified in believing some further proposition. But perhaps there are other versions that yield the stronger conclusion. Indeed, in surveying the literature one will discover versions that differ from (A2) in one or both of the following respects:

1. Their starting points (the conditions of which they seek to establish) are cases of being justified in believing that one knows (is justified in believing) that *p*, rather than, more generally, cases of being justified in believing that *p*.
2. They are concerned to establish what is necessary for *showing* that *p*, rather than what is necessary for *being justified* in believing that *p*.

Let's consider whether regress arguments with one or the other of these features will yield iterative foundationalism.

First let's consider an argument that differs from (A2) only in the first respect. In his essay "Theory of Knowledge" in a volume devoted to the history of twentieth-century American philosophy, R. M. Chisholm[12] launches a regress argument as follows:

> To the question "What justification do I have for thinking that I know that *a* is true?" one may reply: "I know that *b* is true, and if I know that *b* is true then I also know that *a* is true". And to the question "What justification do I have for thinking I know that *b* is true?" one may reply:

An adequate treatment of the argument would involve looking into the possibility of an infinite structure of belief and the patterns of justification that can obtain there. Pending such an examination, the most one can say for the argument is that it is clear that mediate justification is possible on alternative *a* and not clear that it is possible on alternative *d*.

[11]See, e.g., Bertrand Russell, *Human Knowledge, Its Scope and Limits* (London: Allen & Unwin, 1948), p. 171; Anthony Quinton, *The Nature of Things* (London: Routledge & Kegan Paul, 1973), p. 119.

[12]*Philosophy* (Englewood Cliffs, N.J.: Prentice-Hall, 1964). Because of the ambiguity of the term 'knowledge claim', formulations and criticisms of the argument are often ambiguous in the present respect. When we ask how a "knowledge claim" is justified, we may be asking what it takes to justify an assertion that *p* or we may be asking what it takes to justify a claim that one knows that *p*. Thus, e.g., we find Arthur Danto beginning the argument by speaking of *m* being justified in asserting *s* but then sliding into a consideration of what it takes to justify "claims to know" (*Analytical Philosophy of Knowledge* [New York: Cambridge, 1968], pp. 26–28).

"I know that c is true, and if I know that c is true then I also know that b is true". Are we thus led, sooner or later, to something, n, of which one may say "What justifies me in thinking I know that n is true is simply the fact that n is true"? (p. 263)

Chisholm then supports an affirmative answer to this last question by excluding other alternatives in a manner similar to that of (A2).

Now the crucial question is: why does Chisholm conclude not just that mediate justification of claims to know requires *some* immediately justified beliefs, but that it requires immediately justified *epistemic* beliefs? Of course, having granted the general position that any mediately justified belief rests on some immediately justified belief(s), one might naturally suppose that mediately justified *epistemic* beliefs will rest on immediately justified *epistemic* beliefs. But we should not assume that all cases of mediate knowledge rest on foundations that are similar in content. On the contrary, every version of foundationalism holds that from a certain set of basic beliefs one erects a superstructure that is vastly different from these foundations. From knowledge of sense data one derives knowledge of public physical objects, from knowledge of present occurrences one derives knowledge of the past and future, and so on. So why suppose that *if* mediate epistemic beliefs rest on foundations, those foundations will be epistemic beliefs? We would need some special reason for this. And neither Chisholm nor, to my knowledge, anyone else has given any such reason. All rely on essentially the same argument as (A2), which at most yields the weaker conclusion. They seem to have just assumed uncritically that the foundations on which epistemic beliefs rest are themselves epistemic.[13]

Thus, altering the regress argument in the first way does not provide

[13]Lest this assumption still seem obvious to some of my readers, let me take a moment to indicate how mediate epistemic knowledge might conceivably be derived from non-epistemic foundations. Let's begin the regress with Chisholm and follow the line of the first ground he mentions: that I justifiably believe that b. (To simplify this exposition I am replacing 'know' with 'justifiably believe' throughout.) By continuing to raise the same question we will at last arrive at a c such that I have *immediate* justification for believing that c. Here my justification (for believing that c) will shift from one or more other justified beliefs to the appropriate "warrant-increasing" property. What is then required at the next stage is a justification for supposing the belief that c to have this property, and for supposing that this property does confer warrant. It is highly controversial just how claims like these are to be justified, but, in any event, at this point we have exited from the arena of explicit claims to being justified in a certain belief; what needs justification from here on are beliefs as to what is in fact the case, and beliefs as to what principles of evaluation are valid, not beliefs as to my epistemic relation to these matters. And, without attempting to go into the details, it seems plausible that, if a foundationalist view is tenable at all, these sorts of beliefs will rest on the same sort of foundation as other factual and evaluative beliefs.

grounds for iterative foundationalism. Let's turn to the second modification. In order to maximize our chances, let's combine it with the first and consider what it would take to *show*, for some *p*, that I am justified in believing that *p*.[14] It is easy to see how one might be led into this. One who accepted the previous argument might still feel dissatisfied with simple foundationalism. "You have shown," he might say, "that it is *possible* to be justified in believing that *p* without having any immediately justified epistemic belief. But are we *in fact* justified in believing any *p*? To answer that question you will have to *show*, for some *p*, that you are justified in believing it. And the question is, what is required for that? Is it possible to do that without immediately justified epistemic belief?"

Now if we are to show, via a regress argument, that immediately justified epistemic belief is necessary for showing that I am justified in believing any *p*, it must be because some requirement for showing sets up a regress that can be stopped only if we have such beliefs. What could that requirement be? Let's see what is required for showing that *p*. Clearly, to show that *p* I must adduce some other (possibly compound) proposition, *q*. What restrictions must be put on a *q* and my relations thereto?

(1) It is true that *q*.[15]
(2) *q* constitutes adequate grounds for *p*.

These requirements give rise to no regress, or at least none that is vicious. Even if no proposition can be true without some other proposition's being true, there is nothing repugnant about the notion of an infinity of true propositions. Hence we may pass on.

---

[14] I have not located a clear-cut example of a regress argument with this starting point and with the conclusion in question. Nevertheless, the prospect seems tempting enough to be worth deflating. Moreover, it forces us to raise interesting questions concerning the concept of showing.

Just as the ambiguity of 'knowledge claim' led to versions of the regress argument being indeterminate with respect to the earlier feature, so the process-product ambiguity of terms like 'justification' and 'justified' often make it uncertain whether a philosopher is talking about what it takes for a belief to *be* justified or about what it takes to *justify* a belief in the sense of *showing* it to be justified. See, e.g., C. I. Lewis, *An Analysis of Knowledge and Valuation* (La Salle, Ill.: Open Court, 1946), p. 187; Leonard Nelson, "The Impossibility of the 'Theory of Knowledge'," in Chisholm and Swartz, *Empirical Knowledge*, p. 8.

[15] It may also be required that *p* be true, on the ground that it makes no sense to speak of my having shown what is not the case. ('Show' is a success concept.) I neglect this point since it has no bearing on our present problem.

(3) I am justified in believing that q.[16]

This requirement clearly does give rise to a regress, viz., that already brought out in (A2). We have seen that immediately justified epistemic belief is not required to end that regress; so again we may pass on.

(4) I am justified in believing that I am justified in believing that q.

I am not prepared to admit this requirement, my reasons being closely connected with the point that one may be justified in believing that q without even believing that one is so justified, much less being justified in believing that one is so justified. However, it is not necessary to discuss that issue here. Even if (4) is required, it will simply set up a regress of the sort exemplified by Chisholm's argument, an argument we have seen to have no stronger conclusion than simple foundationalism.

(5) I am able to show that q.

This looks more promising. Clearly this requirement gives rise to a regress that is different from that of (A2). If I can show that p by citing q only if I am able to show that q, and if, in turn, I am able to show that q by citing r only if I am able to show that r, it is clear that we will be able to avoid our familiar alternatives of circularity and infinite regress only if at some point I arrive at a proposition that I can show to be correct without appealing to some other proposition. In deciding whether this argument provides support for iterative foundationalism, we must consider first whether requirement (5) is justified and, second, whether immediately justified epistemic belief would stop the regress so generated.

The requirement looks plausible. For, if I cannot show that q, then it looks as if I won't be able to settle whether or not it is the case that q, and in that case how can I claim to have settled the question about p? But this plausibility is specious, stemming from one of the protean

---

[16]One may contest this requirement on the grounds that, if I have produced what is in fact a true adequate ground, that is all that should be demanded. And it may be that there is some "objective" concept of showing of which this is true. Nevertheless where we are interested in whether *Jones* has shown that p (rather than just whether "it has been shown that p", where perhaps all we are interested in is whether there *are* true adequate grounds), it seems that we must adopt this requirement in order to exclude wildly accidental cases in which Jones is asserting propositions at random and just happens to hit the mark.

forms assumed by that confusion of levels typified by the confusion of knowing that p with knowing that one knows that p. It's quite true that an inability to show that q will prevent me from showing *that I have shown that p*; for to do the latter I have to show that the grounds I have cited for p are correct. But why suppose that it also prevents me from showing that p? Can't I prove a theorem in logic without being able to prove that I have proved it? The former requires only an ability to wield the machinery of first order logic, which one may possess without the mastery of metalogic required for the second. Similarly, it would seem that I can show that p, by adducing true adequate grounds I am justified in accepting, without being able to *show* that those grounds are true.

But even if requirement (5) were justified and the show-regress were launched, immediately justified epistemic beliefs would be powerless to stop it. Let's say that I originally set out to show that I am justified in believing that a, and in the regress of showings thus generated I eventually cite as a ground *that I am immediately justified in believing that z* (call this higher level proposition "Z"), where I am in fact immediately justified in believing that Z. How will this latter fact enable me to *show* that Z? As a result of being immediately justified in believing that Z, I may have no doubt about the matter; I may feel no need to show *myself* that Z. But of course that doesn't imply that I *have shown* that Z. However immediate my justification for accepting Z, I haven't *shown* that Z unless I adduce grounds for it that meet the appropriate conditions. And once I do that, we are off to the races again. The regress has not been stopped. In the nature of the case it cannot be stopped. In this it differs from the original regress of *being* justified. *Showing* by its very nature requires the exhibition of grounds. Furthermore, grounds must be different from the proposition to be shown. (This latter follows from the "pragmatic" aspect of the concept of showing. To show that p is to present grounds that one can justifiably accept without already accepting p. Otherwise showing would lack the point that goes toward making it what it is.) Hence, there are no conceivable conditions under which I could show that p without citing other propositions that, by requirement (5), I must be able to show. If we accept requirement (5), if an infinite structure of abilities to show is ruled out, and if circularity is unacceptable, it follows that it is impossible ever to show anything. (That would seem to be an additional reason for rejecting [5].) Since immediately justified epistemic belief would do nothing to stop the regress, this kind of regress argument can provide no support for iterative foundationalism.

III. Functions of Foundationalism

Thus, although simple foundationalism is strongly supported by (A2), we have failed to find any argument that supports iterative foundationalism. And the second level argument strikes at the latter but not the former. Hence it would seem that foundationalism has a chance of working only in its simple form. This being the case, it is of some interest to determine the extent to which simple foundationalism satisfies the demands and aspirations that foundationalism is designed to satisfy, other than stopping the regress of justification. I shall consider two such demands.

Answering Skepticism

Skepticism assumes various forms, many of which no sort of foundationalism could sensibly be expected to answer. For example, the extreme skeptic who refuses to accept anything until it has been shown to be true and who will not allow his opponent any premises to use for this purpose obviously cannot be answered, whatever one's position. Talking with him is a losing game. Again there are more limited skepticisms in which one sort of knowledge is questioned (e.g., knowledge of the conscious states of other persons) but others are left unquestioned (e.g., knowledge of the physical environment). Here the answering will be done, if at all, by finding some way of deriving knowledge of the questioned sort from knowledge of the unquestioned sort. The role of a general theory of knowledge will be limited to laying down criteria for success in the derivation, and differences over what is required for foundations would seem to make no difference to such criteria.

The kind of "answer to skepticism" that one might suppose to be affected by our difference is that in which the skeptic doubts that we have any knowledge, a successful answer being a demonstration there is some. One may think that the possession of immediate epistemic knowledge will put us in a better position to do that job. Whether it does, and if so how, depends on what it takes to show that one knows something. The discussion of showing in Section II yielded the following conditions for S's showing that *p:*

(1) It is true that *p*.
(2) *S* cites in support of *p* a certain proposition *q* such that:
   (A) It is true that *q*.
   (B) *q* is an adequate ground for *p*.
   (C) S is justified in believing *q*.

We rejected the further conditions that S be able to show that q. However, since we are here concerned with showing something to a skeptic, it may be that some further requirement should be imposed. After all, we could hardly expect a skeptic to abandon his doubt just on the *chance* that his interlocuter is correct in the grounds he gives. The skeptic will want to be given some reason for supposing those grounds to be correct, and this does not seem unreasonable. But we can't go back to the unqualified requirement that every ground adduced be established or even establishable without automatically making showing impossible. Fortunately there is an intermediate requirement that might satisfy a reasonable skeptic while not rendering all showing impossible. Let's require that S be able to show that r, for any r among his grounds concerning which his audience has any real doubt. This differs from the unqualified requirement in leaving open the possibility that there will be grounds concerning which no reasonable person who has reflected on the matter will have any doubt; and if there be such, it may still be possible for S to succeed in showing that p. Thus we may add to our list of conditions:

(D) If there is real doubt about q, S is able to show that q.

Now when p is 'S knows that a', the question is whether one or more of these conditions is satisfiable only if S has immediately justified epistemic beliefs. Let's consider the conditions in turn. As for (1), S can in fact know that a without having any directly justified epistemic belief, even if it should be the case that one can't know that a without knowing that one knows that a. For, as we saw in Section II, there is no reason to doubt that all justified beliefs *that one knows or is justified in believing something* are themselves *mediately* justified. As for (2A) and (2B), there should be no temptation to suppose that they depend on iterative foundationalism. As for whether the grounds are true, that is clearly quite independent of my epistemic situation vis-à-vis those grounds, and hence quite independent of whether I have any immediately justified epistemic beliefs, here or elsewhere. Even if one or more of the grounds should themselves be claims to knowledge, the question of what is required for their truth can be handled in the same way as requirement (1). And adequacy, being a matter of relations between propositions, cannot depend on what sort of justification S has for one or another belief. As for (2C), the discussion in Sections I and II failed to turn up any reasons for supposing that immediately justified epistemic belief is required for my being justified in believing anything. That leaves (2D). But this has already been covered. To satisfy (2D) I have to be able to *show* that (some of) my grounds are true. But that will not require conditions that are different in kind from those already discussed. Hence we may conclude that iterative foundationalism is not a presupposition of our showing that we do have knowledge. Of course it remains an open question whether we are in fact capable of showing that we know something. But if we are incapable, it is not because of the lack of immediately justified epistemic belief.

Self-consciously Reconstructing Knowledge from the Foundations

Suppose that we are assailed by general doubts as to whether we really know anything. In order to lay such doubts to rest we seek as many items as possible of which we can be absolutely certain, each on its own apart from any support from anything else we might know, since at that initial stage we are not supposing, with respect to any particular item, that it counts as knowledge. Having identified a number of such isolated certainties, we proceed to seek ways in which further knowledge can be established on that basis, thus validating as much knowledge as possible. Here is an enterprise that really does require iterative foundationalism. If the enterprise is to succeed, then we must, with respect to at least the initial certainties, be immediately justified not only in believing the proposition in question to be true but also in believing that we are immediately justified in believing it to be true. For otherwise, how could we identify the proposition in question as one of the foundations? We can't be mediately justified in supposing ourselves to know it immediately, for at that stage we have nothing else to go on to provide a basis for that higher level belief.

Obviously, my description of this enterprise is modeled on Descartes' procedure in the *Discourse* and *Meditations*. Nevertheless, there are differences, more marked in the *Meditations*, but present in both. For one thing, Descartes was not working with a true-justified-belief conception of knowledge, and so what he says has to be "translated" into contemporary "justification" talk. More crucially, Descartes does not rest content with an immediate recognition of isolated certainties. He requires a discursive proof of their status, thus giving rise to the notorious Cartesian circle.[17] We might think of the program I have sketched as

---

[17] In Essay 12 I argue that even where the premises of an argument for the reliability of a source of belief are taken from that same source, that does not prevent one from using that argument to show that the source is reliable. This has obvious applications to the Cartesian circle, a point that is, in effect, brought out by James van Cleve in his "Foundationalism, Epistemic Principles and the Cartesian Circle," *Philosophical Review*, 88, no. 1 (1979), 55–91.

the Cartesian program, translated into "justification" talk, and without the requirement that the status of the foundations be established by an appeal to the omnipotence and goodness of God.

If iterative foundationalism is both without strong support and subject to crushing objections, it looks as if we will have to do without a self-conscious reconstruction of knowledge. How grievous a loss is this? Why should anyone want to carry out such a reconstruction? Well, if knowledge does have a foundational structure, it seems intolerable that we should be unable to spell this out. And it may seem that such a spelling out would have to take the present form. But that would be an illusion. If there are foundations, one can certainly identify them and determine how other sorts of knowledge are based on them without first taking on the highly artificial stance assumed by Descartes. One can approach this problem, as one approaches any other, making use of whatever relevant knowledge or justified belief one already possesses. In that case immediate epistemic knowledge is by no means required, just as we have seen it is not required to show that one is justified in holding certain beliefs. If iterative foundationalism is false, we can still have as much epistemic knowledge as you like, but only after we have acquired quite a lot of first level knowledge. And why should that not satisfy any epistemic aspirations that are fitting for the human condition?

IV. Envoi

As we have seen, the main reason for adopting foundationalism is the seeming impossibility of a belief's being mediately justified without resting ultimately on immediately justified belief. And the main reason for rejecting it (at least the main antecedent reason, apart from the difficulties of working it out) is that reason one version of which we found in the quotation from Aune. That is, it appears that the foundationalist is committed to adopting beliefs in the absence of any reasons for regarding them as acceptable. And this would appear to be the sheerest dogmatism. It is the aversion to dogmatism, to the apparent arbitrariness of putative foundations, that leads many philosophers to embrace some form of coherence or contextualist theory, in which no belief is deemed acceptable unless backed by sound reasons.

The main burden of this paper is that with simple foundationalism one can have the best of both arguments; one can stop the regress of justification without falling into dogmatism. We have already seen that Aune's form of the dogmatism argument does not touch simple foun-

dationalism. For that form of the argument attacks only the un-
grounded acceptance of claims *to knowledge or justification;* and simple
foundationalism is not committed to the immediate justification of any
such higher level claims. But one may seek to apply the same argument
to lower level beliefs. Even simple foundationalism, the critic may say,
must allow that some beliefs may be accepted in the absence of any
reasons for supposing them to be true. And this is still arbitrary dogmatism. But the simple foundationalist has an answer. His position
does not require anyone to accept any belief without having a reason
for doing so. Where a person *is* immediately justified in believing that
p, he may find adequate reasons for the higher level belief that he is
immediately justified in believing that *p.* And if he has adequate reasons for accepting this epistemic proposition, it surely is not arbitrary
of him to accept the proposition that *p.* What better reason could he
have for accepting it?

Lest the reader dismiss this answer as a contemptible piece of sleight-
of-hand, let me be more explicit about what is involved. Though the
simple foundationalist requires *some* immediately justified beliefs in
order to terminate the regress of justification, his position permits him
to recognize that all epistemic beliefs require mediate justification.
Therefore, for any belief that one is immediately justified in believing,
one *may* find adequate reasons for accepting the proposition that one is
so justified. The curse (of dogmatism) is taken off immediate justification at the lower level, just by virtue of the fact that propositions at the
higher level are acceptable only on the basis of reasons. A foundational
belief, *b,* is immediately justified just because some valid epistemic principle lays down conditions for its being justified which do not include
the believer's having certain other justified beliefs. But the believer will
be justified in believing *that* he is immediately justified in holding *b* only
if he has *reasons* for regarding that principle as valid and for regarding
b as falling under that principle. And if he does have such reasons, he
certainly cannot be accused of arbitrariness or dogmatism in accepting
b. The absence of reasons for *b* is "compensated" for by the reasons for
the correlated higher level belief. Or, better, the sense in which one can
have reasons for accepting an immediately justified belief is necessarily
different from that in which one can have reasons for accepting a
mediately justified belief. Reasons in the former case are necessarily
"meta" in character; they have to do with reasons for regarding the
belief as justified. Whereas in the latter case, though one *may* move up a
level and find reasons for the higher level belief that the original belief
is mediately justified, it is also required that one have adequate reasons
for the lower level belief itself.

We should guard against two possible misunderstandings of the above argument. First, neither simple foundationalism nor any other epistemology can guarantee that one will, or can, find adequate reasons for a given epistemic proposition, or for any other proposition. The point rather is that there is nothing in the position that rules out the possibility that, for any immediately justified belief that one has, one can find adequate reasons for the proposition that one is so justified. Second, we should not take the critic to be denying the obvious point that people are often well advised, in the press of everyday life, to adopt beliefs for which they do not have adequate reasons. We should interpret him as requiring only that an *ideal* epistemic subject will adopt beliefs only for good and sufficient reason. Hence he insists that our epistemology must make room for this possibility. And, as just pointed out, simple foundationalism does so.

The dogmatism argument may be urged with respect to *showing* that *p*, as well as with respect to accepting the proposition that *p*. That is, the critic may argue that foundationalism is committed to the view that "foundations cannot be argued for". Suppose that in trying to show that *p* I adduce some grounds, and, the grounds being challenged, I try to show that they are true, and . . . in this regress I finally arrive at some foundation *f*. Here, according to the critic, the foundationalist must hold that the most I can (properly) do is simply *assert f*, several times if necessary, and with increasing volume. And again this is dogmatism. But again simple foundationalism is committed to no such thing. It leaves something for the arguer to do even here, viz., try to establish the higher level proposition that he is immediately justified in believing that *f*. And, if he succeeds in doing this, what more could we ask? Unless someone demands that he go on to establish the grounds appealed to in that argument—to which again the simple foundationalist has no objection in principle. Of course, as we saw earlier, the demand that one establish every ground in a demonstration is a self-defeating demand. But the point is that the simple foundationalist need not, any more than the coherence theorist, mark out certain points at which the regress of showing *must* come to an end. He allows the possibility of one's giving reasons for an assertion whenever it is appropriate to do so, even if that assertion is of a foundation.

Has Foundationalism
Been Refuted?

The battle over foundationalism in epistemology has recently been escalated with the publication of two works in which that position is subjected to detailed criticism, Frederick L. Will's *Induction and Justification*[1] and Keith Lehrer's *Knowledge*.[2] In both cases, however, the attack is directed to features of the position that are by no means essential to foundationalism and that do not appear in its most defensible form, what I shall call 'Minimal Foundationalism'. This paper will be devoted to supporting this claim and to suggesting that if one wishes to dispose of foundationalism he must concentrate his fire on its strongest form.

I. Will's Criticism

Will formulates foundationalism as follows:

There is a class of claims, cognitions, that are known in a special direct, certain, incorrigible way; and all epistemic authority resides in these. The philosophical question of the epistemic status of any claim is always a question of the relation of that claim to this class of first cognitions. A claim can be established to be a genuine example of knowledge, or at least a claim worthy of some kind of reasonable adherence, only if it can be disclosed to be, if not a first cognition itself, in some degree authenti-

From *Philosophical Studies*, 29, no. 5 (1976), 287–305. Copyright © 1976 by D. Reidel Publishing Company, Dordrecht-Holland. Reprinted by permission of Kluwer Academic Publishers.
[1]Ithaca: Cornell University Press, 1974.
[2]Oxford: Clarendon Press, 1974.

cated by one or more of such cognitions. It must be possible somehow, beginning with such cognitions, by a finite set of steps in an acceptable procedure to arrive at the claim in question as a conclusion and, by virtue of this, as a justified result. (p. 142)

Elsewhere these "first cognitions" are characterized as "infallible" (p. 203), "indubitable" (p. 172), "self-justifying" (p. 190), and enjoying "logical independence from every other possible cognition" (p. 200). Will's objections to the position are focused on the claims of independence and incorrigibility, the latter understood as the impossibility of justified rejection or revision.

The doctrine advanced concerning these alleged first steps in cognition, like that concerning consequent ones, is that . . . in discriminating a quality of one's own visual experience (e.g., the redness of the after-image) one is participating in a practice that extends, and depends for its success upon conditions which extend, far beyond the subject as an individual human being. (p. 197).

And just because of this, one's supposition that one's sensation is of a certain character is liable both to error and to revision.

If knowing any truth about a sensation, if indeed *having* a sensation of the kind that is specified in that truth, involves the employment and sound working of a vast array of equipment and resource extending far beyond any individual and what can be conceived to be private to him, then the possibility that this equipment and resource is not in place and working soundly cannot be discounted in the philosophical understanding of the knowledge of such truth. If the sound discrimination of the sensation of X, in its character *as* X, can be made only by correctly utilizing something further, say, Y, and if, in a case like this, discrimination of a sensation as X can be made while yet, for some reason, Y is not being used correctly, then a discrimination of X need not be a sound discrimination. (p. 203)

Will's attack on incorrigibility and infallibility embodies a salutary emphasis on the possibility and importance of failings other than error.

There are a variety of ways in which a discrimination may go wrong without being mistaken, without yielding anything sufficiently close to a good performance to be rightly called an error. And there are also a variety of ways in which a discrimination can exhibit its corrigibility other than by going wrong, by yielding somehow an unsuccessful individual performance. . . . Like every other mode of response, modes of sensory discrimination exhibit their liability to change, improvement, deterioration and obsolescence in the dependence they exhibit at all points upon individual and social needs and the conditions under which these needs are filled. (p. 207)

If I were concerned in this paper with the soundness of Will's criticism, there are a number of matters into which I should have to go. For one thing, there is the question of whether he thinks that the dependence of, for instance, sensory discriminations, on social practices, *itself* contradicts a central tenet of foundationalism, or whether he makes this point only as a basis for showing corrigibility. And this of course depends on how he interprets the *independence* he supposes foundationalism to ascribe to first cognitions. Although he is not as explicit about this as one might wish, there are indications that he supposes foundationalism to be committed to the view that the possibility of first cognitions *in no way* depends on the existence of anything outside one's momentary state of mind (e.g., p. 203); in that case the dependence he (surely correctly) alleges would be itself an argument against the position. Again it is not clear that his vigorous and penetrating attack on incorrigibility really is based on the claim that all cognition depends on social practices. Would not Will's points about the inherent possibility of any procedure's being misused and about the liability of any conceptual scheme to be scrapped for a better one apply even to a disembodied mind that is alone in the universe (assuming, contra Wittgenstein and Will, that one can speak intelligibly of a solipsistic mind as using procedures and conceptual schemes)? But my concern in this paper is limited to showing that even if we freely grant the force of his arguments, a significant brand of foundationalism is left standing.

Let's suppose, then, that Will has shown both that all cognition depends (not just in fact but, as he claims, with a kind of theoretical necessity [pp. 198–99]) on social practices, and that no cognitions are incorrigible. Does that dispose of foundationalism? Hardly. Though foundationalists have often taken their foundations to be incorrigible,[3] they need not have done so in order to be distinctive foundationalists. To flesh out this claim I shall formulate a "Minimal Foundationalism", the weakest, and hence least vulnerable, doctrine that has enough bite (of the right sort) to deserve that title.

It will be useful to build up to the formulation in several stages. In the most unspecific terms a foundationalist is one who supposes that knowledge forms a structure, most components of which are supported by a certain subset of components that are not themselves sup-

[3]The case of independence is more complicated. See below for some discussion of this.

ported by the former. To make this less metaphorical we have to specify the mode of support involved. Most contemporary formulations (including those of our critics) employ some form of a justified-true-belief conception of knowledge, in that they take something like S's being justified in truly believing that *p* as at least a necessary condition for S's knowing that *p*.[4] In these terms we can specify the relevant mode of support as justification. The rest of knowledge is supported by the foundations and not vice versa, just in that it depends on the foundations for the justification of the beliefs involved, and not vice versa. Two further considerations will enable us to make this formulation more perspicuous.

(1) First a useful bit of terminology. Where what justifies a belief includes[5] the believer's possessing certain other justified beliefs (those that embody his evidence or reasons for the initial belief), we may speak of *mediately (indirectly)* justified belief. And where what justifies a belief does not include any such thing (any other justified belief of that person) we may speak of *immediately (directly)* justified belief. Correspondingly, a case of knowledge in which the justification requirement is satisfied by mediate justification may be called *mediate (indirect) knowledge;* and a case in which the justification requirement is satisfied by immediate justification will be called *immediate (direct)* knowledge.

(2) We should make more explicit just how mediate justification is thought to depend on immediately justified belief. The idea is that although the other beliefs that are involved in the justification of a given belief may themselves be mediately justified, if we continue determining at each stage how the beliefs involved are justified, we will arrive, sooner or later, at a set of beliefs each of which is immediately justified. This will not, in general, be a single line of descent, for typically the mediately justified belief with which we start will rest on several beliefs, each of which in turn will rest on several beliefs. So the general picture is that of multiple branching from the original belief.

Taking account of all this, we may formulate Minimal Foundationalism as follows.

(I) Every mediately justified belief stands at the base of a (more or less) multiply branching tree structure at the tip of each branch of which is an immediately justified belief.

[4]It often goes unnoticed that the seventeenth-century foundationalists often taken as paradigmatic, Descartes and Locke, were *not* working with any such conception of knowledge, and hence that they did *not* envisage the structure of knowledge as a structure of justification of belief.

[5]Only "includes" because other requirements are also commonly imposed in these cases, e.g., that the first belief be "based" on the others, and, sometimes, that the believer realize that these other beliefs do constitute adequate grounds for the first.

Knowledge seems to have been mislaid in the course of our discussion, but it is easily relocated. Foundationalism is thought of as dealing with knowledge just because one thinks of the justified beliefs in question as satisfying the other requirements for knowledge. One can, if he likes, build into (I) an explicit restriction to cases of knowledge.

(II) In every case of mediate knowledge the mediately justified belief involved stands at the base of a (more or less) multiply branching tree structure at the tip of each branch of which is an immediately justified belief that satisfies the other requirements for knowledge.

The fact remains, however, that the structure definitive of foundationalism comes into the picture via the justification of belief. Hence (I) gives what is essential to the position, and that is what I shall be discussing under the title of 'Minimal Foundationalism'.

There are certain differences between (I) and Will's formulation that are not directly relevant to our present concerns. For example, Will thinks of foundationalism in terms of how one is to *show* that a nonbasic belief is justified, whereas (I) is in terms of what it is for a nonbasic belief to *be* justified.[6] But of course it follows from (I) that the way to *show* that a nonbasic belief is justified is roughly the way Will specifies. Again, (I) is in terms of 'belief', whereas Will uses terms like 'claim' and 'cognition'. It lies outside the purview of this paper to argue that 'belief' is the term we need, but I am confident it could be successfully argued.

What *is* directly to the point is that the targets of Will's criticism are not to be found in Minimal Foundationalism. What that position requires of a foundation is only that it be immediately justified, justified by something other than the possession of other justified beliefs. And to say that a certain person is immediately justified in holding a certain belief is to say nothing as to whether it could be shown defective by someone else or at some other time.[7] Still less is it to say that it enjoys

---

[6]Talk of a belief "being justified" or the "justification" of a belief is ambiguous. The justification of a belief might be the process of showing it to be justified, or it might be the status that it is thereby shown to have. Likewise 'his belief is justified' might mean that it has been shown to have the status in question, or it might just mean that it does have that status. This ambiguity typically makes it difficult to interpret discussions of epistemic justification. In this paper I shall restrict '. . . is justified' to the latter meaning—*having* the epistemically desirable status. I shall use '. . . is shown to be justified' to express the other concept.

[7]Will also argues, in essentially the same way, against the supposition that derived claims can be incorrigible. I take it to be even more obvious that foundationalism need not attribute incorrigibility to nonbasic beliefs, even if it should require basic beliefs to be incorrigible. For the principles of mediate justification might countenance logical connections (e.g., of an inductive sort) that do not transfer incorrigibility.

the absolute independence opposed by Will. A minimal foundation *is* independent of every other cognition in that it derives its justification from none. But that by no means implies that it is nomologically possible for such a belief to occur without a supporting context of social practices. And it is the latter mode of independence that Will rejects.

Will attempts to show that "absolute" independence and incorrigibility, as well as infallibility, are required if a cognition is to serve as a foundation.

> The crucial aspect of the alleged first cognitions that are taken to be expressed in basic empirical propositions is their logical independence from every other possible cognition. This character of epistemic atoms is essential to them, essential to their role as self-justifying grounds for other claims. If they are not logically independent, other cognitions may serve as grounds for them; and this is incompatible with their role as members of the justification sequence with which the sequence of questions must stop, because no more can possibly be asked. From this independence follows their incorrigibility, and given this incorrigibility . . . they will have to be certain in a very strong sense that implies infallibility. (pp. 200–201)

Ten pages earlier there is a similar line of argument, starting from the basic demand for a foundation that it "can be established in utter independence from other claims" (p. 190), which I take to be roughly equivalent to being "members of the justification sequence with which the sequence of questions must stop". Thus we have a chain of alleged implications that runs—*can be established without dependence on other claims→independence from every other cognition→incorrigibility→infallibility.*

As against this I would suggest that neither the starting point nor any of the succeeding links in the chain have been shown to be required by foundationalism.

It may look as if "can be established in utter independence from other claims" is just precisely what we have said Minimal Foundationalism requires of its foundations. However, there is a subtle but highly significant difference between '*is justified* without dependence on other claims' and 'can be *established* without dependence on other claims'. I might well *be* immediately justified in believing, for example, that I feel depressed, without being able to "establish" this (i.e., *show* that it is true), either with or without dependence on other "claims". In fact it is not at all clear what would count as such a showing; perhaps the strongest candidate would be my showing that I am justified in believing that I feel depressed. But of course to do that requires far more conceptual and dialectical sophistication than would normally be possessed by those who *are* justified in holding such beliefs. In view of that, it is fortunate that Minimal Foundationalism does not require one to be able to *show* that his foundations have the required status, but only that they *do* have them.[8]

In the quotation above "logical independence" is said to be entailed by the capability of being established without reliance on other claims. Perhaps it is, but only in the sense in which a contradiction entails everything. I don't see what sense can be attached to showing or establishing *p* without adducing some grounds *q*, not identical with *p*. If when asked to show that *p* I simply reiterate my assertion that *p*, I have clearly not *shown* that *p;* this follows just from the concept of showing. Even if my belief is self-justifying, so that nothing outside the belief is required to justify me in holding it, what follows from that, if anything follows concerning showing, is that there is no need for me to show that *p* is true; it certainly does not follow that I *can* show that *p* just by asserting that *p*. So the requirement that it be possible to establish that *p* without dependence on other cognitions is a self-contradictory one. And the more sensible requirement that we have seen to be intrinsic to foundationalism, that the claim *be justified* otherwise than by relation to other cognitions, does *not* entail that the claim is "logically independent of all other possible cognitions". Indeed it is not at all clear what is meant by the latter, but let's take its denial to involve what Will says it involves, viz., that other cognitions may serve as grounds. Does this prevent the putative foundation from being immediately justified? Will thinks so. "Claims are said to be self-justifying ones only when they alone, and no other claims whatever, may be advanced in their support." (p. 201).[9] But I see no merit in this. To say that a belief is immediately justified is just to say that there are conditions *sufficient* for its justification that do not involve any other justified beliefs of that believer. This condition could be satisfied even if the believer has other justified beliefs that could serve as grounds. Overdetermination is an epistemic as well as a causal phenomenon. What fits a belief to serve as a foundation is simply that it doesn't *need* other justified beliefs in order to be justified itself. It can be accepted *whether or not* there are grounds. Clearly the existence of grounds does not prevent its having that status.

---

[8]Will's adherence to the stronger requirement is no doubt connected with the fact that he, along with many foundationalists, construes the regress argument in terms of a regress of *showing* justification rather than a regress of *being* justified. See below, p. 55.

[9]Another difficulty with the argument under consideration is the incorrect identification of 'immediately justified' (not by relation to other cognitions) and 'self-justified'. We shall let that pass for now, returning to it in connection with Lehrer where it plays a larger role in the argument.

As for the next link in the chain, I suppose that if foundations were 'logically independent' of other claims in such a way as to render them insusceptible of mediate justification, it would follow by the same token that they could not be shown mistaken on the basis of other claims. But since we have seen no reason to attribute the former to foundations, we are left with no basis for the attribution of incorrigibility. Will elsewhere gives other arguments for incorrigibility, but they also involve features that go beyond Minimal Foundationalism. For example, "incorrigibility derives from the assignment of certain claims to the position of fixed and absolute beginnings in the justification process" (p. 191).[10] And if we require maximal stability for the structure of justification, we shall indeed have to rule out the possibility that any foundation loses its credentials. But all that is required by Minimal Foundationalism is that the mediately justified beliefs a person has at any moment rest (at that moment) on certain immediately justified beliefs. This in no way implies that the set of immediately justified beliefs changes from moment to moment *only* by adding new members. Items can also drop out, whether by refutation or otherwise. That will only mean that mediately justified beliefs that essentially depended on those delinquents will drop out as well.

We may, finally, note that the derivation of infallibility from incorrigibility fares no better.

> Since incorrigibility without truth is a dubious merit for any set of truth claims to have, since incorrigible error is of the worst kind, and since the aspiration to truth of any item in the corpus of human knowledge is taken to depend upon these alleged incorrigibile claims, they must, in their splendid isolation, be incorrigibly true. Infallibility as a requirement derives in the theory from incorrigibility. (p. 190)

This may indicate why infallibility is attractive to foundationalists (or any other seeker after truth), but it does nothing to show that a claim *cannot* be incorrigible without being infallible; indeed by acknowledging the conceivability of incorrigible error Will acquiesces in the denial of that.[11] Nor does it do anything to show that only infallible claims can

---

[10]Cf. Lehrer: "If basic beliefs were refutable by non-basic ones, then all that was justified by basic beliefs might be undone if those basic beliefs themselves were refuted. In this case, we would be lacking a foundation for justification" (p. 79). Lehrer cannot be whole-hearted in his advocacy of this argument, for he later acknowledges the possibility of corrigible foundations.

[11]Lehrer argues that incorrigibility does entail infallibility; more specifically he argues for the contrapositive: ". . . if the justification of basic beliefs did not guarantee their truth, then such beliefs would be open to refutation on the grounds that, though they are

play the foundational role. No doubt, in order to be a foundation a belief must carry a strong presumption of truth; this it enjoys just by virtue of being justified. But that is quite different from *impossibility* of falsity.[12]

II. Lehrer's Criticism

Lehrer's formulation of foundationalism runs as follows:

> It is possible to give a more precise characterization of foundation theories by specifying the conditions that must be met for a belief to be basic. The first is that a basic statement must be self-justified and must not be justified by any non-basic belief. Second, a basic belief must either be irrefutable, or, if refutable at all, it must only be refutable by other basic beliefs. Third, beliefs must be such that all other beliefs that are justified or refuted are justified or refuted by basic beliefs. A theory of justification having these features is one in which there are basic beliefs which are self-justified and neither refutable nor justifiable by non-basic beliefs and which justify and refute all non-basic beliefs that are justified or refuted. These basic beliefs constitute the foundation of all justification. (pp. 76–77)

This, like Minimal Foundationalism, is (appears to be) in terms of what it is to *be* justified, rather than what it takes to *show* justification; but, like Will, Lehrer tacks on a requirement of incorrigibility (here interpreted as impossibility of error). As noted in footnotes 10 and 11, Lehrer claims, like Will, that incorrigibility and infallibility are required for foundations, and devotes a longish chapter (chapter 4) to arguing that there are not nearly enough incorrigible beliefs to serve as foundations for others. In spite of that he goes on in the following chapter to acknowledge the conceivability of a theory built on corrigible foundations. Our task here will be to determine whether his objections against this latter form of the theory tell against Minimal Foundationalism.

---

self-justified, they are in fact false" (p. 79). It remains, however, to be shown that the mere possibility of being false necessarily carries with it the possibility that we should be able to show that it is false.

[12]Elsewhere Will appeals to Chisholm's notion that what renders a foundation justified is simply the fact that makes it true (p. 201, fn. 5). Where a belief is justified in this way, it cannot be justified without being true. But that is not to say that no such belief can be false. And in any event that is only one possible form of immediate justification. (See below.)

For an illuminating critique of other arguments designed to show that foundations must be incorrigible or infallible, see A. M. Quinton, *The Nature of Things* (London: Routledge & Kegan Paul Ltd., 1973), chap. 6.

Lehrer attacks the theory both on the basic and the nonbasic level. As for the former, he considers whether the beliefs that we need for foundations are "self-justified". After arguing that "independent information" is required for the justification of perceptual beliefs, Lehrer admits that for the justification of some beliefs, for instance, those concerning one's own current states of consciousness, no "information" is required over and above "semantic information" that is needed for understanding the meaning of the statement, and hence that they may be self-justified (p. 111). But *how* is this possible? In particular, "What defence can be given of this epistemological principle telling us that beliefs of this sort are self-justified?" (p. 112). There is a lengthy and, to my mind, persuasive argument against the common position that such principles are true by virtue of the meanings of terms (pp. 112–19). The other alternatives he considers are that "the belief that the principle is true is basic" (p. 121), and that by taking such beliefs to be self-justified we will be able to explain how other beliefs are justified (p. 121). The objection to the first of these alternatives is that: "This manoeuvre, though logically consistent, opens the door to the most rampant forms of speculation. Anyone wishing to argue that he knows anything whatever can then claim that what he knows is a basic belief. When asked to defend this claim, he can again retort that it is a basic belief that this belief is basic, and so on." (p. 152). The second alternative is rejected on the basis of the argument considered below, which seeks to show that foundationalism cannot account for the justification of nonbasic empirical beliefs.

How damaging is this criticism to Minimal Foundationalism? Taking it *à pied de la lettre*, not at all. Minimal Foundationalism does not require that any belief be self-justified, but only that some beliefs be immediately justified; and the former is only one possible form of the latter. A belief is *self*-justified, in a literal sense, if it is justified just by virtue of being held, just by virtue of being the sort of belief it is (e.g., a belief by a person that he is currently thinking so-and-so). But that is by no means the only kind of immediate justification. The following also constitute live possibilities for the justification of, for example, a belief by a person that he currently feels depressed.

(1) Justified by its truth, in other words by the fact that makes it true, the fact that he does now feel depressed.[13]

[13]See Sydney Shoemaker, *Self-Knowledge and Self-Identity* (Ithaca: Cornell University Press, 1963), p. 216; and R. M. Chisholm, *Theory of Knowledge* (Englewood Cliffs, N.J.: Prentice-Hall, 1966), pp. 26–27.

(2) Justified by the believer's awareness of his feeling depressed, where this is a nonpropositional kind of awareness that does not necessarily involve any belief or judgment, justified or otherwise.[14]
(3) Justified by being formed, or being held, in certain kinds of circumstances, for instance, being wide awake, alert, in full possession of one's faculties.

If what it takes to justify my belief that I am feeling depressed is what is specified by (1), (2), or (3), then more is required than the mere existence of the belief.[15]

But although it is an extremely important point that immediate justification is not confined to self-justification, this is too easy a way with Lehrer's argument. For whatever mode of immediate justification we think attaches to beliefs about one's current states of consciousness, the question can still be raised as to what defense can be given of the epistemological principle that beliefs of this sort are justified under these conditions. This is a profound and difficult problem that must certainly be faced by foundationalism, and I cannot hope to go into it properly here. I shall have to content myself with arguing that Lehrer has not shown this to be a fatal difficulty for Minimal Foundationalism.

First let us note that this is a problem for any epistemology, foundationalist or otherwise, that employs the concept of epistemic justification. It is incumbent on any such epistemology to specify the grounds for principles that lay down conditions for beliefs of a certain sort to count as justified. I believe that a sober assessment of the situation would reveal that no epistemology has been conspicuously successful at this job. Before using this demand as a weapon against foundationalism the critic should show us that the position he favors does a better job.[16]

Rather than spend more time on these legalistic "burden of proof" considerations, I should like to turn to a point that is more directly

---

[14]See B. Russell, *Problems of Philosophy* (London: Oxford University Press, 1912), p. 77; and G. E. Moore, "The Refutation of Idealism," in *Philosophical Studies* (London: Kegan Paul, Trench, Trubner, 1922), pp. 24–25, and "The Nature and Reality of Objects of Perception," in ibid., pp. 70–71.

[15]'Self-justified' is often used in an undiscriminating way, to range over more or less of the terrain of immediate justification. Lehrer himself, just after stressing the requirement that basic beliefs be "self-justified", says that "Empiricists think that experience can guarantee the truth of the basic beliefs" (p. 78). That sounds more like (2).

[16]No doubt Lehrer takes himself to have shown this in the exposition of his own position in chap. 8. I cannot discuss that in this paper.

relevant to my interest in revealing gratuitous accretions to Minimal Foundationalism. My own view as to how foundationalism (or any other epistemology) should test a principle of justification is that it should use empirical evidence to determine whether beliefs approved by the principle are reliable, that is, can be depended on to be (at least usually) correct. I suspect that Lehrer, along with most of my readers, would react to this by saying that whatever the merits of this suggestion for other epistemologies, it is obviously unavailable for foundationalism. Since it is definitive of that position to insist that a foundation does not depend on any other belief for its justification, how can a foundationalist countenance the deployment of empirical evidence to validate the foundations? Well, to see how this is possible we have to uncover a distinction closely analogous to the one mentioned earlier between a basic belief's *being justified* and *being established* (or shown to be justified). The distinction in question is that between (a) knowing (being justified in believing) that I am depressed (when that is a basic belief), and (b) knowing (being justified in believing) that I immediately know (am justified in believing) that I feel depressed. Clearly it is definitive of foundationalism to hold that (a) does not depend on any other beliefs' being justified, but it is in no way essential to foundationalism to deny that (b) is so dependent. Minimal Foundationalism would be committed to the latter denial only if one could not be immediately justified in believing that p without also being immediately justified in believing that he is immediately justified in believing that p. But why suppose that? Even if justification on the lower level necessarily carries with it justification of the belief that one is so justified, it would not follow that the justification of the higher level belief is *immediate*. It could be, rather, that being justified in believing that p automatically puts one in possession of the evidence he needs for being *mediately* justified in believing that he is immediately justified in believing that p. And in any event, why suppose that being justified in believing that p necessarily carries with it being justified in believing that one is so justified? It would seem that those who have not attained the level of epistemological reflection have no justification for believing anything about their being epistemically justified. And when one does come to be justified in accepting some higher level epistemic belief, is this not typically on the basis of ratiocination? In particular it may be, as Lehrer in effect suggests, that I will have to formulate some general principle of justification and find adequate reasons for accepting it before I can become justified in believing that I am immediately justified in believing that p. And in that case perhaps empirical evidence for the reliability of beliefs that satisfy this principle will be the crucial reason in support of the principle.[17]

Let's return to Lehrer's argument that foundationalism can provide no adequate reason for accepting a principle that declares beliefs concerning one's own current conscious states to be immediately justified in some way, for example, to be self-justified. The burden of the last paragraph is that this argument will work only if Lehrer can exclude the possibility of a foundationalist's providing adequate empirical support for such principles. And he can do this only by saddling foundationalism with the gratuitous demand that in addition to basic beliefs' *being* immediately justified, one must be immediately justified in taking them to be immediately justified. Once again the argument tells only against a position that makes claims it need not make in order to be a foundationalism.

On the level of nonbasic beliefs Lehrer's argument proceeds from what he terms "the fundamental doctrine of foundation theories", viz., that "justification, whether it is the self-justification of basic beliefs, or the derivative justification of non-basic beliefs, guarantees truth" (pp. 78–79). When we consider the justification of nonbasic beliefs by evidence, "The consequence which follows is that evidence never *completely* justifies a belief in such a way as to guarantee the truth of the belief unless the probability of the statement on the basis of the evidence is equal to one" (p. 149). Indeed, we can apply the same considerations to basic beliefs. "If we now consider the question of how probable a belief must be in order to be self-justified, an analogous argument shows that the belief must have an initial probability of one" (p. 150). And this implies that practically no contingent beliefs could be justified. "For any strictly coherent probability function, no statement has an initial probability of one unless it is a logical truth, and in infinite languages no non-

---

[17]In Essay 1 I explore the differences between Minimal Foundationalism and a kind that requires, for each basic belief, that one also be immediately justified in believing that one is immediately justified in believing it.

It is very common in discussions of foundationalism to state the position so as only to require immediate justification or knowledge at the first level, but then to glide into the stronger requirement. Will's formulation of the position quoted above embodies no requirement that one have immediate knowledge *of* the epistemic status of "first cognitions". But still we find him saying things like "beginning items of knowledge . . . whose philosophical validation as knowledge must be capable of being made out in complete independence of the institution and the instruments of criticism and evaluation that the institution provides" (p. 160) and ". . . a level of foundational items in knowledge, items the status of which as knowledge is in a special way not subject to challenge" (p. 175). In these latter passages he is representing foundationalism as requiring that the *epistemic status* of the foundations be knowable without dependence on other cognitions.

general statement has an initial probability of one unless it is a logical truth. Hence, with the exception of certain general statements in infinite languages, completely justified basic beliefs would have to be restricted to logical truths, and completely justified non-basic beliefs would have to be restricted to logical consequences of completely justified basic beliefs. . . . We would be locked out of the realm of the contingent, and skepticism would reign supreme there." (p. 151).

I will not have time to go into the way Lehrer derives these conclusions from the "fundamental doctrine". Again I shall have to restrict myself to considering whether the argument, if valid, is damaging to Minimal Foundationalism. And here that reduces to the question whether Minimal Foundationalism holds that "justification guarantees truth".

Unfortunately it is not at all clear what this is supposed to mean. A natural interpretation would be that justification necessitates truth, that it is impossible for a justified belief to be false. And that seems to be what Lehrer means initially. In the paragraph in which he introduces the "fundamental doctrine", he says, "Basic beliefs are basic because they cannot be false; their truth is guaranteed". (78). But when in the next chapter he comes to recognize the possibility of basic beliefs that are corrigible, he analogizes the epistemic guarantee of truth to a manufacturer's guarantee of soundness, and points out that in neither case is the existence of the guarantee incompatible with the absence of what is guaranteed. (p. 102). But then hasn't the "fundamental doctrine" become vacuous? On *any* (sensible) conception of justification it carries at least a strong presumption of truth. And isn't that as much of a guarantee as a manufacturer's guarantee? It looks at this point as if "guarantee of truth" has become indistinguishable from "justification". But then in chapter 6, where the argument currently under consideration occurs, Lehrer seems to have drifted into a conception midway between 'necessitates truth' and 'carries a strong presumption of truth', but without telling us just what this is. Indeed the only real clue we have is the claim quoted above, that a belief must have a probability of one if its justification is to guarantee its truth. Perhaps it is something like this: to say that the justification of a belief *guarantees* its truth is to say that it comes as close as possible to necessitating the truth of the belief. But whether or not that is just the way to put it, it is clear that so long as 'justification guarantees truth' has the consequence for both basic and nonbasic beliefs alleged by Lehrer in the present argument, that doctrine is no part of Minimal Foundationalism. It is quite possible for some beliefs to be immediately justified and for other beliefs to be mediately justified on the basis of the former, without any of them receiving a probability of one. At least there is nothing in the general notions of immediate and mediate justification to support any such requirement. No doubt, the higher the probability the stronger the justification, but why should a foundationalist have to insist on a maximally strong justification? What is there about *foundationalism*, as contrasted with rival orientations, that necessitates such a demand? The distinctive thing about foundationalism is the *structure* of justification it asserts; and this structure can be imposed on justifications of varying degrees of strength. Once more a band of camp followers has been mistaken for the main garrison.

III. The Status of Minimal Foundationalism

One may grant that Minimal Foundationalism is untouched by the criticisms we have been discussing and yet feel that this is of little import, just because that position is so minimal as to have lost the features that give foundationalism its distinctive contours. My answer to that is simply to point out that when we formulate the main argument for foundationalism, the regress argument, in the only form in which it gives any support to that position, the version that emerges is precisely what I have been calling Minimal Foundationalism. The regress argument may be formulated as follows.

> Suppose we are trying to determine whether S is mediately justified in believing that p. To be so justified he has to be justified in believing certain other propositions, $q, r, \ldots$, that are suitably related to p (so as to constitute adequate grounds for p). Let's say we have identified a set of such propositions each of which S believes. Then he is justified in believing that p only if he is justified in believing each of these propositions. And for each of these propositions, $q, r, \ldots$ that he is not immediately justified in believing, he is justified in believing it only if he is justified in believing some other propositions that are suitably related to it. And for each of these latter propositions. . . .
>
> Thus in attempting to give a definitive answer to the original question we are led to construct a more or less extensive tree structure, in which the original belief and every other putatively mediately justified belief forms a node from which one or more branches issue, in such a way that every branch is a part of some branch that issues from the original belief. Now the question is: what form must be assumed by the structure in order that S be mediately justified in believing that p? There are the following conceivable forms for a given branch.

(A) It terminates in an immediately justified belief.
(B) It terminates in an unjustified belief.
(C) The belief that p occurs at some point (past the origin), so that the branch forms a loop.
(D) The branch continues infinitely.

Of course some branches might assume one form and others another.

The argument is that the original belief will be mediately justified only if every branch assumes form (A). Positively it is argued that on this condition the necessary conditions for the original belief's being mediately justified are satisfied, and negatively it is argued that if any branch assumes any other form, they are not.

(A) Where every branch has form (A), each branch terminates in an immediately justified belief that is justified without the necessity for further justified beliefs. Hence justification is transferred along each branch right back to the original belief.
(B) For any branch that exhibits form (B), no element, including the origin, is justified, at least by this structure. Since the terminus is not justified, the prior element, which is justified only if the terminus is, is not justified. And since it is not justified, its predecessor, which is justified only if it is, is not justified either. And so on, right back to the origin, which therefore itself fails to be justified.
(C) Where we have a branch that forms a closed loop, again nothing on that branch, including the origin, is justified, so far as its justification depends on this tree structure. For what the branch "says" is that the belief that p is justified only if the belief that r is justified, and that belief is justified only if . . . , and the belief just before the looping back is justified only if the belief that p is justified. So what this chain of necessary conditions tells us is that the belief that p is justified only if the belief that p is justified. True enough, but that still leaves it open whether the belief that p *is* justified.
(D) If there is a branch with no terminus, that means that no matter how far we extend the branch, the last element is still a belief that is mediately justified if at all. Thus as far as this structure goes, wherever we stop adding elements, we still have not shown that the conditions for the mediate justification of the original belief are satisfied. Thus the structure does not exhibit the original belief as mediately justified.

Hence the original belief is mediately justified only if every branch in the tree structure terminates in an immediately justified belief. Hence every mediately justified belief stands at the base of a (more or less) multiply branching tree structure at the tip of each branch of which is an immediately justified belief.

I do not claim that this argument is conclusive; I believe it to be open to objection in ways I will not be able to go into here. But I do feel that it gives stronger support to foundationalism than any other regress argument. And clearly it yields, at most, Minimal Foundationalism. All that it takes to avoid the three alternatives deemed unacceptable by this argument is a belief at the tip of each branch that is in fact immediately justified. These beliefs do not have to incorrigible, infallible, or indubitable to perform this function. Their justification does not have to "guarantee" their truth in any sense in which that goes beyond just being justified. They do not have to be incapable of mediate justification. They do not even have to be true, though if they were generally false, the structure they support would be of little interest. Their *occurrence* can depend on various external conditions. They do not have to be self-justified, in a strict sense, as contrasted with other modes of direct justification. Nor is it necessary that the believer can show them to be immediately justified; still less is it necessary that he *immediately* know that they are immediately justified. All that is needed to satify the demands of the argument is that a belief that *is* immediately justified in some way or other terminate each chain of mediate justification. Since Minimal Foundationalism does guarantee this, it can hardly be maintained that it lacks the distinctive epistemological force characteristic of foundationalism.

Within the confines of this paper I cannot properly support my claim that the above is the only version of the regress argument that supports any form of foundationalism; to do so would involve examining them all. I will, however, say a word about a version that one frequently encounters in both friend and foe, including Will and Lehrer. This is the version that, ignoring the fine print, differs from the above version only in being concerned with *showing justification* rather than with *being justified*.[18] In this second version the argument is that if we start with a mediately justified belief and proceed to show it to be justified by citing its grounds, and then showing them to be justified, and . . . , then again the only alternative to circularity, infinite regress or ending in something not shown to be justified, is to arrive, along each strand of justification, at some belief that can be *shown* to be justified in some way that does not involve adducing other beliefs. This form of the argument does indeed have a conclusion markedly stronger than Minimal Foun-

[18]Because of the ambiguity pointed out in fn. 6, it is often unclear which version is being expounded. But our two authors are unmistakably dealing with the second version. Will, indeed, explicitly distinguishes these versions on p. 178, and his criticisms on pp. 183–84 are clearly directed against the second version. For Lehrer's discussion see pp. 15–16 and pp. 155–57.

dationalism, but unfortunately, as pointed out above in another connection, this conclusion is logically incoherent. It is conceptually impossible to *show* that a belief is justified, or show that anything else, without citing propositions we take ourselves to be justified in believing. Hence this form of the argument does not support any form of foundationalism, or any other position.

IV. Conclusion

Will and Lehrer are to be commended for providing, in their different ways, important insights into some possible ways of developing a nonfoundationalist epistemology. Nevertheless if foundationalism is to be successfully disposed of, it must be attacked in its most defensible, not in its most vulnerable, form. Although Will and Lehrer reveal weaknesses in historically important forms of foundationalism, it has been my aim in this paper to show that their arguments leave untouched the more modest and less vulnerable form I have called 'Minimal Foundationalism', a form approximated to by the most prominent contemporary versions of the position.[19] It is to be hoped that those who are interested in clearing the decks for an epistemology without foundations will turn their critical weapons against such modest and careful foundationalists as Chisholm, Danto, and Quinton.

[19]The closest approximation is found in Quinton, *The Nature of Things*. The versions of Chisholm, *Theory of Knowledge,* and Arthur Danto, *Analytical Philosophy of Knowledge* (Cambridge: Cambridge University Press, 1968), are also much closer to Minimal Foundationalism than to the positions attacked by Will and Lehrer.

What's Wrong with
Immediate Knowledge?

In this essay I will consider what seem to me the most interesting current arguments for the impossibility of immediate knowledge. I shall conclude that they all fail to foreclose that possibility. I shall not explicitly argue that the possibility is realized, though it will become clear in the course of my argument where I think that obvious examples are to be found.

Attacks on immediate knowledge are nothing new. They were a staple of nineteenth-century absolute idealism[1] and were prominent also in its American offshoot, pragmatism.[2] But after a hiatus from roughly 1920 to 1950, these attacks have been resumed in English-speaking philosophy, with the revival of pragmatist and holistic ways of thinking in such philosophers as Quine, Sellars, Rorty, and Davidson. I feel that the time is ripe for a critical review of these arguments in their most recent guises. Before starting on that I should make it explicit that my rejection of these arguments does not imply that I consider everything in recent pragmatism, holism, and coherence theories to be unsound.

From *Synthese*, 55 (1983), 73–95. Copyright © 1983 by D. Reidel Publishing Co., Dordrecht, Holland, and Boston, U.S.A. Reprinted by permission of Kluwer Academic Publishers.

[1]Bernard Bosanquet, *Logic or the Morphology of Knowledge* (London: Oxford University Press, 1911), bk. 2, chap. 9. F. H. Bradley, *Essays on Truth and Reality* (Oxford: Clarendon Press, 1914), chap. 8. Bradley, *The Principles of Logic*, 2d ed. (London: Oxford University Press, 1922), Terminal Essay II. Brand Blanshard, *The Nature of Thought* (London: George Allen & Unwin, 1939), chap. 25–28.

[2]C. S. Peirce, "Questions Concerning Certain Faculties Claimed for Man," in *Collected Papers*, ed. C. Hartshorne and P. Weiss (Cambridge: Harvard University Press, 1934), vol. 5. John Dewey, *Logic: The Theory of Inquiry* (New York: Henry Holt, 1938), chap. 8.

I

Let me specify at the outset in what sense I will be defending the possibility of *immediate* knowledge, since the term is by no means unambiguous. The rough idea is that whereas *mediate* knowledge depends for its status as knowledge on other knowledge, *immediate* knowledge does not. Mediate knowledge is, immediate knowledge is not, *mediated* by other knowledge. To make this more precise we will have to dig down into the concept of knowledge, and that takes us into highly controversial territory. If we could suppose that knowledge is true justified belief, plus some fourth requirement to avoid Gettier-type counterexamples, we could make the distinction between mediate and immediate knowledge hang on the distinction between mediate and immediate justification, which could then be explained as follows.

   (I) S is *mediately* justified in believing that p—S is justified in believing
      that p by virtue of some relation this belief has to some other justi-
      fied belief(s) of S.
  (II) S is *immediately* justified in believing that p—S is justified in believing
      that p by virtue of something other than some relation this belief has
      to some other justified belief(s) of S.

However, some contemporary epistemologists think that what converts true belief into knowledge is reliability rather than justification, where a "reliable" true belief is one that has originated, and/or is sustained, in a way that is generally reliable, that will generally produce true rather than false beliefs.[3] To further compound the confusion, some reliability theorists take reliability to *be,* or to be an adequate criterion for, justification.[4] In this essay I want to avoid these controversies so as to focus on the issues raised by the arguments I will be examining. I can do this by leaving open just exactly what it is that plays the role in the concept of knowledge that many contemporary theorists assign to justification. I shall coin a neutral term, 'epistemization', for the function performed by whatever fills this role. That is, an "epistemizer" will be what converts true belief into knowledge, perhaps subject to some further condition for avoiding Gettier counterexamples. Justification and reliability will be two leading candidates for the role of epistemizer (or

---

[3]D. M. Armstrong, *Belief, Truth, and Knowledge* (London: Cambridge University Press, 1973), chap. 12–15. Alvin I. Goldman, "What Is Justified Belief?", in *Justification and Knowledge,* ed. G. S. Pappas (Dordrecht: D. Reidel, 1979). Marshall Swain, *Reasons and Knowledge* (Ithaca: Cornell University Press, 1981).

[4]Goldman, "What Is Justified Belief?"; Swain, *Reasons and Knowledge.*

the same candidate, depending on how 'justification' is explained).[5] We can then distinguish between mediate and immediate epistemization in the same terms we used above for distinguishing mediate and immediate justification.

> (III) S's belief that p is *mediately* epistemized — S's belief that p is epistemized by some relation this belief has to some other epistemized belief(s) of S.
>
> (IV) S's belief that p is *immediately* epistemized — S's belief that p is epistemized by something other than some relation this belief has to some other epistemized belief(s) of S.

Putative mediate epistemizers include (a) having adequate evidence for the belief in question and (b) the belief in question having been arrived at by inference in a way that will generally produce true beliefs. Immediate epistemization is a wastebasket category. It embraces *any* form of epistemization that does not involve relations to other epistemized beliefs of the same subject. Hence the range of conceivable immediate epistemizers is much wider. Popular candidates include (a) immediate experience of what the belief is about, (b) for certain special cases, simply the truth of the belief, or the fact that it is believed or understood, (c) facts about the origin of the belief, for instance, the fact that a certain perceptual belief arose from normal perceptual processes.

Plausible candidates for immediate knowledge include one's knowledge of the simplest logical and mathematical truths: 'No proposition is both true and false', '$2 + 3 = 5$'—and one's knowledge of one's own current states of consciousness: 'I feel relieved', 'I am thinking about next summer's vacation'. In both sorts of cases it seems implausible to suppose that one knows the item in question only by virtue of knowing or being justified in believing something else, on which the first knowledge is based. Requests for evidence or reasons for one's first-person current conscious state attributions are clearly out of place. "What do you mean, what reason do I have for supposing that I feel relieved? I just do, that's all."[6] Again, although '$2 + 3 = 5$' can be derived from

---

[5] I will continue to use the term 'justification' when discussing epistemologists who think of knowledge in those terms. I shall use 'epistemization' when I am striving for maximum generality.

[6] The inappropriateness of the request for reasons here has moved some to deny that this is a case of knowledge. That move, I believe, would have to be defended with the same arguments we shall be criticizing in the body of the paper. Since these arguments are directed against the possibility of immediate knowledge, they can be used either to discard the immediacy and keep the knowledge, or to discard the knowledge and keep the immediacy.

other propositions (as can 'I feel relieved', for that matter), one normally feels no need to do so or to be able to do so, in order to know it to be the case. It seems that we can *see* that 2 + 3 = 5, just by considering that proposition itself. A simple perceptual belief, for example, that there is a tree in front of me, or if you prefer, that I see a tree in front of me, is a more controversial case. A normal adult could provide a reason if pressed: "It looks like a tree" or "I am having the kind of experience I would have if I were seeing a tree". But it seems that a being too unsophisticated to come up with any such reasons could still have perceptual knowledge that there is a tree in front of him just by virtue of forming that belief by normal perceptual processes in normal circumstances.

I should make it explicit that what I am going to be defending in this paper is what we may call "wholly immediate knowledge". Recently it has been pointed out by several writers that one might think of certain beliefs as justified partly immediately and partly mediately, in such a way that the belief has justification sufficient for knowledge only by combining the two sources.[7] Thus it might be that a perceptual belief is justified to some extent just by being formed by normal perceptual processes in normal circumstances, but that this is not sufficient for knowledge (even given truth and whatever may be required over and above justification and truth). In addition, the belief would have to "cohere" with other things one knows, or it would have to be supported by reasons for supposing that the conditions of perception are normal. In that instance we might speak of a case of perceptual knowledge as "partly immediate" since part of what epistemizes the belief is something other than its relation to other justified beliefs of the same subject. This is an interesting suggestion and worthy of careful examination, but in this paper I shall restrict myself to the question of the possibility of wholly immediate knowledge.

The question of the possibility of immediate knowledge is frequently assimilated to the question of the viability of foundationalism, but the

[7]See, e.g., Roderick Firth, "Coherence, Certainty, and Epistemic Priority," *Journal of Philosophy*, 61 (1964) 545–77. This should not be confused with prima facie immediate justification, where the justification, when it comes off, is wholly immediate, but where the justification could be "overriden" or "defeated" if conditions are not propitious. (John Pollock, *Knowledge and Justification* [Princeton: Princeton University Press, 1974], chap. 2; Roderick M. Chisholm, *Theory of Knowledge*, 2d ed. [Englewood Cliffs, N.J.: Prentice-Hall, 1977], chap. 4.) Thus one might take the perceptual belief that there is a tree in front of one to be prima facie justified merely by one's having a certain visual experience; then if conditions are abnormal in a certain way that justification is "overridden". Here it is not required for justification that one have one or more other justified beliefs related in a certain way to the target belief.

questions are distinct. Foundationalism is a theory of the structure of knowledge. It holds, to put it briefly, that all mediate epistemization ultimately rests on immediately epistemized beliefs. Trace back a chain of mediate epistemization and you will eventually reach an immediately epistemized belief. Clearly foundationalism entails the possibility of immediate epistemization, but not vice versa. One could recognize that some beliefs are immediately epistemized but deny that mediate epistemization always rests on such beliefs, as foundationalism maintains. I will not be discussing the contentions of one or another version of foundationalism, other than the possibility of immediate epistemization.

Much of the attack on immediate knowledge has focused on some particular putative immediate epistemizer. The concept of immediate awareness has been extensively criticized, in absolute idealism, in pragmatism, and in more recent writings.[8] The notion of a belief's being "self-justified" has come in for a good deal of attack.[9] Such opponents often assume that disposing of their chosen target will amount to the elimination of immediate knowledge. But even where such arguments succeed in unmasking a particular alleged epistemizer, they fail in their more ambitious task, because of the indefinite plurality of possible immediate epistemizers. Even if there is something radically wrong with the concept of an immediate experience of a particular or of a fact, there is still the claim that some beliefs are self-warranted, the claim that some beliefs are epistemized by a reliable noninferential origin, and so on. One could set out to discredit all the immediate epistemizers that have actually been put forward, one by one. But at best such a procedure would fail to show that all possibilities have been eliminated.

In this paper I am going to confine myself to arguments that are directed against *any* sort of immediate epistemization and immediate knowledge. In keeping with this restriction I shall even forgo considering an important argument to the effect that wherever an immediate justification for a belief is defeasible we can be (sufficiently) justified in the belief only if we are justified in believing that no defeating circumstances obtain.[10] Since there are putative immediate justifications that do not seem to have this prima facie character, for example, my justifi-

---

[8]For an influential recent attack see Wilfrid Sellars, "Empiricism and the Philosophy of Mind," in *Science, Perception, and Reality* (New York: Humanities Press, 1963).

[9]See, e.g., Bruce Aune, *Knowledge, Mind, and Nature* (New York: Random House, 1967); Keith Lehrer, *Knowledge* (London: Oxford University Press, 1974); F. L. Will, *Induction and Justification* (Ithaca: Cornell University Press, 1974).

[10]See, e.g., Georges Dicker, *Perceptual Knowledge* (Dordrecht: D. Reidel, 1980), chap. 1.

cation for supposing that I feel tired now, or for supposing that $2 + 3 = 5$, this argument, even if successful, would not rule out all immediate knowledge.

II

As a preliminary to examining the arguments I take most seriously, I shall dispose of some tempting but misdirected arguments that turn out to hit some other target instead.

(1) First I will briefly note that some theorists seem to suppose that the beliefs involved in immediate knowledge must be infallible, incorrigible, or indubitable,[11] and hence that by showing that none of our beliefs enjoy those immunities, one will have shown that there can be no immediate knowledge. At least opponents of "foundational" or "basic" beliefs, which must be immediately epistemized to fill that role, have often supposed that such beliefs must enjoy such immunities.[12] But a moment's reflection will assure us that there is nothing in the concept of immediate epistemization, any more than in the concept of mediate epistemization, that limits its application to beliefs that *cannot* (in some significant sense) be mistaken, refuted, or reasonably doubted.

(2) I have a sense that it is a rather widely shared view that a belief can be immediately epistemized only if it *in no way* depends on other knowledge of the same subject, only if it could be held without the subject's knowing anything else; though I must confess to some difficulty in finding this explicitly affirmed in print.[13] In any event, if that were a condition of immediate knowledge, it would be a serious liability, for there are powerful reasons for denying the possibility of knowledge that is isolated to that extent. Speaking with absolute generality, it is plausible to hold that I can't know something of the form 'x is P' without having general knowledge as to what it is for something to be P. And getting down to standard putative cases of immediate knowledge, it is a widely held view that I can't have knowledge only of my own conscious states. Such knowledge, and hence any particular instance of such knowledge, presupposes that I know something about the ways in which states of consciousness are manifested in publicly

---

[11]For the distinction between these terms, see Essay 10.

[12]See, e.g., Aune, *Knowledge, Mind, and Nature,* chap. 2 and Will, *Induction and Justification,* chap. 7; and for a response see Essay 2 in this volume.

[13]In Will, *Induction and Justification,* p. 203, there is a passage that might be interpreted in this way.

observable behavior and demeanor. And as for '2 + 3 = 5' and the like, it is very plausible to hold that one could not have knowledge of a particular arithmetical truth without knowing at least some significant part of a larger arithmetical system. If one tried to teach a child that 2 + 3 = 5 while keeping him ignorant of, for instance, '1 + 1 = 2', he would fail miserably. Of course, these contentions can be, and have been, controverted. But since I will be arguing that they are, in any event, irrelevant to the issue of immediate knowledge, I need not defend them. It is enough that they have been held with some show of reason.

I want to deny that the cases of dependence just cited are incompatible with the existence of immediate knowledge. How can this be? Well, it all depends on the sort of dependence involved. Immediate knowledge requires independence of other knowledge, so far as the epistemization of belief is concerned. Immediate knowledge is knowledge in which the belief involved is not *epistemized* by a relation to other knowledge or epistemized belief of the same subject. But in the above cases what is alleged is that the very *existence* of the belief depends on other knowledge. Unless I know what it is to be P, I can't so much as form the belief that x is P, for I lack the concept of P. Unless I know something about outward criteria of conscious states, I cannot so much as form the belief that I feel tired, for I lack the concept of feeling tired. Unless I know something about the rest of the number system, I cannot so much as form the belief that 2 + 3 = 5, for I lack the requisite concepts. But all this says nothing as to what *epistemizes* the belief, once formed, and it is on this that the classification into immediate or mediate depends. The question of what epistemizes a belief only arises once the belief is formed. That question *presupposes* the existence of the belief and hence presupposes any necessary conditions of that existence. It is then a further question whether the belief is epistemized and, if so, by what. Hence it is a further question whether that epistemization is mediate or immediate. To suppose that the conditions for forming the belief are themselves conditions of epistemization, and hence determinative of the choice between mediate and immediate, is to confuse levels of questioning. It would be like arguing that since a necessary condition of my making a request (orally) is that I have vocal chords, part of what justifies me in making that request is that I have vocal chords. The existence of immediate knowledge is quite compatible with a thoroughgoing coherence theory of concepts, according to which one could not have a single concept without having a whole system of concepts, and even with the further view that the possession of a system of concepts requires having various pieces of knowledge involving those concepts.[14]

(3) It is very plausible to suppose that *any* belief, however it arose, can be evaluated for truth, justification, or rationality by reference to reasons or evidence. However I came to believe that $2 + 3 = 5$ or that there is a tree in front of me, or even that I feel tired, it is possible, for me or for someone else, to look for reasons for supposing that it is true or false. And sometimes such reasons can be found. There is even some plausibility in holding that it is always, in principle, possible to find such reasons. But whether or not the latter claim is correct, it will at least follow that any belief is subject to assessment in terms of reasons or evidence. And it has been thought that this is incompatible with supposing that any belief is immediately epistemized. But again this is just a confusion. To say that a belief is immediately epistemized is not to imply that it could not *also* be mediately epistemized, even at the same time. It is only to say that there *is* an epistemization, not involving other knowledge or epistemized belief of the same subject, that is sufficient for knowledge.[15] Epistemic overdetermination is just as possible as the causal variety. Just as the existence of one set of causally sufficient conditions does not rule out the possibility of another set, so the existence of one (mediate) epistemization is quite compatible with the existence of another (immediate) one.

III

Now I turn to the criticisms I will take more seriously. They all involve what we may call the "Level Ascent" argument. According to this argument, when we consider any putative bit of immediate knowledge, we find that the belief involved really depends for its epistemization on some higher level reasons that have to do with its epistemic status, with the *reliability* of its mode of formation, or with what it is that is supposed to epistemize the belief. In recent decades the Level Ascent argument has been prominent in the writings of Wilfrid Sellars, and I shall first look at its Sellarsian form.[16] It may be doubted that Sellars

---

[14]See Firth, "Coherence, Certainty, and Epistemic Priority."

[15]Note that (IV) does *not* read: "S's belief that p is *immediately* epistemized—S's belief is epistemized *only* by something other than some relation this belief has to some other epistemized belief(s) of S." The 'only' was omitted specifically to allow for the possibility that the belief might also (contemporaneously) be mediately epistemized. A parallel point holds for (III).

[16]No doubt, Sellars' best known sally in this arena is his attack on "giveness" and the idea that foundational beliefs are justified by virtue of formulating what is given in a

can be counted among the foes of immediate knowledge, for he is wont to present his position as a sort of synthesis of foundationalism and coherentism.[17] But as we shall see, the foundationalist ingredient in the brew does not include any recognition of full-blooded immediate knowledge.

The earliest explicit rejection of immediate knowledge known to me in Sellars' works comes in an oft-quoted section of "Empiricism and the Philosophy of Mind" (EPM), first published in 1956. Having disposed, to his satisfaction, of the view that the "authority" of observational reports stems from their correctly formulating the content of non-propositional awarenesses that are "self-authenticating", Sellars goes on to consider what alternative there might be. He begins with the following possibility.

> An overt or covert token of 'This is green' in the presence of a green item . . . expresses observational knowledge if and only if it is a manifestation of a tendency to produce overt or covert tokens of 'This is green'—given a certain set—if and only if a green object is being looked at in standard conditions. (p. 167)

This is what has since come to be known as a reliability account of observational knowledge. What makes this a case of knowledge is that the belief (or in this case the statement) stems from a habit that can be relied on to produce true beliefs (statements). This would be one form of the view that such knowledge is immediate knowledge, for the specified necessary and sufficient condition does not require the subject to have other knowledge or justified belief. But Sellars does not accept this account. It "won't do as it stands" (p. 167). Although the "authority" of the report stems from "the fact that one can infer the presence of a green object from the fact that someone makes this report" (p. 167), that is, from the fact that the report was a manifestation of a reliable

---

nonpropositional cognitive act. But because of my limitation to *general* arguments against immediate knowledge, I will not be discussing that aspect of his polemic.

For different reactions to the Level Ascent argument see Ernest Sosa, "The Raft and the Pyramid," *Midwest Studies in Philosophy* 5 (1980), where it is called the "Doxastic Ascent" argument, and R. G. Meyers, "Sellars' Rejection of Foundations," *Philosophical Studies*, 39 (1981), 61–78.

[17]In speaking of Firth, "Coherence, Certainty, and Epistemic Priority," he refers to "one aspect of his enterprise, which is, as I would put it, to reconcile as far as possible the claims of those who stress warrantedness grounded in explanatory coherence (among whom I count myself) with the claims of those who stress the non-inferential warrantedness of certain empirical statements (among whom I also count myself)". "More on Givenness and Explanatory Coherence," in *Justification and Knowledge*, ed. G. S. Pappas (Dordrecht: D. Reidel, 1979), p. 174.

tendency, still "to be the expression of knowledge, a report must not only have authority, this authority must *in some sense* be recognized by the person whose report it is" (p. 168). In other words, "no tokening by *S now* of 'This is green' is to count as 'expressing observational knowledge' unless it is also correct to say of *S* that he *now* knows the appropriate fact of the form *X is a reliable symptom of Y*, namely that . . . utterances of 'This is green' are reliable indicators of the presence of green objects in standard conditions of perception . . ." (p. 169). In still other terms, Jones does not *know* that this is green unless he is *able* to take the formation of his statement (belief) in these circumstances as a reason for supposing that a green object is present (p. 168). Since what is required for knowing that this is green (over and above true belief, that is to say, what is required for epistemization) includes Jones's having certain specific pieces of knowledge and the ability to use them to support the proposition in question, Sellars is clearly denying that observational knowledge is or can be immediate knowledge, as that term was explained above. His reason for denying it clearly falls under our Level Ascent rubric. One's belief counts as knowledge only if one knows something about the epistemic status of that belief, viz., that it counts as a reliable sign of the fact believed. And, equally clearly, this move could be used against *any* claim to immediate knowledge.

The exposition in EPM leaves things insufficiently explicit in at least two respects. The first and less serious has to do with the way in which the view is supposed to give something to the foundationalist. In an oft-quoted passage, Sellars writes:

> There is clearly some *point* to the picture of human knowledge as resting on a level of propositions—observation reports—which do not rest on other propositions in the same way as other propositions rest on them. On the other hand, I do wish to insist that the metaphor of 'foundation' is misleading in that it keeps us from seeing that if there is a logical dimension in which other empirical propositions rest on observation reports, there is another logical dimension in which the latter rest on the former. (p. 170)

The discussion in EPM, summarized in the previous paragraph, makes clear the way in which Sellars thinks that observation reports rest on other propositions, but not the way in which he thinks that they do not (i.e., the way in which others rest on them). The second and more serious respect is that no adequate support is given for the position. The author just lays it down that "to be the expression of knowledge, a report must not only have authority, this authority must *in some sense* be recognized by the person whose report it is" (p. 168).[18]

Are other writings of Sellars more explicit in these two respects? The most systematic presentation of Sellars' general epistemology known to me is the third of the Matchette lectures, given in 1971 at the University of Texas and published under the general title of "The Structure of Knowledge" (SK) in *Action, Knowledge and Reality: Critical Studies in Honor of Wilfrid Sellars,* ed. H. N. Castañeda (Indianapolis: Bobbs-Merrill, 1975). There we shall find that though the first lack is filled, the second is not.[19]

In the third of these lectures, entitled "Epistemic Principles", he makes two distinctions between observation reports and, for example,

[18]To be sure, Sellars prefaces this remark with "For we have seen that . . .", but it is not clear to me just where in the essay he supposes it to have been seen. Perhaps he was thinking of this passage: "Statements pertaining to this level, in order to 'express knowledge' must not only be made, but, so to speak, must be worthy of being made, *credible,* that is, in the sense of worthy of credence. Furthermore, and this is a crucial point, they must be made in a way which *involves* this credibility. For where there is no connection between the making of a statement and its authority, the assertion may express *conviction,* but it can scarcely be said to express knowledge" (p. 164). If this is intended to be an argument for the crucial claim quoted above from p. 168, then I will have to retract my statement that Sellars "just lays it down". But if this be support, it is quite inadequate to the task. I will agree that knowledge requires some connection between "the making of a statement and its authority", i.e., in this case, between the making of a statement and the fact that it was made in circumstances in which it is likely to be true. A merely accidental concatenation of the two would be a case in which it was just a matter of luck that the statement was true, and being right by accident is not knowledge. But, and this is the crucial point, Sellars' candidate for the connection is not the only possibility. Sellars thinks that if there is to be a "connection", it will have to be a relatively sophisticated one in second intention; it will have to be that the speaker makes her statement in recognition that the circumstances are propitious for its truth. But there is a humbler candidate, the one that is already built into the initial suggestion that Sellars thinks we must go beyond, viz., that the statement "is a manifestation of a tendency to produce overt or covert tokens of 'This is green'—given a certain set—if and only if a green object is being looked at in standard conditions" (p. 167). That is, the mere fact that the particular utterance is a manifestation of a general tendency to make such utterances only in truth-conducive circumstances is *itself* a "connection between the statement and its authority" that removes the case from the class of lucky guesses or accidental hits; and this is true whether or not the speaker knows *that* the circumstances are propitious. What we need from Sellars is a reason for thinking that this simpler "connection" is not enough, and that the higher-level-knowledge connection is required for knowledge of the lower level proposition.

[19]In another prime source for Sellars' general epistemology, "More on Givenness and Explanatory Coherence," he *assumes* that it is reasonable to accept introspective, perceptual, and memory (IPM) judgments only because it is reasonable to accept the higher level judgment that IPM judgments are generally true (pp. 177, 178, 180). But in that article the focus is on what it takes to be justified in those higher level judgments, and as a result the claim about what it takes to be justified in IPM judgments is not even discussed, much less adequately supported.

the generalizations that are traditionally thought to be based on them. First (a point that was at least implicit in EPM), the former differs from the latter in being "non-inferential" in the sense that they are not, typically, arrived at on the basis of inference of any sort. They are formed "spontaneously" (pp. 324, 342). But this is not a difference in epistemic status, at least not according to Sellars' lights. It does not constitute a way in which observation reports "do not *rest* on other propositions in the same way as other propositions *rest* on them". Sellars spells out the distinctively epistemic difference as follows. The way in which other propositions rest on observation reports is given by the following schema:

> I have good reasons, all things considered, for believing *p*;
> *So, p;*
> So, I have good reasons, all things considered, for believing *q*. (p. 335)

Here we are justified in believing *q* because it "can be correctly inferred, inductively or deductively, from other beliefs which we are justified in holding" (p. 336). But the way in which an observation report is justified is given by the following schema:

> I just thought-out-loud 'Lo! Here is a red apple'
> (no countervailing conditions obtain);
> So, there is good reason to believe that there is a red apple in front of me.
>
> . . .
>
> Notice that although the justification of the belief that there is a red apple in front of (Jones) is an inferential justification, it has the peculiar character that its essential premise asserts the occurrence of the very same belief in a specific context. It is this fact which gives the appearance that such beliefs are *self-justifying* and hence gives the justification the appearance of being *non-inferential*. (p. 342)

Thus the respect in which an observation report does not *rest* on other justification of other beliefs *on the same level*. The beliefs that Jones must be justified in believing, in order that he be justified in believing B (that there is a red apple in front of him), are beliefs *about* B, that it occurred in certain circumstances that satisfy certain conditions. In fn. 12 on p. 342 Sellars refers to a passage in his essay "Phenomenalism", in which he says that the kind of credibility generated for B by the above schema is a "trans-level credibility" (*Science, Perception, and Reality*, p. 88).[20]

---

[20]In scrutinizing the above schemata one may be struck by the fact that in the second schema, unlike the first, the premises make no reference to the justification of any other

Thus the thesis that observation reports do not rest on other propositions, as Sellars understands that thesis, does not imply that they express immediate knowledge, as we have explained that notion. Sellars remains committed to the thesis that I know that there is a red apple before me only if I know the relevant facts about what gives my utterance its "authority".

But what about some reason for accepting this position? Here SK is less satisfactory, though the hints are broader than in EPM. For one thing, Sellars talks as if it is central to the concept of justification that it involves having reasons for the justificandum.

> Presumably, to be justified in believing something is to have good reasons for believing it, as contrasted with its contradictory. (p. 332)

> Is it not possible to construe 'I know that-p' as essentially equivalent to 'p, and I have reasons good enough to support a guarantee. . . '? (p. 333)

Against this background, the question:

> If knowledge is justified true belief, how can there be such a thing as self-evident knowledge? And if there is no such thing as self-evident knowledge, how can *any* true belief be, in the relevant sense, justified? (p. 332)

hangs:

> ultimately on a distinction between two ways in which there can be, and one can have, good reasons for believing that-p. (p. 334)

That distinction is the one between same-level and trans-level reasons that we have just been discussing.

Well, *if* it is essential to the epistemic justification of a belief that the believer have adequate reason for her belief, then there can be no immediate justification, and, if justification is necessary for knowledge, no immediate knowledge. But unless that claim is itself defended in some way, it is too close to the question at issue to advance the discussion. It is very close indeed; the principle of justification through reasons alone is precisely what the partisan of immediate knowledge is

---

beliefs of the subject. And from this one may infer that Sellars supposes that the justification of observational beliefs depends in no way on the justification of other beliefs. But this is *not* Sellars' position. He is committed to holding both that an observational belief can be correctly inferred from the premises of the appropriate schema of the second sort, *and* that such a belief is justified only if the believer knows, or is justified in believing, those premises. (See, e.g., p. 342.)

denying. For to have reasons for a belief is to have other knowledge or justified belief that supports the belief in question. And immediate justification is justification for which that is not required.

We may find something far enough back to advance the discussion, by considering the way in which Sellars hints that *all* justification is higher level in character. It always consists of showing, or of the capacity to show, that one's belief is justified, or reasonable, or that one has adequate reasons for it. Note that the two schemata of justification that were cited on p. 68 have as their conclusion not the proposition the justification of the belief in which is in question, but rather a higher level proposition to the effect that the subject has good reasons, or that there are good reasons, to believe the lower level proposition. And of the second schema Sellars says, "Like all justification arguments, it is a higher-order thinking" (SK, p. 342). One could wish the author to be more explicit, but this does suggest that Sellars is thinking of epistemic justification in general as consisting of, or requiring, the *capacity* of the subject to produce adequate reasons for supposing that it is reasonable to believe the proposition justified.

If this is the case, then justification does require adequate reasons, for I couldn't have the capacity to produce adequate reasons without there being such reasons to produce. But why should we suppose that this *is* required for epistemic justification? We frequently take ourselves to know things with respect to which we have no such capacity. I often suppose myself to know that my wife is upset about something, where I would be hard pressed to specify how I can tell, that is, hard pressed to specify what makes it reasonable for me to believe this. The same goes for much of our supposed knowledge about history, geography, and physical regularities. In the face of all this, why should we accept the thesis that justification essentially involves the capacity to demonstrate reasonableness?

It is tempting to suppose that Sellars has fallen victim to the pervasive confusion between the activity of *justifying* a belief—*showing* the belief to be reasonable, credible, or justified—and a belief's *being* justified, where this is some kind of epistemic state or condition of the believer vis-à-vis that belief, rather than something he is or might be *doing*.[21] There are enough locutions that are ambiguous between these two to provide a spawning ground for the confusion. ('The belief is justified.' 'What does it take to justify the belief?') One who has fallen

---

[21]"The essential point is that in characterizing an episode or state as that of *knowing*, we are not giving an empirical description of that episode or state; we are placing it in the logical space of reasons, of justifying and being able to justify what one says." (EPM, p. 169.)

into the confusion will realize, of course, that we can't require S to have actually gone through the activity of justifying B in order to be justified in accepting B. But if still in the toils of the confusion, he is likely to take it as obvious that at least S must be *capable* of justifying B in order to *be* justified in accepting B.[22]

But perhaps Sellars' higher level slant on justification has a more respectable origin. Perhaps he is simply exhibiting the widespread tendency of epistemologists to think of knowledge as the exclusive possession of critically reflective subjects, where being "critically reflective" essentially involves the tendency to ask, and the capacity to answer, questions as to what it is that justifies one's beliefs or makes them reasonable. If one has to be that kind of subject in order to have knowledge, then knowledge does require what Sellars says it does. But it seems clear that none of us satisfy that antecedent condition with respect to all our beliefs, and that many human subjects, and all lower animals, satisfy it with respect to few or none of their beliefs. An examination of the epistemic status of one's beliefs is a highly sophisticated exercise that presupposes a massive foundation of less rarefied cognitive achievements. Presumably epistemology is not limited to understanding the condition of philosophers and other choice spirits who have achieved a considerable ability in making explicit what it takes to render one or another sort of belief rational. It is, more generally and more basically, an attempt to understand the nature and conditions of such cognitive achievements as getting accurate information about the immediate environment through perception, one's awareness of what one is thinking or feeling at the moment, and one's recollection of what happened to one in the past. If terms like 'knowledge' are confined to the cognitive achievements of critically reflective subjects, we shall have to find a new term for the territory in its full extent.

The above should not be taken to imply, nor does it imply, that reflective knowledge of one's knowledge and of the epistemic status of one's beliefs is not valuable; nor does it imply that there are not impor-

[22]Although I am perhaps too much given to seeing instances of another confusion, a level confusion between, e.g., being justified in believing *that p* and being justified in believing *that one is justified in believing that p* (Essays 2 and 6), I can hardly find Sellars guilty of this charge, in view of what we have already noted to be his clear recognition of the distinction. It is worthy of note, though, that if one did fail to make the distinction, as many epistemologists do, this could easily lead one to the Level Ascent argument. For, clearly, in order to be justified in the higher level belief *that one is justified in the lower level belief*, one must have reasons that have to do with the epistemic status of that lower level belief. And so if one fails to distinguish the two justifications, one will automatically take it that such reasons are required for being justified in the lower level belief. It may be that such a confusion plays a role in Bonjour's position, to be discussed below, but I will not pursue that possibility.

tant goals for the attainment of which it is necessary. It would seem to be required for answering skepticism, for being fully self-conscious about one's cognitive situation, and, more generally, for doing epistemology, an activity I am scarcely in a position to brand as pointless. But all this is quite compatible with the point just urged that one can genuinely have propositional knowledge without being capable, and especially without being fully capable, of a reflective assessment of that knowledge. We must not confuse epistemology with its own subject matter.

IV

In his essay "Can Empirical Knowledge Have a Foundation?"[23] Laurence Bonjour mounts an argument against immediate knowledge that displays many of the features of Sellars' attack. Let's consider whether Bonjour does any better by way of providing support for the crucial contentions of that attack.

Bonjour is concerned to show the impossibility of "basic beliefs", beliefs that are justified otherwise than by other justified beliefs, what we have been calling "immediately justified beliefs". The central argument runs as follows.

> If basic beliefs are to provide a secure foundation for empirical knowledge, if inference from them is to be the sole basis for the justification of other empirical beliefs, then that feature, whatever it may be, in virtue of which a belief qualifies as basic must also constitute a good reason for thinking that the belief is true.[24] If we let 'φ' represent this feature, then for a belief B to qualify as basic in an acceptable foundationist account, the premises of the following argument must themselves be at least justified;
> (i) Belief B has feature φ.
> (ii) Beliefs having feature φ are highly likely to be true.
> ___
> Therefore, B is highly likely to be true.
>
> . . . And if we now assume, reasonably enough, that for B to be justified for a particular person (at a particular time) it is necessary,

[23]*American Philosophical Quarterly*, 15 (1978), 1–13.
[24]Bonjour supports this claim, cogently in my opinion, as follows. ". . . knowledge requires *epistemic* justification, and the distinguishing characteristic of this particular species of justification is, I submit, its essential or internal relationship to the cognitive goal of truth. . . . A corollary of this conception of epistemic justification is that a satisfactory defense of a particular standard of epistemic justification must consist in showing it to be truth-conducive, i.e., in showing that accepting beliefs in accordance with its dictates is likely to lead to truth (and more likely than any proposed alternative)" (p. 5).

not merely that a justification for *B* exist in the abstract, but that the person in question be in cognitive possession of the justification, we get the result that *B* is not basic after all since its justification depends on that of at least one other empirical belief. (pp. 5–6)

It is clear that this argument passes my test for a *general* argument against immediate knowledge. The argument is quite indifferent as to what the feature φ is. It could be "formulating the content of an immediate awareness" or "being a true self-presenting proposition" or "being formed by a reliable perceptual process" or what-you-will, and the argument will be just as strong, or just as weak.

As already indicated, I am not at all disposed to quarrel with the claim that premises (i) and (ii) must be true whenever B is immediately (or mediately) justified (and hence that the conclusion must be true as well since it is a valid argument). To admit so much is no more than to agree that any justifying feature must be "truth-conducive". But this is perfectly compatible with the existence of immediate knowledge. The premise "B is justified by virtue of having feature φ, which is truth-conducive" has no tendency to support "B is justified by the fact that the subject has adequate reasons for it". It is the further requirement that is the clinker: "For B to be justified for a particular person (at a particular time) it is necessary, not merely that a justification for B exist in the abstract, but that the person in question be in cognitive possession of it." In other words, in order that I be justified in accepting B, I must know, or be justified in believing, the premises of the above argument. And why should we suppose that? Again, unless some significant grounds are adduced, our opponent of immediate knowledge has done nothing more impressive than to affirm the contradictory.

Now Bonjour, like Sellars, roundly affirms that justification, in general, requires possession of adequate reasons by the subject (pp. 5, 7). And so, as in Sellars, when confronted with a putatively basic belief, we are driven to higher level reasons. But, again, this by itself is to repeat the position rather than to defend it. In Bonjour's article there is rather more ground than in Sellars for suspecting a confusion between *justifying a belief* and *being justified in a belief*. After enunciating "the traditional conception of knowledge as *adequately justified true belief*" he writes: "Now the most natural way to justify a belief is by producing a justificatory argument. . . ." The obvious suggestion is that "justified" in the conditions for knowledge means "having been the target of a successful activity of justifying", rather than, for instance, "it's being all right for the subject to hold it". He backs out of this in the next paragraph when he writes, "a person for whom a belief is inferentially justified need not have explicitly rehearsed the justificatory argument in question to others or even to himself", but he feels he is still left with the requirement that "the inference be available to him if the belief is called into question by others or by himself . . . and that the availability of inference be, in the final analysis, his reason for holding the belief" (p. 2). And three pages later, after opining that "the very idea of an epistemically basic empirical belief is extremely paradoxical", he supports the opinion by writing: "For on what basis is such a belief *to be justified,* once appeal to further empirical beliefs is ruled out?" (p. 5; emphasis mine; see also the first paragraph of p. 8).

However, Bonjour also has a way of defending the demand for reasons that is different from anything in Sellars, and we ought to consider that. In spelling out the concept of justification that is involved in his argument he writes:

> Knowledge requires *epistemic* justification and the distinguishing characteristic of this particular species of justification is, I submit, its essential or internal relationship to the cognitive goal of truth. Cognitive doings are epistemically justified, on this conception, only if and to the extent that they are aimed at this goal—which means roughly that one accepts all and only beliefs which one has good reason to think are true. To accept a belief in the absence of such a reason, however appealing or even mandatory such acceptance might be from other standpoints, is to neglect the pursuit of truth; such acceptance is, one might say, *epistemically irresponsible.* My contention is that the idea of being epistemically responsible is the core of the concept of epistemic justification. (p. 5)

Some of the transitions in this line of thought are unconvincing as they stand. Accepting "all and only beliefs which one has good reason to think are true" is by no means the same thing as aiming at the goal of truth, even if we modify the former to "accepting all and only beliefs that one *takes oneself to* have good reasons to think are true". To suppose it is obvious that they come to the same thing is to assume the anti-immediacy thesis that is at issue. But what I want to focus on at the moment is the support given this transition by what follows—the conception of justification as epistemic responsibility.

To think of epistemic justification as amounting to epistemic responsibility is to treat the former as a normative concept, one that belongs to a circle of concepts that includes duty, obligation, blame, reproach, right, and wrong. Bonjour is thinking of being justified in believing that *p* as either having done one's epistemic duty in so believing, or as not having violated any epistemic duty in so believing. If we want to keep epistemic justification in line with other species of the genus, we will have to opt for the latter. What I am justified in *doing* is not always something I have an obligation to do, but it is always something that I am permitted to do, something the doing of which does not violate any obligations. To say that I am justified in taking a taxi to the airport (and charging it to my expense account) is not to imply that I have a duty to take a taxi, rather than a bus; it is only to imply that I am allowed to do so, that doing so does not violate any regulations. So let's say that, on a normative construal, S's being justified in believing that p amounts to S's not violating any epistemic obligation in believing that p.^A

This pushes the question back to "Why should we suppose that one who believes that p without having adequate reason for supposing p to be true is violating any intellectual obligation?" If I have acquired a propensity to form perceptual beliefs in circumstances favorable to their truth, why suppose that I am violating some epistemic obligation by manifesting that propensity, where I don't have any good reason for supposing that the circumstances are propitious? Why wouldn't an acceptable set of epistemic norms permit me to form beliefs in that way? So far as I can see, Bonjour would have to reply as follows.

> To be responsible in my doxastic decisions I have to make them in the light of the reasons available to me, for that is all I have to go on. Therefore what is required of me as a seeker after truth, as a cognitive subject, is that I decide between believing that p and refraining from that belief on the basis of whatever relevant reasons are available to me. To make the decision on any other basis or in any other way would be to flout my intellectual obligations. It would be "epistemically irresponsible".[25]

If this is the way the wind blows, then it shows, first of all, that Bonjour is assuming that obligations and the like attach directly to believing and refraining from believing, and hence that he is assuming believing and the reverse to be under voluntary control. "Ought implies can." He is assuming that, with respect to each candidate for belief, the subject has a choice as to whether or not to believe it. This voluntaristic version of a normative conception of justification can be

---

[25] In considering the reliabilist position that S knows that p provided S has a true belief that p that was formed in a reliable manner (whether or not S knows it to be reliable), Bonjour writes: "But P himself has no reason at all for thinking that B is likely to be true. From his perspective, it is an accident that the belief is true. And thus his acceptance of B is no more rational or responsible from an epistemic standpoint than would be the acceptance of a subjectively similar belief for which the external relation in question failed to obtain" (p. 8).

contrasted with an nonvoluntaristic version according to which belief is not, either in general or ever, under voluntary control, and intellectual obligations attach rather to the various things people can do (voluntarily) to affect their belief-forming process.[B] Second, even granted the voluntarism, Bonjour's demand for reasons would not be supported by a severely objectivist version, on which a believing's being in accord with my obligations is simply a matter of whether that believing is *in fact* in violation of any obligation, whatever I believe, know, or justifiably believe about the matter. If one of my obligations is to refrain from a perceptual belief if the conditions of perception are abnormal, then whether I violated that obligation in believing that p would be a matter of whether, in fact, the conditions were abnormal, not on whether I believed, knew, or justifiably believed that the conditions are abnormal. On that version justification hangs on the way things are, rather than on what reasons I have that bear on the question. To squeeze a universal demand for reasons out of the concept of justification, Bonjour will have to be using a more subjective version of a voluntaristic normative conception, according to which one has satisfied one's obligations in a belief *iff* one knows or is justified in believing that the objective requirements have been satisfied. On that reading it *will* be the case that one is proceeding as one ought in believing that p only if one has adequate reason for supposing that q, where q amounts to whatever is required by the relevant (objective) epistemic obligations.[C]

Thus we have found one not disreputable ground for the universal demand for reasons. But however respectable, the subjective-voluntaristic-normative conception of justification is not immune from criticism, especially as regards the claim that justification in this sense is a necessary condition of knowledge. I myself am disinclined to allow that justification on any normative conception is necessary for knowledge. The reason for this is as follows. Normative conceptions like obligation and reproach apply only to beings that are capable of governing their conduct in accordance with norms, principles, or rules. It is for lack of this capacity that we refrain from using such concepts in application to very small children and lower animals. But surely these creatures are not devoid of knowledge. Both infants and dogs acquire knowledge about their immediate physical environment through perception. If Bonjour denies this last claim we have an opposition quite similar to the earlier opposition between Sellars and myself as to whether subjects should be credited with knowledge only to the extent that they are capable of critical reflection on the epistemic status of their beliefs.

But even if we employ some sort of normative conception of justification, there are strong objections to a voluntaristic version thereof. It seems clear that belief is not, in general, under direct voluntary control. When I seem to myself to see a truck coming down the street, or when I am in any of the innumerable situations, perceptual and otherwise, where it seems obvious to me that something is or is not the case, I do not have the capacity to believe *or* refrain from believing at will, as I choose. If in the above situation I were to set myself to refrain from believing that a truck is coming down the street, perhaps in order to prove to myself that I can, I wouldn't know how to begin. I wouldn't know what button to push. (Of course, I can undertake a regimen that is designed to gradually wean myself away from reliance on the senses; but even if I should succeed in this, that is a different story. There are many things not themselves under direct voluntary control that I can affect by what I do, e.g., my health and my wealth.) Whether I can ever believe at will is a matter I will not go into. However that question is resolved, it is clear that belief is not always, or even generally, a matter of choice. Hence a conception of justification that presupposes voluntary control of belief cannot be applied to belief in general. On that construal, justification cannot be a general requirement for knowledge.[26]

Thus in Bonjour, as in Sellars, the contention that putatively immediate knowledge really rests on higher level reasons itself rests on a foundation of sand.[27,28]

[26]For the concepts of justification mentioned here, as well as others, see Essays 4 and 5.

[27]The considerations of Sections III and IV can also be used against the position Michael Williams takes in his book *Groundless Belief* (New Haven: Yale University Press, 1977). I have not explicitly discussed his arguments in the body of the paper, for he does not squarely oppose the possibility of any immediate knowledge as does Sellars and Bonjour. He recognizes the possibility that, e.g., perceptual beliefs might be justified just by virtue of having been reliably formed, even if the subject knows nothing about that (p. 69). But he holds that if that is the whole story, such beliefs do not meet the foundationalist's requirements since a "potential infinite regress of justification" has not been closed off (p. 69). This is because empirical facts will have to be produced to justify the supposition that the perceptual beliefs in question *were* reliably produced. "To say that there is an *empirical* presumption in favor of beliefs of a certain kind being true is to trace the prima-facie credibility of these beliefs to further general facts and thus to lead ourselves back into the very regress from which *intrinsically* credible beliefs are supposed to liberate us" (p. 76; see also pp. 158–61). Of course, if someone makes the higher level statement that certain perceptual beliefs are reliably produced and therefore credible, he will need reasons for that statement and *he* will not be at the terminus of a regress of justification. But that does not imply that the perceptual believer in question needs reasons to be justified in holding his first-level perceptual beliefs, and hence it doesn't imply that *he* is not at the terminus of a regress of justification. (See Essay 1) Williams does nothing to support that claim, and if he were to support it with considerations of the sort deployed by Sellars and Bonjour, the same responses would be in order.

[28]This paper has profited greatly from comments by Robert Audi and Jonathan Bennett.

Notes

A. For an extended discussion of normative conceptions of epistemic justification (there termed "deontological"), see Essay 5.

B. Again, see Essay 5, Sections VI and VII, for details.

C. See Essay 4, Section III, where various "modes" of epistemic obligation (and other sorts of obligation and justification) are distinguished. There the one under consideration at this point is called a "cognitive" mode.

PART II

THE NATURE OF EPISTEMIC JUSTIFICATION

Concepts of
Epistemic Justification

I

Justification, or at least 'justification', bulks large in recent
epistemology. The view that knowledge consists of true justified belief
(+ . . .) has been prominent in this century, and the justification of
belief has attracted considerable attention in its own right. But it is
usually not at all clear just what an epistemologist means by 'justified',
just what concept the term is used to express. An enormous amount of
energy has gone into the attempt to specify conditions under which
beliefs of one or another sort are justified; but relatively little has been
done to explain *what it is* for a belief to be justified, what that is for
which conditions are being sought.[1] The most common procedure has
been to proceed on the basis of a number of (supposedly) obvious cases
of justified belief, without pausing to determine what property it is of
which these cases are instances. Now even if there were some single
determinate concept that all these theorists have implicitly in mind, this

---

From *The Monist*, 68, no. 1 (1985). Reprinted by permission of the editor.

[1]Of late, a number of theorists have been driving a wedge between what it is to *be* P or
what *property* P is, on the one hand, and what belongs to the *concept* of P or what is the
meaning of P on the other. Thus it has been claimed that *what heat is* is determined by the
physical investigation into the nature of heat, whether or not the results of that investigation are embodied in our *concept* of heat or in the meaning of 'heat'. (See Saul Kripke,
"Naming and Necessity," in *Semantics of Natural Language*, ed. D. Davidson and G. Harman [Dordrecht: D. Reidel, 1972].) I shall take it no such distinction is applicable to
epistemic justification, that here the only reasonable interpretation to be given 'what it is'
is 'what is involved in the concept' or 'what the term means'. If someone disagrees with
this, that need not be a problem. Such a person can simply read, e.g., 'what concept of
justification is being employed' for 'what justification is taken to be'.

procedure would be less than wholly satisfactory. For in the absence of an explicit account of the concept being applied, we lack the most fundamental basis for deciding between supposed intuitions and for evaluating proposed conditions of justification. And in any event, as philosophers we do not seek merely to speak the truth, but also to gain an explicit, reflective understanding of the matters with which we deal. We want to know not only when our beliefs are justified, but also what it is to enjoy that status. True, not every fundamental concept can be explicated, but we shall find that much can be done with this one.

And since, as we shall see in this paper, there are several distinct concepts that are plausibly termed "concepts of epistemic justification", the need for analysis is even greater. By simply using 'justified' in an unexamined, intuitive fashion, the epistemologist is covering up differences that make important differences to the shape of a theory of justification. We cannot fully understand the stresses and strains in thought about justification until we uncover the most crucial differences between concepts of epistemic justification.

Not all contemporary theorists of justification fall under these strictures. Some have undertaken to give an account of the concept of justification they are using.[2] But none of them provide a map of this entire conceptual territory.

In this essay I am going to elaborate and interrelate several distinct concepts of epistemic justification, bringing out some crucial issues involved in choosing between them. I shall give reasons for disqualifying some of the contenders, and I shall explain my choice of a winner. Finally I shall vouchsafe a glimpse of the enterprise for which this essay is a propaedeutic, that of showing how the differences between these concepts make a difference in what it takes for the justification of belief, and other fundamental issues in epistemology.

Before launching this enterprise, we must clear out of the way a confusion between one's *being* justified in believing that *p*, and one's *justifying* one's belief that *p*, where the latter involves one's *doing* something to show that *p*, or to show that one's belief was justified, or to exhibit one's justification. The first side of this distinction is a state or

[2]I think especially of R. M. Chisholm, *Theory of Knowledge*, 2d ed. (Englewood Cliffs, N.J.: Prentice-Hall, 1977), chap. 1; Carl Ginet, *Knowledge, Perception, and Memory* (Dordrecht: D. Reidel, 1975), chap. 3; A. I. Goldman, "What Is Justified Belief?", in G. S. Pappas, ed., *Justification and Knowledge* (Dordrecht: D. Reidel, 1979) and *Epistemology and Cognition* (Cambridge: Harvard University Press, 1986); M. B. Naylor, "Epistemic Justification," *American Philosophical Quarterly*, 25 (January, 1988), 49–58; N. Wolterstorff, "Can Belief in God Be Rational If It Has No Foundations?", in *Faith and Rationality*, ed. A. Plantinga and N. Wolterstorff (Notre Dame, Ind.: University of Notre Dame Press, 1983).

condition one is in, not anything one does or any upshot thereof. I might *be* justified in believing that there is milk on the table because I see it there, even though I have done nothing to show that there is milk on the table or to show that I am justified in believing there to be. It is amazing how often these matters are confused in the literature. We will be concentrating on the "be justified" side of this distinction, since that is of more fundamental epistemological interest. If epistemic justification were restricted to those cases in which the subject carries out a "justification", it would *obviously* not be a necessary condition of knowledge or even of being in a strong position to acquire knowledge. Most cases of perceptual knowledge, for example, involve no such activity.[3]

II

Let's begin our exploration of this stretch of conceptual territory by listing a few basic features of the concept that would seem to be common ground.

(1) It applies to beliefs, or alternatively to a cognitive subject's having a belief. I shall speak indifferently of S's belief that *p* being justified and of S's being justified in believing that *p*. This is the common philosophical concept of belief, in which S's believing that *p* entails neither that S knows that *p* nor that S does not know that *p*. It is not restricted to conscious or occurrent beliefs.

(2) It is an evaluative concept, in a broad sense in which this is contrasted with 'factual'. To say that S is justified in believing that *p* is to imply that there is something all right, satisfactory, in accord with the way things should be, about the fact that S believes that *p*. It is to accord S's believing a positive evaluative status.

(3) It has to do with a specifically *epistemic* dimension of evaluation. Beliefs can be evaluated in different ways. One may be more or less prudent, fortunate, or faithful in holding a certain belief. Epistemic justification is different from all that. Epistemic evaluation is undertaken from what we might call the "epistemic point of view". That point of view is defined by the aim at maximizing truth and minimizing falsity in a large body of beliefs. The qualification "in a large body of beliefs" is needed because otherwise one could best achieve the aim by

---

[3]It may be claimed that the activity concept is fundamental in another way, viz., by virtue of the fact that one is justified in believing that *p* only if one is *capable* of carrying out a justification of the belief. But if that were so, we would be justified in far fewer beliefs than we suppose. Most human subjects are quite incapable of carrying out a justification of any perceptual or introspective beliefs.

restricting one's beliefs to those that are obviously true. That is a rough formulation. How large a body of beliefs should we aim at? Is any body of beliefs of a given size, with the same truth-falsity ratio, equally desirable, or is it more important, epistemically, to form beliefs on some matters than others? And what relative weights should be assigned to the two aims at maximizing truth and minimizing falsity? We can't go into all that here; in any event, however these issues are settled, it remains true that our central cognitive aim is to amass a large body of beliefs with a favorable truth-falsity ratio. For a belief to be epistemically justified is for it, somehow, to be awarded high marks relative to that aim.

(4) It is a matter of degree. One can be more or less justified in believing that *p*. If, e.g., what justifies one is some evidence one has, one will be more or less justified depending on the amount and strength of the evidence. In this paper, however, I shall, for the sake of simplicity, treat justification as absolute. You may, if you like, think of this as the degree of justification required for some standard of acceptability.

III

Since any concept of epistemic justification is a concept of some condition that is desirable or commendable from the standpoint of the aim at maximizing truth and minimizing falsity, in distinguishing different concepts of justification we will be distinguishing different ways in which conditions can be desirable from this standpoint. As I see it, the major divide in this terrain has to do with whether believing and refraining from believing are subject to obligation, duty, and the like. If they are, we can think of the favorable evaluative status of a certain belief as consisting in the fact that in holding that belief one has fulfilled one's obligations, or refrained from violating one's obligations, to achieve the fundamental aim in question. If they are not so subject, the favorable status will have to be thought of in some other way.

I shall first explore concepts of the first sort, which I shall term 'deontological',[4] since they have to do with how one stands, in believing

---

[4]I am indebted to Alvin Plantinga for helping me to see that this term is more suitable than the term 'normative' that I had been using in earlier versions of this paper. The reader should be cautioned that 'deontological' as used here does not carry the contrast with 'teleological' that is common in ethical theory. According to that distinction a deontological ethical theory, like that of Kant's, does not regard principles of duty or obligation as owing their status to the fact that acting in the way they prescribe tends to realize certain desirable states of affairs, whereas a teleological theory, like Utilitarianism, holds that this is what renders a principle of obligation acceptable. The fact that we are not

that *p,* vis-à-vis duties or obligations. Most epistemologists who have attempted to explicate justification have set out a concept of this sort.[5] It is natural to set out a deontological concept on the model of the justification of behavior. Something I *did* was justified just in case it was *not in violation* of any relevant duties, obligations, rules, or regulations, and hence was not something for which I could rightfully be blamed. To say that my expenditures on the trip were justified is not to say that I was obliged to make those expenditures (e.g., for taxis), but only that it was all right for me to do so, that in doing so I was not in violation of any relevant rules or regulations. And to say that I was justified in making that decision on my own, without consulting the executive committee, is not to say that I was required to do it on my own (though that *may* also be true); it is only to say that the departmental by-laws permit the chairman to use his own discretion in matters of this kind. Similarly, to say that a belief was deontologically justified is not to say that the subject was obligated to believe this, but only that he was permitted to do so, that believing this did not involve any violation of relevant obligations. To say that I am justified in believing that salt is composed of sodium and chlorine, since I have been assured of this by an expert, is not to say that I am obligated to believe this, though this might also be true. It is to say that I am permitted to believe it, that believing it would not be a violation of any relevant obligation, for example, the obligation to refrain from believing that *p* in the absence of adequate reasons for doing so. As Carl Ginet puts it, "One is *justified* in being confident that *p* if and only if it is not the case that one ought not to be confident that *p;* one could not be justly reproached for being confident that *p.*"[6]

Since we are concerned specifically with the *epistemic* justification of belief, the concept in which we are interested is not that of *not violating obligations of any sort in believing,* but rather the more specific concept of *not violating "epistemic", "cognitive", or "intellectual" obligations in believing.* Where are such obligations to be found? If we follow out our earlier specification of the "epistemic point of view", we will think of our basic

---

using 'deontological' with this force is shown by the fact that we are thinking of epistemic obligations as owing their validity to the fact that fulfilling them would tend to lead to the realization of a desirable state of affairs, viz., a large body of beliefs with a favorable truth-falsity ratio.

[5]See Chisholm, *Theory of Knowledge,* chap. 1; Ginet, *Knowledge, Perception, and Memory,* chap. 3; Naylor, "Epistemic Justification"; Wolterstorff, "Can Belief in God Be Rational?" In my development of deontological concepts in this paper I have profited from the writings of all these people and from discussions with them.

[6]*Knowledge, Perception, and Memory,* p. 28. See also A. J. Ayer, *The Problem of Knowledge* (London: Macmillan, 1956), pp. 31–34; Chisholm, *Theory of Knowledge,* p. 14; Naylor, "Epistemic Justification," p. 51.

epistemic obligation as that of doing what we can to achieve the aim at maximizing truth and minimizing falsity within a large body of beliefs. There will then be numerous more specific obligations that owe their status to the fact that fulfilling them will tend to the achievement of that central aim. Such obligations might include *to refrain from believing that p in the absence of sufficient evidence* and *to accept whatever one sees to be clearly implied by something one already believes (or, perhaps, is already justified in believing).*[7] Of course other positions might be taken on this point.[8] One might suppose that there are a number of ultimate, irreducible intellectual duties that cannot be derived from any basic goal of our cognitive life. Or alternative versions of the central aim might be proposed. Here we shall think in terms of the basic aim we have specified, with more specific obligations derived from that.

Against this background we can set out our first concept of epistemic justification as follows, using 'd' for 'deontological':

(I) S is J_d in believing that *p iff* in believing that *p* S is not violating any epistemic obligations.

There are important distinctions between what we may call "modes" of obligation, justification, and other normative statuses. These distinctions are by no means confined to the epistemic realm. Let's introduce them in connection with moral norms for behavior. Begin with a statement of obligation in "objective" terms, a statement of the objective state of affairs I might be said to be obliged to bring about. For example, it is my obligation as a host to make *my guest, G, feel welcome.* Call that state of affairs 'A'. We may think of this as an *objective* conception of my obligation as a host. I have fulfilled that obligation *iff* G feels welcome.[9] But suppose I did what I sincerely believed would bring about A? In that case surely no one could blame me for dereliction of duty. That suggests a more *subjective* conception of my obligation as *doing what I believed was likely to bring about A.*[10] But perhaps I should not

---

[7]These examples are meant to be illustrative only; they do not necessarily carry the endorsement of the management.

[8]Here I am indebted to Alvin Plantinga.

[9]A weaker objective conception would be this. My obligation is to do what in fact is *likely* to bring about A. On this weaker conception I could be said to have fulfilled my obligation in (some) cases in which A is not forthcoming.

[10]We could also subjectivize the aimed at result, instead of or in addition to subjectivizing what it takes to arrive at that result. In this way one would have subjectively fulfilled one's obligation if one had done what one believed to be one's obligation. Or, to combine the two moves to the subjective, one would have subjectively fulfilled one's obligation if one had done what one believed would lead to the fulfillment of what one believed to be one's obligation. But sufficient unto the day is the distinction thereof.

be let off as easily as that. "You should have realized that what you did was not calculated to make G feel welcome." This retort suggests a somewhat more stringent formulation of my obligation than the very permissive subjective conception just specified. It suggests that I can't fulfill my obligation by doing just anything I happen to believe will bring about A. I am not off the hook unless *I did what the facts available to me indicate will have a good chance of leading to A.* This is still a subjective conception in that what it takes to fulfill my obligation is specified from my point of view; but it takes my point of view to range over not all my beliefs, but only my justified beliefs. This we might call a *cognitive* conception of my obligation.[11] Finally, suppose that I did what I had adequate reason to suppose would produce A, and I did produce A, but I didn't do it for that reason. I was just amusing myself, and I would have done what I did even if I had known it would not make G feel welcome. In that case I might be faulted for moral irresponsibility, however well I rate in the other modes. This suggests what we may call a motivational conception of my obligation as *doing what I believed (or was justified in believing) would bring about A, in order to bring about A.*

We may sum up these distinctions as follows:

(II) S has fulfilled his *objective* obligation *iff* S has brought about A.

(III) S has fulfilled his *subjective* obligation *iff* S has done what he believed to be most likely to bring about A.

(IV) S has fulfilled his *cognitive* obligation *iff* S did what he was justified in believing to be most likely to bring about A.

(V) S has fulfilled his *motivational* obligation *iff* S has done what he did because he supposed it would be most likely to bring about A.

We can make analogous distinctions with respect to the justification of behavior or belief, construed as the absence of any violation of obligations.[12] Let's indicate how this works out for the justification of belief.

(VI) S is *objectively* justified in believing that *p iff* S is not violating any objective obligation in believing that *p*.

(VII) S is *subjectively* justified in believing that *p iff* S is not violating any subjective obligation in believing that *p*.

---

[11] I would call this "epistemic obligation", except that I want to make these same distinctions with respect to epistemic obligation, and so I don't want to repeat the generic term for one of the species.

[12] Since we are tacitly restricting this to epistemic justification, we will also be, tacitly, restricting ourselves to intellectual obligations.

(VIII) S is *cognitively* justified in believing that *p iff* S is not violating any cognitive obligation in believing that *p*.

(IX) S is *motivationally* justified in believing that *p iff* is not violating any motivational obligation in believing that *p*.

If we assume that only one intellectual obligation is relevant to the belief in question, viz., the obligation to believe that *p* only if one has adequate evidence for *p*, we can be a bit more concrete about this.

(X) S is objectively justified in believing that *p iff* S has adequate evidence for *p*.[13]

(XI) S is subjectively justified in believing that *p iff* S believes that he possesses adequate evidence for *p*.

(XII) S is cognitively justified in believing that *p iff* S is justified in believing that he possesses adequate evidence for *p*.[14]

(XIII) S is motivationally justified in believing that *p iff* S believes that *p* on the basis of adequate evidence, or, alternatively, on the basis of what he believed, or was justified in believing, was adequate evidence.

I believe that we can safely neglect (XI). To explain why, I will need to make explicit what it is to have adequate evidence for *p*. First, a proposition, *q*, is adequate evidence for *p* provided they are related in such a way that if *q* is true then *p* is at least probably true. But I *have* that evidence only if I believe that *q*. Furthermore I don't "have" it in such a way as to thereby render my belief that *p* justified unless I know or am justified in believing that *q*. An unjustified belief that *q* wouldn't do it. If I believe that Begin has told the cabinet that he will resign, but only because I credited an unsubstantiated rumor, then even if Begin's having told the cabinet that he would resign is an adequate indication that

---

[13]Since this is all on the assumption that S does believe that *p*, we need not add that to the right hand side in order to get a sufficient condition.

[14]Note that (XI), (XII), and some forms of (XIII) are in terms of higher level beliefs about one's epistemic status vis-à-vis *p*. There are less sophisticated sorts of subjectivization. For example:

S is subjectively justified in believing that *p iff* S believes that *q*, and *q* is evidence for *p*.

(For the reason this does not count as having adequate evidence see the next paragraph in the text.)

Or even more subjectively:

S is subjectively justified in believing that *p iff* S believes that *q* and bases his belief that *p* on his belief that *q*.

The definitions presented in the text do not dictate what we should say in the case in which S does not have the higher level belief specified in (XI) and (XII), but satisfies either of the above conditions. A thorough treatment of modes of normative status would have to go into all of this.

he will resign, I will not thereby be justified in believing that he will resign.

Now I might very well *believe* that I have adequate evidence for q even though one or more of these conditions is not satisfied. I might mistakenly believe that my evidence is adequate support, and I might mistakenly suppose that I am justified in accepting it. But, as we have just seen, if I am not justified in accepting the evidence for p, then my believing it cannot render me justified in believing that p, however adequate that evidence. I would also hold, though this is perhaps more controversial, that if the evidence is not in fact adequate, my having that evidence cannot justify me in believing that p. Thus, since my believing that I have adequate evidence is compatible with these non-justifying states of affairs, we cannot take subjective justification, as defined in (XI), to constitute epistemic justification.

That leaves us with three contenders. Here I will confine myself to pointing out that there is a strong tendency for J_d to be used in a cognitive rather than a purely objective form. J_d is, most centrally, a concept of freedom from blameworthiness, a concept of being "in the clear" so far as one's intellectual obligations are concerned. But even if I don't have adequate evidence for p, I could hardly be blamed for believing that p (even assuming, as we are in this discussion, that there is something wrong with believing in the absence of adequate evidence), provided I am justified in supposing that I have adequate evidence. So long as that condition holds, I have done the right thing, or refrained from doing the wrong thing, so far as I am able to tell; and what more could be required of me? But this means that it is (XII), rather than (X), that brings out what it takes for freedom from blame, and so brings out what it takes for being J_d.[15]

What about the motivational form? We can have J_d in any of the first three forms with or without the motivational form. I can have adequate evidence for p and believe that p, whether or not my belief is based on that evidence; and so for the other two. But the motivational mode is parasitic on the other modes, in that the precise form taken by the

---

[15]We have been taking it that to be, e.g., subjectively or cognitively justified in believing that p is not to be violating any subjective or cognitive obligations in believing that p. That means that if we opt for cognitive justification, we are committed to giving a correspondingly cognitive formulation of what intellectual obligations one has. But that isn't the only way to do it. We could leave all the obligations in a purely objective form, and vary the function that goes from obligation to justification. That is, we could say that one is subjectively justified if one believes that one has not violated an (objective) obligation (or, perhaps, believes something that is such that, given one's objective obligations, it implies that none of those obligations have been violated). And a similar move could be made for the other modes.

motivational mode depends on the status of the (supposed) evidence on which the belief is based. This "unsaturated" character of the motivational mode is reflected in the threefold alternative that appears in our formulation of (XIII). If S bases his belief that p on actually possessed adequate evidence, then (XIII) combines with (X). If the evidence on which it is based is only believed to be adequate evidence, or only justifiably believed to be adequate evidence, then (XIII) combines with (XI) or (XII). Of course, it may be based on actually possessed adequate evidence, which is justifiably believed to be such, in which case S is justified in all four modes. Thus the remaining question concerning J_d is whether a "motivational rider" should be put on (XII). Is it enough for J_d that S be justified in believing that he has adequate evidence for p, or should it also be required that S's belief that p be based on that evidence? We will address this question in Section v in the form it assumes for a quite different concept of justification.[16]

---

[16]Here are a couple of examples of the attraction of (XII) for J_d. Chisholm, *Theory of Knowledge*, presents an informal explanation of his basic term of epistemic evaluation, 'more reasonable than' in terms of an "intellectual requirement". The explanation runs as follows. "One way, then, of re-expressing the locution "p is more reasonable than q for S at t" is to say this: S is so situated at t that his intellectual requirement, his responsibility as an intellectual being, is better fulfilled by p than by q" (p. 14). The point that is relevant to our present discussion is that Chisholm states our basic intellectual requirement in what I have called "cognitive" rather than "objective" terms, and with a motivational rider. "We may assume that every person is subject to a purely intellectual requirement— that of trying his best to bring it about that, for every proposition h that he considers, he accepts h if and only if h is true" (p. 14). The "requirement" is that one *try one's best* to bring this about, rather than that one do bring it about. I take it that to try my best to bring about a result, R, is to do what, so far as I can tell, will bring about R, insofar as that is within my power. (It might be claimed that so long as I do what I believe will bring about R, I am trying my best, however irresponsible the belief. But it seems to me that so long as I am not acting on the best of the indications available to me, I am not "trying my best". The motivational rider comes in too, since unless I do what I do *because* I am taking it to (have a good chance to) lead to R, I am not trying at all to bring about R.

Of course, Chisholm is speaking in terms of fulfilling an intellectual obligation rather than, as we have been doing, in terms of not violating intellectual obligations. But we are faced with the same choice between our "modes" in either case.

For a second example I turn to Wolterstorff, "Can Belief in God Be Rational?" Wolterstorff's initial formulation of a necessary and sufficient condition of justification (or, as he says, "rationality") for an "eluctable" belief of S that p is: *S lacks adequate reasons for ceasing from believing that p* (164). But then by considerations similar to those we have just adduced, he recognizes that even if S does not in fact have adequate reason for ceasing to believe that p, he would still be unjustified in continuing to hold the belief if he were "rationally obliged" to believe that he does have adequate reason to cease to believe that p. Moreover Wolterstorff recognizes that S would be justified in believing that p if, even though he does have adequate reason to cease from believing that p, he is rationally justified in supposing that he doesn't. Both these qualifications amount to recognizing that what is crucial is not what reasons S has in fact, but what reasons S is justified in supposing himself to have. The final formulation, embodying these and other qualifications, runs as follows:

IV

We have explained *being J$_d$ in believing that p* as *not violating any intellectual obligations in believing that p*. And, in parallel fashion, being J$_d$ in refraining from believing that p would consist in not having violated any intellectual obligations in so doing. But if it is possible for me to violate an obligation in refraining from believing that p, it must be that I can be obliged, under certain conditions, to believe that p. And, by the same token, if I can violate obligations in believing that p, then I can be obliged to refrain from believing that p. And this is the way we have been thinking of it. Our example of an intellectual obligation has been the obligation to refrain from believing that p in the absence of adequate evidence. On the other side, we might think of a person as being obliged to believe that p if confronted with conclusive evidence that p (where that includes the absence of sufficient overriding evidence to the contrary).

Now it certainly looks as if I can be obliged to believe or to refrain from believing, only if this is in my direct voluntary control; only if I can, here and now, believe that p or no just by willing (deciding, choosing . . .). And that is the way many epistemologists seem to construe the matter. At least, many formulations are most naturally interpreted in this way. Think back, for example, on Chisholm's formulation of our intellectual obligation, cited in n16. Chisholm envisages a person thinking of a certain proposition as a candidate for belief, considering what grounds there might be for belief or refraining from belief, and then effectively choosing belief or abstention on the basis of those considerations.[17] Let's call the version of J$_d$ that presupposes direct voluntary control over belief (and thus thinks of an obligation to believe as an obligation to bring about belief here and now), 'J$_{dv}$' ('v' for 'voluntary').

I find this assumption of direct voluntary control over belief quite unrealistic. There are strong reasons for doubting that belief is usually, or perhaps ever, under direct voluntary control. First, think of the beliefs I acquire about myself and the world about me through experi-

---

A person s is rational in his eluctable and innocently produced belief *Bp* if and only if S does believe p and either:

  (i) S neither has nor ought to have adequate reason to cease from believing p, and is not rationally obliged to believe that he *does* have adequate reason to cease; or

  (ii) S does have adequate reason to cease from believing p but does not realize that he does, and is rationally justified in that. (p. 168)

[17]Chisholm, *Theory of Knowledge*, p. 14. See also Ginet, *Knowledge, Perception, and Memory*, p. 36.

ence—through perception, self-consciousness, testimony, and simple reasoning based on these data. When I see a car coming down the street, I am not capable of believing or disbelieving this at will. In such familiar situations the belief-acquisition mechanism is isolated from the direct influence of the will and under the control of more purely cognitive factors.

Partisans of a voluntary control thesis will counter by calling attention to cases in which things don't appear to be so cut and dried: cases of radical underdetermination by evidence, as when a general has to dispose his forces in the absence of sufficient information about the position of enemy forces; or cases of the acceptance of a religious or philosophical position where there seem to be a number of equally viable alternatives. In such cases it can appear that one makes a decision as to what to believe and what not to believe. My view on these matters is that insofar as something is chosen voluntarily, it is something other than a belief or abstention from belief. The general chooses to proceed on the working assumption that the enemy forces are disposed in such-and-such a way. The religious convert to whom it is not clear that the beliefs are correct has chosen to live a certain kind of life, or to selectively subject himself to certain influences. And so on. But even if I am mistaken about these kinds of cases, it is clear that for the vast majority of beliefs nothing like direct voluntary control is involved. And so J_{dv} could not possibly be a generally applicable concept of epistemic justification.

If I am right in rejecting the view that belief is, in general or ever, under direct voluntary control, are we foreclosed from construing epistemic justification as freedom from blameworthiness? Not necessarily. We aren't even prevented from construing epistemic justification as the absence of obligation-violations. We *will* have to avoid thinking of the relevant obligations as obligations to believe or refrain from believing, on the model of obligations to answer a question or to open a door, or to do anything else over which we have immediate voluntary control.[18] If we are to continue to think of intellectual obligations as having to do with believing, it will have to be more on the model of the way in which obligations bear on various other conditions over which one lacks direct

---

[18]Note that I am not restricting the category of *what is within my immediate voluntary control* to "basic actions". Neither of the actions just mentioned would qualify for that title. The category includes both basic actions and actions that involve other conditions, where I can ordinarily take it for granted that those conditions are satisfied at the moment of choice. Thus my point about believing is not just that it is not a basic action, but that it is not even a nonbasic action that is under my effective immediate control. For further discussion of this point see Essay 5.

voluntary control but which one can influence by voluntary actions, such conditions as being overweight, being irritable, being in poor health, or having friends. I can't institute, nullify, or alter any of those conditions here and now just by deciding to do so. But I can do things at will that will influence those conditions, and in that way they may be to some extent under my indirect control. One might speak of my being obliged to be in good health or to have a good disposition, meaning that I am obliged to do what I can (or as much as could reasonably be expected of me) to institute and preserve those states of affairs. Since, however, I think it less misleading to say exactly what I mean, I will not speak of our being obliged to weigh a certain amount or to have a good disposition, or to believe a proposition; I will rather speak of our having obligations to do what we can, or as much as can reasonably be expected of us, to influence those conditions.[19]

The things we can do to affect our believings can be divided into (1) activities that bring influences to bear, or withhold influences from, a particular situation, and (2) activities that affect our belief-forming habits. (1) includes such activities as checking to see whether I have considered all the relevant evidence, getting a second opinion, searching my memory for analogous cases, and looking into the question of whether there is anything markedly abnormal about my current perceptual situation. (2) includes training myself to be more critical of gossip, talking myself into being either more or less subservient to authority, and practicing greater sensitivity to the condition of other people. Moreover it is plausible to think of these belief-influencing activities as being subject to intellectual obligations. We might, for instance, think of ourselves as being under an obligation to do what we can (or what could reasonably be expected of us) to make our belief-forming processes as reliable as possible.[A]

All this suggests that we might frame a deontological conception of justification according to which one is epistemically justified in believing that *p iff* one's believing that *p* is not the result of one's failure to fulfill one's intellectual obligations vis-à-vis one's belief-forming and maintaining activities. It would, again, be like the way in which one is or isn't to blame for other conditions that are not under direct voluntary control but that one can influence by one's voluntary activities. I am to blame for being overweight (being irritable, being in poor health, being without friends) only if that condition is in some way due to my own

[19]For other accounts of the indirect voluntary control of belief see Naylor, "Epistemic Justification," pp. 55–56, and Wolterstorff, "Can Belief in God Be Rational?", pp. 153–55.

past failures to do what I should to limit my intake or to exercise or whatever. If I would still be overweight even if I had done everything I could and should have done about it, then I can hardly be blamed for it. Similarly, we may say that I am subject to reproach for believing that *p*, provided that I am to blame for being in that doxastic condition, in the sense that there are things I could and should have done, such that if I had done them I would not now be believing that *p*. If that is the case, I am unjustified in that belief. And if it is *not* the case, if there are no unfulfilled obligations the fulfilling of which would have inhibited that belief formation, then I am justified in the belief.

Thus we have arrived at a deontological concept of epistemic justification that does not require belief to be under direct voluntary control. We may label this concept 'J_{di}' ('i' for 'involuntary'). It may be more formally defined as follows:

> (XIV) S is J_{di} in believing that *p* at *t iff* there are no intellectual obligations that (1) have to do with the kind of belief-forming or sustaining habit the activation of which resulted in S's believing that *p* at *t*, or with the particular process of belief formation or sustenance that was involved in s's believing that *p* at *t*, and (2) which are such that:
> (A) S had those obligations prior to *t*.
> (B) S did not fulfill those obligations.
> (C) If S had fulfilled those obligations, S would not have believed that *p* at *t*.[20]

As it stands, this account will brand too many beliefs as unjustified, just because it is too undiscriminating in the counterfactual condition, C. There are ways in which the nonfulfillment of intellectual obligations can contribute to a belief acquisition without rendering the belief unjustified. Suppose that I fail to carry out my obligation to spend a certain period in training myself to observe things more carefully. I use the time thus freed up to take a walk around the neighborhood. In the course of this stroll I see two dogs fighting, thereby acquiring the belief that they are fighting. There was a relevant intellectual obligation I didn't fulfill, which is such that if I had fulfilled it I wouldn't have

---

[20]Our four "modes" can also be applied to J_{di}. Indeed, the possibilities for variation are even more numerous. For example, with respect to the *subjective* mode we can switch from the objective fact to the subject's belief with respect to (a) the circumstances of a putative violation, (b) whether there was a violation, and (c) whether the violation was causally related to the belief formation in question. We will leave all this as an exercise for the reader.

acquired that belief. But if that is a perfectly normal perceptual belief, it is surely not thereby rendered unjustified.

Here the dereliction of duty contributed to belief formation simply by facilitating access to the data. That's not the kind of contribution we had in mind. The sorts of cases we were thinking of were those most directly suggested by the two sorts of intellectual obligations we distinguished: (a) cases in which the belief was acquired by the activation of a habit that we would not have possessed had we fulfilled our intellectual obligations; (b) cases in which we acquire, or retain, the belief only because we are sheltered from adverse considerations in a way we wouldn't be if we had done what we should have done. Thus we can avoid counterexamples like the above by reformulating C as follows:

(C) If S had fulfilled those obligations, then S's belief-forming habits would have changed, or S's access to relevant adverse considerations would have changed, in such a way that S would not have believed that *p* at *t*.

But even with this refinement J_{di} does not give us what we expect of epistemic justification. The most serious defect is that it does not hook up in the right way with an adequate truth-conducive ground. I may have done what could reasonably be expected of me in the management and cultivation of my doxastic life and still hold a belief on outrageously inadequate grounds. There are several possible sources of such a discrepancy. First, there is what we might call "cultural isolation". If I have grown up in an isolated community in which everyone unhesitatingly accepts the traditions of the tribe as authoritative, then if I have never encountered anything that seems to cast doubt on the traditions and have never thought to question them, I can hardly be blamed for taking them as authoritative. There is nothing I could reasonably be expected to do what would alter that belief-forming tendency. And there is nothing I could be expected to do that would render me more exposed to counterevidence. (We can suppose that the traditions all have to do with events distant in time and/or space, matters on which I could not be expected to gather evidence on my own.) I am J_{di} in believing these things. And yet the fact that it is the tradition of the tribe that *p* may be a very poor reason for believing that *p*.

Then there is deficiency in cognitive powers. Rather than looking at the more extreme forms of this, let's consider a college student who just doesn't have what it takes to follow abstract philosophical reasoning, or exposition for that matter. Having read Book IV of Locke's *Essay*, he believes that it is Locke's view that everything is a matter of opinion, that one person's opinion is just as good as another's, and that what is true for me may not be true for you. And it's not just that he didn't work hard enough on this particular point, or on the general abilities involved. There is nothing that he could and should have done such that had he done so, he would have gotten this straight. He is simply incapable of appreciating the distinction between "One's knowledge is restricted to one's own ideas" and "Everything is a matter of opinion". No doubt teachers of philosophy tend to assume too quickly that this description applies to some of their students, but surely there can be such cases, cases in which either no amount of time and effort would enable the student to get straight on the matter, or it would be unreasonable to expect the person to expend that amount of time or effort. And yet we would hardly wish to say that the student is justified in believing what he does about Locke.

Other possible sources of a discrepancy between J_{di} and epistemic justification are poor training that the person lacks the time or resources to overcome, and an incorrigible doxastic incontinence. ("When he talks like that, I just can't help believing what he says.") What this spread of cases brings out is that J_{di} is not sufficient for epistemic justification; we may have done the best we can, or at least the best that could reasonably be expected of us, and still be in a very poor epistemic position in believing that p; we could, blamelessly, be believing p for outrageously bad reasons. Even though J_{di} is the closest we can come to a deontological concept of epistemic justification if belief is not under direct voluntary control, it still does not give us what we are looking for.[B]

V

Thus neither version of J_d is satisfactory. Perhaps it was misguided all along to think of epistemic justification as freedom from blameworthiness. Is there any alternative, given the nonnegotiable point that we are looking for a concept of epistemic evaluation? Of course there is. By no means all evaluation, even all evaluation of activities, states, and aspects of human beings, involves the circle of terms that includes 'obligation', 'permission', 'right', 'wrong', and 'blame'. We can evaluate a person's abilities, personal appearance, temperament, or state of health as more or less desirable, favorable, or worthwhile, without taking these to be within the person's direct voluntary control and so subject to obligation in a direct fashion (as with J_{dv}), and without making the evaluation depend on whether the person has done what she should to influence these states (as with J_{di}). Obligation and blame need not come into it at all. This is most obvious when we are dealing with matters that are not even under indirect voluntary control, like one's basic capacities or bodily build. Here when we use positively evaluative terms like 'gifted' or 'superb', we are clearly not saying that the person has done all she could to foster or encourage the condition in question. But even where the condition is at least partly under indirect voluntary control, as with personal appearance or state of health, we need not be thinking in those terms when we take someone to present a pleasing appearance or to be in splendid health. Moreover, we can carry out these evaluations from a certain point of view. We can judge that someone has a fine bodily constitution from an athletic or from an aesthetic point of view, or that someone's manner is a good one from a professional or from a social point of view.

In like fashion one can evaluate S's believing that p as a good, favorable, desirable, or appropriate thing without thinking of it as fulfilling or not violating an obligation, and without making this evaluation depend on whether the person has done what she could to carry out belief-influencing activities. As in the other cases, it could simply be a matter of the possession of certain good-making characteristics. Furthermore, believings can be evaluated from various points of view, including the epistemic, which, as we have noted, is defined by the aim at maximizing truth and minimizing falsity. It may be a good thing that S believes that p for his peace of mind, or from the standpoint of loyalty to the cause, or as an encouragement to the redoubling of his efforts. But none of this would render it a good thing for S to believe that p from the epistemic point of view. To believe that p because it gives peace of mind or because it stimulates effort may not be conducive to the attainment of truth and the avoidance of error.

All of this suggests that we can frame a concept of epistemic justification that is "evaluative", in a narrow sense of that term in which it contrasts with 'deontological', with the assessment of conduct in terms of obligation, blame, right, and wrong. Let's specify an "evaluative" sense of epistemic justification as follows:

(XV) S is J_e in believing that p *iff* S's believing that p, as S does, is a good thing from the epistemic point of view.

This is a way of being commendable from the epistemic point of view that is, or can be, quite different from the subject's not being to blame for any violation of intellectual obligations.[21] The qualification "as S

---

[21] I must confess that I do not find 'justified' an apt term for a favorable or desirable state or condition, when what makes it desirable is cut loose from considerations of

does" is inserted to make it explicit that in order for S to be J_e in believing that p, it need not be the case that any believing of p by S would be a good thing epistemically, much less any believing of p by anyone. It is rather that there are aspects of *this* believing of p by S that make it a good thing epistemically. There could conceivably be person-proposition pairs such that any belief in that proposition by that person would be a good thing epistemically, but this would be a limiting case and not typical of our epistemic condition.

Is there anything further to be said about this concept? Of course we should avoid building anything very substantive into the constitution of the concept. After all, it is possible for epistemologists to differ radically as to the conditions under which one or another sort of belief is justified. When this happens, they are at least sometimes using the same concept of justification; otherwise they wouldn't be disagreeing over what is required for justification, though they could still disagree over which concept of justification is most fundamental or most useful. Both our versions of J_d are quite neutral in this way. Both leave it completely open as to what intellectual obligations we have, and hence as to what obligations must not be violated if one is to be justified. But while maintaining due regard for the importance of neutrality, I believe that we can go beyond (XV) in fleshing out the concept.

We can get a start on this by considering the following question. If goodness from an epistemic point of view is what we are interested in, why shouldn't we identify justification with truth, at least extensionally? What could be better from that point of view than truth? If the name of the game is the maximization of truth and the minimization of falsity in our beliefs, then plain unvarnished truth is hard to beat. This consideration, however, has not moved epistemologists to identify justification with truth, or even to take truth as a necessary and sufficient condition for justification. The logical independence of truth and justification is a staple of the epistemological literature. But why should this be? It is obvious that a belief might be J_d without being true and vice versa, but what reason is there for taking J_e to be independent of truth?

I think the answer to this has to be in terms of the "internalist" character of justification. When we ask whether S is justified in believing that p, we are, as we have repeatedly been insisting, asking a question from the standpoint of an aim at truth; but we are not asking whether things are in fact as S believes. We are getting at something

---

obligation and blame. Nevertheless, since the term is firmly ensconced in the literature as the term to use for any concept that satisfies the four conditions set out in Section II, I will stifle my linguistic scruples and employ it for a nondeontological concept.

more "internal" to S's "perspective on the world". This internalist feature of justification made itself felt in our discussion of J_d when we pointed out that to be J_{dv} is to fail to violate any relevant intellectual obligations, *so far as one can tell;* it is to be J_{dv} in what we call the "cognitive" mode. With respect to J_e the analogous point is that although this is goodness vis-à-vis the aim at truth, it consists not in the beliefs fitting the way the facts actually are, but something more like the belief's being true "so far as the subject can tell from what is available to the subject". In asking whether S is J_e in believing that p, we are asking whether the truth of p is strongly indicated by what S has to go on; whether, given what S had to go on, it is at least quite likely that p is true. We want to know whether S had *adequate grounds* for believing that p, where *adequate* grounds are those sufficiently indicative of the truth of p.^C

If we are to make the notion of *adequate grounds* central for J_e, we must say more about it. A belief has a certain ground, G, when it is "based on" G. What is it for a belief, B, to be *based on* G? That is a difficult question. So far as I know, there is no fully satisfactory general account in the literature, nor am I able to supply one. But we are not wholly at a loss. We do have a variety of paradigm cases; the difficulty concerns just how to generalize from them and just where to draw the line. When one infers p from q and *thereby* comes to accept p, this is a clear case of basing one belief on another. Again, when I come to believe that this is a tree because this visually appears to me to be the case, that is another paradigm; here my belief that that is a tree is based on my visual experience, or, if you prefer, on certain aspects of that experience. The main difficulties arise with respect to cases in which no conscious inference takes place but in which we are still inclined to say that one belief is based on another. Consider, for instance, my forming the belief that you are angry on seeing you look and act in a certain way. I perform no conscious inference from a proposition about your demeanor and behavior to a proposition about your emotional state. Nevertheless, it seems plausible to hold that I did learn about your demeanor and behavior through seeing it, and that the beliefs I thereby formed played a crucial role in my coming to believe that you are angry. More specifically, it seems that the former beliefs gave rise to the latter belief; that if I hadn't acquired the former, I would not have acquired the latter; and, finally, that if I am asked why I suppose that you are angry, I would cite the behavior and demeanor as my reason (perhaps only as "the way he looked and acted"). How can we get this kind of case together with the conscious-inference cases into a general account? We might claim that they are all cases of inference, some of them being unconscious. But there are problems as to when we are justified in imputing unconscious inferences. We might take it that what lets in our problem cases is the subject's disposition to cite the one belief(s) as his reason for the other belief; and then make our general condition a disjunction of conscious inference from q and a tendency to cite q as the reason. But then what about subjects (small children and lower animals) that are too unsophisticated to be able to answer questions as to what their reasons are? Can't their beliefs be based on something when no conscious inference is performed? Moreover, this disjunctive criterion will not include cases in which a belief is based on an experience, rather than on other beliefs. A third suggestion concerns causality. In all the cases mentioned thus far it is plausible to suppose that the belief that q was among the causes of the belief that p. This suggests that we might try to cut the Gordian knot by boldly identifying "based on" with "caused by". But this runs into the usual difficulties of simple causal theories. Many items enter into the causation of a belief, for example, various neurophysiological happenings, that clearly don't qualify as even part of what the belief is based on. To make a causal account work, we would have to beef it up into "caused by q in a certain way". And what way is that? Some way that is paradigmatically exemplified by our paradigms? But how to state this way in such a fashion that it applies equally to the nonparadigmatic cases?[22]

In the face of these perplexities our only recourse is to keep a firm hold on our paradigms and work with a less than ideally determinate concept of a relationship that holds in cases that are "sufficiently like" the paradigms. That will be sufficient to do the job over most of the territory.[23]

Let's return to "grounds". What a belief is based on we may term the ground of the belief. A ground, in a more dispositional sense of the term, is the sort of item on which a belief can be based. We have already cited beliefs and experiences as possible grounds, and these would seem to exhaust the possibilities. Indeed, some epistemologists would find this too generous already, maintaining that beliefs can be based

[22]There are also problems as to where to draw the line. What about the unconscious "use" of perceptual cues for the depth of an object in the visual field or for "size constancy"? And however we answer that particular question, just where do we draw the line as we move further and further from our initial paradigms?

[23]For some recent discussion of 'based on' see M. Swain, *Reasons and Knowledge* (Ithaca: Cornell University Press, 1981), chap. 3, and G. S. Pappas, "Basing Relations", in Pappas, ed., *Justification and Knowledge*. One additional point I do need to make explicit is this. I mean 'based on' to range over both what initially gave rise to the belief, and what sustains it while it continues to be held. To be precise, one should speak of *what the belief is based on at time t*. If t is the time of acquisition, one is speaking of what gave rise to the belief; if t is later than that, one is speaking of what sustains the belief.

only on other beliefs. They would treat perceptual cases by holding that the belief that a tree is over there is based on the *belief that* there visually appears to me to be a tree over there, rather than, as we are suggesting, on the visual appearance itself. I can't accept that, largely because I doubt that all perceptual believers have such beliefs about their visual experience,[24] but I can't pause to argue the point. Suffice it to say that since my opponents' position is, to be as generous as possible, controversial, we do not want to build a position on this issue into the *concept* of epistemic justification. We want to leave open at least the *conceptual* possibility of *direct* or *immediate* justification by experience (and perhaps in other ways also), as well as *indirect* or *mediate* justification by relation to other beliefs (inferentially in the most explicit cases). Finally, to say that a subject *has adequate* grounds for her belief that *p* is to say that she has other justified beliefs, or experiences, on which the belief could be based and which are strongly indicative of the truth of the belief. The reason for the restriction to *justified* beliefs is that a ground shouldn't be termed adequate unless it can confer justification on the belief it grounds. But we noted earlier that if I infer my belief that *p*, even by impeccable logic, from an *unjustified* belief that *q*, the former belief is not thereby justified.[25]

To return to the main thread of the discussion, we are thinking of S's being J_e in believing that *p* as involving S's having adequate grounds for that belief. That is, we are thinking of the possession of those adequate grounds as constituting the goodness of the belief from the epistemic point of view. The next thing to note is that the various "modes" of J_d apply here as well.

Let's begin by noting an objective-subjective distinction. To be sure, in thinking of J_e as *having truth-indicative grounds within one's "perspective on the world"*, we are already thinking of it as more subjective than flat-out truth. But within that perspectival conception we can set the requirements as more objective or more subjective. There is more than one respect in which the possession of adequate grounds could be "subjectivized". First, there is the distinction between the existence of

---

[24]For an interesting discussion of this point see A. Quinton, *The Nature of Things* (London: Routledge & Kegan Paul, 1973), chap. 7. My opponent will be even more hard pressed to make out that beliefs about one's own conscious experience are based on other beliefs. His best move here would be either to deny that there are such beliefs or to deny that they are based on anything.

[25]No such restriction would be required just for having grounds (of some sort), though even here the word 'ground' by itself carries a strong suggestion that what is grounded is, to some extent, supported. We need a term for anything a belief might be based on, however vainly. 'Ground' carries too much positive evaluative force to be ideally suitable for this role.

the ground and its adequacy. S is *objectively* J_e in believing that p if S (a) does in fact have grounds that are (b) in fact adequate grounds for that belief. A (more or less) *subjective* version would replace (a) or (b) or both with the requirement that the subject believe this to be the case. Of the two partially subjective versions, it may well be doubted that the one in which only (a) is subjectivized is possible. For if I believe mistakenly that I have grounds for the belief, can there be any matter of fact as to whether those nonexistent grounds are adequate? Perhaps. If my belief is specific enough as to what grounds I am supposing myself to possess, it could be objectively true or false that such grounds would be adequate. But in any event, lacking time to go into all possible variations, I shall confine attention to the subjectivization of (b). So our first two modes will be:

(XVI)   Objective—S does have adequate grounds for believing that p.

(XVII) Subjective—S has grounds for believing that p and he believes them to be adequate.

And here too we have a "justified belief", or "cognitive" variant on the subjective version.

(XVIII) Cognitive—S has grounds for believing that p and he is justified in believing them to be adequate.

We can dismiss (XVII) by the same arguments we brought against the subjective version of J_d. The mere fact that I believe, however unjustifiably or irresponsibly, that my grounds for believing that p are adequate could scarcely render me justified in believing that p. If I believe them to be adequate just because I have an egotistical penchant to overestimate my powers, that could hardly make it rational for me to believe that p. But here we will not find the same reason to favor (XVIII) over (XVI). With J_d the cognitive version won out because of what it takes for blameworthiness. But whether one is J_e in believing that p has nothing to do with whether he is subject to blame. It depends rather on whether his believing that p is a *good thing* from the epistemic point of view. And however justifiably S believes that his grounds are adequate, if they are not, then his believing that p on those grounds is not a good move in the truth-seeking game. Even if he isn't to blame for making that move, it is a bad move nonetheless. Thus J_e is properly construed in the objective mode.

We are also confronted with the question of whether J_e should be construed "motivationally". Since we have already opted for an objective reading, the motivational version will take the following form:

(XIX) Motivational—S's belief that *p* is based on adequate grounds.

So our question is whether it is enough for justification that S *have* adequate grounds for his belief, whether used or not, or whether it is also required that the belief be based on those grounds. We cannot settle this question on the grounds that were available for J_{dv}, since with J_e we are not thinking of the subject as being obliged to take relevant consideration into account in *choosing* whether to believe that *p*.

There is something to be said on both sides of this issue. In support of the first, source-irrelevant position (XVI without XIX), it can be pointed out that S's *having a justification* for believing that *p* is independent of whether S does believe that *p;* I can have adequate grounds for believing that *p*, and so *have* a justification, even though I do not in fact believe that *p*. Hence it can hardly be a requirement for having a justification for *p* that my nonexistent belief have a certain kind of basis. Likewise my having adequate grounds for believing that *p* is sufficient for this being *a rational thing for me to believe.* But, says the opponent, suppose that S does believe that *p*. If simply having adequate grounds were sufficient for this belief to be justified, then, provided S does have the grounds, her belief that *p* would be justified however frivolous the source. But surely a belief that stems from wishful thinking would not be justified, however strong one's (unutilized) grounds for it.[26]

Now the first thing to say about this controversy is that both antagonists win, at least to the extent that each of them is putting forward a viable concept, and one that is actually used in epistemic assessment. There certainly is the concept of *having* adequate grounds for the belief that *p*, whether or not one does believe that *p*, and there equally certainly is the concept of one's belief being based on adequate grounds. Both concepts represent favorable epistemic statuses. *Ceteris paribus,* one is better off believing something for which one has adequate grounds than believing something for which one doesn't. And the same

[26]For some recent discussion of this issue see G. Harman, *Thought* (Princeton: Princeton University Press, 1973), chap. 2; K. Lehrer, *Knowledge* (New York: Oxford University Press, 1974), chap. 6; R. Firth, "Are Epistemic Concepts Reducible to Ethical Concepts?", in *Values and Morals,* ed. A. I. Goldman and J. Kim (Dordrecht: D. Reidel, 1978); R. Foley, "Epistemic Luck and the Purely Epistemic," *American Philosophical Quarterly,* (1984).

can be said for the contrast between having a belief that is based on adequate grounds and having one that isn't. Hence I will recognize that these are both concepts of epistemic justification, and I will resist the pressure to decide which is *the* concept.

Nevertheless, we can seek to determine which concept is more fundamental to epistemology. On this issue it seems clear that the motivational concept is the richer one and thereby embodies a more complete account of a belief's being a good thing from the epistemic point of view. Surely there is something epistemically undesirable about a belief that is generated in an intellectually disreputable way, however adequate the unutilized grounds possessed by the subject. If, possessing excellent reasons for supposing that you are trying to discredit me professionally, I nevertheless believe this, not for those reasons but out of paranoia, in such a way that even if I didn't have those reasons I would have believed this just as firmly, it was undesirable from the point of view of the aim at truth for me to form that belief as I did. So if we are seeking the most inclusive concept of what makes a belief a good thing epistemically, we will want to include a consideration of what the belief is based on. Hence I will take (XIX) as the favored formulation of what makes a belief a good thing from the epistemic point of view.

I may add that (XVI) can be seen as derivative from (XIX). To simply *have* adequate grounds is to be in such a position that *if* I make use of that position as a basis for believing that *p*, I will thereby be justified in that belief. Thus (XVI) gives us a concept of a potential for (XIX); it is a concept of having resources that are sufficient for believing justifiably, leaving open the question of whether those resources are used.

The next point to be noted is that (XIX) guarantees only prima facie justification. As often noted, it is quite possible for my belief that *p* to have been formed on the basis of evidence that in itself adequately supports *p*, even though the totality of the evidence at my disposal does not. Thus the evidence on which I came to believe that the butler committed the murder might strongly support that hypothesis, but when arriving at that belief I was ignoring other things I know or justifiably believe that tend to exculpate the butler; the total evidence at my disposal is not sufficient support for my belief. In that case we will not want to count my belief as justified all things considered, even though the grounds *on the basis of which* it was formed were themselves adequate. Their adequacy is, so to say, *overridden* by the larger perspectival context in which they are set. Thus (XIX) gives us prima facie justification, what will be justification provided it is not canceled by further relevant factors. Unqualified justification requires an additional condition to the effect that S does not also have reasons that suffice to override the justification provided by the grounds on which the belief is based. Building that into (XIX), we get:

(XX) Motivational—S's belief that p is based on adequate grounds, and S lacks overriding reasons to the contrary.

Even though (XX) requires us to bring in the unused portions of the perspective, we cannot simplify the condition by ignoring the distinction between what provides the basis and what doesn't, and make the crucial condition something like "The totality of S's perspective provides adequate support". For then we would run up against the considerations that led us to prefer (XIX) to (XVI).

We have distinguished two aspects of our evaluative concept of justification, the strictly evaluative portion—goodness from the epistemic point of view—and the very general statement of the relevant good-making characteristic, *based on adequate grounds in the absence of overriding reasons to the contrary.* In taking the concept to include this second component we are opting for the view that this concept, though unmistakably evaluative rather than "purely factual" in character, is not so purely evaluative as to leave completely open the basis on which this evaluative status supervenes. I do not see how to justify this judgment by reference to any more fundamental considerations. It is just that in reflecting on epistemic justification, thought of in evaluative (as contrasted with deontological) terms, it seems clear to me that the range of possible bases for epistemic goodness is not left completely open by the concept, that it is part of what we mean in terming a belief justified, that the belief was based on adequate grounds (or, at least, that the subject had adequate grounds for it).[27] Though this means that J_e is not maximally neutral on the question of what it takes for justification, it is still quite close to that. It still leaves open whether there is immediate justification and if so on the basis of what, how strong a ground is needed for justification, what dimensions of strength there are for various kinds of grounds, and so on.

Let's codify our evaluative concept of justification as follows:

(XXI) S is J_{eg} in believing that p *iff* S's believing that p, as S did, was a good thing from the epistemic point of view, in that S's belief that

---

[27]Even though we have opted for the 'based on' formulation as giving us the more fundamental concept of epistemic justification, we have also recognized the 'has adequate grounds' formulation as giving us a concept of epistemic justification. Either of these will introduce a "basis of evaluative status" component into the concept.

> *p* was based on adequate grounds and S lacked sufficient overriding reasons to the contrary.

In the subscript, 'g' stands for 'grounds'.

My supposition that all justification of belief involves adequate grounds may be contested. This does seem incontrovertible for beliefs based on other beliefs and for perceptual beliefs based on experience. But what about beliefs in self-evident propositions where the self-evidence is what justifies me in the belief?[28] On considering the proposition that two quantities equal to the same quantity are equal to each other, this seems obviously true to me; and I shall suppose, though this is hardly uncontroversial, that in those circumstances I am justified in believing it. But where are the adequate grounds on which my belief is based? It is not that there are grounds here about whose adequacy we might well have doubts; it is rather that there seems to be nothing identifiable as grounds. There is nothing here that is distinguishable from my belief and the proposition believed, in the way evidence or reasons are distinct from that for which they are evidence or reasons, or in the way my sensory experience is distinct from the beliefs about the physical world that are based on it. Here I simply consider the proposition and straightaway accept it. A similar problem can be raised for normal beliefs about one's own conscious states. What is the ground for a typical belief that one feels sleepy?[29] If one replies "One's consciousness of one's feeling of sleepiness", then it may be insisted, with some show of plausibility, that where one is consciously feeling sleepy, there is no difference between one's feeling sleepy and one's being conscious that one is feeling sleepy.[D]

This is a very large issue that I will not have time to consider properly. Suffice it to say that one may treat these as limiting cases in which the ground, though real enough, is minimally distinguishable either from the belief it is grounding or from the fact that makes the belief true. In the first-person belief about one's own conscious state the ground coincides with the fact that makes the belief true. Since the fact believed is itself an experience of the subject, there need be nothing "between" the subject and the fact that serves as an indication of the latter's presence. The fact "reveals itself" directly. Self-evident propositions require separate treatment. Here I think that we can take the *way* the proposition appears to one, variously described as "obviously true",

---

[28]This latter qualification is needed, because I might accept a self-evident proposition on authority. In that case I was not, so to say, taking advantage of its self-evidence.

[29]We are not speaking here of a belief that one *is* sleepy. There a ground is readily identifiable—one's feeling of sleepiness.

"self-evident", and "clear and distinct", as the ground on which the belief is based. I accept the proposition because it *seems* to me so obviously true. This is less distinct from the belief than an inferential or sensory experiential ground, since it has to do with how I am aware of the proposition. Nevertheless, there is at least a minimal distinctness. I can form an intelligible conception of someone's failing to believe that *p*, where *p* seems obviously true. Perhaps this person has been rendered unduly skeptical by overexposure to the logical paradoxes.

VI

Let's go back to the idea that the "based on adequate grounds" part of J_{eg} is there because of the "internalist" character of justification. Contrasts between internalism and externalism have been popular in epistemology lately, but the contrast is not always drawn in the same way. There are two popular ways, both of which are distinct from what I have in mind. First there is the idea that justification is internal in that it depends on what support is available for the belief from "within the subject's perspective", in the sense of what the subject knows or justifiably believes about the world.[30] This kind of internalism restricts justification to mediate or discursive justification, justification by reasons. Another version takes "the subject's perspective" to include whatever is "directly accessible" to the subject, accessible just on the basis of reflection; internalism on this version restricts justifiers to what is directly accessible to the subject.[31] This, unlike the first version, does not limit us to mediate justification, since experience can be taken to be at least as directly accessible as beliefs and knowledge.[E]

In contrast to both these ways of drawing the distinction, what I take to be internal about justification is that whether a belief is justified depends on what it is based on (grounds); and grounds must be other psychological state(s) of the same subject. I am not absolutely certain that grounds are confined to beliefs and experiences, even if experiences are not confined to sensations and feelings but also include, e.g., the way a proposition seems obvious to one, and religious and aesthetic experiences; but these are the prime candidates, and any other exam-

---

[30]See L. Bonjour, "Externalist Theories of Empirical Knowledge," *Midwest Studies in Philosophy*, 5 (1980); K. Bach, "A Rationale for Reliabilism," *The Monist*, 68, 2 (April 1985); H. Kornblith, "Ever since Descartes," *The Monist*, 68, 2 (April 1985).

[31]See A. I. Goldman, "The Internalist Conception of Justification," *Midwest Studies in Philosophy*, 5 (1980); Chisholm, *Theory of Knowledge*, chap. 4, pp. 63–64; Ginet, *Knowledge, Perception, and Memory*, pp. 34–37.

ples must belong to some kind of which these are the paradigms. So in taking it to be conceptually true that one is justified in believing that *p* *iff* one's belief that *p* is based on an adequate ground, I take justification to be "internal" in that it depends on the way in which the belief stems from the believer's psychological states, which are "internal" to the subject in an obvious sense. What would be an externalist contrast with this kind of internalism? We shall see one such contrast in a moment, in discussing the relation of J_{eg} to reliabilism. Moreover, it contrasts with the idea that one can be justified in a certain belief just because of the status of the proposition believed (necessary, infallible). My sort of internalism is different from the first one mentioned above, in that experiences as well as beliefs can figure as grounds. And it is different from the second if, as I believe, what a belief is based on may not be directly accessible. This will be the case if, as seems plausible, much belief formation goes on below the conscious level. It would seem, for example, that, as we move about the environment, we are constantly forming short-term perceptual beliefs without any conscious monitoring of this activity.[F]

The most prominent exponents of an explicitly nondeontological conception of epistemic justification have been reliabilists, who have either identified justification with reliability[32] or have taken reliability to be an adequate criterion of justification.[33] The reliability that is in question here is the reliability of belief formation and sustenance.[34] To say that a belief was formed in a reliable way is, roughly, to say that it was formed in a way that can be depended on generally to form true rather than false beliefs, at least from inputs like the present one, and at least in the sorts of circumstances in which we normally find ourselves.[35] Thus if my visual system, when functioning as it is at present in yielding my belief that there is a tree in front of me, generally yields true beliefs about objects that are fairly close to me and directly in front of me, then my present belief that there is a tree in front of me was formed in a reliable manner.

Now it may be supposed that J_{eg}, as we have explained it, is just reliability of belief formation with an evaluative frosting. For where a belief is based on adequate grounds, that belief has been formed in a reliable fashion. In fact, it is plausible to take reliability as a *criterion* for

---

[32]Swain, *Reasons and Knowledge,* chap. 4.

[33]Goldman, "What Is Justified Belief?"

[34]For simplicity I shall couch the ensuing formulations solely in terms of belief formation, but the qualification 'or sustenance' is to be understood throughout.

[35]These two qualifications testify to the difficulty of getting the concept of reliability in satisfactory shape; and there are other problems to be dealt with, e.g., how to identify the general procedure of which the present belief formation is an instance.

adequacy of grounds. If my grounds for believing that *p* are not such that it is generally true that beliefs like that formed on grounds like that are true, they cannot be termed 'adequate'. Why do we think that wanting State to win the game is not an adequate reason for supposing that it has won, whereas the fact that a victory has been reported by several newspapers is an adequate reason? Surely it has something to do with the fact that beliefs like that when formed on the first sort of grounds are not *generally* true, while they are *generally* true when formed on grounds of the second sort. Considerations like this may lead us to suppose that J_{eg}, in effect, identifies justification with reliability.[36]

Nevertheless the internalist character of justification prevents it from being identified with reliability, and even blocks an extensional equivalence. Unlike justification, reliability of belief formation is not limited to cases in which a belief is based on adequate grounds within the subject's psychological states. A reliable mode of belief formation *may* work through the subject's own knowledge and experience. Indeed, it is plausible to suppose that all of the reliable modes of belief formation available to human beings are of this sort. But it is quite conceivable that there should be others. I might be so constituted that beliefs about the weather tomorrow which apparently just "pop into my mind" out of nowhere are in fact reliably produced by a mechanism of which we know nothing, and which does not involve the belief being based on anything. Here we would have reliably formed beliefs that are not based on adequate grounds from within my perspective, and so are not J_{eg}.

Moreover, even within the sphere of beliefs based on grounds, reliability and justification do not necessarily go together. The possibility of divergence here stems from another feature of justification embodied in our account, the way in which unqualified justification requires not only an adequate ground but also the absence of sufficient overriding reasons. This opens up the possibility of a case in which a belief is formed on the basis of grounds in a way that is in fact highly reliable, even though the subject has strong reasons for supposing the way to be unreliable. These reasons will (or may) override the prima facie justifi-

---

[36]An alternative to explicating 'adequate' in terms of reliability would be to use the notion of conditional probability. G is an adequate ground for a belief that *p* just in case the probability of *p* on G is high. And since adequacy is closely related both to reliability and to conditional probability, they are presumably closely related to each other. Swain, *Reasons and Knowledge*, chap. 4, exploits this connection to explicate reliability in terms of conditional probability, though in a more complex fashion than is indicated by these brief remarks.

cation provided by the grounds on which the belief was based. And so S will not be justified in the belief, even though it was reliably generated. Consider, in this connection, a case presented by Alvin Goldman.[37]

> Suppose that Jones is told on fully reliable authority that a certain class of his memory beliefs are almost all mistaken. His parents fabricate a wholly false story that Jones suffered from amnesia when he was seven but later developed *pseudo*-memories of that period. Though Jones listens to what his parents say and has excellent reasons to trust them, he persists in believing the ostensible memories from his seven-year-old past.

Suppose that Jones, upon recalling his fifth birthday party, believes that he was given an electric train for his fifth birthday because, as it seems to him, he remembers being given it.[38] By hypothesis, his memory mechanism is highly reliable, and so his belief about his fifth birthday was reliably formed. But this belief is not adequately supported by the *totality* of what he justifiably believes. His justifiable belief that he has no real memory of his first seven years overrides the support from his ostensible memory. Thus Jones is not J_{eg} in his memory belief, because the "lack of overriding reasons to the contrary" requirement is not satisfied. But reliability is subject to no such constraint. Just as reliable mechanisms are not restricted to those that work through the subject's perspective, so it is not a requirement on the reliability of belief formation that the belief be adequately supported by the totality of the subject's perspective. However many and however strong the reasons Jones has for distrusting his memory, the fact remains that his memory beliefs are still reliably formed. Here is another way in which the class of beliefs that are J_{eg} and the class of reliably formed beliefs can fail to coincide.[39]

[37]"What Is Justified Belief?", p. 18.

[38]If you have trouble envisaging his trusting his memory in the face of his parents' story, you may imagine that he is not thinking of that story at the moment he forms the memory belief.

[39]In the article in which he introduces this example, "What Is Justified Belief?", Goldman modifies the "reliability is a criterion of justification" view so that it will accommodate the example. The modified formulation runs as follows:

> If S's belief in p at t results from a reliable cognitive process, and there is no reliable or conditionally reliable process available to S which had it been used by S in addition to the process actually used, would have resulted in S's not believing p at t, then S's belief in p at t is justified. (p. 20)

In the case cited there is such an alternative reliable process, viz., one that takes account of the total evidence. The revised criterion yields the correct result in this case. This move, however, leaves unshaken the point that in this case Jones's belief *is* reliably formed but unjustified. That remains true, however the revised criterion applies to the case.

I would suggest that, of our candidates, J_{eg} most fully embodies what we are looking for under the heading of "epistemic justification". (1) Like its deontological competitors it is an evaluative concept, in a broad sense, a concept of a favorable status from an epistemic point of view. (2) Unlike J_{dv}, it does not presuppose that belief is under direct voluntary control. (3) Unlike J_{di}, it implies that the believer is in a strong epistemic position in believing that p, that is to say, that there is something about the way in which he believes that p that renders it at least likely that the belief is true. Thus it renders it intelligible that justification is something we should prize from an epistemic point of view. (4) Unlike the concept of a reliable mode of belief formation it represents this "truth-conductivity" as a matter of the belief's being based on an adequate ground within the subject's own cognitive states. Thus it recognizes the "internalist" character of justification; it recognizes that in asking whether a belief is justified we are interested in the prospects for the truth of the belief, given what the subject "has to go on". (5) Thus the concept provides broad guidelines for the specification of conditions of justification, but within those guidelines there is ample room for disagreement over the precise conditions for one or another type of belief. The concept does not leave us totally at a loss as to what to look for. But in adopting J_{eg} we are not building answers to substantive epistemological questions into the concept. As the only candidate to exhibit all these desiderata, J_{eg} is clearly the winner.

VII

It may be useful to bring together the lessons we have learned from this conceptual exploration.

(1) Justifying, an activity of showing or establishing something, is much less central for epistemology than is "being justified", as a state or condition.

(2) It is central to epistemic justification that *what justifies* is restricted to the subject's "perspective", to the subject's knowledge, justified belief, or experience.

(3) Deontological concepts of justification are either saddled with an indefensible assumption of the voluntariness of belief (J_{dv}) or allow for cases in which one believes that p without having any adequate ground for the belief (J_{di}).

(4) The notion of one's belief being based on adequate grounds incorporates more of what we are looking for in a concept of epistemic

justification than the weaker notion of having adequate grounds for belief.

(5) Justification is closely related to reliability, but because of the perspectival character noted in (2), they do not completely coincide; much less can they be identified.

(6) The notion of believing that p in a way that is good from an epistemic point of view in that the belief is based on adequate grounds (J_{eg}) satisfies the chief desiderata for a concept of epistemic justification.

VIII

The ultimate payoff of this conceptual exploration is the increased sophistication it gives us in dealing with substantive epistemological issues. Putting our scheme to work is a very large enterprise, spanning a large part of epistemology. In conclusion I will give one illustration of the ways in which our distinctions can be of help in the trenches. For this purpose I will restrict myself to the broad contrast between J_{dv} and J_{eg}.

First, consider what we might term "higher level requirements" for S's being justified in believing that p. I include under that heading all requirements that S know or justifiably believe something *about* the epistemic status of p, or about the strength of S's grounds for p. This would include requirements that S be justified in believing that:

(1) R is an adequate reason for p (where R is alleged to justify S's belief that p).[40]

(2) Experience e is an adequate indication that p (where e is alleged to justify S's belief that p).[41]

On J_{eg} there is no temptation to impose such requirements. If R *is* an adequate reason (e is an adequate indication), then if one believes that p on that basis, one is *thereby* in a strong position, epistemically; and the further knowledge, or justified belief, that the reason is adequate (the

---

[40] See, e.g., D. Armstrong, *Belief, Truth, and Knowledge* (London: Cambridge University Press, 1973), p. 151; B. Skyrms, "The Explication of 'S Knows that P,'" *Journal of Philosophy*, 64 (1967), 373–89.

[41] See, e.g., W. Sellars, "Empiricism and the Philosophy of Mind," in *Science, Perception and Reality* (London: Routledge & Kegan Paul, 1963), pp. 168–69; L. Bonjour, "Can Empirical Knowledge Have a Foundation?", *American Philosophical Quarterly*, 15 (1978), 5–6; Lehrer, *Knowledge*, pp. 103–5.

experience is an adequate indication), though no doubt quite important and valuable for other purposes, will do nothing to improve the
truth-conduciveness of one's believing that p. But on J_{dv} we get a different story. If it's a question of being blameless in believing that p, it
can be persuasively argued that this requires not only forming the
belief on what is in fact an adequate ground, but doing so in the light of
the realization that the ground is an adequate one. If I decide to believe
that p without knowing whether the ground is adequate, am I not
subject to blame for proceeding irresponsibly in my doxastic behavior,
whatever the actual strength of the ground? If the higher level requirements are plausible only if we are using J_{dv}, then the dubiousness of
that concept will extend to those requirements.[42]

In the above paragraph we were considering whether S's being justified in believing that his ground is adequate is a *necessary* condition of
justification. We can also consider whether it is sufficient. Provided that
S is justified in believing that his belief that p is based on an adequate
ground, G, does it make any difference, for his being justified in believing that p, whether the ground *is* adequate? Our two contenders will
line up here as they did on the previous issue. For J_{eg} the mere fact that
S is justified in supposing that G is adequate will cut no ice. What J_{eg}
requires is that S *actually be* in an epistemically favorable position; and
although S's being justified in supposing G to be adequate is certainly
good evidence for that, it doesn't *constitute* being in such a position.
Hence J_{eg} requires that the ground of the belief actually be an adequate one. As for J_{dv}, where it is a question of whether S is blameworthy in believing that p, what is decisive is how S's epistemic position
appears within S's perspective on the world. If, so far as S could tell, G
is an adequate ground, then S is blameless, that is, J_{dv}, in believing that
p on G. Nothing else could be required for justification in that sense. If
S has chosen his doxastic state by applying the appropriate principles in
the light of all his relevant knowledge and justified belief, then he is
totally in the clear. Again the superior viability of J_{eg}, as over against
J_{dv}, should tip the scales in favor of the more objective requirement of
adequacy.[43] G

[42]In Essay 3 I develop at much greater length this kind of diagnosis of Bonjour's
deployment of a higher level requirement in his argument against immediate knowledge
in "Can Empirical Knowledge Have a Foundation?"

[43]Ancestors of this essay were presented at SUNY at Albany, SUNY at Buffalo, Calvin
College, Cornell University, University of California at Irvine, Lehigh University, Uni-
versity of Michigan, University of Nebraska, Syracuse University, and the University of
Western Ontario. I wish to thank members of the audience in all these institutions for
their helpful comments. I would like to express special appreciation to Robert Audi, Carl
Ginet, George Mavrodes, Alvin Plantinga, Fred Schmitt, and Nicholas Wolterstorff for
their penetrating comments on earlier versions.

Notes

A. For a fuller discussion of modes of voluntary control of belief, and for a fuller presentation of deontological conceptions of epistemic justification, see Essay 5.

B. In Essay 5, Section VII, there are replies to criticisms of the treatment of the two cases discussed here, as well as a presentation of further cases.

C. See Essay 9 for a fuller development of this idea.

D. In Essay 11 I use considerations like this, among others, to support the idea that such beliefs are "self-warranted" rather than justified by being based on an adequate ground. For the conflict between the position of this essay and Essay 9, on the one hand, and Essay 11, on the other, see endnote G of Essay 11.

E. See Essay 8 for an extended discussion of these modes of internalism.

F. In Essay 9 this last consideration is harmonised with an accessibility form of internalism by construing the latter to require only that the ground be the *sort* of thing that is *typically* directly accessible to its possessor.

G. For further discussion of this see Essay 8.

The Deontological Conception
of Epistemic Justification

I. The Deontological Conception

The terms 'justified', 'justification', and their cognates are most naturally understood in what we may term a "deontological" way, as having to do with obligation, permission, requirement, blame, and the like. We may think of *requirement, prohibition,* and *permission* as the basic deontological terms, with *obligation* and *duty* as species of requirement, and with *responsibility, blameworthiness, reproach, praiseworthiness, merit, being in the clear,* and the like as normative consequences of an agent's situation with respect to what is required, prohibited, or permitted. More specifically, when we consider the justification of *actions,* something on which we have a firmer grip than the justification of beliefs, it is clear that to be justified in having *done* something is for that action not to be in violation of any relevant rules, regulations, laws, obligations, duties, or counsels, the ones that govern actions of that sort. It is a matter of the action's being *permitted* by the relevant system of principles.[1] To say that the action was justified does not imply that it was

This essay originally appeared in J. E. Tomberlin, ed., *Philosophical Perspectives,* 2, Epistemology (1988). It is reprinted by permission of the editor and Ridgeview Publishing Company.

[1] Robert Audi has suggested that for me *to have justifiably done A* it is also necessary that I did it *because* it was permitted by the relevant system of principles (though this is not required, he says, for *A's having been justified for me*). This would be on the analogy of the distinction between S's *being justified in believing that p,* and *the proposition that p's being justified for S.* This may be right, but I am unable to go into the matter that fully here. The point I need for this paper is that *permission,* rather than *requirement,* by the relevant principles is *necessary* for the justification of action.

required or obligatory, only that its negation was not required or obligatory. This holds true whether we are thinking of moral, legal, institutional, or prudential justification of actions. To say that Herman was (morally) justified in refusing to take time out from writing his book to join in a peace march is to say that the relevant moral principles do not require him to march; it is not to say that he is morally obliged to stick to writing his book, though that may be true also. Likewise to say that Joan was legally justified in leaving the state is to say that her doing so contravened no law; it is not to say that any law required her to do so. Finally, consider my being justified in giving my epistemology class a take-home final rather than one to be taken in the classroom. Here we might be thinking of institutional justification, in which case the point would be that no regulations of my department, college, or university require a classroom final exam; but my being so justified does not imply that any regulations require a take-home exam. Or we might be thinking of pedagogical justification, in which case the point would be that sound pedagogical principles allow for a take-home exam for this kind of course, not that they require it; though, again, the latter might be true also.

The most natural way of construing the justification of beliefs is in parallel fashion. To say that S is justified in believing that p at time t is to say that the relevant rules or principles do not forbid S's believing that p at t. In believing that p at t, S is not in contravention of any relevant requirements. Again, it is not to say that S is required or obligated to believe that p at t, though that might also be true. With respect to beliefs we can again distinguish various modes of justification: moral, prudential, and epistemic. These may diverge. I may, for example, be morally justified in trusting my friend (believing that he is well intentioned toward me), and I may even be morally required to do so, even though, since all my evidence tends strongly against it, the belief is not epistemically justified. In this paper our concern is with epistemic justification. How is that distinguished from the other modes? The justification of anything, H, consists in H's being permitted by the relevant principles: epistemic, moral, or whatever. Thus the crucial question is: What distinguishes epistemic principles from moral principles? Well, the "epistemic point of view" is characterized by a concern with the twin goals of believing the true and not believing the false. To set this out properly we would have to go into the question of just how these goals are to be weighted relative to each other, and into a number of other thorny issues; but suffice it for now to say that epistemic principles for the assessment of belief will grade them in the light of these goals. Just how this is done depends on the conception of justification with which one is working. On a deontological conception of justification, the principles will *forbid* beliefs formed in such a way as to be likely to be false and either *permit* or *require* beliefs formed in such a way as to be likely to be true.[2] Thus on the deontological conception of the epistemic justification of belief that is as close as possible to the standard conception of the justification of action, to be justified in believing that p at t is for one's belief that p at t not to be in violation of any epistemic principles, principles that permit only those beliefs that are sufficiently likely to be true.[3] Let's say, for example, that beliefs in generalizations are permitted only if based on adequate inductive evidence, otherwise forbidden, and that a perceptual belief that p is permitted only if (a) it is formed on the basis of its perceptually seeming to one that p and (b) one does not have sufficient overriding reasons; otherwise it is forbidden. One will be justified in a belief of the specified sort if the relevant necessary conditions of permissibility are satisfied; otherwise the belief will be unjustified.

Since this is the natural way to use 'justification', it is not surprising that it is the one most often formulated by those who seek to be explicit about their epistemic concepts. Perhaps the most eminent contemporary deontologist is Roderick Chisholm.[4] Because of the complexities of Chisholm's view, however, I shall take as my model deontologist Carl Ginet. He sets out the conception with admirable directness.

> One is *justified* in being confident that p if and only if it is not the case that one ought not to be confident that p; one could not be justly reproached for being confident that p.[5]

[2]Principles having to do with the way a belief is formed is not the only possibility here. A deontologist might prefer to make the permissibility of a belief depend on what evidence or grounds the subject *has* for the belief, rather than on the grounds that were actually used as a basis in the formation of the belief. Again, she might prefer to make permissibility depend on whether the belief is formed in the right way or on the basis of an adequate ground, *so far as the subject can tell*, rather than on the actual chances of the belief's being true. Since these differences are not germane to the issues of this paper, I have chosen to state the matter in terms of my position, according to which the actual adequacy of the basis on which a belief was formed is crucial for its justificatory status.

[3]This formulation is itself subject to both internalist and externalist versions (in fact to several varieties of each), depending on whether the "likelihood" is objective or "within the subject's perspective". Moreover, as foreshadowed in the last sentence in the text, this version of a deontological conception is only the one that is closest to the usual concept of the justification of actions; in the course of this essay it will be found not to be viable and will be replaced by a deontological conception that is further from the action case.

[4]See Roderick Chisholm, "Lewis' Ethics of Belief," in *The Philosophy of C. I. Lewis*, ed. P. A. Schilpp (La Salle, Ill.: Open Court, 1968); *Theory of Knowledge*, 2d ed. (Englewood Cliffs, N.J.: Prentice-Hall, 1977); "A Version of Foundationalism," in *The Foundations of Knowing* (Minneapolis: University of Minnesota Press, 1982).

[5]Carl Ginet, *Knowledge, Perception, and Memory* (Dordrecht: D. Reidel, 1975), p. 28. Other epistemologists who explicitly endorse a deontological conception are Laurence

The Nature of Epistemic Justification

Now this conception of epistemic justification is viable only if beliefs are sufficiently under voluntary control to render such concepts as *requirement, permission, obligation, reproach,* and *blame* applicable to them. By the time-honored principle that "Ought implies can", one can be obliged to do A only if one has an effective choice as to whether to do A.[6] It is equally obvious that it makes no sense to speak of S's being permitted or forbidden to do A if S lacks an effective choice as to whether to do A.[7] Therefore the most fundamental issue raised by a formulation like Ginet's is as to whether belief is under voluntary control. Only if it is can the question arise as to whether the epistemic justification of beliefs can be construed deontologically. As we shall see, there are various modes of voluntary control that have usually not been fully distinguished in the literature and that require separate treatment. I will be arguing in this paper that (a) we lack what I will call direct voluntary control over beliefs, (b) that we have only a rather weak degree of "long range" voluntary control over (only) some of our beliefs, and (c) that although our voluntary actions can influence our beliefs, the deontological notion of justification based on this indirect influence is not the sort of notion we need for the usual epistemological purposes to which the term 'justification' is put.

Bonjour, *The Structure of Empirical Knowledge* (Cambridge: Harvard University Press, 1985), chap. 1; Paul Moser, *Empirical Justification* (Dordrecht: D. Reidel, 1985), chaps. 1, 4; Margery Naylor, "Epistemic Justification," *American Philosophical Quarterly*, 25, no. 1 (1988), 49–58; Alvin Plantinga, "Reason and Belief in God," in *Faith and Rationality*, ed. A. Plantinga and N. Wolterstorff (Notre Dame, Ind.: University of Notre Dame Press, 1983); Nicholas Wolterstorff, "Can Belief in God Be Rational If It Has No Foundations?", in ibid.; John Pollock, *Contemporary Theories of Knowledge* (Totowa, N.J.: Rowman & Littlefield, 1986), pp. 7–8. It should be noted that Plantinga makes it explicit that he would be just as happy with a conception in terms of "excellence" rather than in terms of freedom from blame. This indifference has since shifted to a definite preference for the latter. See his "Positive Epistemic Status and Proper Function," *Philosophical Perspectives*, 2 (1988). Alvin Goldman, though a reliabilist, also advocates a deontological conception in *Epistemology and Cognition* (Cambridge: Harvard University Press, 1986), chap. 4.

[6]Various exceptions to the principle have been noted recently. See, e.g., Michael Stocker, "'Ought' and 'Can'," *Australasian Journal of Philosophy*, 49, no. 3 (1971), 303–16. However, none of the exceptions involve kinds of actions that are not normally under voluntary control. Hence they have no tendency to show that one could be required or forbidden to believe while one generally lacks voluntary control over beliefs. The formulations in this paragraph should be taken as requiring that one normally have voluntary control over one's beliefs, not that one has voluntary control over a particular belief in a particular situation.

[7]As we have pointed out, for an action or whatever to be justified in a deontological sense is for it to be *permitted*, rather than required. Thus it is the necessity of an effective choice for something to be *permitted* that is crucial here.

II. The Problem of Voluntary Control of Belief

There are many locutions that encourage us to think of believing as subject to requirement, prohibition, and permission. We say "You shouldn't have supposed so readily that he wouldn't come through", "You have no right to assume that", "I had every right to think that she was honest", "I ought to have given him the benefit of the doubt", and "You shouldn't jump to conclusions". We also often seem to suggest the voluntary control of belief: "I finally decided that he was the man for the job", "Make up your mind; is it coreopsis or isn't it?", "I had to accept his testimony; I had no choice" (the suggestion being that in other cases one does have a choice). And philosophers frequently fall in with this, speaking of a subject's being in a situation in which he has to decide whether to accept, reject, or "withhold" a proposition.[8] All these turns of phrase, and many more, seem to imply that we frequently have the capacity to effectively decide or choose what we are to believe, and hence that we can be held responsible for the outcome of those decisions. It is natural to think of this capacity on the model of the maximally direct control we have over the motions of our limbs and other parts of our body, the voluntary movements of which constitute "basic actions", actions we perform "at will", just by an intention, volition, choice, or decision to do so, things we "just do", not "by" doing something else voluntarily. Let's call the kind of control we have over states of affairs we typically[9] bring about by basic actions, "basic voluntary[10] control". If we do have voluntary control of beliefs, we have the same sort of reason for supposing it to be basic control that we have for supposing ourselves to have basic control over the (typical) movements of our limbs, viz., that we are hard pressed to specify any voluntary action by doing which we get the limbs moved or the beliefs engendered. Hence it is not surprising that the basic voluntary control thesis has had distinguished proponents throughout the history of philosophy, for example, Augustine, Aquinas, Descartes, Kierkegaard, and

[8]See, e.g., Chisholm, *Theory of Knowledge,* pp. 14–15.
[9]This qualification is needed because things we can bring about by a basic action, e.g., a movement of one's arm, we *can* also bring about by doing something else, as when one lifts one arm by moving the other arm.
[10]I will often omit the modifier 'voluntary' in speaking of control. In this paper it is always to be tacitly understood.

Newman.[11] Though distinctly out of favor today, it still has its defenders.[12]

Before critically examining the thesis, we must make some distinctions that are important for our entire discussion. First, note that although the above discussion is solely in terms of belief, we need to range also over propositional attitudes that are contrary to belief. Chisholm speaks in terms of a trichotomy of "believe", "reject", and "withhold" that p.[13] Since rejecting p is identified with believing some contrary of p, it brings in no new kind of propositional attitude; but withholding p, believing neither it nor any contrary, does. The basic point to be noted here is that one has control over a given type of state only if one also has control over some field of incompatible alternatives. To have control over believing that p is to have control over whether one believes that p or not, that is, over whether one believes that p or engenders instead some incompatible alternative.[14] The power to choose A at will *is* the power to determine at will whether it shall be A or (some form of) not-A. Therefore, to be strictly accurate we should say that our problem concerns voluntary control over propositional attitudes. Although in the sequel the formulation will often be in terms of belief, it should be understood as having this more general bearing.

Second, something needs to be said about the relation between the control of *actions* and of *states of affairs*. Thus far we have been oscillating freely between the two. Now a belief, in the psychological sense that is being used here (as contrasted with the abstract sense of that which is believed), is a more or less long-lived *state* of the psyche, a modification of the wiring that can influence various actions and reactions of the subject so long as it persists. And the same holds for other propositional attitudes. Thus in speaking of voluntary control of beliefs, we have been speaking of the control of states. But couldn't we just as well speak of the voluntary control of, and responsibility for, the action of bringing about such states: accepting, rejecting, or withholding a prop-

---

[11]Most of these people limit their voluntarism to cases in which it is not clear to the subject whether the belief is true or false. For an excellent account of the history of thought on this subject, with many specific references, see Louis Pojman, *Religious Belief and the Will* (London: Routledge & Kegan Paul, 1986).

[12]See, e.g., Carl Ginet, "Contra Reliabilism," *The Monist*, 68, no. 2 (1985), and Jack Meiland, "What Ought We To Believe? The Ethics of Belief Revisited," *American Philosophical Quarterly*, 17 (1980). Neither of these maintains that belief is always under basic voluntary control.

[13]*Theory of Knowledge*, chap. 1.

[14]To be sure, one might lack the power to determine which of a number of incompatible alternatives is realized, but one could not have the power to choose A at will without also having the power to determine at will that some contrary of A (at least not-A) is realized.

osition, forming a belief, or refraining from believing?[15] The two loci of responsibility and control may seem strictly correlative, so that we can equally well focus on either. For one exercises voluntary control over a type of state, C, by voluntarily doing something to bring it about or inhibit it. And from the other side, every action can be thought of as the bringing about of a state of affairs. Whenever we are responsible for a state of affairs by virtue of having brought it about, we may just as well speak of being responsible for the action of bringing it about. There are the following reasons, however, for proceeding in terms of states.

First, in holding that beliefs are subject to deontological evaluation since under voluntary control, one need not restrict oneself to beliefs that were formed intentionally by a voluntary act. I can be blamed for believing that *p* in the absence of adequate evidence, even though the belief was formed quite automatically, not by voluntarily carrying out an intention to do so. Provided believing in general is under voluntary control, any belief can be assessed deontologically. It is enough that I could have adopted or withheld the proposition by a voluntary act, had I chosen to do so.

Another consideration that decisively favors the focus on states is that, as we shall see later, there is a way in which one can be responsible and blameworthy for a state of belief, or other state, even if one lacks the capacity to bring about such states intentionally.

The final preliminary note is this. Our issue does not concern free will or freedom of action, at least not in any sense in which that goes beyond one's action's being under the control of the will. On a "libertarian" conception of free will this is not sufficient; it is required in addition that both A and not-A be causally possible, given all the causal influences on the agent. And other requirements may be imposed concerning agency. A libertarian will, no doubt, maintain that if deontological concepts are to apply to believings in the same way as to overt actions, then all of his conditions for freedom will have to apply to believings as well. In this essay, however, I shall only be concerned with the issue of whether believings are under voluntary control. If, as I shall argue, this condition is not satisfied for believings, that will be sufficient to show that they are not free in the libertarian sense as well.

[15]I understand "accepting" a proposition as an activity that gives rise to a belief. Therefore, unlike Keith Lehrer, "The Gettier Problem and the Analysis of Knowledge" (in *Justification and Knowledge*, ed. G. S. Pappas [Dordrecht: D. Reidel, 1979]), and others, I am not using the term in such a sense that one could accept a proposition without believing it; though, of course, the belief engendered by an acceptance may be more or less long lived. I also recognize processes of belief formation that do not involve any activity of acceptance.

III. Basic Voluntary Control

Let's turn now to a critical examination of the basic control thesis, the thesis that one can take up at will whatever propositional attitude one chooses. Those who have attacked this view are divided between those who hold that believing at will is logically impossible and those who hold that it is only psychologically impossible, a capacity that we in fact lack though one we conceivably could have had.[16] I cannot see any sufficient reasons for the stronger claim, and so I shall merely contend that we are not so constituted as to be able to take up propositional attitudes at will. My argument for this, if it can be called that, simply consists in asking you to consider whether you have any such powers. Can you, at this moment, start to believe that the United States is still a colony of Great Britain, just by deciding to do so? If you find it too incredible that you should be sufficiently motivated to try to believe this, suppose that someone offers you $500,000,000 to believe it, and you are much more interested in the money than in believing the truth. Could you do what it takes to get that reward? Remember that we are speaking about believing at will. No doubt, there are things you could do that would increase the probability of your coming to believe this, but that will be discussed later. Can you switch propositional attitudes toward that proposition just by deciding to do so? It seems clear to me that I have no such power. Volitions, decisions, or choosings don't hook up with anything in the way of propositional attitude inauguration, just as they don't hook up with the secretion of gastric juices or cell metabolism. There could conceivably be individual differences in this regard. Some people can move their ears at will, while most of us cannot. However, I very much doubt that any human beings are endowed with the power of taking on propositional attitudes at will. The temptation to suppose otherwise may stem from conflating that power with others that we undoubtedly do have but that are clearly distinct.[17] If I were to set out to bring myself into a state of belief that *p,* just by an act of will, I might assert that *p* with an expression of conviction, or dwell favorably on the idea that *p,* or imagine a sentence expressing *p* emblazoned in the heavens with an angelic chorus in the background intoning the Kyrie of Mozart's Coronation Mass. All this I can do at will, but none of

[16]The best-known defense of the logical impossibility claim is by Bernard Williams, "Deciding to Believe," in *Problems of the Self* (Cambridge: Cambridge University Press, 1972). It has been criticized by, inter alia, Trudy Govier, "Belief, Values, and the Will," *Dialogue,* 15 (1976), and by Barbara Winters, "Believing at Will," *Journal of Philosophy,* 76 (1979).

[17]It may also stem from misdiagnoses of a sort to be presented shortly.

this amounts to taking on a belief that *p*. It is all show, an elaborate pretence of believing. Having gone through all this, my doxastic attitudes will remain just as they were before; or if there is some change, it will be a *result* of these gyrations.

We should not suppose that our inability to believe at will is restricted to propositions that are obviously false. The inability also extends, at least, to those that are obviously true. A few pages back we made the point that voluntary control attaches to contrary pairs, or to more complex arrays of alternatives. If the sphere of my effective voluntary control does not extend both to A and to not-A, then it attaches to neither. If I don't have the power to choose between A and not-A, then we are without sufficient reason to say that I did A *at will*, rather than just doing A, accompanied by a volition. It is even more obvious, if possible, that responsibility, obligation, and their kindred attach to doing A only if the agent has an effective choice between doing and not doing A. If I would still have done A whatever I willed, chose, or preferred, I can hardly be blamed for doing it.

Thus, even if I willingly, or not unwillingly, form, for instance, perceptual beliefs in the way I do, it by no means follows that I form those beliefs at will, or that I have voluntary control over such belief formation, or that I can be held responsible or blameworthy for doing so. It would have to be true that I have effective voluntary control over whether I do or do not believe that the tree has leaves on it when I see a tree with leaves on it just before me in broad daylight with my eyesight working perfectly. And it is perfectly clear that in this situation I have no power at all to refrain from that belief. And so with everything else that seems perfectly obvious to us. We have just as little voluntary control over ordinary beliefs formed by introspection, memory, and simple uncontroversial inferences.

The discussion to this point will suggest to the voluntarist that he can still make a stand on propositions that do not seem clearly true or false and hold that there one (often) has the capacity to adopt whatever propositional attitude one chooses. In religion, philosophy, and high level scientific matters it is often the case that, so far as one can see, the relevant arguments do not definitively settle the matter one way or the other. I engage in prolonged study of the mind-body problem or of the existence of God. I carefully examine arguments for and against various positions. It seems to me that none of the positions have decisively proved their case, even though there are weighty considerations that can be urged in support of each. There are serious difficulties with all the competing positions, though, so far as I can see, more than one contender is left in the field in each case. So what am I to do? I could just abandon the quest. But alternatively I could, so it seems, simply decide to adopt one of the positions and/or decide to reject one or more of the contenders. Is that not what I must do if I am to make any judgment on the matter? And isn't that what typically happens? I decide to embrace theism or epiphenomenalism, and forthwith it is embraced.

There are also practical situations in which we are confronted with incompatible answers to a certain question, none of which we see to be clearly true or false. Here we often do not have the luxury of leaving the field; since we must act in one way rather than another, we are forced to form, and act on, some belief about the matter. It would be a good idea for me to plant these flowers today if and only if it will rain tomorrow. But it is not at all clear to me whether tomorrow will be rainy. I must either plant the flowers today or not, and it would surely be unwise to simply ignore the matter, thereby in effect acting un- critically on the assumption that it will not rain tomorrow. Hence the better part of wisdom would be to make some judgment on the matter, the best that I can. On a larger scale, a field commander in wartime is often faced with questions about the current disposition of enemy forces. But often the information at his disposal does not tell him just what that disposition is. In such a situation is it not clear that, weighing available indications as best he can, he simply decides to make a certain judgment on the matter and act on that? What else can he do?

Before responding to these claims I should point out that even if they were correct, it would still not follow that a deontological concep- tion of justification is adequate for epistemology. For the voluntarist has already abandoned vast stretches of the territory. He has given up all propositions that seem clearly true or false, and these constitute the bulk of our beliefs. Controversial and difficult issues force themselves on our attention, especially if we are intellectuals, just because we spend so much of our time trying to resolve them. But if we survey the whole range of our cognitive operations, they will appear as a few straws floating on a vast sea of items about none of which we entertain the slightest doubt. Consider the vast number of perceptual beliefs we form about our environment as we move about in it throughout our waking hours, most of them short-lived and many of them uncon- scious. By comparison the controversial beliefs we have in religion, politics, philosophy, and the conduct of our affairs are negligible in number, however significant they may be individually. Hence if only the uncertain beliefs are under voluntary control, that will not enable us to form a generally applicable deontological concept of epistemic justification.[18]

To return to our philosopher, gardener, and military commander, I would suggest that in each case the situation is better construed in some way other than as initiating a belief at will.[19] The most obvious suggestion is that although in these cases the supporting considerations are seen as less conclusive, here too the belief follows automatically, without intervention by the will, from the way things seem at the moment to the subject. In the cases of (subjective) certainty belief is determined by that sense of certainty, or, alternatively, by what leads to it, the sensory experience or whatever; in the cases of (subjective) uncertainty belief is still determined by what plays an analogous role, the sense that one alternative is more likely than the others, or by what leads to that. Thus when our philosopher or religious seeker "decides" to embrace theism or the identity theory, what has happened is that at that moment this position seems more likely to be true, seems to have weighter considerations in its favor, than any envisaged alternative. Hence S is, *at that moment,* no more able to accept atheism or epiphenomenalism instead, than he would be if theism or the identity theory seemed obviously and indubitably true. This can be verified by considering our capacities in a situation in which the above conditions are not satisfied; theism and atheism, or the various contenders on the mind-body issue, really seem equally likely to be true, equally well or ill supported. If that were strictly the case (and perhaps it seldom is), then could S adopt, for example, theism, just by choosing to do so? When I contemplate that

---

[18]Ginet disagrees. He holds that "we can interpret an ascription of unjustifiedness to a belief that the subject cannot help having as saying that, if the subject were able to help it, she ought not to hold the belief" (*Knowledge, Perception, and Memory*, p. 183). Thus we can extend a deontological concept of justification to irresistible beliefs by invoking a counterfactual. I have two comments to make on this move. (1) This renders epistemic justification quite different from the justification of action, where 'justified' and other deontological terms are withheld from actions the subject couldn't help performing. (2) Insofar as we can make a judgment as to what would be permitted or forbidden were a certain range of involuntary states within our voluntary control, it will turn out that the deontological evaluation is simply a misleading way of making evaluations that could be stated more straightforwardly and more candidly in other terms. Suppose that we judge that if we had voluntary control over the secretion of gastric juices, then we ought to secrete them in such a way as to be maximally conducive to health and a feeling of well being; e.g., we should not secrete them so as to produce hyperacidity. But since gastric juices are not within our voluntary control, this would seem to be just a misleading way of saying that a certain pattern of secretion is desirable or worthwhile. The deontological formulation is a wheel that moves nothing else in the machine.

[19]Cf. Pojman, *Religious Belief and the Will*, chap. 13, for excellent diagnoses of putative cases of basic control of beliefs.

possibility, it seems to me that I would be as little able to adopt theism at will as I would be if it seemed obviously true or obviously false. Here, like Buridan's ass, I am confronted with (subjectively) perfectly equivalent alternatives. If it were a choice between actions, such as that confronting the ass, I need not perish through indecision. I could arbitrarily make a choice, as we often do in a cafeteria line when two alternative salads look equally tempting. (Some people negotiate this more quickly than others.) But doxastic choice is another matter. How *could* I simply choose to believe one rather than the other when they seem exactly on a par with respect to the likelihood of truth, especially when that subjective probability is rather low? To do so would be to choose a belief in the face of the lack of any significant inclination to suppose it to be true. It seems clear to me that this is not within our power.[20]

The above account in terms of comparative subjective probability might be correct for all our cases, theoretical and practical. Thus the military commander might adopt the supposition about the disposition of enemy forces that seems to him at the moment best supported by the reports at his disposal. But I believe that there are cases, both theoretical and practical, in which the upshot is not triggered by some differential subjective probability of the alternatives. I have already argued that in those cases the upshot cannot be the formation of a belief, whether at will or otherwise. But then what? Here is one possibility. What S is doing is to resolve to act as if *p* is true, adopt it as a basis for action. This is often a correct description of situations like the military commander's. He may well have said to himself: "I don't know what the disposition of enemy forces is; I don't even have enough information to make an educated guess. But I have to proceed on some basis or other, so I'll just assume that it is H and make my plans accordingly." This is not to form the belief that the disposition is H; it is not to *accept* the proposition that the disposition is H, except as a basis for action. It would simply be incorrect to describe the commander as *believing* that the disposition of enemy forces is H, or having any other belief about the matter. He is simply proceeding on a certain assumption, concerning the truth of which he has no belief at all. One may also make an assumption for theoretical purposes, in order to see how it "pans out", in the hope that one will thereby obtain some additional reasons for supposing it to be true or false. Thus a scientist can adopt

---

[20]In maintaining that one cannot believe that *p* without its at least seeming to one that *p* is more probable than any envisaged alternative, I am not joining Richard Swinburne (*Faith and Reason* [Oxford: Clarendon Press, 1981], chap. 1) in supposing that to believe that *p* is just to take *p* to be more probable than some alternative(s).

"as a working hypothesis" the proposition that the atomic nucleus is positively charged, draw various consequences from it, and seek to test those consequences. The scientist need not *form the belief* that the atomic nucleus is positively charged in order to carry out this operation; typically he would be doing this because he didn't know what to believe about the matter. Likewise a philosopher might take materialism as a working hypothesis to see how it works out in application to various problems. There may also be blends of the theoretical and the practical. One may adopt belief in God, or some more robust set of religious doctrines, as a guide to life, setting out to try to live in accordance with them, seeking to act and feel one's way into the religious community, in order to determine how the doctrines work out in the living of them, both in terms of how satisfactory and fulfilling a life they enable one to live and in terms of what evidence for or against them one acquires.

Where the "acceptance" of a proposition in the absence of a significant subjective probability is not the adoption of a working hypothesis, there are other alternatives. (1) S may be seeking, for whatever reason, to bring himself into a position of believing *p*; and S or others may confuse this activity, which can be undertaken voluntarily, with believing or judging the proposition to be true. (2) As noted earlier, S may assert that *p*, overtly or covertly, perhaps repeatedly and in a firm tone, and this, which can be done voluntarily, may be confused with a "judgment" that *p*, of the sort that inaugurates a state of belief. (3) S may align herself, objectively and/or subjectively, with some group that is committed to certain doctrines—a church, a political party, a movement, a group of thinkers—and this, which can be done voluntarily, may be confused with coming to believe those doctrines. I am convinced that the analysis of a wide variety of supposed cases of believing at will in the absence of significant subjective probability would reveal that in each case forming a belief that *p* has been confused with something else. Thus I think that there is a strong case for the proposition that no one ever acquires a belief at will. But even if I am wrong about that, the above considerations do at least show that it is of relatively rare occurrence, and that it certainly cannot be used as the basis for a generally applicable deontological concept of epistemic justification.

IV. Nonbasic Immediate Voluntary Control

The demise of basic control, however, is by no means the end of "voluntarism", as we may term the thesis that one has voluntary control of propositional attitudes. Many deontologists, after disavowing any commitment to what they usually call "direct voluntary control of belief" and what we have called "basic voluntary control", proceed to insist that beliefs are subject to what they term "indirect voluntary control".[21] All of them use the term 'indirect control' in an undiscriminating fashion to cover any sort of control that is not "direct", that is, basic. As a result they fail to distinguish between the three sorts of nonbasic control I shall be distinguishing.[22] Some of their examples fit one of my three categories, some another. The ensuing discussion will show important differences between these three modes of control.

To get into this, let's first note that we take many familiar nonbasic overt actions to be voluntary (and their upshots to be under voluntary control) in a way that is sufficient for their being required, permitted, and prohibited. Consider opening a door, informing someone that p, and turning on a light. To succeed in any of these requires more than a volition on the part of the agent; in each case I must perform one or more bodily movements and these movements must have certain consequences, causal or conventional, in order that I can be said to have performed the nonbasic action in question. In order for it to be true that I opened a certain door, I must pull it, push it, kick it, or put some other part of my body into suitable contact with it (assuming that I lack powers of telekinesis), and this must result in the door's coming to be open. In order to inform H that p, I must produce various sounds, marks, or other perceptible products, and either these products must fall under linguistic rules in such a way as to constitute a vehicle for asserting that p (if we are thinking of informing as an illocutionary act), or H, upon perceiving these products, must be led to form the belief that p (if we are thinking of informing as a perlocutionary act). Hence actions like these are not immediately consequent on a volition and so are not strictly done "at will". Nevertheless I might be blamed for my failure to turn on the light when it was my obligation to do so. The point is that in many cases we take the extra conditions of success for granted. We suppose that if the agent will just voluntarily exert herself, the act will be done. Here we might say that the action, and its upshot, is under the "immediate voluntary control" of the agent (more strictly, *nonbasic* immediate voluntary control), even though more than an act

---

[21]See, e.g., Alvin Goldman, "The Internalist Conception of Justification," *Midwest Studies in Philosophy*, 5 (1980); Plantinga, "Reason and Belief in God"; Wolterstorff, "Can Belief in God Be Rational?"; Moser, *Empirical Justification*, chap. 4; Matthias Steup, "The Deontic Conception of Epistemic Justification," *Philosophical Studies*, 53, no. 1 (1988).

[22]Even the extended treatment in Pojman, *Religious Belief and the Will*, fails to make any distinctions within "indirect control".

of will is required of the agent. I call this "immediate"[23] control since the agent is able to carry out the intention "right away", in one uninterrupted intentional act, without having to return to the attempt a number of times after having been occupied with other matters.[24] I will use the term "direct control" for both basic and immediate control. It is clear that if beliefs were under one's immediate control, that would suffice to render them susceptible to deontological evaluation.

But are beliefs always, or ever, within our immediate voluntary control? Our discussion of this will be largely a rerun of the discussion of basic control, with some added twists. As in the earlier discussion we can first exempt most of our doxastic situations from serious consideration. With respect to almost all normal perceptual, introspective, and memory propositions, it is absurd to think that one has any such control over whether one accepts, rejects, or withholds the proposition. When I look out my window and see rain falling, water dripping off the leaves of trees, and cars passing by, I no more have immediate control over whether I accept those propositions than I have basic control. I form the belief that rain is falling willy-nilly. There is no way I can inhibit this belief. At least there is no way I can do so *on the spot,* in carrying out an uninterrupted intention to do so. How would I do so? What button would I push? I could try asserting the contrary in a confident tone of voice. I could rehearse some skeptical arguments. I could invoke the Vedantic doctrine of *maya.* I could grit my teeth and command myself to withhold the proposition. But unless I am a very unusual person, none of these will have the least effect. It seems clear that nothing any normal human being can do during the uninterrupted operation of an intention to reject the proposition that it is raining (in the above situation) will have any chance at all to succeed. And the same can be said for inferential beliefs in which it is quite clear to one that the conclusion is correct. Since cases in which it seems perfectly clear to the subject what is the case constitute an enormously large proportion (I would say almost all) of propositions that are either the object of a definite attitude or considered as a candidate for such, the considerations of this paragraph show that immediate voluntary

---

[23]When the 'nonbasic' qualifier is omitted, 'immediate' is hardly a felicitous term for something that contrasts with basic control. Nevertheless, I shall, for the sake of concision, mostly speak in terms of 'immediate control'. The 'nonbasic' qualifier is to be understood.

[24]This notion of doing something "right away" will serve to distinguish the present form of direct control from the next.

control cannot be a basis for the application of deontological concepts to most of our propositional attitudes.

But what about situations in which it is not clear whether a proposition is true or false? This is where voluntarists tend to take their stand. After all, they say, that is what inquiry is for, to resolve matters when it is not clear what the correct answer is. One certainly has voluntary control over whether to keep looking for evidence or reasons, and voluntary control over where to look, what steps to take, and so on. Since one has control over those matters, that amounts to what I have called immediate voluntary control over one's propositional attitudes.

> If self-control is what is essential to activity, some of our beliefs, our believings, would seem to be acts. When a man deliberates and comes finally to a conclusion, his decision is as much within his control as is any other deed we attribute to him. If his conclusion was unreasonable, a conclusion he should not have accepted, we may plead with him: "But you needn't have supposed that so-and-so was true. Why didn't you take account of these other facts?" We assume that his decision is one he could have avoided and that, had he only chosen to do so, he could have made a more reasonable inference. Or, if his conclusion is not the result of a deliberate inference, we may say, "But if you had only stopped to think", implying that, had he chosen, he could have stopped to think. We suppose, as we do whenever we apply our ethical or moral predicates, that there was something else the agent could have done instead.[25]

To be sure, the mere fact that one often looks for evidence to decide an unresolved issue does not show that one has immediate control, or any other sort of control, over one's propositional attitudes. That also depends on the incidence of success in these enterprises. And sometimes one finds decisive evidence and sometimes one doesn't. But let's ignore this complexity and just consider whether there is a case for immediate control of propositional attitudes in the successful cases.

No, there is not, and primarily for the following reason. These claims ignore the difference between doing A in order to bring about E, for some definite E, and doing A so that some effect within a certain range will ensue. In order that the "looking for more evidence" phenomenon would show that we have immediate voluntary control over propositional attitudes in basically the way we do over the positions of doors and light switches, it would have to be the case that the search for evidence was undertaken with the intention of taking up a certain particular attitude toward a particular proposition. For only in that

[25]Chisholm, "Lewis' Ethics of Belief," p. 224.

case would the outcome show that we have exercised voluntary control over *what* propositional attitude we take up. Suppose that I can't remember Al Kaline's lifetime batting average and I look it up in the baseball almanac. I read there the figure .320, and I thereby accept it. Does that demonstrate my voluntary control over my belief that Kaline's lifetime batting average was .320? Not at all. At most it shows that I have immediate voluntary control over whether I take up *some* propositional attitude toward *some* proposition ascribing a lifetime batting average to Kaline. This is not at all analogous to my exercising my capacity to get the door open whenever I choose to do so. Its nearest analogue in that area would be something like this. I am a servant and I am motivated to bring the door into whatever position my employer chooses. He has an elaborate electronic system that involves automatic control of many aspects of the household, including doors. Each morning he leaves detailed instructions on household operations in a computer. Doors can only be operated through the computer in accordance with his instructions. There is no way in which I can carry out an intention of my own to open or to close a door. All I can do is to actuate the relevant program and let things take their course. Since the employer's instructions will be carried out only if I actuate the program, I am responsible for the doors' assuming whatever position he specified, just as I was responsible for taking up some attitude or other toward some proposition within a given range. But I most emphatically am not responsible for the front door's being open rather than closed, nor can I be said to have voluntary control over its specific position. Hence it would be idle to apply deontological concepts to me vis-à-vis the specific position of the door: to forbid me or require me to open it, or to blame or reproach me for its being open. I had no control over that; it was not subject to my will. And that's the way it is where the only voluntary control I have over my propositional attitudes is to enter onto an investigation that will eventuate in some propositional attitude or other, depending on what is uncovered. That would be no basis for holding me responsible for believing that *p* rather than rejecting or withholding it, no basis for requiring me or forbidding me to believe that *p*, or for reproaching me for doing so.

If Chisholm's claim is only that one can voluntarily put oneself in a position from which some doxastic attitude to *p* will be forthcoming (or perhaps that one can put oneself in a position such that a desirable doxastic attitude to *p* will be forthcoming), *this* capacity extends to all sorts of propositions, including those over which we obviously have no voluntary control. Consider propositions concerning what is visible. I have the power to open my eyes and look about me, thereby putting myself in a position, when conditions are favorable, to reliably form propositions about the visible environment. Again, with respect to past experiences I can "search my memory" for the details of my experiences of the middle of yesterday, thereby, usually, putting myself in an excellent position to reliably form beliefs about my experiences at that time. No one, I suppose, would take this to show that I have immediate voluntary control over what I believe about the visible environment or about my remembered experiences. And yet this is essentially the same sort of thing as the search for additional evidence, differing only in the type of belief-forming mechanism involved.

I suspect that deontologists like Chisholm secretly suppose that the additional evidence, rather than "automatically" determining the doxastic attitude, simply puts the subject in a position to make an informed choice of an attitude. That is, despite their official position, they really locate the voluntary control in the moment of attitude formation rather than in the preliminary investigation, thus in effect taking the direct voluntary control position. But then, faced with the crashing implausibility of that position, they think to save the application of deontological concepts by pushing the voluntary control back to the preliminary search for decisive considerations. It is, then, their secret, unacknowledged clinging to the basic control thesis that prevents them from seeing that voluntary control of the investigative phase has no tendency to ground the deontological treatment of propositional attitudes. I must confess that I have no real textual evidence for this speculation, and that I am attracted to it by the fact that it explains an otherwise puzzling failure of acute philosophers to see the irrelevance (to this issue) of our voluntary control over the conduct of inquiry.

Thus far I have been considering one way in which deontologists seek to defend a claim of immediate voluntary control over beliefs. We have seen that way to fail by irrelevance, since it has to do with voluntarily putting oneself in a position to form the most rational attitude, whatever that may be, rather than voluntarily taking up some specific attitude. However, there is no doubt but that people do sometimes set out to get themselves to believe that *p*, for some specific *p*. People try to convince themselves that X loves them, that Y will turn out all right, that the boss doesn't really have a negative attitude toward them, that the Red Sox will win the World Series, that materialism is true, or that God exists. Epistemologists don't like to cite such disreputable proceedings as a ground for the application of deontological concepts. To try to get oneself to believe that *p*, prior to being in a good position to tell whether *p* is true or not, is not a procedure to be commended from the epistemic standpoint. Nevertheless, these undertakings have to be considered in a comprehensive survey of possible modes of voluntary control. Proceeding in that spirit, the point to note here is that such goings-on provide no support for a supposition of *immediate* voluntary control over belief. For such enterprises can be successfully carried out only as long-term projects. If I, not currently believing that X loves me, were to set out to bring about that belief in one fell swoop, that is, during a period of activity uninterruptedly guided by the intention to produce that belief, then, unless I am markedly abnormal psychologically, I am doomed to failure. We just don't work that way. Again, I wouldn't know what button to push. My only hope of success would lie in bringing various influences to bear upon myself and shielding myself from others, in the hope of thereby eventually moving myself from disbelief to belief. This might include dwelling on those encounters in which X had acted lovingly toward me, shutting out evidences of indifference or dislike, encouraging romantic fantasies, and so forth. Thus this sort of enterprise belongs, rather, to the category of *long-range voluntary control,* a topic to which we now turn.

V. Long-range Voluntary Control

We have seen that we cannot plausibly be credited with either sort of direct control over our propositional attitudes. Taking up such an attitude can be neither a basic action like raising one's arm nor a non-basic action like flipping a switch. Hence the deontological treatment of belief can borrow no support from the applicability of deontological terms to actions like these. But the possibility still remains that we have more long-range voluntary control over belief. The considerations of the last paragraph encourage this supposition, at least for some cases. Before examining this possibility I will firm up the distinction between this type of control and the previous one.

In introducing the notion of "immediate control" I said that when one has this species of control over a type of state, C, one is able to bring about a C "right away, in one uninterrupted intentional act". When conditions are propitious, one can get a door open, get a light on, get one's shoes on, or tell Susie the mail has come, by doing various things under the direction of a single uninterrupted intention to bring about that state of affairs. One does not have to return to the attempt a number of times after having been occupied with other matters.[26] And

---

[26]I should make it explicit that I do not suppose that an intention must be conscious, much less focally conscious, during all the time it is playing a role in guiding behavior.

since one is not ordinarily capable of keeping an intention in an active state for more than a relatively short period of time, the sorts of actions over which one has immediate control must be capable of execution within a short time after their inception.

Long-range control is simply the foil of immediate control. It is the capacity to bring about a state of affairs, C, by doing something (usually a number of different things) repeatedly over a considerable period of time, interrupted by activity directed to other goals. One has this sort of control, to a greater or lesser degree, over many things: one's weight, cholesterol concentration, blood pressure, and disposition; the actions of one's spouse or one's department. One can, with some hope of success, set out on a long-range project to reduce one's weight, improve one's disposition, or get one's spouse to be more friendly to the neighbors. The degree of control varies markedly among these examples. I have, within limits, complete control over my weight; only sufficient motivation is required to achieve and maintain a certain weight. My ability to change my disposition or to change behavior patterns in my spouse is much less. But all these cases, and many more, illustrate the point that one can have long-range control over many things over which one lacks direct control. I cannot markedly reduce my weight right away, by the uninterrupted carrying out of an intention to do so, for instance, by taking a pill, running around the block, or saying "Abracadabra". But that doesn't nullify the fact that I have long-range control.

It does seem that we have some degree of long-range voluntary control over at least some of our beliefs. As just noted, people do set out on long-range projects to get themselves to believe a certain proposition, and sometimes they succeed in this. Devices employed include selective exposure to evidence, selective attention to supporting considerations, seeking the company of believers and avoiding nonbelievers, self-suggestion, and more bizarre methods like hypnotism. By such methods people sometimes induce themselves to believe in God, in materialism, in communism, in the proposition that they are loved by X, and so on. Why doesn't this constitute a kind of voluntary control that grounds deontological treatment?

Well, it would if, indeed, we do have sufficient control of this sort. Note that people could properly be held responsible for their attitudes toward propositions in a certain range only if those who set out to intentionally produce a certain attitude toward such a proposition, and made sufficient efforts, were frequently successful.[27] For only if we are

[27] I am not saying that S could be held responsible for taking attitude A toward p only if S himself had in fact been successful in intentionally bringing about that attitude. The

generally successful in bringing about a goal, G, when we try hard enough to do so, do we have effective control over whether G obtains. And if I don't have effective control over G, I can hardly be held to blame for its nonoccurrence. Even if I had done everything I could to produce it, I would have had little chance of success; so how could I rightly be blamed for its absence? (I might be blamed for not *trying* to produce it or for not trying hard enough, but that is another matter.) This is a generally applicable principle, by no means restricted to the doxastic sphere. If I am so constituted that the most I can do with respect to my irritability is to make it somewhat less likely that it will exceed a certain (rather high) average threshold, I can hardly be blamed for being irritable.

It is very dubious that we have reliable long-range control over any of our beliefs, even in the most favorable cases, such as beliefs about religious and philosophical matters and about personal relationships. *Sometimes* people succeed in getting themselves to believe (disbelieve) something. But I doubt that the success rate is substantial. To my knowledge there are no statistics on this, but I would be very much surprised if attempts of this sort bore fruit in more than a very small proportion of the cases. In thinking about this, let's first set aside cases in which the attempt succeeds because the subject happens onto conclusive evidence that would have produced belief anyway without deliberate effort on his part to produce belief. These are irrelevant because the intention to believe that p played no effective role. Thus we are considering cases in which the subject is swimming against either a preponderance of contrary evidence or a lack of evidence either way. S is fighting very strong tendencies to believe when and only when something seems true to one. Some of these tendencies are probably innate and some engendered or reinforced by socialization; in any event they are deeply rooted and of great strength. To combat or circumvent them one must exercise considerable ingenuity in monitoring the input of information and in exposing oneself to nonrational influences. This is a tricky operation, requiring constant vigilance as well as considerable skill, and it would be very surprising if it were successful in a

---

requirement is rather that p be the sort of proposition toward which people generally are usually successful in bringing about a certain attitude when they try hard enough to do so. If the more stringent requirement were adopted, for actions generally, it would prevent us from holding S responsible for a purely habitual action where he could have successfully carried out an intention to refrain from that action if he had had such an intention. For in that case the action was not in fact the carrying out of a specific intention to perform it. Nevertheless, provided the agent could have inhibited the action had he formed an intention to do, we would feel justified in holding him responsible for it.

significant proportion of the cases. I am not suggesting that it is unusual for people to form and retain beliefs without adequate grounds, reasons, or justification. This is all too common. But in most such cases the proposition in question seems clearly true, however ill supported. The typical case of prejudice is not one in which S manages to believe something contrary to what seems to him to be the case or something concerning which he has no definite impression of truth or falsity. It is a case in which his socialization has led it to seem clearly true to him that, for example, blacks are innately inferior.

Thus a long-range control thesis does not provide much grounding for deontologism, even for the sorts of propositions people do sometimes try to get themselves to believe or disbelieve. Much less is there any such grounding for those propositions with respect to which people don't normally even try to manipulate their attitudes. We have already noted that most of our beliefs spring from doxastic tendencies that are too deeply rooted to permit of modification by deliberate effort. Most of the matters on which we form beliefs are such that the project of deliberately producing belief or disbelief is one that is never seriously envisaged, just because it is too obvious that there is no chance of success. Thus even if we were usually successful when we set out to produce a propositional attitude, the voluntary control thus manifested would not ground the application of deontological concepts to beliefs generally. So, once again, the most we could conceivably have (and I have argued that we do not in fact have even that) would fall short of a generally applicable deontological concept of justification.

VI. Indirect Voluntary Influence: A Different Deontological Conception of Epistemic Justification

Up to this point I have been examining the support for a deontological conception of epistemic justification provided by the treatment of propositional attitude formation on the model of intentional action. We have considered whether, or to what extent, it is in our power to carry out an intention to take up a certain propositional attitude, either at will (basic control), or while uninterruptedly guided by the intention to do so (immediate control), or as a complex long-term project (long-range control). We have seen that for most of our beliefs we have control of none of these sorts, and that for the others we have, at most, some spotty and unreliable control of the long-range sort. I conclude that we do *not* generally have the power to carry out an intention to take up a certain propositional attitude. Insofar as the conception of epistemic justification as *believing as one is permitted to* depends on that assumption, it must be rejected. The inauguration of propositional attitudes simply does not work like intentional action.

However, this is not necessarily the end of the line for the deontologist. He has another move. We can be held responsible for a state of affairs that results from our actions even if we did not produce that state of affairs intentionally, provided it is the case that something we did (didn't do) and should have not done (done) was a necessary condition (in the circumstances) of the realization of that state of affairs, that is to say, provided that state of affairs would not have obtained had we not done (done) something we should not have done (done). Suppose that, although I did not do anything with the intention of bringing about my cholesterol buildup, still I could have prevented it if I had done certain things I could and should have done, for instance, reduce fat intake. In that case I could still be held responsible for the condition; it could be my fault. This is a way in which deontological concepts can be applied to me, with respect to a certain state of affairs, even though that state of affairs did not result from my carrying out an intention to produce it.

This suggests that even if propositional attitudes are not under our effective voluntary control, we might still be held responsible for them, provided we could and should have prevented them; provided there is something we could and should have done such that if we had done it we would not have had the attitude in question. If this is the case, it could provide a basis for the application of deontological concepts to propositional attitudes, and, perhaps, for a deontological concept of epistemic justification, one that bypasses the above critique. Let's use the term 'indirect voluntary influence' for this kind of voluntary control, or better, "voluntary impact" we may have on our beliefs.

It may be helpful to display in outline form the various modes of voluntary control we have distinguished.

   (I) Direct control
      (A) Basic control
      (B) Nonbasic immediate control
  (II) Long-range control
 (III) Indirect influence

Now it does seem that we have voluntary control over many things that influence belief. These can be divided into (1) activities that bring influences to bear, or withhold influences from, a particular situation involving a particular candidate, or a particular field of candidates, for belief, and (2) activities that affect our general belief-forming habits or tendencies.[28] There are many examples of (1). With respect to a particular issue, I have voluntary control over whether, and how long, I consider the matter, look for relevant evidence or reasons, reflect on a particular argument, seek input from other people, search my memory for analogous cases, and so on. Here we come back to the activities that people like Chisholm wrongly classify as the intentional inauguration of a propositional attitude. Although the fact that it is within my power to either look for further evidence or not does not show that I have voluntary control over what attitude I take toward p, it does show that I have voluntary control over influences on that attitude. The second category includes such activities as training myself to be more critical of gossip, instilling in myself a stronger disposition to reflect carefully before making a judgment on highly controversial matters, talking myself into being less (more) subservient to authority, and practicing greater sensitivity to the condition of other people. It is within my power to do things like this or not, and when I do them with sufficient assiduity I make some difference to my propositional attitude tendencies, and thus indirectly to the formation of such attitudes.[29]

Actually, there would be no harm in including in the first category attempts to bring about a certain specific attitude, and the successful carrying out of such an attempt when and if that occurs. For these too would be things over which we have voluntary control that influence our propositional attitudes. The point of stressing other things is that, since our earlier discussions have provided reason for thinking that such attempts are rarely successful, I want to emphasize the point that even if we are never successful in carrying out an intention to believe (reject, withhold) p, still there are many things over which we have voluntary control that do have a bearing on what propositional attitudes are engendered.

Thus it will sometimes be the case that had we performed (not performed) some voluntary actions A, B, . . . , we would have (not have)

[28]See Wolterstorff, "Can Belief in God Be Rational?", for an excellent discussion of these modes of influence.

[29]Note that the activities in this second category are even further removed from the intentional formation of a certain belief than those in the first, which themselves are clearly distinct from any such thing. The activities in the first category are concerned with a small number of alternatives for attitude formation. Though the activities are not undertaken with the aim of taking up one particular attitude from this field, they are directed to seeking out influences that will resolve *this* indeterminancy in some way or other. The activities in the second group, however, are directed much more generally to our tendencies of attitude formation on a wide variety of topics and in a wide variety of situations. But the most important point is that in neither case do the activities in question involve the carrying out of an intention to take up a particular propositional attitude.

taken up some attitude we did not (did) take up. The only remaining question is as to whether deontological concepts apply to the sorts of activities we have been discussing. Is it ever the case that we ought or ought not to engage in some activity of searching for new evidence or refraining from doing so? Is it ever the case that we ought (ought not) to strive to make ourselves more (less) critical of gossip or more (less) sensitive to contrary evidence? Deontologists typically aver that we have *intellectual* obligations in such matters, obligations rooted in our basic intellectual obligation to seek the true and avoid the false, or, alternatively, rooted in our basic aim, need, or commitment to believe the true and avoid believing the false. Let's go along with our opponents on this point. I can do so with a clear conscience, since I am seeking to show that even if we admit this, and make the other concessions I have been making, a deontological conception of epistemic justification is not viable.

Thus it will sometimes be the case, when I believe that p, that I would not have done so had I done various things in the past that I could and should have done but failed to do. Suppose that I accept some idle gossip to the effect that Jim is trying to undermine Susie's position as chair of the department. It may be that had I been doing my duty by way of making myself more critical of gossip, and by way of checking into this particular matter, I would not have formed that belief or would not have retained it for so long. In that case I could be held responsible for believing this in the same way as that in which I can be held responsible for my cholesterol buildup. I can be properly blamed for it, even though I did not intentionally bring it about.

Note that this application of deontological concepts to beliefs is a derivative one. What is primarily required, permitted, and forbidden are the voluntary activities we ranged in two categories, various sorts of activities that influence belief. Deontological concepts are applied to beliefs only because of some relation these attitudes have to those primary targets of permission, and the like. This asymmetrical relation of dependence attaches to all those cases in which one is responsible for a state of affairs without being responsible for an action of intentionally bringing it about.

Now let's consider just what deontological terms can be applied to beliefs in this derivative way and how this application is to be understood. Remember that we are taking requirement, prohibition, and permission to be the basic deontological concepts. When dealing with intentional actions, it is best to think first of general principles that lay down conditions under which an action of a certain sort is required, forbidden, or permitted, and then consider a particular action to have one of these statuses because it exemplifies some general principle. Thus if we take the forming of a belief to be an intentional action, we will envisage general principles that hold, for instance, that it is forbidden to believe that p in the absence of sufficient evidence. Then if I form a particular belief without sufficient grounds, that belief is forbidden, or, if you prefer, I have violated a prohibition in forming that belief. We can then apply other deontological terms like 'responsible', 'blame', and 'praise' on this basis. If one intentionally does something that falls under a principle of one of the above sorts, one is responsible for what one has done. If in doing it one has violated a requirement or a prohibition, one can rightly be blamed for it. If one has not violated any requirement or prohibition, one is justified in doing it.

But on the present way of looking at the matter, we can have no principles laying down conditions under which a belief is required, forbidden, or permitted, just because we lack sufficient voluntary control over belief formation. What the relevant principles will require, and so forth, are activities that are designed to influence factors that, in turn, will influence belief formation.[30] Hence there is no basis for taking a particular belief to be required, prohibited, or forbidden. And so if we are to say, on the rationale given above, that one can be responsible and blameworthy for a belief, that will be the case even though the belief is not prohibited. If one is puzzled by this, the cure comes from realizing that responsibility and blame supervene on requirement, prohibition, and permission in two quite different ways. First, and most simply, one is to blame for doing something forbidden or for failing to something required. But second, one is also to blame for the obtaining of some fact if that fact would not have obtained if one had not behaved in some manner for which one is to blame in the first sense, that is, for doing something forbidden or failing to do something required.

So far, in discussing indirect influence, we have seen that one can be to blame for a certain propositional attitude provided one wouldn't have that attitude had one not failed to conform to some intellectual requirement or prohibition. But this formulation must be refined. On reflection it turns out to be too broad. There are certain ways in which dereliction of duty can contribute to belief formation without render-

---

[30]Thus the closest we get to the principle mentioned above would be something like: "One should do what one can to see to it that one is so disposed as to believe that p only when that belief is based on adequate evidence". Hence the power to do things that influence belief formation can be thought of as, inter alia, a higher level capacity to get ourselves into, or make it more likely that we will be in, a condition that would be required of us if we had sufficient voluntary control over belief.

ing the subject blameworthy for forming that belief. Suppose that I fail to carry out my obligation to spend a certain period in training myself to look for counterevidence. I use the time thus freed up to take a walk around the neighborhood. In the course of this stroll I see two dogs fighting, thereby acquiring the belief that they are fighting. There was a relevant intellectual obligation I didn't fulfill, which is such that if I had fulfilled it I wouldn't have acquired that belief. But if that is a perfectly normal perceptual belief, I am surely not to blame for having formed it.[31]

Here the dereliction of duty contributed to belief formation simply by facilitating access to the data. That is not the kind of contribution we had in mind. The sorts of cases we were thinking of were those most directly suggested by the two sorts of intellectual obligations we distinguished: (a) cases in which we acquire or retain the belief only because we are sheltered from adverse considerations in a way we wouldn't have been had we done what we should have done; (b) cases in which the belief was acquired by the activation of a habit we would not have possessed had we fulfilled our intellectual obligations. Thus we can avoid counterexamples like the above by the following reformulation:

(I) S is (intellectually) to blame for believing that *p iff* If S had fulfilled all her intellectual obligations, then S's belief forming habits would have changed, or S's access to relevant adverse considerations would have changed, in such a way that S would not have believed that *p*.

Another issue has to do with the "absoluteness" of the counterfactual involved in this formulation. (I) involves the flat requirement that S *would not have believed that p* under these conditions. But perhaps S is also blameworthy for believing that *p* if some weaker condition holds, for instance, that it would be much less likely that S would have believed that *p* had S fulfilled her intellectual obligations. Of course, the relation between this and (I) depends on one's account of counterfactuals. For present purposes we need not enter this forbidding swamp. I am shortly going to argue that the concept of epistemic justification that emerges from (I) is inadequate for epistemology, and that argument will not rest on taking the counterfactual to be stronger or weaker.

We can now move on to developing a deontological notion of epistemic justification that is based on the above. One point is obvious: when S is to blame for believing that *p*, that belief is not justified. But

---

[31]I am indebted to Emily Robertson for calling this problem to my attention.

that will presumably cover only a tiny proportion of beliefs. What about the others?

One possibility would be to treat being justified as the mirror image of being unjustified. To justifiably believe that *p*, then, is for one's belief that *p* to be to one's credit. That is, one is justified in believing that *p* *iff* one wouldn't have believed that *p* unless one had fulfilled one's intellectual obligations in some way: by doing what is intellectually required of one or by refraining from doing what one is intellectually forbidden to do. This might seem to leave us with precious few justified beliefs. How many of our beliefs have intellectually dutiful deeds as an essential part of their ancestry? But before embracing that conclusion we should remember that part of the formulation that has to do with refraining from doing what is forbidden. The formulation does not imply that we are justified only where some positive act of duty is in the causal ancestry. One might argue that it is always open to us to engage in attempts to build up disreputable belief-forming tendencies, for example, wishful thinking; and that often we wouldn't have the perfectly respectable beliefs we do have if we had engaged in that enterprise with sufficient vigor. But even so, it still remains that no such counterfactual would hold for beliefs that are beyond the reach of voluntary endeavors, like typical perceptual, memory, and introspective beliefs. No amount of striving after wishful thinking would dislodge most of these. Hence they would fall outside the scope of justified belief on this construal.

There is a simple way to set up the justified-unjustified distinction on the basis of (I) without coming into so violent a conflict with our ordinary judgments. We can take any belief that is not unjustified by the above criterion to be justified. On this construal, 'unjustified' would be the term that "wears the trousers" (Austin), and 'justified' would simply be its negation. A belief is justified *iff* the subject is not intellectually to blame for holding it. This brings us back to the deontological conception of justification advocated by Ginet and others. Remember that we quoted Ginet as saying that one is justified provided that "one could not be justly reproached for being confident that *p*". The only difference is that whereas Ginet was thinking of blame as attaching to belief as something that is itself under voluntary control, we are thinking of it in the more complex, derivative way developed in this section.

VII. Critique of This New Conception

The upshot of the paper thus far is that the only viable deontological conception of justification is the one that identifies being justified in believing that *p* with not being intellectually to blame for believing that *p*, in a sense of 'to blame for' explicated in (I). To put this into a canonical formula:

(II) S is justified in believing that *p* *iff* it is not the case that if S had fulfilled all her intellectual obligations, then S's belief-forming habits would have changed, or S's access to relevant adverse considerations would have changed, in such a way that S would not have believed that *p*.

What follows the *iff* is, of course, the denial of the account of being to blame for a belief given by (I). "Of course", since on this conception, being justified in believing that *p* is just not being to blame for believing that *p*.

In the remainder of the paper I shall present reasons for denying that (II) gives us a concept of justification that is what we are, or should be, looking for in epistemology. I shall point out ways in which one can be justified according to (II), and yet not justified in any way that is crucial for epistemological concerns; and, conversely, that one can be justified in an epistemologically crucial way and yet not deontologically justified, as spelled out by (II). But first a terminological disclaimer. My linguistic intuitions tell me that 'justified' and its cognates are properly used only in a deontological sense. To be justified in doing or believing . . . something just *is* to not have violated any relevant rules, norms, or principles in so doing, believing. . . . If, as I believe, most epistemologists use 'justified' for some quite different notion, they are speaking infelicitously. However, this way of talking is so firmly entrenched that I shall go along with it, albeit with an uneasy linguistic conscience.

If I am to argue that (II) does not amount to real epistemic justification, I must proceed on the basis of some assumption as to what epistemic justification really is. I have no time to argue for any such assumption at the tag end of this paper.[32] Hence I shall argue the point separately for two different conceptions, one more externalist, the other more internalist.[33] I shall devote most of the time to my favorite conception, which is basically externalist with an internalist twist. Let me begin by briefly explaining that.

Start from the idea of forming a belief in such a way as to be in a

[32]For a defense of a particular conception of epistemic justification see Essay 9. For an account of some differences in concepts of epistemic justification, together with a brief defense of a chosen alternative, see Essay 4.
[33]For an account of the varieties of internalism and externalism see Essay 8.

good position to get a true belief. Call this, if you like, a "strong position" conception of justification.[34] One is justified in believing that p only if that belief that p was formed in such a way as to make it at least very likely that the belief is true, or, as is sometimes said, only if it was formed in a "truth-conducive" way.[35] Reliability theory is a natural way of further developing the notion: the belief is justified only if it was formed in a *reliable* fashion, one that can generally be *relied* on to produce true beliefs. Note that there is no guarantee that the subject will be aware of the crucial aspects of the mode of formation, much less of the fact that that mode is truth conducive; that is what makes this conception externalist. My internalist twist consists in also requiring that the belief be based on a "ground" that the subject can be aware of fairly readily. This twist does not negate the externalism. I do not also require that the subject be aware, or have the capacity to become aware, that the ground is an adequate one or that the belief was formed in a reliable or a truth-conducive way. My internalist qualification will play no role in what follows. The argument will depend solely on the requirement that the ground be in fact an adequate one (sufficiently indicative of the truth of the belief). I mention my internalist twist only to point out that the ensuing argument against (II) does not depend on embracing the most extreme form of externalism.

The first point to mention about (II) is that the concept does not apply at all to subjects that lack sufficient sophistication, reflectiveness, or freedom to be subject to intellectual requirements, prohibitions, and the like. This includes lower animals and very young children as well as the mentally defective. But I don't want to stress this consideration, since it can be plausibly argued that the notion of epistemic justification has no significant application to such subjects either. If I went along with the popular view that justification is necessary for knowledge, I would resist this claim, for it is clear to me that lower animals and very young children often know what is going on in their environment. But since I am prepared to recognize knowledge without justification, I am free to acknowledge that the notion of epistemic justification gets a foothold only where subjects are capable of evaluating their own doxastic states and those of others and responding to those evaluations appropriately. Hence the discussion will be restricted to normal adult humans, to whom deontological concepts are applicable.

Next I shall explore ways in which one may be deontologically justi-

---

[34]In Essay 4 this is called an "evaluative" conception, evaluative from the "epistemic point of view".

[35]A more detailed account would look into the epistemic status of the belief at times subsequent to its formation as well. We must forgo that in this brief discussion.

fied in a belief without forming the belief in a truth-conducive way. But first, how we are to tell when one is free of blame in forming a belief? That depends on whether the belief stemmed, in the specified way, from any failure of obligations. But how are we to think of those obligations? I am not now asking about the content of our intellectual obligations. As for that, I shall simply draw on the illustrations given earlier. I am asking rather: how much is a person obliged to do along these lines in a particular situation? And the main point is that we must distinguish between "counsels of perfection" and what it is reasonable to expect of a person. With world enough and time we could require people to carry out an exhaustive investigation of each witness, search through all the relevant literature for considerations pertinent to each candidate for belief, check each calculation ten times, and so on. But we simply do not have time for all that. Even if we were exclusively devoted to the search for truth, we would not be able to do that for all the matters on which we need to form beliefs. And given that we have various other commitments and obligations, it is doubly impossible. Hence, abandoning counsels of perfection, let us say that one can properly be blamed for a belief only if that belief stems, in the specified way, from failures to do what could reasonably be expected of one; simply failing to do what would be ideally adequate is not enough.

In Essay 4, I present two examples of subjects who are deontologically justified but in a poor position to get the truth. One is a case of cultural isolation. S has lived all his life in an isolated primitive community where everyone unhesitatingly accepts the traditions of the tribe as authoritative. These have to do with alleged events distant in time and space, about which S and his fellows have no chance to gather independent evidence. S has never encountered anyone who questions the traditions, and these traditions play a key role in the communal life of the tribe. Under these conditions it seems clear to me that S is in no way to blame for forming beliefs on the basis of the traditions. He has not failed to do anything he could reasonably be expected to do. His beliefs about, for example, the origins of the tribe stem from what, so far as he can see, are the best grounds one could have for such beliefs. And yet, let us suppose, the traditions have not been formed in such a way as to be a reliable indication of their own truth. S is deontologically justified, but he is not believing in a truth-conducive way.

The first half of this judgment has been challenged by Matthias Steup, who takes a hard line with my tribesman.

> No matter how grim the circumstances are, if an agent holds a belief contrary to evidence, it is within his power, given that he is a *rational*

agent, to *reflect* upon his belief and thereby to find out that he had better withhold it, or even assent to its negation. Being a rational agent, I would say, involves the capacity to find out, with respect to any belief, whether or not it is being held on good grounds.[36]

Hence, contrary to my judgment, S is not free of intellectual blame and so is not deontologically justified.

I think that Steup is displaying an insensitivity to cultural differences. He supposes that there are standards recognized in all cultures that determine what is adequate evidence, or good enough grounds, for one or another kind of belief. That does not seem to me to be the case. There may very well be transcultural epistemic standards, such as consistency and reliability, but I see no reason to suppose that they are sufficient to settle all issues as to what counts as adequate reasons or grounds. On the contrary, the criteria for this vary significantly from one culture to another. The judgments of adequacy of grounds that are transmitted across generations will differ across cultures. Hence what can reasonably be expected of a subject with respect to, for instance, critical examination of beliefs and their bases will differ across cultures. We require adults in our culture to be critical of "tradition", but this is a relatively recent phenomenon, given the time humans have been on earth; it cannot be reasonably required of everyone in every society. Note that I am not saying that what *is* adequate evidence varies with the culture. I am no cultural relativist. On the contrary. My judgment that S's belief lacks adequate grounds was based on the supposition that there are objective standards for adequacy of grounds that hold whatever is accepted in one or another culture. But that is just the point. Deontological justification is sensitive to cultural differences because it depends on what can reasonably be expected of one, and that in turn depends on one's social inheritance and the influences to which one is exposed. But truth conducivity does not so depend. Hence they can diverge.

The other case I presented was a "cognitive deficiency" case. It concerned a college student who doesn't have what it takes to follow abstract philosophical exposition or reasoning. Having read parts of Book IV of Locke's *Essay*, he takes it that Locke's view is that everything is a matter of opinion. He is simply incapable of distinguishing between that view and Locke's view that one's knowledge is restricted to one's own ideas. There is nothing he could do, at least nothing that could reasonably be expected of him, given his other commitments and obli-

---

[36]Steup, "The Deontic Conception of Epistemic Justification," p. 78.

gations, that would lead him to appreciate that difference. Hence he cannot be blamed for interpreting Locke as he does; he is doing the best he can. But surely this belief is outrageously ill grounded, based as it is on the student's dim-witted impressions of Locke.

Steup challenges this case by claiming that even if the student is incapable of attaining a better understanding of Locke, he could have done something that would have led him to withhold acceptance of the interpretation in question, viz., ask himself "Do I understand Locke's *Essay* well enough to be justified in assenting to this interpretation?".[37] Now, as Steup intimates, I certainly don't want to depict the case in such a way that the student is incapable of asking himself this question. I do, however, want to construe it in such a way that asking the question would not lead him to withhold assent. The case I have in mind is one in which the student feels quite confident of his reading; this is definitely the way it strikes him, and he has no tendency to doubt it (at least not prior to seeing the grade he gets on the final exam). Certainly that scenario is a possible one, and it, too, illustrates the possibility of a gap between deontological justification and truth-conducive justification.

However, it may have been poor strategy to trot out this hapless student as one of only two cases, for it undoubtedly raises too many controversial issues. Moreover, it may give the impression that counterexamples based on cognitive deficiency are limited to such extreme and, we may hope, such unusual cases as this, whereas in fact they are all too common. We have such a case whenever one forms a belief, on poor grounds, on something beyond one's intellectual capacity; and this is surely a common occurrence. Just consider a person who forms the belief that socialism is contrary to Christianity, for the reasons that are often given for this view by the New Right, and who is intellectually incapable of figuring out how bad these reasons are.

However, cultural isolation and cognitive deficiency cases only scratch the surface. We have so far been considering cases that are either rather extreme in our culture or come from a very different culture. But there are other sorts of cases that are around us every day. I am thinking particularly of those in which we lack the time or resources to look into a matter in an epistemically ideal fashion. Consider the innumerable beliefs each of us forms on testimony or authority. Most of what we believe, beyond what we experience personally, comes from this source. Ideally we would check out each source to make sure that it is reliable before accepting the testimony. But who has time for that? We can do it in special cases where the matter is of particular

[37]Ibid., p. 80.

importance, but no one could do it for even a small percentage of the items proferred by others for our belief. Nor is it a real option to withhold belief save where we do run a check. That would leave our doxastic structure so impoverished we would not be able to function in our society. Practically everything we believe about science, history, geography, and current affairs is taken on authority. Moreover, even if we had the time to check up on each authority, in most cases we lack the resources for making an informed judgment. For the same reason that I cannot engage in astrophysics on my own, I am in no position to determine who is a competent authority in the field, except by taking the word of other alleged authorities. Thus in most cases in which I uncritically accept testimony I have done as much as could reasonably be expected of me. And now let us consider those cases in which the authority is incompetent or the witness is unreliable. There we are forming a belief on an objectively unreliable basis, though deontologically justified in doing so. One could hardly deny that this happens significantly often.

This same pattern is found outside the sphere of testimony. Consider perception. Sometimes peoples' eyes deceive them because of physiological or psychological malfunctioning, or because of abnormalities in the environment (cleverly constructed imitations, unusual conditions of the medium, and the like). Should we check for such abnormalities each time we are on the verge of forming a perceptual belief? Obviously we have no time for this, even if our perceptual belief-forming mechanisms were sufficiently under voluntary control. Hence, except where there are definite indications that things are off, we will not have failed in our intellectual obligations if we simply form perceptual beliefs unself-consciously and uncritically; and hence we are deontologically justified in doing so. But now consider cases in which our visual impressions are misleading, even though we are not aware of any indications of this. There one is forming beliefs on an unreliable basis, though deontologically justified in doing so.

Next consider irresistible beliefs and belief tendencies. If it is strictly impossible for me to alter a certain belief or tendency, then I can hardly be expected to do so. But some of these irresistible beliefs may be formed in an unreliable fashion. The most obvious examples concern strong emotional attachments that are, in practice, unshakeable. For many people their religious, or irreligious, beliefs have this status, as do beliefs concerning one's country, one's close relations, or one's political party. Such beliefs are often not formed in a truth-conducive fashion. But the person cannot be blamed for having something she can't help having, and so we get our discrepancy once more.

Finally, consider timing problems. Suppose that I come to realize that it is incumbent on me to look more fully into matters relevant to basic religious issues: the existence of God, the conditions of salvation, the authority of Scriptures, and so on. I have deeply rooted beliefs on these matters; I am not going to throw them over just because I am reopening the questions, nor am I obliged to do so. And even if suspension of belief would be ideally required, it is not a real possibility for me until I see conclusive negative evidence. In any event, I enter onto my investigation. Let's say that the investigation reveals that my beliefs were ill founded all along. As soon as I see that, I cease to believe, either immediately or after some period of readjustment. But while the investigation is proceeding, something that might occupy many years, I am deontologically justified in continuing to hold the beliefs, for I am not obliged to give them up, even if I could, just because questions have been raised; and yet they are not held on truth-conducive grounds. Again our discrepancy. And again it would seem that such cases are quite frequent.

This completes my case for the possibility, and the actuality, of deontological justification without truth-conducive justification. Even if I am mistaken about the possibility or actuality of some of the above cases, I can safely ignore the possibility that I am mistaken about all. We may take it that our deontological formula, (II), fails to capture what we are looking for in epistemology under the rubric of 'justification', when we are looking for something in the neighborhood of "being in a favorable position in believing that p", favorable from the standpoint of the aim at believing the true and avoiding believing the false.

But we can have discrepancies in the opposite direction as well: believing on an adequately truth-conducive ground while not deontologically justified. This possibility will be realized where: (1) I form a belief that p on ground G; (2) G is in fact an adequate ground for that belief; (3) if I had reflected critically on this belief-forming proclivity, as I should have done, I would have found sufficient reasons to doubt its adequacy, and as a result this belief would not have been formed. Here is an example. Let's suppose that it is incumbent on me to look into the credentials of anyone on whose word I believe something of practical importance. An acquaintance, Broom, tells me that Robinson, whom we are considering for a position in my department, has just been made an offer by Princeton. The press of affairs and my instinctive confidence in Broom lead me to neglect my duty and accept Broom's report uncritically. If I had looked into the matter, I would have found strong evidence that Broom is untrustworthy in such matters. This evidence, however, would have been misleading, and in fact Broom is extremely scrupulous and reliable in reporting such things. Thus I formed the belief on an objectively adequate ground, but had I done my intellectual duty I would have mistrusted the ground and hence not formed the belief. I was justified on truth-conductivity standards but not according to (II).

I have been seeking to show that the deontological conception of justification, the only one of that ilk we have found to be internally viable, fails to deliver what is expected of justification if those expectations include truth conducivity. But not all contemporary epistemologists go along with this; in particular, the most extreme internalists do not. Not that they sever justification altogether from the aim at attaining the true and avoiding the false. They hold, to put it into my terms, that for a belief to be justified it is necessary, not that its ground be in fact such as to render it likely that the belief is true, but that the subject be justified in supposing this, that the belief appear to be truth-conducive "from the subject's own perspective on the world".[38] Although this kind of internalism is developed in various ways, by no means all of which exactly fit the formula given in the last sentence, we cannot go into all that in this paper. I shall work with the characterization just given.

I believe this view to be subject to an infinite regress of requirements of justification, and to other fatal difficulties.[39] My present concern, however, is to point out divergencies between it and (II) and hence to show that the deontological conception runs afoul of both externalism and internalism. After the lengthy discussion just completed I can be briefer here. The general point is that even after one has done everything that is reasonably expected of one intellectually, it is by no means guaranteed that one is justified in supposing that the ground of one's belief is an adequate one. Let's glance at a few of the cases just presented in connection with my moderate externalism. First, the point with respect to irresistible beliefs is precisely the same. If a belief is irresistible, then no matter how intellectually virtuous I am, I will form that belief whether or not I am justified in supposing its ground to be an adequate one. Turning to resistible beliefs, let's note first that we often do not have time to look into whether the ground of the belief is an adequate one. In such cases (assuming the belief doesn't stem from some other failure to

[38]See, e.g., Richard Foley, *The Theory of Epistemic Rationality* (Cambridge: Harvard University Press, 1987), esp. chaps. 1–3; Bonjour, *The Structure of Empirical Knowledge*, chap. 1; Richard Fumerton, *Metaphysical and Epistemological Problems of Perception* (Dordrecht: D. Reidel, 1985), chap. 2; Keith Lehrer, "The Coherence Theory of Knowledge," *Philosophical Topics*, 14, no. 1 (1986).

[39]For details see Essay 8.

carry out intellectual obligations) one would be deontologically justified; but, assuming that a failure to consider the matter would prevent one from being justified in supposing one's ground to be adequate, one would not satisfy internalist requirements.[40] Again, consider another version of lack of cognitive powers. It seems plausible to suppose that many cognitive subjects are simply incapable of engaging in a rational consideration of whether the grounds of their beliefs (at least many sorts of beliefs, for instance, those involving complex inductive grounds) are adequate ones. Even if they raise the question, they are not capable of coming to well-grounded conclusions. These people might have done everything that could reasonably be expected of them in an intellectual way, and yet, because of their inability to effectively submit the grounds of their beliefs to a critical assessment, would not be justified in supposing the ground of a certain belief to be sufficient. Again, deontological justification without internalist justification.

The internalist may reply that we have set our standards for higher level justification too high. It is only necessary that one *have* a justification for believing the ground of one's lower level belief to be an adequate one; and this does not require that one have actually formed any such higher level belief. That is, what should be required is that one be in possession of sufficient evidence for the proposition that the ground in question is adequate, whether or not one has actually made use of that evidence to support a belief in the adequacy of the ground. But we will still get divergencies. The irresistible beliefs will still pose problems. One can't be faulted for holding those beliefs, whether or not one is in possession of adequate evidence for a correlated higher level belief in adequacy. And again it seems that in cases of lack of time I could be deontologically justified in believing that *p*, whether or not I have sufficient evidence for supposing that ground of that belief to be adequate. Finally, in cases of deficient cognitive powers one could not be faulted for failure of intellectual obligations in believing that *p*, even if one lacks evidence for the belief in the adequacy of grounds.

Moreover, here too we get the possibility of internalist justification without deontological justification. Consider one who is justified in supposing the ground of her belief that the hostages are in Iran to be an adequate one. That is, the information and general principles at her disposal indicate her evidence to be sufficient. She is internalistically

---

[40]Some epistemologists understand 'S is justified in believing that *p*' to mean something like 'If S were to believe that *p*, in S's present situation, that belief would be justified'. On this understanding the above requirement does not hold. However, I have throughout the paper been understanding 'S is justified in believing that *p*' as 'S justifiably believes that *p*'.

justified in this belief about the hostages. Yet had she engaged in further investigation, as she should have done, her internal perspective would have been enlarged and corrected in such a way that she would no longer be justified in this higher level belief. Her total knowledge and justified belief would then have indicated that her evidence for this proposition is not sufficient. Here we have internalist justification without deontological justification.

Thus the deontological conception embodied in (II) matches an internalist conception of justification no better than it matches an externalist one. I conclude that there is nothing to be said for the deontological conception, the only one that is not vitiated by internal flaws, as a fundamental concept for epistemology. This is not to deny that it is an interesting and important concept. There are, no doubt, contexts in which it is highly relevant to consider whether a person has failed in any intellectual duty and what bearing this has on the fact that he now believes that *p*. We would want to consider this if, for example, we were engaged in training the person to be more intellectually responsible or to improve his belief-forming tendencies. But we have seen that these deontological issues are not central to the basic concerns of epistemology with truth and falsity, whether this is conceived externalistically as the formation of propositional attitudes in such a way as to maximize truth and minimize falsity, or internalistically as the formation of propositional attitudes in accordance with what is indicated by the subject's perspective as to the chances for maximizing truth and minimizing falsity. Deontological justification is not epistemic justification.

VIII. Conclusion

Let's draw the threads of this paper together. We have examined several forms of a deontological conception of epistemic justification in terms of freedom from blame in taking up a certain propositional attitude. All of these but one was seen to be untenable by reason of requiring a degree of control over our propositional attitudes that we do not enjoy. The only version that escapes this fate was seen to be not the sort of concept we need to play a central role in epistemology. Therefore, despite the connotations of the term, we are ill advised to think of epistemic justification in terms of freedom from blame for believing.[41]

[41]Thanks are due to Robert Audi and Jonathan Bennett for very useful comments on this paper. I have profited from discussions with Carl Ginet about these issues.

Level Confusions
in Epistemology

Uncovering confusions in each other's work is a favorite, almost, one sometimes suspects, the sole, occupation of contemporary American philosophers. I am surely not the only member of this class who has to resist temptations to spend a disproportionate amount of time on such activities. After all, it is so much easier than presenting and defending substantive theses. And it is a lot of fun. Like the rest of fallen humanity, I resist temptation only part of the time, and this is, I fear, the other part. In this paper I will be engaged in uncovering what I take to be some fundamental and pervasive confusions in contemporary epistemology. However, in this instance I have more solid reasons than usual for spending time in confusion spotting. I do think that epistemology is one area in which the practitioners, even (or perhaps especially) the most significant ones, have fallen into certain confusions that have profoundly influenced their systematic constructions. Hence by revealing those confusions one can make an important contribution to the development of epistemology with relatively little effort. At least that is my claim for what I am doing in this paper. You can form your own judgment as to whether it is correct.

The confusions to which I will be calling your attention all involve sloughing over the distinction between epistemic levels, proceeding as if what is true of a proposition, belief, or epistemic state of affairs on one level is ipso facto true of a correlated proposition, belief, or epistemic state of affairs on another. The levels I have in mind are those

From *Midwest Studies in Philosophy*, 5 (1980), 135–50. Reprinted by permission of the editors.

built up by the introduction and iteration of epistemic or pistic operators: 'know that', 'believe that', 'is justified in believing that', and so on. Thus if we begin with any proposition, p, we can build a structure of epistemic levels by using various epistemic operators.

(I) p
    S believes that p.
    S believes that S believes that p.
    . . . .

(II) p
    S is justified in believing that p.
    S is justified in believing that S is justified in believing that p.
    . . . .

(III) p
    S knows that p.
    S knows that S knows that p.
    . . . .

We can also have "mixed" items. *S knows that p* can give rise to the higher level *S believes that S knows that p* or the equally higher level *S is justified in believing that S knows that p*. My purposes in this paper do not require me to develop precise criteria for determining the relative levels of any two such items. The confusions we will be disclosing are all between items that are obviously on different levels.

I

My first example concerns the concept of immediate (direct) justification. The contrast between mediate (indirect) and immediate (direct) justification can be most simply and most fundamentally stated as follows.

(1) To say that a belief is mediately justified is to say that what justifies it includes some other justified beliefs of the same subject.[1]
(2) To say that a belief is immediately justified is to say that what justifies it does not include some other justified beliefs of the same subject.

This generic characterization of immediate justification is purely negative. Anyone who holds that some beliefs are immediately justified

---

[1]We are leaving open the question of what else is required for mediate justification over and above the possession of certain other justified beliefs.

will have some conception of what can justify beliefs in such a way that no other justified beliefs of the same subject are involved in the justification.

Now the confusion about immediate justification I will be exploring consists just in this: it is confusedly supposed that for S's belief that *p* to be immediately justified, it is required that the higher level belief that *S is justified in believing that p,* or that *S knows that p,* itself be immediately justified; or, even more confusedly, that this is what the immediate justification of S's belief that *p* consists in. Full-blown examples of this confusion can be found in Roderick Chisholm and in Panayot Butchvarov.[2] I will restrict my attention to Chisholm.

Chisholm's version of immediate justification is what we may call truth-justification, justification of a belief by its truth or by the fact that makes it true. To follow Chisholm's presentation of this, a short terminological digression will be required. Chisholm distinguishes several grades of epistemic justification, one of the higher of which is 'evident'. (The exact definition of 'evident' and its distinction from other grades need not concern us here.) The term 'evident' is applied to propositions; if a proposition, *p*, is evident for a subject, S, then S is justified (to a high degree) in believing that *p*. Chisholm tends to use the term 'justified' in a nondiscriminating way to range over all grades of justification.

In the recently published second edition of his *Theory of Knowledge*[3] Chisholm defines his basic notion of immediate justification for empirical beliefs as follows.

D2.1 *h* is *self-presenting* for S at *t* = *Df. h* is true at *t;* and necessarily, if *h* is true at *t,* then *h* is evident for S at *t.* (p. 22)[4]

This conforms to the generic notion of immediate justification I presented above. But Chisholm also presents his version of immediate justification in a quite different way. He introduces his conception of the directly evident by considering the ways in which one might answer

[2]Panayot Butchvarov, *The Concept of Knowledge* (Evanston, Ill.: Northwestern University Press, 1970), pt. I, section 6.
[3]Roderick Chisholm, *Theory of Knowledge,* 2d ed. (Englewood Cliffs, N.J.: Prentice-Hall, 1977).
[4]One other terminological guide to the quotations that follow. In the first edition of *Theory of Knowledge* (1966), Chisholm used the term 'directly evident' for the concept expressed above by the term 'self-presenting'. In the second edition the former term is officially reserved for a wider concept, but much of the material that was retained from the first edition still used 'directly evident' in the way 'self-presenting' was defined above. I will use the term 'directly evident' for the concept just defined.

the "Socratic" questions "What justification do you have for thinking you know this thing to be true?" or "What justification do you have for counting this thing as something that is evident?" (p. 17).

> In many instances the answers to our questions will take the following form: "What justifies me in thinking that I know that *a* is *F* is the fact it is evident to me that *b* is *G*". . . . This type of answer to our Socratic questions shifts the burden of justification from one claim to another. For we may now ask, "What justifies me in counting it as evident that *b* is *G*?" or "What justifies me in thinking I know that *b* is *G*?". . . . We might try to continue *ad indefinitum*, justifying each new claim that we elicit by still another claim. Or we might be tempted to complete a vicious circle. . . . But if we are rational beings, we will do neither of these things. For we will find that our Socratic questions lead us to a proper stopping place. . . . Let us say provisionally that we have found a proper stopping place when the answer to our question may take the following form:
>   What justifies me in thinking I know that *a* is F is simply the fact that *a* is F.
> Whenever this type of answer is appropriate, we have encountered the *directly evident*. (pp. 18–20)

In this passage and others we get a different picture of what makes a proposition directly evident. According to the definition D2.1, what makes a true proposition, *p*, directly evident for S, is that its truth makes *it* evident for S; whereas according to the passage just quoted what makes *p* directly evident is that its truth makes evident (justifies)[5] S's higher level belief that S knows that *p* (or that it is evident to S that *p*). The two passages give different answers to the question: what does the truth of *p* have to justify in order that *p* be *directly* evident?

There is fairly strong textual evidence that Chisholm simply does not see that the two accounts are different, or, at least, that the realization of their difference is not effectively operative in his mind when he is presenting his position. Not only do we find each account reflected in numerous passages. We even find Chisholm juxtaposing them in the same discussion.

---

[5]What are we to make of the fact that in D2.1 Chisholm speaks of *p* being made *evident* by the fact that *p*, whereas in the passage just quoted he speaks of the higher level proposition being *justified* by the fact that *p*? Does this indicate that Chisholm is less sure about the degree of justification conferred by the fact that *p* on the higher level proposition than about the degree of justification it confers on the proposition that *p*? Or does he think that the propositions on both levels are made *evident* by the fact that *p*? For present purposes it is not necessary to settle this question. The point with which we are concerned is simply the relation between claims to some justificatory role of the fact that *p* on the two levels.

Thinking and believing provide us with paradigm cases of the directly evident. Consider a reasonable man who . . . believes that Albuquerque is in New Mexico, and suppose him to reflect on the philosophical question, "What is my justification for thinking that I know . . . that I believe that Albuquerque is in New Mexico?". . . . The man could reply in this way: "My justification for thinking I know . . . that I believe that Albuquerque is in New Mexico, is simply the fact . . . that I do believe that it is in New Mexico". And this reply fits our formula for the directly evident:

What justifies me in thinking I know that *a* is F is simply the fact that *a* is F.

Our man has stated his justification for a proposition merely by reiterating that proposition. (p. 21)

Obviously it is the higher level conception of direct evidence that is being employed throughout most of this passage. But the very last sentence constitutes a reversion to the lower level conception. If the proposition for which the man is stating his justification was the higher level proposition *I know that I believe that Albuquerque is in New Mexico,* then he did *not* state his justification by reiterating the proposition. For what he enunciated in stating his justification was not that proposition, but its lower level correlate, *I believe that Albuquerque is in New Mexico.* Thus he stated his justification for *p* by reiterating *p* only if the *p* in question were that lower level proposition.

Of course it may be that Chisholm is not *confusing* the two levels but is presenting the matter in such a way as to reflect his *conviction* that, for self-presenting propositions, the truth of *p* generates justification on both levels. Indeed, in a later part of the book Chisholm does espouse, and argue for, a level-bridging principle that might seem to have this consequence.

. . . if a proposition is evident and if one considers the proposition, then it is evident that the proposition is evident. (p. 114)

This principle does ensure a transfer of evidence from a proposition, *p,* to the higher level proposition that *it is evident that p,* given that S considers the matter. But it by no means follows from this that the source of evidence is the same on the two levels; hence it does not follow that where the truth of *p* suffices to make *p* evident, *it* will also suffice to make *it is evident that p* evident. The principle quoted above is quite compatible with its being the case that where *it is evident that p* (for some self-presenting proposition, *p*) becomes evident to S upon considering the matter, what makes the higher level proposition evident is not the mere truth of *p,* but something that is uncovered in the process of consideration. And Chisholm evinces no awareness that the thesis that the truth of p generates evidence on the higher level as well as the lower is one that needs to be scrutinized and defended, whether on the basis of the above principle or otherwise.

In any event, the important philosophical question is not what is or is not going on in Chisholm's mind, but whether the thesis that the source of evidence is the same on the two levels has important consequences that are likely to pass unnoticed if one simply assumes the thesis without explicitly realizing that one is doing so. I will now point out some of those consequences.

First, if one saddles one's account of immediate justification with the claim that the same kind of justification extends to one or more correlated higher level propositions, the plausibility of one's account will be reduced. This is certainly the case with Chisholm. Whatever our ultimate judgment in the matter, it is not totally implausible to suppose that one is justified in beliefs about what one is currently feeling, sensing, or thinking just by the fact that one *is* so feeling, sensing, or thinking. But is it equally plausible that I am justified in supposing that *it is evident to me that I feel tired* just by the fact that I feel tired? Can I be justified in supposing that a certain proposition has a certain epistemic status for me, *just by feeling tired*? One's initial doubts in this matter are increased by considering Chisholm's definition of 'evident'.

> D1.5 h is evident for S = Df (i) h is beyond reasonable doubt for S and (ii) for every i, if accepting i is more reasonable for S than accepting h, then i is certain for S. (p. 12)

And the definition of 'certain' runs:

> D1.4 h is certain for S = Df h is beyond reasonable doubt for S, and there is no i such that accepting i is more reasonable for S than accepting h. (p. 10)

Leaving aside what it takes to be justified in supposing the acceptance of one proposition to be more reasonable than the acceptance of another, and leaving aside what it takes to be justified in supposing that a certain proposition is beyond reasonable doubt, let us concentrate on the rest of what is involved in a proposition's being evident, viz., a certain comparative epistemic status vis-à-vis all other propositions. More specifically, this comparative status consists in its being the case that no other propositions enjoy a more favorable epistemic status for S except those that enjoy the highest possible epistemic status. Now, is it credible that I should be justified in a belief that is, in part, about the epistemic status of a given proposition vis-à-vis the entire class of propositions, *just by virtue of feeling tired?* At the very least, the claim to higher level truth-justification raises questions that are quite different from the claim to lower level truth-justification. Chisholm has saddled his theory with a considerable liability by adding on the higher level claim.[6]

Moreover, Chisholm need not have taken on this additional liability in order for direct evidence to play its intended role in his system. The course of Chisholm's exposition, and the structure of his theory, makes it clear that the main function of directly evident propositions in his system is to stop the regress of justification and serve as foundations of knowledge. I have argued elsewhere that the demands of the regress argument are amply satisfied by first level immediate justification and that a foundationalist epistemology based on propositions that enjoy only first level immediate justification will be in at least as strong a position as any other foundationalism.[7] It is true that Chisholm's methodology requires what we might call "high accessibility" to one's own epistemic states. This position is reflected in the quote from p. 114 given above and in other pronouncements in that same section of the book, such as Chisholm's version of the KK thesis.

(K4) If S considers the proposition that he knows that p, and if he does know that p, then he knows that he knows that p. (p. 116)

However, it remains to be shown that high accessibility requires that what justifies the higher level proposition that *it is evident to S that p*, or that *S knows that p*, be the *same* as what justifies p itself. Chisholm has not so argued, and I am dubious about the prospects.

An equally serious consequence of a confusion of levels (or of an uncritical assumption that correlated propositions on two levels enjoy the same justification) is that the range of candidates for immediate justification is sharply restricted. It is a striking fact that most epistemologists who work with something like our distinction between mediate and immediate justification are markedly penurious in the modes of immediate justification they consider. Chisholm is typical in this

---

[6]Similar points can be made for other conceptions of immediate justification. If we hold with Russell, C. I. Lewis, and many others, that beliefs about one's current sensory data are justified by the fact that one is "directly aware" of those data, this has a certain initial plausibility, one that is not shared by the correlated higher level claim that one is justified in believing that one is justified in holding such beliefs by virtue of being directly aware of sensory data.

[7]Essay 1.

regard. He simply notes that when a proposition is rendered evident by its own truth it is thereby *directly* evident, and he fails to consider whether there are other possibilities. Other epistemologists are equally narrowly preoccupied with immediate awareness or with self-evidence as sources of immediate justification.[8] One particularly unfortunate consequence of this parochialism is an obliviousness to the possibility that a belief might be immediately justified by having originated in a certain way, for example, justified by having been produced by a reliable belief-producing mechanism.[9] Whatever the reason for Chisholm's ignoring immediate awareness, or Lewis' ignoring truth-justification, it seems quite plausible to suppose that the level confusion we have been discussing is responsible for the widespread neglect of immediate justification by origin. For if one takes it that what immediately justifies S in believing that p will ipso facto immediately justify S in believing that *S is justified in believing that p,* then one will restrict the range of immediate justifiers to those one supposes will be capable of justifying the higher level, as well as the lower level belief. As we have seen in discussing Chisholm, it is by no means obvious that the modes of immediate justification favored by level confusers do meet this requirement; perhaps a judicious assessment would reveal that none do. Nevertheless, it seems much *more* obvious that the fact that a belief was produced by a reliable psychological mechanism is *not* sufficient to justify a belief *about* the epistemic status of that belief; for we are often in the dark concerning the reliability, or other features, of what produces our beliefs. Hence in failing to distinguish between justification on the two levels, one will be led to ignore the possible epistemic relevance of the actual mode of belief production.

Indeed, even where the possibility is considered, level confusions may play a decisive role in its evaluation. Consider the following passage from Keith Lehrer's book *Knowledge.*[10]

> Thus, if something looks red to a person, he cannot justifiably conclude that it is red from the formula that red things look red in standard conditions to normal observers, he would also need to know that the conditions are standard and that he is normal. Independent information is, therefore, required for the justification of this perceptual belief. . . .
> More generally, to justify such a belief requires the information that the conditions that surround a man and the state he is in are such that when

[8]For two of the rare attempts to critically compare different putative direct justifiers, see Essay 11 and Butchvarov, *The Concept of Knowledge,* chap. 1, sec. 6.
[9]For a presentation of this possibility see Alvin I. Goldman, "Discrimination and Perceptual Knowledge," *Journal of Philosophy,* 73 (1976), 771–91.
[10]Keith Lehrer, *Knowledge* (Oxford: Oxford University Press, 1974).

something looks red in conditions of this sort to a person in his state, then it is red.

   . . . Since a man may hallucinate, he cannot justifiably conclude he sees something as opposed to merely hallucinating unless he has information enabling him to distinguish hallucination from the real thing. (pp. 103–104)

Let us agree that a person to whom x looks red cannot be justified in a perceptual belief that x is red unless "the conditions that surround" him and "the state he is in are such that when something looks red in conditions of this sort to a person in his state, then it is red". But why should we also require that the person *have that information, know* (justifiably believe) that this is so. Why is it not enough that it *be* so? As we read on, it becomes transparently clear that Lehrer is falling into a level confusion.

   . . . the need for independent information arose from the need to determine whether the circumstances in which a person finds himself are those in which a man may justifiably conclude that he is seeing a typewriter or seeing something red.

   . . . when a great deal . . . hinges on the matter of whether the person saw a bear-print or something else, . . . then we start to ask serious questions. We seek to determine if the person has information enabling him to decide whether he is seeing things of the sort he says he sees. (p. 105)

Well of course if *that* is what we are (he is) after, we (he) need "independent information". If he is trying to determine whether he is (really) seeing a bear-print (which involves determining whether his perceptual belief that there was a bear-print in a certain place was justified), or trying to determine whether the circumstances of his perception were such as to justify his perceptual belief, then *of course* he needs evidence of the sort mentioned. But that is just to say that he needs such evidence in order to be justified in the higher level epistemic belief that his original perceptual belief was justified (and to be justified in the beliefs that support that epistemic belief). Lehrer can get from this incontrovertible truth to his central claim that such information is required for the perceptual belief to be justified only by confusing the two problems—the justification of the perceptual belief and the justification of the higher level belief that the perceptual belief is justified.

If one restricts oneself to sources of immediate justification that, one supposes, survive a transition to higher levels, the kinds of beliefs one takes to be susceptible of immediate justification will be likewise restricted. Historically, this has meant a restriction (for a posteriori knowledge) to beliefs concerning the believer's current states of consciousness. The insuperable difficulties encountered in the attempt to build the whole of a posteriori knowledge on such a slim basis have been more than amply documented. Our discussion reveals the role level confusion has played in generating the supposition that no more extended foundation is available.

Indeed, if one does not distinguish between justification on different levels, one may be, confusedly, led to reject the whole concept of immediate justification. Consider the following argument from Bruce Aune's book *Knowledge, Mind, and Nature*.[11]

> I would venture to say that any spontaneous claim, observational or introspective, carries almost no presumption of truth, when considered entirely by itself. If we accept such a claim as true, it is only because of our confidence that a complex body of background assumptions—concerning observers, standing conditions, the kind of object in question—and, often, a complex mass of further observations all point to the conclusion that it is true.
>
> Given these prosaic considerations, it is not necessary to cite experimental evidence illustrating the delusions easily brought about by, for example, hypnosis to see that no spontaneous claim is acceptable wholly on its own merits. On the contrary, common experience is entirely adequate to show that clear-headed men never accept a claim merely because it is made, without regard to the peculiarities of the agent and of the conditions under which it is produced. For such men, the acceptability of every claim is always determined by inference. If we are prepared to take these standards of acceptability seriously, we must accordingly admit that the traditional search for intrinsically acceptable empirical premises is completely misguided. (pp. 42–43)

Here Aune is arguing that beliefs are justified only by inference (from other propositions known, or justifiably believed), which is equivalent to the denial that there are any immediately justified beliefs. But a close reading will reveal that the considerations he advances seem to yield that conclusion only if one is confusing levels. The solid points that Aune makes in support of that claim are the following.

> If we accept such a claim [observational or introspective] as true, it is only because of our confidence that a complex of background assumptions . . . all point to the conclusion that it is true.
>
> . . . clear-headed men never accept a claim merely because it is made, without regard to the peculiarities of the agent and of the conditions

[11]Bruce Aune, *Knowledge, Mind, and Nature* (New York: Random House, 1967).

under which it is produced. For such men, the acceptability of every claim is always determined by inference.

Now in making these points Aune is not really considering what would justify the *issuer* of an introspective or observational claim, but what it would take to justify "us" in accepting his claim; he is considering the matter from a third-person perspective. And it is clear that I cannot be immediately justified in accepting *your* introspective or observational claim. If I am so justified, it is because I am justified in supposing that you issued a claim of that sort, that you are in a normal condition and know the language, and so on. But that is only because I, in contrast to you, am justified in believing that p (where what you claimed is that p) only if I am justified in supposing that *you are justified in believing that p*. My access to p is through your access. It is just because my justification in believing p presupposes my being justified in believing that you are justified, that my justification has to be indirect. Thus what Aune's argument supports is the necessity for inferential backing for any higher level belief to the effect that some person is justified in believing that p. Only a failure to distinguish levels leads him to suppose that he has shown that *no* belief can be immediately justified.

II

Next let us consider the bearing of level confusions on the requirements for *mediate* justification. If the justification is mediate, there must be some other proposition, q, that is related to p and to S's belief that p in certain ways. Exactly what ways are necessary? The following requirements are accepted by virtually all who have considered the matter.

(1) q is related to p in a way that is "appropriate"[12] for purposes of justification.
(2) S believes that q.
(3) S is justified in believing that q.[13]

[12]If one should try to give a general criterion for "appropriateness", it might be something like this: q is related to p "appropriately" *iff* the truth of q will thereby either guarantee the truth of p, or at least make the truth of p likely. In other words, the relationship is, or tends to be, truth-preserving.

[13]The rationales for (2) and (3) are fairly obvious. How can the fact that q is "appropriately" related to p do anything to justify *me* in believing that p unless I "have" this adequate ground, unless I am in a position to appropriate the epistemic benefits contained therein? And I cannot do this unless it is at least something I believe. And unless I am *justified* in believing it, how can justification (for me) be transferred along the appropriate propositional relation? Some would go further and require that I *know* that q.

Most of the discussion of mediate justification has centered on (1). How must propositions, for instance, about sensory appearances, be related to, for instance, propositions about physical objects in the environment of the perceiver, to serve as adequate grounds for the latter? Must there be an entailment? Will some sort of inductive evidence relationship do? Or is there some special "evidence-conferring" relationship involved?

Again, there is widespread agreement that there must be some "psychological" connection between S's belief that q and S's belief that p. They cannot just lie "side by side" in his mind: q must be "his reason," or at least one of his reasons for believing that p. This is often taken to imply that the belief that p have been produced by the belief that q, or that the former be causally *sustained* by the latter. Sometimes this is further specified to require that S have *inferred* p from q, or now be disposed to do so. But whether or not inference is required, there is general agreement that some restrictions must be put on the mode of generation. So let us put as the fourth condition:

(4) S's belief that p was produced by, or is causally sustained by, S's belief that q, in the right way.

Now we come to further alleged conditions that, I want to suggest, depend for their plausibility on level confusions. For one thing, various writers[14] hold that if S's belief that q is to constitute an adequate basis for S's belief that p, not only must q be appropriately related to p, but S must *know*, or at least justifiably believe, that this is so.

(5) S is justified in believing that q is appropriately related to p.

It seems to me that this is too sophisticated as a general requirement for mediate justification, especially if we take mediate justification to be required for mediate knowledge. Surely creatures like dogs and pre-verbal children can have mediate knowledge. My dog knows that I am preparing to take him for a walk, and he knows that because he sees me getting out his chain. But such creatures have no concepts of deductive, inductive, or other relations between propositions and hence are quite incapable of believing, much less justifiably believing, that such relations obtain. Even where S has the relevant concepts, he may not be

---

[14]D. M. Armstrong, *Belief, Truth, and Knowledge* (Cambridge: Cambridge University Press, 1973), p. 151. Brian Skyrms, "The Explication of 'X knows that p'," *Journal of Philosophy*, 64 (June 22, 1967), 374.

justified in supposing that appropriate relations obtain. He may just unthinkingly assume (truly) that, for example, his local newspaper is a reliable source of local news. Does this prevent him from learning (coming to know) about local happenings from reading his newspaper (from his knowledge that these happenings are reported in the newspaper)?

Those who introduce condition (5) fail to give anything like a full-dress defense of it. Its proponents seem to take it as having sufficient intrinsic plausibility to make an explicit defense unnecessary. My diagnosis is that this plausibility largely stems from level confusion. It does seem that I cannot be justified in the higher level belief that *my belief that q mediately justifies me in believing that p* unless I am justified in supposing that *q* is appropriately related to *p*. For unless I am justified in supposing that, how could I be justified in supposing that the appropriate justification relation holds between the beliefs? And so if one does not distinguish between being mediately justified in believing that *p* and being justified in believing that *one is mediately justified in believing that p*, then one will naturally suppose that what is required for the latter is also required for the former.

Another widespread requirement is:

(6) S is able, or disposed, to cite *q* as what justifies his belief that *p*.

Here, for example, is C. I. Lewis, disavowing the necessity for a conscious inference from *q* to *p*, and replacing that requirement with a combination of (4) and (6).

> ... whether the ground of judgment is or is not explicitly in mind, is hardly the pertinent consideration, because it could not plausibly be taken to mark the important distinction between attitudes of B having positive cognitive value and those which lack it. Rather the pertinent distinction is between cases in which if the judgment be challenged by ourselves or others, we should be able to assign a basis of it which, whether explicitly thought of in drawing the judgment or not, is so related to it that we could truly say "If it were not for that, I should not have so judged".[15]

Again (6) would seem to be much too sophisticated a requirement, especially if justification is required for knowledge. There are knowing creatures who lack the sophistication, or even the linguistic skills, to

[15]C. I. Lewis, *An Analysis of Knowledge and Valuation* (La Salle, Ill.: Open Court, 1946), p. 328.

respond to challenges by specifying the basis of their beliefs. They include creatures that do not have the use of language as well as language users who do not (yet) have any concept of epistemic justification. Even those sophisticated enough to engage in this kind of palaver may be unable, in particular cases, to identify the real and sufficient bases of their belief. Why, then, has this requirement seemed right to many? Here, too, level confusion may play an important role. Requirement (6) seems more plausible as a requirement for being justified in accepting the higher level proposition that *S is justified in believing that p.* One might well think that I cannot be justified in a claim to justification unless I can point out what does the justifying. But here we cannot pin all the blame on level confusion. For, in truth, (6) is questionable as a requirement for higher level justification as well. Why must I be able to *specify, cite,* or *formulate* what it is that justifies me in believing that *p,* in order to *be* justified in supposing that I *am* so justified? This is a special form of the old question of whether I can be justified in accepting a relatively unspecific or general proposition without being able to specify the particular fact(s) that makes it true. It has many forms: can I not be justified in supposing that there are a lot of dots on that surface without being able to say how many? Can I not be justified in believing that there is someone in the room without being able to say who is in the room? Of course it remains to be seen exactly how one could be justified in supposing, unspecifically, that one is (somehow) justified in believing that *p* without being able to say precisely what justifies one. But surely this possibility should not be dismissed without a hearing.

In the light of the point just made, perhaps the main villain in this piece is another widespread confusion in epistemology—one we are not really exploring in this essay—the confusion between 'justification' in the sense of *being* justified and 'justification' in the sense of "showing that one is justified". If one fails to keep that distinction in mind, one is liable to suppose that in order to *be* justified in believing that *p* one must be *able* at least to "justify" one's belief that *p* in the sense of showing that one is justified, that is to say, exhibiting what it is that justifies one. And that would explain the plausibility of (6).

III

Finally let us consider the role of level confusion in certain forms of skeptical argument. First, look at what may conveniently be called "Cartesian skepticism" because of its similarity to what we find in Descartes' *Meditations*.[16] The kind of argument I wish to discuss is directed at some particular knowledge claim and is designed to show that the claimer, S, does not know what he is claiming to know. Let us consider a case in which a person is looking out the window and claims to know that a car is parked in front of his house. (He supposes himself to see a car parked there.) The argument will then proceed as follows.

1. If S's present visual experience is being directly produced by an omnipotent spirit, then S does not know (perceptually) that there is a car parked in front of his house.[17]
2. S does not know that his present visual experience is not being directly produced by an omnipotent spirit.
3. Therefore, S does not know (perceptually) that there is a car parked in front of his house.

Questions could be raised about both premises, but I will not go into that. Instead, I will contend that even if both premises were unexceptionable, the conclusion would not follow. Why should we suppose that S's inability to rule out the hypothesis of an abnormal production of his visual experience implies that his visual experience gives him no knowledge of the physical environment? Any answer to this question will have to derive from our rationale for (1). Let us take that rationale to depend on some kind of (at least partly) causal theory of perceptual knowledge. My visual experiences can give me knowledge of a certain physical object only if that object played a role in the chain of causes leading up to that experience. If those experiences would have been produced exactly as they were (given the particular circumstances in which they occurred) even if that object were not there, then those experiences cannot mediate any knowledge of that object. If this be accepted, then (1) is justified. If S's visual experiences were produced directly by an omnipotent spirit, then they would have been produced in precisely this form even if a car had not been parked in front of his house. Hence, in that case, he would not know in this way, would not have visual knowledge, that there is a car parked in front of his house. But how does the conclusion follow from all that (plus [2]). Granted that an *actual* abnormal production inhibits perceptual knowledge, why suppose that the mere fact that S does not know the production was not abnormal rules out S's knowing about the car? If the object I am eating

---

[16]This argument is not supposed to be an exact replica of anything in the *Meditations*.
[17]For a more up-to-date version the omnipotent spirit could be replaced by an ingenious neurophysiologist.

is made of cardboard, it will not nourish me. But suppose I do not know it is not made of cardboard; it by no means follows just from this lack of knowledge that the object will not nourish me. Its nutrient power, or the reverse, depends on what it *is*, not on what I do or do not *know* about it. Why should we suppose the present case is any different?

Here is a slightly different way of putting the matter. I do not know whether what I am eating is made of cardboard. But that fact leaves wide open the possibility that it is not made of cardboard and that it in fact contains nutrients. Similarly, the fact that I do not know whether my present visual experiences are being directly produced by an ingenious neurophysiologist leaves wide open the possibility that in fact they are being produced in the usual way by a chain of causes stemming from a car parked in front of my house. And if that possibility is realized, I do have perceptual knowledge that a car is parked in front of my house. Since premise (2) does not rule out the possibility in question, it (with premise [1]) does not establish that I do not know that a car is parked in front of my house.

But then why is this argument so tempting? Again, a level confusion may be largely responsible. Given a certain assumption, we can derive a higher level correlate of (3) from our two premises, a correlate that replaces *there is a car parked in front of S's house* with *S knows (perceptually) that there is a car parked in front of S's house.*

3A.   Therefore S does not know that he knows (perceptually) that there is a car parked in front of his house.

The assumption in question, a rather controversial one, is that one cannot know that *p* unless one knows, with respect to each of the necessary conditions of *p*, that it obtains. Now according to premise (1), one necessary condition of S's knowing (perceptually) that there is a car parked in front of his house is that his perceptual experience is not produced abnormally. But according to (2), S does not know that this necessary condition obtains. Hence (3A): he does not know that he knows (perceptually) that there is a car parked in front of his house. But, granted that (3A) follows from (1) and (2), why suppose that (3) follows? One possible explanation of this supposition is a *conviction* that one cannot know that *p* without knowing that one knows that *p;* if that were so, then to show that one does not know that one knows that *p* is ipso facto to show that one does not know that *p.* However, not many philosophers hold so strong a level-bridging view. Hence I think that the attractiveness of the original argument is largely due to a level *confusion.* If one fails to distinguish clearly between *p* and *S knows that p,* one will likewise not distinguish between what it takes to know the one and what it takes to know the other.[18]

Finally, let us consider another kind of skeptical argument, in which level confusion also plays an important part. This is what we may call "criterion skepticism"; the classical form is in Sextus Empiricus, *Outlines of Pyrrhonism*, book 2, chapter 4.

> In order to decide the dispute which has arisen about the criterion (of truth), we must possess an accepted criterion by which we shall be able to judge the dispute; and in order to possess an accepted criterion, the dispute about the criterion must first be decided. And when the argument thus reduces itself to a form of circular reasoning the discovery of the criterion becomes impracticable, since we do not allow them to adopt a criterion by assumption, while if they offer to judge the criterion by a criterion we force them to a regress *ad infinitum*. And furthermore, since demonstration requires an approved demonstration, they are forced into circular reasoning.

I should like to work with my own version of an argument suggested by these remarks of Sextus.

> In order for me to be justified in believing that *p*, my belief that *p* must satisfy the conditions laid down by some valid epistemic principle (for epistemic justification). But then I am justified in the original belief only if I am justified in supposing that there is a valid epistemic principle that does apply in that way to my present belief. And in order to be justified in that further belief there must be a valid epistemic principle that is satisfied in *that* case. And in order to be justified in supposing that . . . . This series either doubles back on itself, in which case the justification is cir-

[18]Of course, if (1) were of the form 'If *q*, then not-*p*' rather than of the form 'If *q*, then S doesn't know that *p*', it would be a different ball game. (Where *p* is, in our case, *There is a car parked in front of S's house*, and *q* is *S's present visual experience is being directly produced by an omnipotent spirit*.) For in that case the falsity of *q* is one of the necessary conditions of the truth of *p*, and so (2) tells us that S does not know that this necessary condition holds. And so the same reasoning that led us to take the original argument to show that S does not know that S knows that *p*, would lead us to take this argument to show that S does not know that *p*. Sometimes Cartesian skepticism is presented in this stronger form and sometimes in the weaker form. Thus when *q* is *I am dreaming* and *p* is *I am seated in front of the fire awake*, we have the stronger form, for *q* does imply not-*p*. But in our original example, *q* did not imply not-*p*. My present visual experience's being produced by an omnipotent spirit is quite compatible with there being a car parked in front of my house at the moment. In this paper I am concerned only with the weaker form. It is worthy of note that the stronger form is more vulnerable to the Moore-Malcolm charge of begging the question. For if *q* does imply not-*p*, then the question of whether I know that not-*q* is directly dependent on whether I know that *p*. For if I do know that *p*, which is the point of contention, then, given certain principles of epistemic logic, I ipso facto know that not-*q*.

cular, or it stretches back infinitely. Thus it would appear that claims to justification give rise either to circularity or to an infinite regress.

The level confusion is more readily apparent here than in Cartesian skepticism. This argument has no tendency to show that my being justified in believing that *p* depends on conditions that give rise to an infinite regress. On the argument's own showing, what my *being* justified in believing that *p* depends on is the existence of a valid epistemic principle that applies to my belief that *p*. So long as there *is* such a principle, that belief *is* justified whether I know anything about the principle or not and whether or not I am justified in supposing that there is such a principle. What this latter justification is required for is not my being justified in believing that *p*, but rather my being justified in the higher level belief that *I am justified in believing that p*. I can be justified in that higher level belief only if I am justified in supposing there to be a principle of the right sort. But it is only by a level confusion that one could suppose this latter justification to be required for my being justified in the original lower level belief. The regress never gets started.

This would seem to leave open the possibility that being justified in a higher level belief, such as the belief that *I am justified in believing that p*, does give rise to an infinite regress or circularity. But that would be a mistake of the same kind. To be justified in that higher level belief, there has to be a (higher level) epistemic principle of justification that applies in the right way to the belief in question. But again, all that is required is the *existence* of such a principle. For the justification of that (first order) higher level belief, it is not necessary that I be justified in supposing that there is such a principle, only that there be such. Again, what this last justification is needed for is the justification of the still higher level belief that *I am justified in believing that I am justified in believing that p*. At each stage I can *be* justified in holding a certain belief provided there *is* a valid principle of justification the requirements of which are satisfied by that belief. My knowing or being justified in believing that there is such a principle is required only for the justification of a belief that is of a still higher level vis-à-vis the belief with which we started.

IV

In conclusion, let me suggest a more positive moral from this string of polemics. It should be clear that the level confusions we have been examining naturally lead to ignoring the possibility of what we might call unsophisticated, unreflective first level knowledge or justification, cases in which one knows that p, or is justified in believing that p, but, whether because of conceptual underdevelopment or otherwise, fails to attain the more sophisticated, higher level knowledge (or justified belief) that one has that lower level knowledge or justification. Of course it may not be immediately obvious that there is unreflective knowledge or justification; the question needs careful consideration. But the point is that so long as we are victims of level confusion we cannot even consider the possibility of a purely first level cognition. The new look in epistemology introduced by the "reliability" theories of such thinkers as Dretske, Armstrong, and Goldman is largely built on the claim that first level knowledge is independent of higher level knowledge. We will be able to take this "new look" even experimentally, only to the extent that we can free ourselves from the blinders imposed by level confusion.

Justification

and Knowledge

Anglo-American epistemology of the last few decades has been dominated by the conception of knowledge as true justified belief. Even when its inadequacy was forced onto our attention by Edmund Gettier,[1] the usual reaction has been to enrich the conception by additional conditions, rather than to take a wholly fresh start. In particular, the thesis that being justified in believing that *p* is a necessary condition of knowing that *p* has gone virtually unchallenged.[2] In these remarks I want to give some reasons for rejecting this received opinion.

Unfortunately, this task is greatly complicated by the lack of any single, generally accepted understanding of epistemic justification. Indeed, the term is most frequently employed without any explanation of its meaning, and we are left to make do with such clues as we can glean from intuitive applications of the term.[3] I have elsewhere attempted to delineate and interrelate what I take to be the major conceptions of epistemic justification in the literature.[4] Here I shall draw on some of

Presented at the XVIIth World Congress of Philosophy in Montreal and published in the Congress's *Proceedings*, 5 (1988), edited by Editions Montmorency, Montreal.

[1] "Is Justified True Belief Knowledge?", *Analysis*, 23 (1963), 121–23.

[2] Among the few exceptions are Fred I. Dretske, *Knowledge and the Flow of Information* (Cambridge: MIT Press, 1981), esp. chap. 4; and Robert Nozick, *Philosophical Explanations* (Cambridge: Harvard University Press, 1981), p. 267.

[3] Among those who do attempt to explicate a concept of epistemic justification are Roderick Chisholm, *Theory of Knowledge*, 2d ed. (Englewood Cliffs, N.J.: Prentice-Hall, 1977), chap. 1; Carl Ginet, *Knowledge, Perception, and Memory* (Dordrecht: D. Reidel, 1975), chap. 3; A. I. Goldman, "What Is Justified Belief?", in G. S. Pappas, ed., *Justification and Knowledge* (Dordrecht: D. Reidel, 1979).

[4] Essays 4 and 5.

those results in considering the putative necessity of justification (for knowledge) on several concepts of justification.

I

Let's begin with what we may call a normative conception (J_n).[A] One is J_n in believing that p *iff* one is not violating any intellectual obligations in believing that p. One is in the clear, not subject to blame or reproach (on intellectual grounds) for believing that p.[5] (This is not to say that one is obligated to believe that p, only that the belief is permitted, not contrary to an obligation.) If that is what justification comes to, the concept will apply only to beings that can be subject to obligations, and in particular obligations to conduct their cognitive operations so as to attain truth and avoid falsity. But obligations, and the associated praise, blame, reproach, and so on, attach only to beings that are sufficiently self-conscious and sufficiently sophisticated to be capable of governing their behavior in the light of norms, principles, rules, and the like. And this condition is by no means satisfied by all knowing subjects. Lower animals, very small children, and idiots acquire and utilize much perceptual knowledge concerning the immediate environment; otherwise they would not be able to move around in it successfully.[6] But they are not capable of acting in the light of rules. So J_n is at best a necessary condition for the knowledge possessed by the likes of normal mature human beings. And even this may be too much of a concession. Much of the perceptual knowledge you and I utilize in reacting to our surroundings is acquired and utilized unconsciously. Indeed, it is doubtful that we are capable of consciously attending to all the fine details of the information we receive through perception. And whatever may be the case with respect to our conscious belief acquisitions, it is highly doubtful that we are subject to any intellectual obligations vis-à-vis these inevitably unconscious perceptual beliefs. How could we obliged to accept or reject one of those beliefs when we cannot even be aware of acquiring them?

Thus far I have been working with the most obvious version of J_n, on which the relevant intellectual obligations attach directly to believing.

[5] See Ginet, *Knowledge, Perception, and Memory*, p. 28, for a particularly explicit formulation of this conception.

[6] Partisans of J_n will retort that it is only in a secondary or figurative sense that such beings possess propositional knowledge. But this view, like other denials of univocity, is acceptable only if it is impossible to exhibit a single sense that adequately captures what makes adult human knowledge what it is and *also* applies to lower animals. And, at the very least, this impossibility has not been shown.

They are obligations to accept, or withhold acceptance from, a belief under certain conditions. One such obligation might be: "One should refrain from believing that p if one does not possess adequate evidence that p". This version of J_n presupposes that believing, and refraining from belief, are under direct voluntary control. Otherwise we could not be under an obligation to do so. Let's call this voluntaristic version J_{nv}. Since it is highly dubious, at the very least, that belief *is* under direct voluntary control, this constitutes a reason for denying that J_{nv} applies even to mature human beings, and hence for denying that it is a necessary condition of knowledge, if we have any knowledge. Even if only some of our beliefs are under direct voluntary control, J_{nv} will not be a generally necessary condition of knowledge, if any of the other beliefs count as knowledge. And it does seem that vast stretches of our doxastic life are not subject to direct control by the will. When something seems perfectly obvious to me, whether on the basis of perception, memory, rational intuition, or reasoning, I literally have no choice as to whether to believe it. When in a normal situation I take myself to see a car coming down the street, I have no choice as to whether to believe that there is a car coming down the street. Thus, on more than one count, J_{nv} makes a poor showing as a necessary condition of knowledge.

We can think, however, of epistemic justification in terms of freedom from reproach without taking belief to be under direct voluntary control, provided we take the relevant intellectual obligations to attach not to believings and refrainings themselves, but to things we *can* voluntarily do to influence those believings and refrainings. For example, we can look for more evidence, selectively expose ourselves to various sorts of influences, and train ourselves to be less gullible. We can then take a belief to violate an obligation and so be blameworthy, in a derivative sense, when it stems from violations of such obligations, when we wouldn't have had that belief had we been doing what we should have been doing to influence our doxastic operations. This is like being subject to blame for other matters that are not under direct voluntary control, like being overweight or being irritable. I am blameworthy for being overweight only if there are things I could and should have done, such that if I had done them I would not now be overweight. And to return to belief, I am justified, in this sense, in believing that p, not subject to blame for doing so, provided that belief does not stem from such violations, provided that even if I had done everything I should have done, in the way of belief-influencing activities, I would still be believing that p. Let's call this "involuntaristic" version of J_n, 'J_{ni}'.[B]

J_{ni}, of course, shares with J_{nv} the common failing of all forms of J_n—the limitation to beings that are subject to intellectual obligations. But it also exhibits liabilities of its own. A mature human being might know that p without being J_{ni} in believing that p. Suppose that I have an intellectual obligation to train myself to be more critical of gossip, to investigate the credibility of a person before accepting that person's reports of the doings or conditions of others. Suppose that I fail to carry out this obligation and remain as ready as before to believe pretty much anything anyone tells me. Suppose further that Robinson, a highly reliable and conscientious person, tells me that Taylor, a mutual acquaintance, has just resigned his job. I have never investigated Robinson's credentials and so have no reason to suppose him reliable. Hence if I had engaged in the self-training program I should have undertaken, I would not have believed what Robinson told me, at least not on the spot. Hence I am not J_{ni} in believing, then and there, that Taylor had resigned his job. But, given that Robinson is a highly reliable source of such information, don't I nevertheless come to *know* that Taylor had resigned? Haven't I acquired that *information*, not just acquired a true belief?

II

Even if justification in a normative sense fails to constitute a necessary condition of knowledge, that is by no means the end of the matter. We may also think of epistemic justification as a matter of being "in a strong position (to get the truth)" in believing that p, as forming or holding the belief in such a way or in such circumstances that the belief is at least highly likely to be true.[7] This "strong position" or "truth-conducivity" conception of justification is itself susceptible of development in several different directions.[8] For present purposes, let's think of this in terms of the grounds on which the belief is based.[9] To be justified in believing that p in this sense is for the belief to be based on *adequate*

[7] I myself find it quite infelicitous to use 'justified' for anything other than some kind of absence of blameworthiness, some way of being within what the rules allow. That is, I find any nonnormative use of 'justified' to be misguided. But since "strong position" uses of the term are firmly entrenched in the current literature, I shall swallow these scruples.

[8] For example, with respect to the probability conferred on the proposition believed by the "position", we have various concepts of probability to choose from. And we have various choices as to what is to be included in the position.

[9] The question of what it is for a belief to be *based* on something is itself a difficult one. See, e.g., G. S. Pappas, "Basing Relations," in Pappas, ed., *Justification and Knowledge,* and Marshall Swain, *Reasons and Knowledge* (Ithaca: Cornell University Press, 1981), chap. 3. Without trying to go into the matter properly, I shall be assuming that for a belief to be based on X the belief must be causally dependent on X in some way.

grounds, grounds that provide a sufficiently strong indication of the truth of the belief.[10] C Let's term this concept of justification 'J$_g$'.D

What can count as a "ground"? Some epistemologists will want to restrict grounds to other knowledge or justified belief possessed by the subject. This is to identify grounds with *reasons*, propositions that the subject has come to know or justifiably believe. There is no doubt that grounds can be reasons, but if they can only be reasons, this rules out the possibility of immediate justification, where what puts me in a strong position is not my possession of some other knowledge or justified belief. For example, when I am justified in believing that I feel relaxed, it would seem that what justifies me is not some other information I possess. I would be at a loss to specify any reason I have for supposing this. The same point may hold of ordinary perceptual and memory beliefs, though the matter is controversial. In order to avoid ruling out the possibility of immediate justification, I will construe grounds as including *experiences* as well as *reasons*. Thus in the above case my ground for believing that I feel relaxed is simply my feeling of relaxation.E In this special case the ground coincides with the fact that makes the belief true, but this is by no means required for immediate justification. If my perceptual belief that there is a tree in front of me is immediately justified, the ground is my current visual experience, and this is quite different from what makes the belief true (if it is true), viz., that there is a tree in front of me.

Note that this extension of the category of "grounds" still leaves them restricted to what the subject has "registered" cognitively, what has come within one's ken in some way or other. As we might say, justifiers all fall within the subject's "perspective" on the world.F Whether *I* am justified in believing that the economy is recovering is a function of how the relevant facts are represented in *my* mind, how things appear to *my* thought and experience. Whatever the actual economic trends, whatever reasons there might *be* for supposing this and whatever reasons other people might have, if they have not fallen under my notice, they can't justify *me* in believing that the economy is recovering. This "perspectival" restriction is a key element in the concept of epistemic justification, and decisively distinguishes it from the concept of a belief's being formed in a reliable manner.

Some epistemologists take it to be sufficient for justification that one *have* adequate grounds for the belief, whether or not the belief is based on those grounds.[11] This would leave open the possibility that I am

[10]An even more difficult issue I will have to neglect concerns the conditions of adequacy of grounds. Later in the essay I will touch on one issue concerning adequacy.
[11]See, e.g., Ginet, *Knowledge, Perception, and Memory*, chap. 3; Chisholm, *Theory of*

justified in believing that Jim is trying to get my job, even though my belief stems from paranoid tendencies. (I *have* adequate reasons for believing this, but they are not what lead me to believe it.) For purposes of this paper I shall take J_g to involve the stronger concept of the belief's being *based* on adequate grounds. All my objections to the necessity of justification in this stronger sense (for knowledge) will apply to the weaker concept as well.

We must add one other qualification to J_g before we have a usable concept. It is quite possible for my belief that p to be based on evidence that in itself adequately supports that belief, even though the totality of the evidence at my disposal does not. Thus although the evidence on which I came to believe that the butler committed the murder strongly supports that hypothesis, I was ignoring other things I know that tend to exculpate the butler. In that case we will not want to count my belief as justified. The adequacy of my basis is, so to say, *overridden* by the larger perspectival context within which it is set. Thus we must require of J_g that there be no such overriding contrary reasons.

S's belief that p is J_g—S's belief that p is based on adequate grounds, and S lacks overriding reasons to the contrary.

Now, at long last, we are in a position to consider whether being J_g is necessary for knowledge. Before introducing what I take to be the most decisive objection, I want to consider briefly a consideration that is harder to assess. Can we have knowledge where the belief is based on no grounds at all? Such cases are frequently encountered in the recent literature. Percy often feels certain, for no apparent reason, that the state of the weather in Katmandu is so-and-so. These beliefs that, so far as he can tell, just pop into mind out of nowhere, are invariably correct. In such cases does Percy know what the weather is in Katmandu? Divergent answers are given. The divergence partly comes from differences, or unclarity, over whether there is only a de facto successful track record, or whether it is a lawlike truth that such beliefs are correct. If we adopt the latter alternative, it seems clear to me that Percy does know what the weather is in these cases, though not everyone shares this intuition. At least it is clear that, in this version of the case, Percy is receiving information in a way that nomologically guarantees its correctness. Now what about J_g? Are these beliefs based on adequate grounds, or any grounds at all? Well, this much seems clear. There is

Knowledge; Peter Klein, *Certainty* (Minneapolis: University of Minnesota Press, 1981), pp. 59–60.

something in Percy that is nomologically connected with the metereological facts in question in such a way as to render his beliefs under the effective control of those facts. But this is all totally opaque to him. He has no awareness whatsoever of these connections, or even his end of the connections, short of the belief itself. Hence if "grounds" are to be restricted to items of which the subject is or can be aware, his beliefs are not based on any grounds at all; they do not stem from his cognitive perspective on the world. And so if all I have been saying is correct, this is a (possible) case in which we have knowledge without J_g.

Now I come to what I take to be the most decisive reason for denying that J_g is necessary for knowledge. There are, or could be, cases in which S is receiving information that p in a way that is paradigmatically reliable, tightly under the control of the facts believed, but in which S's total perspective on the world fails to give adequate support to the belief that p. Furthermore, these cases differ from the kind just discussed in that S does have grounds for the belief that p, and grounds that, taken in themselves, are adequate, but he also has adequate "higher level" reasons for regarding these grounds as inadequate. *From his perspective* these higher level grounds cancel out the adequacy of the grounds on which the belief is based, so that the verdict from the perspective as a whole is: not-J_g. And yet S does come to know that p.

Here is a case in point. S has very strong reasons for regarding his sensory experience as an unreliable guide to his present surroundings. All the people with whom he is in contact are in league to convince him that for the past five years he has been subjected to neurophysiological experiments in which, during about half the days in each month, sensory experiences were artificially produced in him in such a way as to be indistinguishable by him from the real thing. According to their story, things have also been so arranged that he has no memory of going to and from the physiological laboratory; moreover the experiences are produced in the laboratory in such a way as to fit smoothly onto the preceeding and following normal periods. And, they say, these experiments are continuing for an indefinite period of time. Thus they convince him that for about half the time his sense experience is a radically unreliable guide to his current situation, and that he cannot tell when this is the case. They produce very impressive evidence. The totality of the evidence available to S strongly supports their story. S believes, and justifiably believes, that his senses are not to be trusted. Nevertheless, from time to time he insensibly slips back into his life-long habit of trusting his senses and forms perceptual beliefs like the rest of us. Suppose that at a certain point our hero has left his study and plunged, Hume-like, into the affairs of the world. He is about to cross a street and seems to see a truck coming down the street. In fact his perceptual belief-forming apparatus is working normally and a truck *is* coming down the street. Forgetting his skepticism for a moment, he waits for the truck to pass before venturing into the street. He acquired a momentary perceptual belief that a truck was coming down the street. That belief, as we have seen, was not J_g, since the total body of evidence available to him indicated that the prima facie support provided by his visual experience was not an adequate support. Nevertheless it seems clear that he did acquire knowledge about his immediate surroundings, more particularly, knowledge that a truck was coming down the street. Given the fact that his senses were functioning in a perfectly reliable and normal fashion, and given the fact that he thereby felt certain that a truck was coming down the street (momentarily forgetting his reasons for doubt), is it not clear that S *learned (ascertained, found out)* that a truck was coming, that he was *cognizant* of the truck, that he received *information* about the state of affairs in the street? Thus he knew that *p* without being J_g in his belief that *p*.[12]

[12]This counterexample may be challenged in the following way. If S really is justified in supposing his senses to be unreliable, then he is no more justified in supposing that people told him about the supposed experiments than he is in supposing a truck to be coming down the street. But then he is not justified in supposing that the experiments took place; hence he has no reason to suppose his senses to be unreliable. In other words the alleged higher level overrider cancels itself. If S is justified, in this way, in supposing his senses to be unreliable, he is *not* justified in that supposition. Hence this is not a case in which he lacks justification for his normal perceptual beliefs.

I acknowledge that S's evidence for the unreliability of his senses cancels out his justification for an essential piece of that evidence, viz., the proposition that certain people said certain things to him. But I deny that this prevents him from being justified in supposing his senses to be unreliable. The crucial point is that the reasons that supply justification for a belief may be *either justifiably believed or known*. What the objection shows is that an essential component of S's reasons for taking his senses to be unreliable is not itself justifiably believed. But that leaves open the possibility that it is known by S, and that possibility is realized. By hypothesis, S's senses are working normally throughout the period. Hence he knows that the persons in question are saying to him what they are saying, just as he knows that a truck is coming down the street. Hence he does have adequate reasons for supposing his senses to be unreliable.

It is true that if he were to think of the above objection and realize that his reasons for the judgment of unreliability recoil upon themselves, this would very likely inhibit his forming a firm belief that his senses are unreliable. He would, most likely, be reduced to a state of confusion, not knowing what to think about the matter. He would then lack the higher level overrider in question, just because he lacked the requisite firm belief. That would not give us a counterexample. But that is not our case. In our case S doesn't think this way. Instead he does form a firm belief that his senses are unreliable, unaware that his reasoning is self-destructive.

It may be objected to my reply, in the second paragraph of this footnote, that the argument is now presupposing what it sets out to prove, that justification is not necessary for knowledge. But it doesn't presuppose that, any more than the original argument does in its judgment that S knows that a truck is coming down the street. In both cases what we do is to make the judgment that, under described conditions, S knows that *p*. We are not

Finally, a consideration that involves going into the conditions for adequacy of grounds. The issue I want to raise is this. Is the kind of adequacy required for J_g an "objective" adequacy, or is it a "perspectival" adequacy, what appears as adequate from the subject's standpoint? Suppose that S believes that p on the basis of ground R? What does it take for R to satisfy the adequacy requirement for J_g? That R confer a sufficiently high probability on p? Or that the total body of evidence available to S indicates that R confers a sufficiently high probability on p? Or both?[13] Thus far in these remarks I have been tacitly assuming a purely objective interpretation. I have been assuming that if the knowledge or experience on which S's belief that p is based is such as to render it highly likely that p is true, then S is J_g in this belief, whether or not S has adequate reasons for supposing that to be so. Thus if my sensory experience is, in fact, a reliable indication of certain facts about my current environment, then I am J_g in beliefs in those facts that are based on that experience, even if I lack sufficient reasons for supposing that reliable indication relation to hold. And if the knowledge about how my wife looks, on which I base the belief that she is angry, really does strongly tend to support the supposition that she is angry, then I am J_g in believing her to be angry, even if I am unable to give adequate support to the judgment that those looks are reliable signs of anger. If we take this position, we are, so to say, imposing a perspectival requirement on justifiers but not on the justifying relation.[G] But many epistemologists want to take that extra step and go whole-hog along the perspectival route. Thus, for instance, many writers require of justification by reasons that the subject be justified in supposing that the reasons are adequate.[14] Some of these also require that those reasons in fact be adequate, and others do not. I do not go along with the view that a

---

employing any general principles, e.g., that justification is not a necessary condition of knowledge, in making this judgment. (If we supposed justification to *be* a necessary condition of knowledge, we would not be making that judgment, but that is another matter.) Moreover, and this is the crucial point, we cannot move one step in evaluating proposed conditions of knowledge without relying on our ability to tell whether a subject knows something in a particular instance. *That* is what is presupposed in the original argument and in our reply to the objection, something that must be presupposed in any serious attack on the problem.

[13]To draw this contrast as I do, I have to be using some "objective" concept of probability.

[14]See, e.g., Ginet, *Knowledge, Perception, and Memory*, pp. 47–52; D. M. Armstrong, *Belief, Truth, and Knowledge* (Cambridge: Cambridge University Press, 1973), p. 151; Brian Skyrms, "The Explication of 'X knows that p'," *Journal of Philosophy*, 64 (June 22, 1967), 374.

justified belief in the adequacy of the grounds for the belief that p is necessary for the belief that p to be justified; but the present point is that if this requirement is imposed we have an additional reason for denying that J_g is necessary for knowledge. For in the two cases just mentioned, in which the belief in the adequacy of the grounds is not adequately supported by the totality of my perspective, I could, so far as I can see, have knowledge nevertheless. So long as I consistently make judgments about the immediate physical environment or about my wife's emotional states on bases that are in fact highly reliable indications of what I am believing, then I *do* acquire knowledge, whether or not I am in a position to defend the claim that those bases are reliable.

III

Finally I should say just a word about the conception of knowledge that underlies the various judgments I have been making. I have been thinking of knowledge as true belief that is formed and/or sustained under the effective control of the fact believed. Provided the true belief is under that kind of constraint, the believer has knowledge, however he may be situated with respect to reasons or grounds, and, if the belief has adequate grounds, how much he knows or justifiably believes as to their adequacy. One encounters many problems in trying to work out this conception of knowledge, and to my knowledge a fully adequate version is still to come, though the best attempt to date is to be found in Fred Dretske's book *Knowledge and the Flow of Information* (mentioned in fn. 2). If one takes this perspective on knowledge, one need not disparage the importance of epistemic justification. Certainly, in any one of several versions of J_g it is often an important question whether S is justified in believing that p, and if so, on what basis. It is unquestionably a central aim of a self-consciously critical intelligence to determine what justification one has, if any, for one's beliefs, and it is a high achievement to answer such questions and to regulate one's cognitive life in accordance with those answers. But, from this perspective on knowledge, it is a fundamental mistake to conflate all this with the question as to the conditions under which a cognitive subject *knows* that p. Perhaps this conflation is but one more example of a professional parochialism, in which, in this case, one supposes that only that kind of knowledge that would satisfy the most stringent philosophical demands deserves the name.

Notes

A. See Essays 4 and 5, where this is called a "deontological" conception of justification.

B. See Essays 4 and 5 for more details.

C. See Essay 9 for a further development of this idea.

D. In Essay 4 this is termed 'J_{eg}'.

E. In Essays 9 and 11 we have somewhat different readings of this kind of case.

F. This particular "internalist" restriction does not conform exactly to either of the two types I discuss in Essay 8. It sounds like what I there call "perspectival internalism"; but it differs from the view so called in Essay 8 in that it allows the perspective to include what is cognitively registered in "experience", even if that is not codified in belief.

G. That distinction is discussed at length in Essays 8 and 9. In those essays reasons are given for imposing what is here called a "perspectival" requirement on justifiers but not on the justifying relation.

PART III

INTERNALISM
AND EXTERNALISM

Internalism and Externalism

in Epistemology

One hears much these days of an epistemological distinction between "internal" and "external." It is often found in discussions of reliabilism in which the critic accuses the reliabilist of violating "internalist" restrictions on justification and of resting content with justification that is "external" to the subject's perspective.[1] But just what distinction is this (are these)? That is not so clear.

As just intimated, those who wield the distinction intend to be contrasting different views on what can confer justification or on what can convert mere true belief into knowledge. The main emphasis has been on justification, and we will continue that emphasis in this paper. In all these discussions it is the internalist position that lays down constraints; the externalist position vis-à-vis a given internalist position is simply the denial that the internalist constraint in question constitutes a necessary condition of justification. Thus our attempts at clarification can be confined to the internalist side.

As the name implies, an "internalist" position will restrict justifiers to items that are *within* something, more specifically, within the subject. But, of course, not everything that is "within" a knowing subject will be admitted as a possible justifier by an internalist. Physiological processes within the subject, of which the subject knows nothing, will not be allowed. Then just where, how, or in what sense, does something have to be "in the subject" in order to pass the internalist test?

Two quite different answers are given to this question in the liter-

From *Philosophical Topics*, 14, no. 1 (1986). Reprinted by permission of the editors.
[1]See, e.g., Laurence Bonjour, "Externalist Theories of Empirical Knowledge," *Midwest Studies in Philosophy*, 5 (1980).

ature. First there is the idea that in order to confer justification something must be within the subject's "perspective" or "viewpoint" on the
world, in the sense of being something that the subject knows, believes,
or justifiably believes. It must be something that falls within the subject's ken, something of which the subject has taken note. Second, there
is the idea that in order to confer justification, something must be
accessible to the subject in some special way, for example, directly
accessible or infallibly inaccessible. We shall explore each of these versions in detail, noting alternative formulations of each, exposing un-
clarities and incoherences, and seeking to develop the strongest form
of each position. We shall consider what can be said for and against
each version, and we shall explore their interrelations. Finally we shall
make some suggestions concerning the most reasonable position to
take on these issues.

I

Let's begin by considering the first form of internalism. In the
essay already cited, Bonjour, in discussing the view that there are "basic
beliefs", has this to say.

> Thus if basic beliefs are to provide a suitable foundation for empirical
> knowledge, . . . then that feature, whatever it may be, in virtue of which
> an empirical belief qualifies as basic, must also constitute an adequate
> reason for thinking that the belief is true. And now if we assume, plausi-
> bly enough, that the person for whom a belief is basic must *himself* possess
> the justification for that belief if *his* acceptance of it is to be epistemically
> rational or responsible, and thus apparently that he must believe *with
> justification* both (a) that the belief has the feature in question and (b) that
> beliefs having that feature are likely to be true, then we get the result that
> this belief is not basic after all, since its justification depends on these
> other beliefs.[2]

The specific conclusion here is that there can be no basic beliefs, no
beliefs that are justified otherwise than on the basis of other beliefs. But
that is not our present concern. We are interested in the constraint on
justification invoked by Bonjour to arrive at this result. That is the
requirement that "that feature, whatever it may be, in virtue of which
an empirical belief qualifies as basic", that is, that feature by virtue of
which it is justified, must be justifiably believed by the subject to attach

[2]Ibid., p. 55.

to that belief if the belief is to be thereby justified. That is, the justifying feature must be part of his "perspective on the world", must be known or justifiably believed by him to obtain if it is to do its justifying work.

Bonjour continues to employ this same understanding of internalism in characterizing the opposed externalist position.

> But according to proponents of the view under discussion, the person for whom the belief is basic need not (and in general will not) have any cognitive grasp of any kind of this reason or of the relation that is the basis for it in order for this basic belief to be justified; all these matters may be entirely *external* to the person's subjective conception of the situation.[3]
>
> When viewed from the general standpoint of the western epistemological tradition, externalism represents a very radical departure. It seems safe to say that until very recent times, no serious philosopher of knowledge would have dreamed of suggesting that a person's beliefs might be epistemically justified simply in virtue of facts or relations that were external to his subjective conception.[4]

Again, in "A Rationale for Reliabilism" Kent Bach writes as follows.

> Internalism requires that a person have "cognitive grasp" of whatever makes his belief justified.[5]

And in "The Internalist Conception of Justification" Alvin Goldman writes:

> Traditional epistemology has not adopted this externalist perspective. It has been predominantly *internalist*, or egocentric. On the latter perspective, epistemology's job is to construct a doxastic principle or procedure *from the inside*, from our own individual vantage point.[6]

---

[3]Ibid.
[4]Ibid., p. 56.
[5]*The Monist*, 68, (April 1985), 247.
[6]*Midwest Studies in Philosophy*, 5 (1980), 32. Later in this essay Goldman considers what conditions should be laid down for the acceptance of a *doxastic decision principle* (DDP). A DDP is a "function whose *inputs* are certain conditions of a cognizer—e.g., his beliefs, perceptual field, and ostensive memories—and whose *outputs* are prescriptions to adopt (or retain) this or that doxastic attitude. . ." (p. 29). Here is what he takes to be "the condition appropriate to *externalism*":
(1) DDP X is right if and only if: X is *actually* optimal.
Whereas the first shot at formulating an appropriate condition for internalism is the following.
(2) DDP X is right if and only if: we are *justified* in believing that X is optimal. (pp. 33–34)

All this would suggest the following formulation of internalism.

>   (1) Only what is within the subject's "perspective" can determine the justification of a belief.

Let's call this version of internalism "perspectival internalism" (henceforth 'PI').

PI needs some refinement before we are ready to consider what can be said for and against it. First, we have been specifying the subject's "perspective" disjunctively as what the subject "knows, believes, or justifiably believes". It will make a considerable difference what choice we make from between these alternatives. For the present let's proceed in terms of justified belief. At a later stage of the discussion we will explicitly consider the three alternatives and justify this decision. This gives us the more specific formulation:

>   (2) Only the justified beliefs of the subject can determine what further beliefs of that subject are justified.

(2) may seem to smell of circularity, but there can be no definitional circularity, since the internalism we are discussing is not concerned with defining "justified"; it is merely laying down one constraint on the provision of justification. There are, of course, well-known problems with making all justification depend on other justified beliefs, and we shall attend to these in due course.

Next we need to consider the way in which the perspective *determines* the justification of belief. But first a terminological matter. Bonjour's formulation is in terms of a "feature" of the belief by which it is justified. Sometimes this is the most natural construal, as when we think of beliefs about one's current conscious states as being justified by virtue of the fact that they, the beliefs, are incorrigible, or by virtue of the fact that they, the beliefs, are "self-warranted". However it is usually more natural to think of the justification of a belief as stemming from its relation to some state of affairs other than itself, as when a belief is justified by virtue of being based on adequate evidence or reasons, or by virtue of arising from a certain sensory experience. To be sure, these ways of talking are mutually translatable. By a well-known grammatical trick we can always take a belief's relation to some external justifying state of affairs to be a property of the belief. And, contrariwise, we can take the fact that belief B is incorrigible to be the state of affairs that justifies it. Hence I shall feel free to use now one construal, now the other, as seems most natural in the particular context. I will most often speak, however, in terms of justifying *facts* or *states of affairs* and will refer to them as "justifiers".

Let's return to the issue concerning the way in which the perspective determines justification. In the first quotation from Bonjour he allows any sort of fact, not just other justified beliefs of the subject, to be a justifier, provided the subject has certain justified beliefs concerning it and its relation to the initial belief. A justifier for a perceptual belief that there is a tree in front of one, can be, for instance, a sensory experience from which that belief sprang. In that case, the belief would be justified by the experience (or by its origin from the experience) only if S justifiably believes that the belief sprang from that experience and that this origin is sufficient for justification. On this version the perspective determines justification by determining what can justify what; but it allows items outside the perspective (items other than justified beliefs of that subject) to function as justifiers.[7]

Here and elsewhere in the paper the following distinction will be useful. A belief is *mediately (indirectly)* justified provided it is justified by virtue of its relations to other justified beliefs of the subject that provide adequate support for it. In such cases the belief is justified by the *mediation* of those other beliefs. If it is justified in any other way it will be said to be *immediately (directly)* justified. In terms of this distinction, the view embodied in the first quotation from Bonjour rules out *purely* immediate justification, justification by something other than other justified beliefs of the subject *alone,* since it holds that an experience can justify a belief only if the subject has certain justified beliefs about the experience and its relation to the belief; but it is hospitable to mixed justification, in which both other justified beliefs *and* something else are required for justification.[8] There is or can be, however, a version of PI that is more radically opposed to immediate justification, one that would "perspectivize" justifiers more thoroughly, by holding that only justified beliefs can *be justifiers.* On this version what justifies a perceptual belief is not the experience itself, or actual origin from the experience, but the justified belief that the experience has occurred or that the belief originated from it.

We have made the distinction between these versions hang on what is

[7]Note that in the passage quoted above Kent Bach says that "internalism requires that a person have 'cognitive grasp' of whatever makes his belief justified". This too would seem to allow that what makes the belief justified could be an item of any (suitable) sort, provided the person has a "cognitive grasp" of it.

[8]Thus although in that passage Bonjour is arguing against the existence of "basic beliefs", i.e., immediately justified beliefs, the argument, if successful, will rule out only *purely* basic beliefs. It will not rule out beliefs a part of whose justification consists in something other than justified beliefs of the same subject.

allowed to count as "a justifier". In the perceptual case both versions require a justified belief that the relevant experience occurs, but they differ as to whether the experience itself can function in a justifying role. But this might be thought a trivial verbal difference, having to do only with where we draw the line between what is doing the justifying, and the conditions under which it is enabled to do so. What difference does it make where that line is drawn? On both views both "the justifier" and "the conditions that must obtain if it is to be a justifier" figure essentially in the conditions that are necessary for the belief in question to be justified. Why does it matter how we divide that set of conditions into what *does* the justifying and what *enables* it to do that justifying?

I agree that the division is not of any great importance. Nevertheless there is an important difference between the versions. For Bonjour's version, in allowing the experience itself into the necessary conditions for justification, under whatever rubric, is imposing a condition for the justification of the perceptual belief over and above those imposed by the more radical alternative. Put it this way. Both versions alike hold that S is justified in believing that p (that there is a tree in front of one) only if S is justified in believing that S has experience E. But Bonjour imposes the additional requirement that S *have* the experience; that is, he requires that the supporting belief be *true*. And this can be seen to mark a decisive superiority of the more radical alternative. We are dealing with a case in which S's belief that he or she has experience E provides him or her with an adequate reason for the perceptual belief. (If more justified beliefs on S's part, about normality or other background conditions, are required for this, let them be included also.) Otherwise the case would fall short of justification by reason of the insufficiency of the alleged ground and we would never get to the problems raised by the internalism-externalism distinction. But if I do justifiably believe that I am having E, and if that constitutes a sufficient reason for my supposing that p, that is surely enough for my being justified in believing that p. To require that my supporting beliefs be *true* might be appropriate if we were laying down requirements for knowledge, but it is clearly too strong a requirement for justification. If, for example, I am justified, to as high degree as you like, in supposing that my car is in my garage, then I am surely *justified* in denying that it is parked in front of the bank, even if, unbeknownst to me, someone had removed it from my garage and parked it in front of the bank. Thus Bonjour's version represents something of an overkill.[9] Let's codify the preferred version.

[9]What I am calling "Bonjour's version" does not represent his considered position, which is more like the other version. The former, however, is suggested by the passage

(3) The only thing that can justify S's belief that *p* is some other justified beliefs of S.

Next let's note a respect in which (3) needs broadening. Recall the important notion of prima facie justification. One is prima facie justified in believing that *p* provided that one is so situated that one will be (unqualifiedly, all things considered) justified in believing that *p*, provided there are no sufficient "overriding"[10] considerations. Thus in a normal perceptual situation in which I take myself to see a tree in front of me, I am thereby prima facie justified in believing that there is a tree in front of me; but this justification can be overridden by abnormalities in the situation, for instance, sensory malfunctioning of various sorts. Now consider what a PI internalist should say about the conditions under which a prima facie justification is overthrown. Does the mere existence of a sufficiently serious malfunctioning suffice? Or would the subject have to know or be justified in believing that this was the case? Clearly it is the second alternative that is in the spirit of PI. Just as the mere fact that a belief was produced in a highly reliable manner cannot justify it, so the mere fact that a belief was generated in an unreliable fashion cannot serve to discredit the belief. In both cases justification, or the lack thereof, depends on how the situation appears within my perspective, that is, on what I know or justifiably believe about it. If and only if I have sufficient reason to think there to be something fishy about this case of perception, will prima facie justification be overthrown. And, indeed, most epistemologists have taken this line about what overrides prima facie justification, even where they haven't also accepted (3) as a constraint on justification.[11] Thus we

---

under discussion. Perhaps Bonjour was led into it there because he was arguing with a partisan of immediate knowledge who claims that a certain nonbelief is sufficient for the justification of a certain belief. Having no reason to deny that the nondoxastic state of affairs obtains, Bonjour simply confined himself to alleging that even if it does obtain, the subject will also have to be justified in believing that it obtains.

[10] I shall use 'overrider' for something that cancels out a prima facie justification. Unlike some theorists I shall refrain from using 'defeater' for this purpose, saving that term (though not using it in this essay) for a fact the mere holding of which prevents a true, overall justified belief from counting as knowledge.

[11] Thus principle (B) in R. M. Chisholm, *Theory of Knowledge*, 2d ed. (Englewood Cliffs, N.J.: Prentice-Hall, 1977), runs as follows:

(B) For any subject S, if S believes, without ground for doubt, that he is perceiving something to be F, then it is beyond reasonable doubt for S that he perceives something to be F.

And 'ground for doubt' is explained as follows.

(D4.3) S believes, *without ground for doubt*, that p = $_{df}$ (i) S believes that p and (ii) no conjunction of propositions that are acceptable for S tends to confirm the negation of the proposition that p. (p. 76)

The PI constraint comes in by requiring "grounds for doubt" that consists in proposi-

should add overriders to the scope of (3). In the interest of concise formulation let us introduce the term 'epistemizer' to range over anything that affects the justification of a belief, positively or negatively. We can then reformulate (3) as:

(4) The only thing that can epistemize S's belief that p is some other justified belief(s) of S.

Now we are in a position to return to the choice between knowledge, belief, and justified belief in the specification of the subject's perspective. To deal with this properly we must note that (4) places severe restrictions on a theory of justification by implying that only *mediate* justification is available. Let's call any theory of justification that recognizes only mediate justification a "discursive" theory. The most prominent discursive theory is coherentism; whether there are any other varieties depends on how narrowly the boundaries of coherentism are drawn, and there is wide variation on this. For the present let's think of coherentism widely, as ranging over any discursive theory.

Next let's distinguish between "positive" and "negative" coherence theories. John Pollock introduced the distinction as follows:

There are two kinds of coherence theories. On the one hand, there are coherence theories which take all propositions to be prima facie justified. According to those theories, if one believes a proposition, P, one is automatically justified in doing so unless one has a reason for rejecting the belief. According to theories of this sort, reasons function primarily in a negative way, leading us to reject beliefs but not being required for the justified acquisition of belief. Let us call these negative coherence theories. The other kind of coherence theory (a positive coherence theory) demands positive support for all beliefs.[12]

In other words, on a positive coherence theory a belief is justified only if it stands in the right relation to justifiers. On a negative coherence theory a belief is justified unless it stands in the wrong relation with overriders. What makes them both coherence theories is that in both cases the epistemizers must be drawn from the subject's propositional attitudes.

Now let's go back to the various sorts of propositional attitudes that

---

tions that are "acceptable" for the subject, in order that the prima facie justification of perceptual beliefs be overthrown.

[12]"A Plethora of Epistemological Theories," in George S. Pappas, ed., *Justification and Knowledge* (Dordrecht: D. Reidel, 1979), p. 101.

might be supposed by PI to make up the subject's perspective: beliefs, justified beliefs, knowledge. In formulations (2), (3), and (4) we chose *justified belief* without explaining or justifying that choice. I now turn to that task.

First, what about the decision between knowledge and justified belief? Here the point is that the more modest constraint is called for. Suppose that I am justified in believing that my car is in the garage, since I left it there this morning and have been away from the house since, no one else has a key to the house or garage, and the neighborhood is remarkably free of crime. In the afternoon I see a car that looks like mine in the parking lot of a bank but believe that it isn't mine, on the grounds of my car's being in my garage. Suppose further that my car has been stolen and this is my car, so I didn't *know* that my car was in the garage even though I was justified in believing this. I am surely justified in believing that the car in the parking lot is not mine, even though the basis for this belief is something I am justified in believing but do not know. Cases like this indicate that it is sufficient for a belief to be a justifier that it be justified; it is not also required that it count as knowledge.

But what about the alternative between any beliefs, on the one hand, and only justified beliefs, on the other? It may seem that we can settle this issue in the same way. Suppose I merely believe that my car is in the garage, just because that is where I normally expect it to be when I don't have it with me; but I am not justified in believing this. On the contrary, I took it to a repair shop to be worked on yesterday; when I believe that it is in my garage, I have temporarily forgotten about this incident, even though I am quite capable of remembering it and would have been remembering it except for this temporary lapse. Again I take my car's being in my garage as a reason for supposing that the car I see in the bank parking lot is not mine. Here it is quite clear that I am not justified in this latter belief by virtue of basing it on an unjustified belief. On the contrary, the fact that I am quite unjustified in supposing my car to be in my garage shows that I don't become justified in some further belief by virtue of basing it on that belief. More generally, it seems that beliefs cannot acquire justification by being brought into relation with unjustified beliefs. One belief cannot "transfer" to another belief a justification it does not possess.

This last argument is, I believe, conclusive for what we might call "local" mediate justification, justification of a particular belief by the evidential or other logical relations in which it stands to one, or a few, other beliefs. Justification can be transferred "locally" only by beliefs that already have it. But the more common sort of discursive theory is a "holistic" coherence theory, one which takes a given belief to be justified, at least in the last analysis, not by its relations to a very few other beliefs "in the vicinity", but by the way in which it fits into some very large system of beliefs. Since the term "coherence theory" derives from the idea that a belief is justified if and only if it "coheres" with such a total system, it will be most natural to restrict the term "coherence theory" to holistic theories. The obvious choice for the system with which a belief must cohere in order to be justified is the totality of the subject's current beliefs. Thus on the most usual sort of coherence theory the subject's "perspective" by reference to which the justification of any particular belief is to be assessed consists of the subject's beliefs, without any further restriction to justified beliefs. Indeed, there could not be such a restriction. For on the kind of (pure) coherence theory we are now considering, a belief is or is not justified just by its relations to the whole of the subject's beliefs. Apart from that coherence with *all* the subject's beliefs there are no justified beliefs to serve as a reference class. Hence by the time the totality of beliefs has been segregated into justified and unjustified it is too late to use the former class as a touchstone to determine whether a given belief is justified. That determination has already been made. Of course, if at a future time the subject has some new beliefs, we can at that time assess their justificatory status, and this determination will be made after the earlier demarcation of the justified from the unjustified beliefs. But that doesn't change the verdict. At that future time, by the terms of the theory, a given belief (new or old) is justified solely on the basis of its coherence with the total set of beliefs the subject has at that time. And so for a pure coherence theory PI should be formulated as follows.

(5) Only the total set of S's beliefs at *t* can function as an epistemizer at *t*.[13]

Since I find pure coherence theories quite unsatisfactory for a variety of reasons, I might seek to rule out (5) on those grounds. But in this essay I did not want to get into *substantive* epistemological issues like those concerning the opposition between foundationalism and coherentism. This essay is designed to be restricted to meta-epistemologi-

[13]To be sure, there are more alternatives than the ones we have mentioned. In his book *Knowledge* (Oxford: Clarendon Press, 1974), Keith Lehrer plumps for a coherence theory in which the test of justification is coherence, not with the actual set of beliefs of the subject but with what Lehrer calls the subject's "corrected doxastic system", that subset "resulting when every statement is deleted which describes S as believing something he would cease to believe as an impartial and disinterested truth-seeker" (p. 190).

cal issues concerning basic epistemological concepts, their explication, interrelations, and suitability for one or another purpose. Thus I shall just point out that the internalism-externalism dispute is mostly carried on by thinkers who believe in local mediate justification. Hence we will ensure maximum contact with that debate if we focus on (4) rather than (5) in the ensuing discussion.

One more point must be laid on the table before we turn to the consideration of what can be said in support of PI. Go back to the initial quotation from Bonjour; we have not yet squeezed it dry. There Bonjour requires for the justification of S's putatively basic belief that S justifiably believe not only that the belief have the "feature" in question but also *that beliefs having that feature are likely to be true*. When we come to the main argument for PI we will see the rationale for this additional higher level requirement. For the moment we need only note its general character. It is clear that Bonjour imposes *this* requirement just because he takes truth conducivity to be required for, as we might say, *justificatory efficacy*. Earlier in the essay he had written that "the distinguishing characteristic" of epistemic justification is "its internal relation to the cognitive goal of truth" (p. 54). Elsewhere Bonjour has laid it down that it is essential to a justifier to be "truth conducive".[14] Thus this additional requirement is really a requirement to the effect that the subject be justified in supposing not only that the putative justifier obtains but also that it be efficacious, that it have what it takes to justify the belief. But he can't come right out and say that. Consider his situation if he were to try. Formulate the additional requirement as: *S justifiably believes that the possession of that feature suffices to justify the belief.* But Bonjour is committed to deny this; his specific contention is that no feature of a belief can be sufficient to justify the belief; the subject must also have certain justified beliefs about that feature.[15] Then how about requiring that the possession of that feature is part of what confers justification on this belief? But we want the requirement to be more specific than that. The two justified beliefs are also part of what confers justification on the belief in this situation, but a different part. We want to specify what part the feature is contributing to the justification. That is what Bonjour is attempting to do with his requirement that S be justified in believing that the feature is probabilifying, that by virtue of having this feature the belief is likely to be true. That will do the job, on

---

[14]"Can Empirical Knowledge Have a Foundation?", *American Philosophical Quarterly*, 15 (January 1978), 5.

[15]Of course the "feature" could be so specified that it included the subject's justified beliefs about another feature. But then it would be this latter feature with respect to which Bonjour is requiring the justified beliefs, and the point would still hold.

the assumption that probabilification is just what it takes for justificatory efficacy. But this is controversial. In fact, other internalists have been in the forefront of denying just this claim.[16] Thus it appears that if we are to give an adequate formulation of this higher level requirement, we must commit ourselves to some highly controversial assumption as to what is required for justification, some highly controversial assumption in substantive epistemology.

Fortunately there is a coward's way out, since we are working with (4), which restricts us to purely mediate justification, rather than with Bonjour's versions. On (4) the only justifiers are other justified beliefs of the same subject. Hence the way in which any justifier has to be related to a belief in order to do its job is to provide "adequate support" or "adequate evidence"; it must be an "adequate reason". No doubt, it is both obscure and controversial what is required for one belief (or the propositional content thereof) to constitute an adequate reason or to provide adequate support for another. But leaving all this aside, and taking cover behind the criterion-neutral term 'adequate', we can put the additional, higher level requirement just by saying that S must justifiably believe that the justifying belief(s) provide adequate support for the justified belief.[17] Tacking this on to our canonical formulation, we get:

(6) Only S's justified beliefs can epistemize S's belief that p, and then only if S justifiably believes that the other justified beliefs in question provide adequate support for p (or for something else, in the case of overriders).

II

We have now explicated PI sufficiently to consider what can be said in its favor. That consideration will lead to further refinements. First let's consider what defense is offered by Bonjour in "Externalist Theories of Empirical Knowledge". The main effort there is devoted to an attack on reliability theories, utilizing an example of alleged clairvoyance. It is stipulated that the subject has a reliable capacity for determining the disposition of distant objects on no apparent basis.

[16]See, e.g., Richard Foley, "What's Wrong with Reliabilism?", *The Monist*, 68 (April 1985).
[17]This requirement for mediate justification is embraced by many epistemologists who do not advocate (4) with its denial of any immediate justification. See, e.g., Carl Ginet, *Knowledge, Perception, and Memory* (Dordrecht: D. Reidel, 1975), pp. 47–49.

Bonjour first argues that if the person has adequate reason for supposing that a belief thus formed is false, or that her clairvoyance is not
reliable, then she is not justified in the clairvoyant beliefs, even though
they are formed reliably. But, as Bonjour acknowledges, this shows
only that the subject's justified beliefs do have a bearing on what other
beliefs are justified, not that they are the only thing that can have this
bearing. Next, he more boldly argues that in the case in which the
subject has no reasons for or against the reliability of her powers or the
truth of the belief (whether or not she believes that the powers are
reliable), she is not justified in holding the beliefs, however reliable her
clairvoyant powers are in fact. However these "arguments" simply consist in Bonjour's displaying his intuitions in opposition to those of his
opponent. A couple of quotations will give the flavor.

> We are now face-to-face with the fundamental—and seemingly ob-
> vious—intuitive problem with externalism: *why* should the mere fact that
> such an external relation (the reliability of the faculty) obtains mean that
> Norman's belief is epistemically justified, when the relation in question is
> entirely outside his ken?
> One reason why externalism may seem initially plausible is that if the
> external relation in question genuinely obtains, then Norman will in fact
> not go wrong in accepting the belief, and it is, *in a sense,* not an accident
> that this is so. But how is this supposed to justify Norman's belief? From
> his subjective perspective, it *is* an accident that the belief is true.[18]

This is more like an appeal to PI than a support for that restriction.
There are, as we shall see, some germs of a more substantial argument
in Bonjour, but they will need developing.
   Nor are we helped by a rather common argument for PI that stems
from a confusion between the *activity* of justifying a belief and the *state*
of a belief's being justified. Here is a good sample.

> In whatever way a man might attempt to justify his beliefs, whether to
> himself or to another, he must always appeal to some belief. There is
> nothing other than one's belief to which one can appeal in the justifica-
> tion of belief. There is no exit from the circle of one's beliefs.[19]

Of course, if I am to carry out the *activity* of justifying a belief, I must
provide an argument for it; I must say something as to why one should
suppose it to be true. And to do this I must employ other beliefs of
mine. In saying what reasons there are for supposing that *p*, I am

[18]"Externalist Theories of Empirical Knowledge," p. 63.
[19]Keith Lehrer, *Knowledge*, pp. 187–88.

expressing other beliefs of mine and contextually implying that I am justified in accepting them. But this all has to do with the activity of *justifying* a belief, *showing* it to be justified. From the fact that I can *justify* a belief only by relating it to other beliefs that constitute a support, it does not follow that a belief can *be justified* only by its relations to other beliefs. Analogously, from the fact that I cannot justify my expenses without saying something in support of my having made them, it does not follow that my expenses cannot *be justified* unless I say something in support of my having made them. Indeed, we all have innumerable beliefs that are commonly taken to be justified but for which we never so much as attempt to produce reasons. It might be argued with some show of plausibility that one can be justified in believing that *p* only if it is *possible* for one to justify that belief; but I cannot imagine any remotely plausible argument for the thesis that I can be justified in believing that *p* only if I *have justified* that belief. Hence the point made by Lehrer about justifying leaves completely intact the possibility that one might *be justified* in a belief by something other than one's other beliefs.

We will have to make the same judgment on an analogous argument from what is involved in *deciding* what to believe. Here is a version by Pollock.

> In deciding what to believe, we have only our own beliefs to which we can appeal. If our beliefs mutually support our believing P, then it would be irrational for us not to believe P and hence belief in P is justified. There is no way that one can break out of the circle of his own beliefs.[20]

Again, even if this shows that I can have no basis other than my own beliefs for a *decision* as to what to believe, it falls far short of showing that nothing can *justify* a belief except other beliefs. For there is no reason to suppose that the only justified beliefs are those the subject *decided* to adopt.

Even though, as will appear in the fullness of time, I am no advocate of PI, I feel that I can improve on the recommendations for that view that can be found in the writings of its supporters. Here is what I take to be the strongest argument for it. I have gleaned the basic idea for this line of argument from various sources, but the development of it is my own.[21]

---

[20]"A Plethora of Epistemological Theories," p. 106. This does not represent Pollock's overall view.

[21]This argument may be thought of as a development of Bonjour's suggestion that the subject must "possess the justification" for the belief "if *his* acceptance of it is to be epistemically rational or responsible". ("Externalist Theories of Empirical Knowledge," p. 55.)

"First let's note that the fact that *q* can enter into the justification for S's believing that *p* only in the guise of S's being justified in believing that *q*. Consider the popular idea that what justifies me in beliefs about my own current conscious states is that such beliefs are infallible, that is, are such that I couldn't mistakenly form such a belief. But how could that fact justify those beliefs unless I were cognizant of the infallibility? If I am unaware of their infallibility, and they have no other justification, am I not proceeding *irresponsibly* in forming such beliefs? Just as the mere fact that X is about to attack me will not justify my striking X unless I have good reason to suppose that he is about to attack me, so the mere fact that current feeling beliefs are infallible can't justify me in accepting them unless I at least have good reason to regard them as infallible. *Pari passu*, the mere fact that I am being appeared to treely cannot render me justified in believing that there is a tree in front of me, unless I am justified in believing that I am being appeared to treely. If I am unaware of the existence of the warrant-conferring fact then, for me, it is just as if it did not exist. How can a fact of which I take no account whatever have any bearing on what it is *permissible* for me to do, in the way of action or of belief? Thus it would seem that my being justified in believing that *q* is at least a *necessary* condition of *q*'s playing a role in justifying my belief that *p*.

But it is also a sufficient condition. Provided I am justified in believing that beliefs about current feelings of the subject are infallible, what more could be required to legitimate those beliefs? Even if they are not in fact infallible, how can that prevent its being *permissible* for me to accept them? If, so far as I can tell, there are facts that strongly support the supposition that *p*, then surely it is *all right* for me to give my assent to *p*. What more could be *demanded* of me? I have done all I can. What the actual facts are over and above what I am most justified in believing is something I cannot be held *responsible* for. Once I have marshaled all the cognitive resources available to me to determine the matter, I have, in my body of justified beliefs, the closest approximation I can make to the actual facts. That is the best I have to go on, and it would be quite unreasonable to suggest that I *ought* to be going on something else instead. What I am justified in believing provides sufficient as well as necessary conditions for the justification of further beliefs."[22]

How does this line of argument go beyond simply displaying inter-

---

[22]Note that what this argument supports is a *positive, local justification* version of PI. But precisely parallel arguments can be given for other versions. For the suggestion of such an argument for a *negative, local justification* version, see the quotation from Wolterstorff in the following footnote. For an argument for a mere belief version, whether local or holistic, see Pollock's "A Plethora of Epistemological Theories," p. 109.

nalist (PI) intuitions? It does so by grounding those intuitions in a particular conception of justification, one that makes epistemic justification a matter of the subject's normative situation, a matter of how the subject's believing that *p* stands vis-à-vis relevant intellectual norms, standards, obligations, duties, and the like. If S's believing that *p* is *not* in contravention of relevant intellectual obligations, then it is *permissible* for him to believe that *p*, he cannot be rightly *blamed* for doing so, it is *all right* for him to hold that belief, he is *in the clear* in so believing. Let's call this a "deontological" conception of epistemic justification. The argument just presented exhibits the PI constraint as flowing from *what justification is,* as thus conceived. Since whether I am justified in believing that *p* depends on whether I could rightfully be blamed or held to account for so believing, then what is crucial for whether I am justified is the way the relevant facts appear from my perspective; justification depends on what the relevant facts are like, *so far as I can tell.* For that is what is crucial for whether I can be blamed for my belief. If and only if my belief is adequately supported *so far as I can tell,* I cannot be blamed for the belief.[23]

Elsewhere I have explored the deontological conception and contrasted it with the very different "strong position" (SP) conception, as well as distinguishing various versions of each.[24] Roughly speaking, to

[23]Here are some adumbrations of this argument. ". . . on the externalist view, a person may be ever so irrational and irresponsible in accepting a belief, when judged in light of his own subjective conception of the situation, and may still turn out to satisfy Armstrong's general criterion of reliability. This belief may in fact be reliable, even though the person has no reason for thinking that it is reliable. . . . But such a person seems nonetheless to be thoroughly irresponsible from an epistemic standpoint in accepting such a belief, and hence not justified, contrary to externalism." (Bonjour, "Externalist Theories of Empirical Knowledge," p. 59.) Here is another adumbration, this time from the standpoint of a negative coherence theory that holds a belief to be justified provided one has no sufficient reason for giving it up. "If a person does not have adequate reason to refrain from some belief of his, what could possibly oblige him to give it up? Conversely, if he surrenders some belief of his as soon as he has adequate reason to do so, what more can rightly be demanded of him? Is he not then using the capacities he has for governing his beliefs, with the goal of getting more amply in touch with reality, as well as can rightly be demanded of him?" (Nicholas Wolterstorff, "Can Belief in God Be Rational?", in Alvin Plantinga and Nicholas Wolterstorff, eds., *Faith and Rationality* [Notre Dame, Ind.: University of Notre Dame Press, 1983], p. 163). Note the crucial occurrence in these passages of terms like 'irresponsible', 'oblige', and 'rightly demanded'. Both these authors, as well as other PI internalists, note the parallel between what is required for epistemic and for ethical justification. In both cases, it is argued, what is required is that the belief or the action be the one to adopt, so far as one can tell from one's own viewpoint on the world.

[24]Essays 4 (where the SP conception is called an "evaluative conception", evaluative from the "epistemic point of view") and 5. For other developments of the deontological conception see Ginet, *Knowledge, Perception, and Memory;* Wolterstorff, "Can Belief in God Be Rational?"; and Margery B. Naylor, "Epistemic Justification," *American Philosophical Quarterly,* 25 (January 1988), 49–58.

be SP justified in believing that p is to believe that p in such a way as to be in a strong position thereby to attain the truth and avoid error. It is to believe that p in a "truth conducive" way. It is for one's belief to have been formed in such a way or on such a basis that one is thereby likely to be believing correctly. Note that each conception omits the crucial emphasis of the other, thereby implicitly denying it to be necessary for justification. Freedom from blameworthiness, being in the clear as far as one's intellectual duties are concerned, is totally ignored by the "strong position" theorist. So long as one forms one's belief in a way that is well calculated to get the truth, it is of no concern how well one is carrying out intellectual duties. Conversely, the deontologist has nothing to say about truth conducivity.[25] So long as I am not violating any intellectual duties, I am "in the clear" in believing that p, whatever my chances for truth. This is not to say that each side denies the importance of what is crucial for the other. The deontologist need not be indifferent to the truth, nor need the "strong position" theorist be uninterested in intellectual duties. But they differ on how these admittedly important matters relate to epistemic justification.

To get a properly rounded picture we should also note a way in which truth-conducivity does typically enter into deontological theories of justification. Even though truth-conducivity does not enter into the meaning of "justified" for the deontologist, he is likely to give it a prominent place when he comes to spell out the content of our most important intellectual obligations. Such theorists typically hold that our basic intellectual obligation is to so conduct our cognitive activities as to maximize the chances of believing the true and avoiding believing the false.[26] Thus even though one may be deontologically justified without thereby being in a favorable position to get the truth, if our basic intellectual obligation is to maximize truth and minimize falsity, one cannot be deontologically justified in a belief unless one is believing in such a way that, so far as one can tell, is well calculated to reach the truth.

Now we can see that just as the deontological conception supports a PI restriction, so an SP conception supports its denial. It is obviously not conceptually necessary that one comes to believe that p in a truth-conducive way only if that belief is well supported by other justified

[25]Bonjour is an exception in trying to combine features of the two conceptions. On the one hand, he argues for PI from a deontological conception of justification. On the other hand, as we have seen, he presupposes the truth-conductivity of justification in formulating his higher level requirement.

[26]Thus Wolterstorff: "Locke assumes—rightly in my judgment—that we have an obligation to govern our assent with the goal in mind of getting more amply in touch with reality." "Can Belief in God Be Rational?", p. 145.

beliefs of the subject. It is clearly possible that there are ways of being in a strong position in one's beliefs other than by basing those beliefs on other justified beliefs. Plausible examples of such other ways are not far to seek. Perceptual beliefs about the physical environment, for example, that the lilies are blooming in the garden, are based on the subject's sensory experience, on the way in which things sensorily appear to one. Furthermore let's make the plausible supposition that one does not typically form beliefs about how one is being sensorily appeared to; the sensory appearance directly gives rise to the belief about the environment. It is not that one says to oneself, even rapidly, implicitly, or below the level of consciousness, "I am having a visual experience of such and such a sort; therefore the lilies are blooming in the garden". No such inference typically takes place, for the premises for such inferences are rarely made objects of belief. Finally, let's make the plausible assumption that our perceptual belief-forming mechanisms are generally reliable, at least for the sorts of perceptual beliefs we typically form, in the sorts of situations we typically encounter. Granting all this, perceptual belief formation constitutes massive support for the thesis that one can form beliefs in a reliable, truth-conducive manner without basing them on other justified beliefs.

Beliefs about one's current conscious states provide even stronger support. It is very plausible to suppose that we have a highly reliable (some would even say infallible) mechanism for the formation of such beliefs. And yet it would be extremely implausible to suppose that these beliefs are formed or held on the basis of reasons. What would such reasons be? It may be suggested that my reason for supposing that I feel sleepy at the moment is that I do believe this and that such beliefs are infallible. But many persons who form such beliefs do not even have the relevant concept of infallibility, much less typically believe that such beliefs are infallible whenever they come to believe such things. Once again we have reason to suppose that beliefs can satisfy the SP conception of justification without satisfying the PI constraint on justification.

Next let's note that the argument we have given for PI supports both the lower level and the higher level requirement laid down in (6). The "lower level requirement" is that the justifier for the belief that p consist of other justified beliefs of the subject, and the "higher level requirement" is that the subject justifiably *believe that* these other justified beliefs provide adequate support for the belief that p. We have been emphasizing the way in which the argument establishes the lower level requirement, but it also lends powerful support to the higher level requirement. For suppose that my belief that p is based on other justified beliefs of mine and, let's suppose, these other justified beliefs provide adequate support for the belief that *p*. But suppose further that I do not justifiably believe that these other beliefs do provide adequate support. In that case, so far as I can tell, I do not have within my perspective adequate support for *p*. Would I not be proceeding irresponsibly in adopting the belief that *p*? Couldn't I properly be held accountable for a violation of intellectual obligations in giving my assent to *p* under those conditions? Therefore if I am to be in the clear in believing that *p*, the belief must not only be based on other justified beliefs of mine; I must also be justified in supposing those beliefs to provide sufficient support for the belief that *p*.

That shows that the higher level justified belief is necessary for justification. We can now proceed to argue that it, together with the lower level requirement, is sufficient. The crucial question here is whether it is also necessary for justification that the other justified beliefs do in fact provide adequate support, that their propositional contents are indeed so related as to make the one an adequate reason for the other. A consideration of conditions of blame, being in the clear, etc., will support a negative answer. For if, going on what I know or justifiably believe about the world, it is clear to me that other justified beliefs of mine adequately support the belief that *p*, what more could be required of me? Even if I am mistaken in that judgment, I made it in the light of the best considerations available to me. I can't be held to blame if I proceed in the light of the best reading of the facts of which I am capable. Hence a *justified belief* that I have adequate support is all that can rightfully be imposed in the way of a higher level requirement.

Now that we have a two-level PI internalism-externalism contrast, there is the possibility of being an internalist on one level and an externalist on another. The two parties disagree both over what can be a justifier and over that by virtue of which a particular item justifies a particular belief. A particularly live possibility of a compromise is an internalism as to what can justify and an externalism as to what enables it to justify. One could be a PI internalist about justifiers by virtue of recognizing only mediate justification, but insist that my belief that *p* is justified by its relations to my belief that *q* if and only if *q* does in fact provide adequate support for *p*. At the end of the paper we shall advocate a similar mediating position, though the internalist component will not be the PI brand.

Now let's consider a way in which what is supported by our argument for PI differs from the formulation of PI with which we have been working. We have represented the deontologist as maintaining that whether S is justified in believing that *p* is solely a function of what other justified beliefs S has. But that cannot be the whole story. Consider a case in which, although the sum total of the justified beliefs I actually possess provides an adequate basis for the belief that *p*, that would not have been the case had I been conducting myself properly. If I had looked into the matter as thoroughly as I should have, I would be in possession of effective *overriders* for my evidence for *p*, and my total body of evidence would not have given sufficient support for the belief that *p*. Here the belief that *p is* adequately supported by the perspective on the world that I actually have, and I justifiably believe that it is; but nevertheless I am not in the clear in believing that *p*, not justified in the deontological sense.

These considerations show that PI must be modified if it is to be supported by a deontological conception of justification. It must include a codicil to the effect that overriders that the subject does not possess, but would have possessed had she been conducting herself as she should have been, also can serve to epistemize beliefs.[27] PI now becomes:

(7) Only S's justified beliefs can epistemize S's belief that *p*, and then only if S justifiably believes that those other justified beliefs provide adequate support for S's belief that *p;* but overriders that S should have had but didn't can cancel out justification provided by the preceding.[28]

[27]There are other ways in which a subject's epistemic situation might have been different from what it actually is had the subject been doing a better job of carrying out her intellectual obligations. In particular, the subject might have had justifiers that she does not actually possess. However it is not at all clear that this and other differences from the actual situation have the same bearing on justification as the lack of overriders that one should have had. Consider a case in which if I had been attending to the matter as I should have I would have had justified beliefs that adequately support the belief that Jones is untrustworthy. As things actually stand I do not have adequate reasons for supposing that. Here, going on the justified beliefs I actually have, we would have to say that I would not be justified in believing that Jones is untrustworthy. But nor does it seem that this judgment would be reversed by the consideration that I would have had adequate support had I been conducting myself properly. Surely we don't want to say that the thing for me to do is to adopt that belief *in the absence of sufficient reasons*, even if I would have had sufficient reasons had I been managing my cognitive activities better.

[28]At a few points in the preceding exposition the need for this qualification was more or less evident. Thus at one point I represented the deontologist as saying that the justification of a given belief depends on the "best representation of the world of which I am currently capable". I have also used such phrases as "one's best judgment of the facts" and "so far as one can tell". All of these phrases point to the "ideal viewpoint" rather than to the actual viewpoint. The best representation of the world of which I am currently capable may not be the representation I actually have. There will be a discrepancy, provided, as is usually the case to some extent, I have not made full use of my opportunities for ascertaining relevant features of the world. The importance of overriders that a subject ought to have but doesn't is well brought out by Wolterstorff, "Can Belief in God Be Rational?", pp. 165–66.

Going back once more to our argument for PI, I now wish to point out that it utilizes a special form of a deontological conception of justification that is limited in ways that render it either totally inapplicable, or at least severely limited in application.

First, it utilizes a concept of justification that assumes beliefs to be under direct voluntary control. The argument takes it that one is justified in believing that *p* if and only if one is not to blame *for believing that p*, if and only if *in that situation this was a belief that one was permitted to choose*. All this talk has application only if one has direct voluntary control over whether one believes that *p* at a given moment. If I lack such control, if I cannot believe or refrain from believing that *p* at will, then it is futile to discuss whether I am *permitted* to believe that *p* at *t* or whether I would be *irresponsible* in choosing to believe that *p* at *t*. And it seems that we just don't have any such control, at least not in general. For the most part my beliefs are formed willy-nilly. When I see a truck coming down the street, I am hardly at liberty either to believe that a truck is coming down the street or to refrain from that belief. Even if there are special cases, such as moral or religious beliefs, where we do have pinpoint voluntary control (and even this may be doubted), it is clear that for the most part we lack such powers.[29]

Not only does the argument in question presuppose direct voluntary control of belief; it considers the requirements for justification only for those beliefs that are acquired by an explicit, deliberate choice. For it arrives at the PI constraint by pointing out that only what I am cognizant of can be taken account of in my *decision* as to whether to believe that *p*. "If I am unaware of their infallibility, . . . am I not proceeding irresponsibly in *forming* such beliefs?" "If, so far as I can tell, there are facts that strongly support the supposition that *p*, then surely it is all right for me to give my assent to *p*." But this fact, that only what I am cognizant of can affect the permissibility of my choice, will imply a *general* constraint on justification only if justification is confined to beliefs that are *chosen* by a deliberate voluntary act. But even if beliefs are *subject to* direct voluntary control, that control need not always be exercised. One can hold that it is always in principle possible to choose whether to believe a given proposition without thereby being committed to the grossly implausible supposition that all our beliefs are in fact acquired by an explicit choice. Even overt actions that are uncontroversially under voluntary control, such as tying one's shoelaces, can be, and often are, performed habitually. Likewise, even if beliefs are as subject to direct voluntary control as tying one's shoelaces, beliefs are

[29]For a discussion of this issue see Essay 5.

often acquired willy-nilly. Hence a concept of epistemic justification that is confined to beliefs acquired by deliberate choice covers only a small part of the territory.

Third, it follows from the point just made that the argument utilizes a concept of justification that evaluates a belief solely in terms of its original acquisition, for the argument has to do with what can determine the permissibility of the *choice* of a belief. But it is often noted by epistemologists that the epistemic status of a belief may change after its acquisition, as the subject comes to acquire or lose support for it. Suppose that after coming to believe that Susie is quitting her job, on the basis of no evidence worthy of the name and hence unjustifiably, I come into possession of adequate evidence for this supposition; let us further suppose that this new evidence now functions as the basis for my belief. In this case my belief comes to be justified *after* its acquisition. Thus a concept of justifiably *acquired* belief is at best only a part of an adequate concept of justified belief.

To be sure, it is not difficult to modify this very restrictive concept, so as to make it more generally applicable. Let's begin by showing how the direct voluntary control assumption can be dropped. It is uncontroversial that our beliefs are under *indirect* voluntary control, or at least subject to influence from our voluntary actions. Even if I can't effectively decide at this moment to stop believing that Reagan is inept, I could embark on a regimen that is designed to improve my assessment of Reagan, and it might even succeed in time. With this possibility of indirect influence in mind, we can reconstrue "intellectual obligations" so that they no longer attach to believings and abstentions therefrom, but to actions that are designed to influence our believings and abstentions. Reinterpreted in this way the argument would be that whether we are justified in believing that p at t would depend on whether prior to t we had done what could reasonably be expected of us to influence that belief. The difference between these two understandings may be illustrated as follows. Suppose that my belief that there is life outside our solar system is inadequately supported by the totality of my justified beliefs. On the direct voluntary control interpretation I have an effective choice, whenever I consider the matter, as to whether to keep believing that or not. It is my duty to refrain from believing it since it is not adequately supported by my "perspective"; since I continue to believe it in defiance of my duty, I am doing something that is not permitted; my belief is not justified. But the matter sorts out differently on the "indirect voluntary control" construal. It is recognized that I lack the capacity to discard that belief at will; at most I have the ability to make various moves that increase the chances of the belief's being abandoned. Hence so long as I am doing as much along that line as could reasonably be expected of me, I can't be faulted for continuing to have the belief; and so it is justified. On either of these interpretations, whether my belief is justified is a function of how things appear in my perspective rather than of how they are in actual fact. So long as life outside the solar system is improbable relative to what I am justified in believing, then my belief is unjustified unless (on the indirect control version) my best efforts have failed to dislodge it.

Next consider how we can lift the other restrictions. We can confine this discussion to the direct control version, since on the indirect control version there was no reason to impose them in the first place. Let's first take the restriction to explicitly chosen beliefs. On the direct control version we can say that the belief is justified provided that it was acquired on such a basis that if the agent had chosen to adopt the belief on that basis he could not have been blamed for doing so. In other words, where the belief, or its furtherance, was not explicitly chosen we can evaluate it, on the deontological conception, by considering whether its basis is such that if it or its furtherance was chosen on that basis the agent would have been in the clear in so choosing.

Now let's see how to lift the restriction to the original acquisition of the belief, and extend the concept to the evaluation of one's continuing to believe that p at times after its original acquisition. Once again the crucial move is to consider what would be the case if we were to make a choice that we did not in fact make. For one thing, we can consider what the judgment would be on my coming to believe this if the belief were voluntarily adopted on the basis of this evidence I possess at present (and analogously for the indirect control version). Or, closer to home, we could consider the possibility that I should now explicitly raise the question of whether to retain the belief, in the light of the evidence I now possess, and should come to a decision to retain it. In that case would I be in the clear in making that decision? If so, I am now justified in retaining the belief.

It is time to take our bearings with respect to these increasingly proliferating variations in a deontological concept of justification. To keep complexity within manageable bounds, I shall formulate a version that is designed to take care both of habitually formed beliefs and post-acquisition influences on justification. I shall formulate this both in a direct control and an indirect control version.

(8) Direct control version. One is justified in believing that p at t if and only if either (a) in choosing at t to adopt or retain the belief that p one was not violating any intellectual obligations, or (b) one's belief

that p at t has such a basis that if one were to decide, in the light of that basis, to retain one's belief that p, one would not be violating any intellectual obligations in so doing.

(9) Indirect control version. One is·justified in believing that p at t if and only if one's believing that p at t does not stem from any violations of intellectual obligations.

Thus it is not difficult to concoct distinctively deontological conceptions of justification that avoid the severe limitations of the concept employed by the argument for PI. But what sort of argument for PI can be constructed on the basis of these alternative conceptions?

The first point is that no case at all can be made for PI on the basis of the indirect control version. According to (9), justification is a function of certain features of the causal history of the belief. Was that history such that if the subject had lived up to her intellectual obligations in the past then she would not have believed that p? This is not a "perspectival" matter. The justified beliefs of the subject do not play any crucial role in determining whether or not that condition was satisfied. It is matter of what actually went on, rather than a matter of how what went on is represented in the subject's viewpoint. Thus (9) supports an externalist position on justification; at least it supports the externalist contrast to PI. Of course we could try to "perspectivize" (9). Any condition for anything that is in terms of what the facts actually are can receive a "perspectival" modification, transforming it into a condition that the facts be represented in a certain way in the subject's perspective. So modified, (9) would become:

(10) S is justified in believing that p if and only if S's belief that p did not, so far as S can tell, stem from S's violations of intellectual obligations.

But (10) is wildly permissive. We rarely have reason to think that one of our beliefs stems from intellectual transgressions. To know about the causal history of beliefs takes research, and we rarely engage in such research. Hence we have very few beliefs about the causal history of our beliefs. And so practically all beliefs, no matter how shoddy or disreputable, will be justified on this criterion. The prospects for support for PI from an indirect control version of a deontological conception are vanishingly small.

Things do not look much rosier from the perspective of (8). According to (8) a belief can be justified on the basis of anything whatsoever, not just other justified beliefs of the subject, provided that one would be in the clear, vis-à-vis one's intellectual obligations, if one were to consider whether to retain the belief in the light of that basis. If one were to engage in such a consideration, one would, of course, be choosing to retain the belief on the basis of other justified beliefs, in particular the belief that that basis obtains. That is the situation envisaged by the restrictive concept employed in the original argument for PI. But the extended concept differs from that precisely by not making the actual obtaining of such a situation necessary for justification. It recognizes that a belief can be justified even if one never does make any decision with respect to it on the basis of what one justifiably believes about its basis. Hence on this modified deontological concept a belief could be justified by being based on some experience, even if the subject in fact has no beliefs about that experience. What is supported by (8) is a denial rather than an affirmation of the PI constraint.

Thus it appears that we have a significant argument for PI only if we utilize a concept of justification that cannot be seriously defended as generally applicable, a concept according to which the justification of beliefs is solely a matter of whether a belief is *chosen* in such a way that this choice does not involve any dereliction of intellectual duty. But we cannot seriously suppose that justified beliefs are restricted to those that are *chosen* in that way, even if some are. Insofar as we are working with an even minimally defensible concept of justification, the argument for PI dissipates.

When we consider the higher level requirement embodied in (7), things look even worse. (7) implies that I will be justified in believing that p on the basis of my justified belief that q only if I am justified in supposing that the latter belief provides adequate support for the former. One reason this darkens the prospects for PI is that it is doubtful that we satisfy that condition very often. Just how often it is satisfied depends on what it takes to be justified in beliefs like that, and that is not at all clear. One thing that is clear for the PI advocate, however, is that to be justified such a belief will have to be mediately justified, since that is the only kind of justification PI recognizes. We will have to have sufficient reasons for supposing that *the belief that q adequately supports the belief that p* if we are to be justified in that higher level belief. How often do we have such reasons? Not very often, I would suggest. Perhaps the following will suffice to indicate the difficulties. Consider perceptual beliefs. If my perceptual belief that it is raining outside is to be mediately justified, this will presumably be on the basis of a justified belief that I am having certain visual experiences, plus perhaps (depending on the requirements we adopt) justified beliefs about the normality of the situation.[30] Now to have adequate reasons for supposing that reasons like that are sufficient support for a perceptual belief about one's environment is to be in the position that many great philosophers have labored to get themselves into when they have wrestled with the problem of how to infer facts about the external world from facts about the sensory experiences of the individual percipient. And even if some philosophers have solved that problem, which I am strongly inclined to deny, it is quite clear that the overwhelming majority of the population is not in possession of any such solution. For a second illustration, consider the point that in order for some non-deductive evidence to be adequate support for a given belief (so that this latter belief is justifiably held), there must be no other justified beliefs of mine that serve to defeat the prima facie support provided by the first-mentioned evidence. Suppose that my reason for supposing that Ray will be in his office today is that today is Wednesday and Ray has a fixed disposition to work in his office on Wednesdays. I have temporarily forgotten, however, that Ray told me last week that he will be out of town on Wednesday of this week. When that justified belief of mine is added to the picture, the total evidence no longer adequately supports the supposition that Ray will be in his office today. This means that I can be justified in supposing that my belief that q renders my belief that p justified only if I am justified in supposing that there is nothing else I am justified in believing such that when that is added to q the conjunction does not adequately support p. And it is difficult to be justified in any claim concerning what is or is not present in the totality of one's justified beliefs.

Thus it is dubious that the higher level requirement of PI is very widely satisfied. If that is required for justification, not many people are justified in many beliefs. But there is an even more serious difficulty with the requirement. It engenders an infinite regress. If in order to be justified in believing that p, I must be justified in believing that my reason, q, adequately supports p, the justification of this later belief requires the justification of a still higher level belief. That is, if r is my reason for supposing that q adequately supports p, I can be justified in supposing that q adequately supports p only if I am justified in supposing that r adequately supports **q adequately supports p.** And my justification for this last belief includes my being justified in a still higher level belief about adequate support. Given PI, I cannot be justified in

---

[30]If this latter sort of reason is required, that constitutes a serious stumbling block, for it seems that we are rarely justified in any such belief, unless the requirements for justification are set very low. But that is not our present concern.

any belief without simultaneously being justified in all the members of an infinite hierarchy of beliefs of ever-ascending level.

Let's make sure we fully appreciate the character of this difficulty. The view that all justification is mediate itself gives rise to a much more widely advertised regress, this one stemming from the lower level requirement that a given belief can be justified only by its relation to another justified belief. The same is true of the justification of this supporting belief; that is to say, it can be justified only by its relation to still another justified belief; and so on ad infinitum. The standard coherentist response to this difficulty is to opt for a circle of justification, rather than an infinite regress, and then to switch from local to holistic justification. I find this response quite inadequate, but this is not the place to go into that. Instead I want to stress the difference in the difficulty entailed by the higher level regress. The preference for a circle over an infinite set is of no avail here. Since there is a regress of *levels,* we are foreclosed from doubling back. No adequate-support belief at an earlier stage will serve to do the job required at a later stage because it will have the wrong content. At each stage what is required is a justified belief to the effect that the "reason for" relationship *at the immediately previous stage* is an adequate one; and no earlier beliefs of that sort in the hierarchy will have been concerned with that particular "reason for" relationship. Hence there is no alternative here to an infinite regress. And, needless to say, it is highly doubtful that any of us is in possession of such an infinite hierarchy of "adequate support" beliefs.

III

PI has not emerged in strong shape from our examination. Let's turn now to the second construal of an internalist constraint on justification, and see if it fares any better. This second construal has to do with the kind of access we can have to justifiers. The general idea is that possible justifiers are restricted to items to which we have a specially favored access. This special access is variously specified as direct, incorrigible, and obtainable just by reflecting. We have already seen Goldman, in "The Internalist Conception of Justification," identifying internalism with PI. Here is an formulation of the second construal from the same essay.

The basic idea of internalism is that there should be guaranteed epistemic access to the correctness of a DDP. No condition of DDP-rightness is acceptable unless we have epistemic access to the DDP that in fact satisfies the condition, i.e., unless we can tell which DDP satisfies it. The internalist's objection to externalism's condition of rightness, i.e., actual optimality, is precisely that cognizers may have no way of telling which DDP satisfies it. Internalism's *own* condition of rightness must, therefore, be such that any cognizer *can tell* which DDP satisfies it.[31]

Another person we cited as a source of PI, Kent Bach, also brings the second version into the picture in "A Rationale for Reliabilism."

> Internalism . . . treats justifiedness as a purely internal matter: if p is justified for S, then S must be aware (or at least be immediately capable of being aware) of what makes it justified and why.[32]

I have found, however, the most elaborate developments of this conception in epistemologists who do not actually employ the "internalism" label. Thus, R. M. Chisholm, in a well-known passage, lays it down that whenever we are justified in a belief, we can determine by reflection what it is that so justifies us.

> We presuppose, second, that the things we know are justified for us in the following sense: *we* can know what it is, on any occasion, that constitutes our grounds, or reason, or evidence for thinking that we know.
> In beginning with what we think we know to be true, or with what, after reflection, we would be willing to count as being evident, we are assuming that the truth we are seeking is "already implicit in the mind which seeks it, and needs only to be elicited and brought to clear reflection".[33]

[31] P. 35. Remember that a DDP is, roughly, a principle that declares certain beliefs to be justified under certain conditions. Therefore the requirement that there be maximal epistemic access to a DDP is an accessibility analogue of what we were calling the "higher level requirement" component of PI. Interestingly enough, when it comes to a high accessibility "lower level requirement" with respect to justifiers, "input to the DDP" in Goldman's lingo, Goldman lays this down on his own, with no hint that it is required by internalism as contrasted with externalism. "If a DDP is to be actually *usable* for making deliberate decisions the conditions that serve as inputs must be *accessible* or *available* to the decision-maker at the time of decision. The agent must be *able to tell*, with respect to any possible input condition, whether that condition holds at the time in question" (p. 30). He even spells this out in such a way that it is *infallible* access that is required. "But what exactly do we mean in saying that a person 'can tell' with respect to a given condition whether or not that condition obtains? Here is a reasonable answer: 'For any person S and time t, if S asks himself at t whether condition C obtains at the time in question, then S will believe that condition C obtains then if and only if it does obtain then" (p. 31).

[32] P. 250. Cf. p. 252.

[33] *Theory of Knowledge*, p. 17. The quotation is from C. I. Lewis, *Mind and the World Order*. It should be acknowledged that in a later essay Chisholm states this assumption only for "some of the things I am justified in believing". See "A Version of Foundationalism," *Midwest Studies in Philosophy*, 5 (1980), 546.

Carl Ginet gives a more elaborate statement of this version of internalism.

> Every one of every set of facts about S's position that minimally suffices to make S, at a given time, justified in being confident that p must be *directly recognizable* to S at that time. By 'directly recognizable' I mean this: if a certain fact obtains, then it is directly recognizable to S at a given time if and only if, provided that S at that time has the concept of that sort of fact, S needs at that time only to reflect clear-headedly on the question of whether or not that fact obtains in order to know that it does.[34]

In the interest of securing a definite target let's focus on the version of special access internalism that requires *direct* access for justifiers, construed along Ginet's lines. I shall refer to this second construal of internalism as "access internalism" (hereinafter 'AI').

Our next order of business should be to consider the relation between the two internalisms. Now that we have completed the laborious process of explicating and refining our conception of PI, we are at last in a position to do this. Are the two conceptions importantly different? Just how are they related? Can one be subsumed under the other? Does one imply the other?

First let's consider the possibility that PI is a special case of AI. Is the restriction of justifiers to the subject's viewpoint a special case of a restriction of justifiers to what is directly accessible? Only if one's own perspective is directly accessible, and this does not seem to be the case. The sum total of my justified beliefs cannot be depended on to spread themselves before my eyes on demand, not even that segment thereof that is relevant to a particular belief under consideration. I may know something that provides crucial evidence for *p* and yet fail to realize this even on careful reflection. We need not invoke Freudian blockages to illustrate this, though they are relevant. It may be that the sheer volume of what I know about, for example, ancient Greek philosophy, is too great for my powers of ready retrieval; or some of this material may be so deeply buried as to require special trains of association to dislodge it. We are all familiar with cases in which something we knew all along failed to put in an appearance when it was needed to advance a particular inquiry. And, remembering our last modification of PI, still less is it the case that *what I would be justified in believing had I been behaving as I ought* is readily available on reflection.

Thus an item may pass the PI test without passing the AI test. PI is not a special case of AI. How about the converse? Is the restriction to

---

[34]*Knowledge, Perception, and Memory*, p. 34.

the directly accessible just a special case of the restriction to the subject's justified beliefs and knowledge? Only if nothing other than my knowledge and justified beliefs is directly accessible to me. But that is clearly not the case. My feelings and other conscious experiences are directly accessible if anything is. And even if it were true, as I see no reason to suppose it to be, that I cannot have a conscious experience without knowing that I do, still the experience is distinguishable from the knowledge of the experience. Hence an item can pass the AI test without passing the PI test. This is what makes it possible for partisans of AI like Chisholm and Ginet to recognize immediate justification and to escape coherentism.

Thus PI and AI look quite independent of one another. But surely they must be closely related in some way. Otherwise how can we understand the fact that they are so persistently lumped together under the "internalism" label? And in fact on closer inspection we can see an interesting connection. We can think of AI as a broadening of PI. Whereas PI restricts justifiers to what the subject already justifiably believes (or, in the modified version, to that plus some of what the subject would justifiably believe under ideal conditions), AI enlarges that to include what the subject *can* come to know just on reflection. It is clear that any item that passes the AI test is something that is readily assimilable into the subject's viewpoint, just on reflection. AI, we might say, enlarges the conception of the subject's perspective to include not only what does in fact occur in that perspective (and what should occur), but also what *could* be there if the subject were to turn his attention to it.

Next let's turn to what can be said in support of AI. We have seen that PI is most plausibly supported on a deontological conception of justification, and the AI constraint has also been defended on that conception. Here we are fortunate to have an explicit statement of the argument from Carl Ginet.

> Assuming that S has the concept of justification for being confident that p, S *ought* always to possess or lack confidence that p according to whether or not he has such justification. At least he ought always to withhold confidence unless he has justification. This is simply what is meant by having or lacking *justification*. But if this is what S ought to do in any possible circumstance, then it is what S *can* do in any possible circumstance. That is, assuming that he has the relevant concepts, S can always tell whether or not he has justification for being confident that p. But this would not be so unless the difference between having such justification and not having it were always directly recognizable to S. And that would not be so if any fact contributing to a set that minimally constitutes S's

having such justification were not either directly recognizable to S or entailed by something directly recognizable to S (so that its absence would have to make a directly recognizable difference). For suppose it were otherwise: suppose that some part of a condition minimally sufficient for S's being justified in being confident that p were *not* entailed by anything directly recognizable to S. Then S's position could change from having such justification to lacking it without there being any change at all in what is directly recognizable to S. But if there is no change in directly recognizable features of S's position, S cannot tell that his position has changed in other respects: no matter how clearheadedly and attentively he considers his position he will detect no change. If it seemed to S before that he had justification for being confident that p then it must still seem so to him. So this sort of justification would be such that it would not always be possible for its subject to tell whether or not he possessed it, which is contrary to what we noted is an obvious essential feature of justification. So there can be no such justification. That is, there can be no set of facts giving S justification for being confident that p that has an essential part that is neither directly recognizable to S nor entailed by something directly recognizable to S.[35]

Note that the conclusion of this argument is not quite the same as the AI thesis I previously quoted from Ginet. According to that thesis, every part of a justifier must be directly recognizable; but the argument purports to show only that a justifier must be either this or *entailed* by what is directly recognizable. Ginet may feel that the additional disjunct makes no significant difference, but this is not the case. One may not be able to spot everything that is entailed by what is directly recognizable; the disjunctive conclusion leaves open the possibility of justifiers that are not wholly identifiable from what is directly recognizable. I shall, however, suppress this difficulty in the ensuing discussion. For the sake of simplicity I shall consider the thesis in the simpler form, bringing in the second disjunct only where it is specially relevant to the point under consideration.

I have said that Ginet argues from a deontological conception of justification, but this may not be obvious from his formulation of the argument. I shall try to make it more obvious. But first let's note that Ginet explicitly lays out such a conception.

One is *justified* in being confident that p if and only if it is not the case that one ought not to be confident that p: one could not be justly reproached for being confident that p.[36]

[35]Ibid., p. 36.
[36]Ibid., p. 28.

This concept does not explicitly appear in the argument, but it is just below the surface. Ginet uses this concept to define the concept of *having a justification* that he employs in the argument.

> I shall take 'S has justification for being confident that p' . . . to mean S is in a position such that if he is, or were to be, confident that p then he is, or would be, justified in being so.[37]

We then get 'is justified in being confident that *p*' defined deontologically, as in the previous quotation. Thus the concept used in the argument is, so to say, the first derivative of a deontological conception. It is the concept of having what it takes to be justified in the deontological sense if one will only make use of those resources.

Before entering onto a critical scrutiny of the argument, let's note some of its features, with special attention to the points we were making concerning the argument for PI. First, the argument should, by rights, apply to overriders of prima facie justification as well as to justifiers. Consider that done. Second, Ginet is obviously presupposing direct voluntary control of belief. Since "in any possible circumstance", "S *ought* always to possess or lack confidence that p according to whether or not he has such justification", this is something that "S *can* do in any possible circumstance". It is always possible for S to stop and consider any actual belief of his, or any candidate for belief, and bring it about then and there that he does or does not adopt or continue to hold the belief according as he has or lacks sufficient justification for it.[38] It is not so clear whether Ginet's concept of justification applies only to beliefs that are acquired by a deliberate choice, and then only in terms of what is true at the moment of acquisition. Let's suppose that he is only assuming the ever-present possibility of a deliberate choice between adopting (continuing) a belief and refraining from doing so, and that to be justified in believing that *p* is to be so situated that if one were, in that situation, to choose to believe that *p* (or continue to do so), one could not be blamed, on intellectual grounds, for that choice.

It will help us to critically evaluate Ginet's argument if we exhibit its skeleton.

[37]Ibid., p. 28.
[38]In "Contra Reliabilism," *The Monist*, 68 (April 1985), Ginet defends this assumption against objections from me. Note that Ginet's argument could easily be recast in an "indirect voluntary control" form. Instead of premising that it is always possible to decide whether or not to believe, or to continue believing, that *p* in the light of the presence or absence of a sufficient justification, one can hold instead that it is always possible to decide whether to do various things to encourage or discourage belief that *p*, in the light of the presence or absence of a sufficient justification. The direct recognizability of justifiers will be as strongly supported by this version as by the original version.

(1) S ought to withhold belief that p if he lacks justification for p.[39]
(2) What S ought to do S can do.
(3) Therefore, S can withhold belief wherever S lacks justification.
(4) S has this capacity only if S can tell, with respect to any proposed belief, whether or not S has justification for it.
(5) S can always tell us this only if justification is always directly recognizable.
(6) Therefore justification is always directly recognizable.

This bare bones rendition should make it apparent where the argument goes astray. It is at step (5). (5) claims that S can tell whether he has justification for a belief only if it is directly recognizable by him whether he does or not. But why should we suppose this? Ginet, in company with almost all contemporary epistemologists, wisely avoids holding that one can know only what is evident to one on simple reflection and what is entailed by that. We know many things only because we have reasons for them in the shape of other things we know, and these reasons are not always deductively related to what they support. Thus direct recognition is only one way to acquire knowledge. Why should we suppose that only this way is available for knowing about justification? That would have to be argued. In the absence of any such argument we are at liberty to deny that justification can always be spotted just by reflection. The argument leaves standing the possibility that S might, in various instances, come to know in some other way whether he has a justification for p.

Consider the ethical analogy that is inevitably suggested by Ginet's argument. There is an exactly parallel argument for the thesis that the justification of actions is always directly recognizable. But that is clearly false. Often I have to engage in considerable research to determine whether a proposed action is justified. If it is a question of whether I would be justified in making a certain decision as department chairman without consulting the executive committee or the department as a whole, I cannot ascertain this just by reflection, unless I have thor-

[39]Ginet recognizes that we are intellectually obligated to refrain from believing that p in the absence of justification, but he wisely holds back from claiming that we are obligated to believe that p wherever we have a justification. The presence of justification gives me a *right* to believe, but I am not obliged to exercise that right; I have a choice as to whether or not to do so. It seems plausible to hold, e.g., that I am justified in believing everything that is entailed by my justified beliefs. But an infinite set of beliefs is so entailed. Thus if I were obligated to believe everything for which I have a justification, I would be in a pretty pickle. Ginet's recognition of this point is evinced by his modifying "S *ought* always to possess or lack confidence that p according to whether or not he has such justification" to "At least he ought always to withhold confidence unless he has justification".

oughly internalized the relevant rules, regulations, by-laws, and so on. Most likely I will have to do some research. Would I be legally justified in deducting the cost of a computer on my income tax return? I had better look up the IRS regulations and not just engage in careful reflection. The situation is similar with respect to more strictly moral justification. Would I be morally justified in resigning my professorship as late as April 12 in order to accept a position elsewhere for the following fall? This depends, inter alia, on how much inconvenience this would cause my present department, what faculty resources there are already on hand for taking up the slack, how likely it is that a suitable temporary replacement could be secured for the coming fall, and so on. There is no guarantee that all these matters are available to me just on simple reflection. Why should we suppose, without being given reasons to do so, that the justification of beliefs is different in this respect?

Let's remember that in the argument we quoted Ginet supported his position by a *reductio* that runs as follows.

(1) Suppose that some part of a justification were not entailed by what is directly recognizable to S.
(2) Then S's position could change from having such justification to lacking it without there being any change in what is directly recognizable to S.
(3) But then S cannot tell that his position vis-à-vis justification has changed.
(4) Therefore if S can always tell what his justificatory situation is, no part of a justification can fail to be directly recognizable.

This argument, in step (3), presupposes a strong foundationalism according to which any knowledge I can have is based on what is directly recognizable to me, and this could well be contested. But even if we go along with this, the argument is unsound. The trouble is in (2), in the assumption that *anything* not entailed by the directly recognizable can change with no change in what is directly recognizable. To assume this is to assume that the nondirectly recognizable is effectively reflected in what is directly recognizable only if the former is entailed by the latter. For if there are other modes of reflection, then a change in the former will sometimes be mirrored in a change in the latter, even when the former is not *entailed* by the latter. For convenience of exposition, let's lump together everything that is not entailed by anything directly recognizable by me as "the world". It is certainly the better part of reason to recognize that much of the world is not adequately reflected in what *I* can directly recognize; if that were not the case, I would be in an immeasurably stronger epistemic position than is the lot of humanity. But to suppose that the world beyond my direct recognition *never* reveals itself in what I can directly recognize would be subversive of the very type of foundationalism this argument presupposes. For in that case the foundations would ground no knowledge of anything beyond themselves except by way of logical deduction. And I am sure that Ginet does not want that. If then a change in "the world" is sometimes reflected in changes in the directly recognizable, why suppose that this is not the case with respect to justification?

Put the matter another way. All that Ginet can extract from his strong foundationalist assumption, his deontological concept of justification, and the "ought implies can" principle, is that it is always possible to determine *from* what is directly recognizable to the subject whether the subject is justified in a certain belief. But that does *not* imply that what does the justifying is itself directly recognizable, or is entailed by what is directly recognizable. It only implies that either it has this status *or* it can be ascertained on the basis of what is directly recognizable.[40]

However, Ginet's argument can easily be transformed into an argument for a more moderate form of AI. To begin with the other extreme, suppose we formulate AI just as the view that to be a justifier an item must be epistemically accessible in some way to the subject. It is not *impossible* for the subject to acquire that bit of knowledge (or justified belief). It does seem that Ginet's argument would establish that much accessibility, granted his premises. If I ought to do something that requires knowing the answer to a certain question, it must be *possible* for me to get that answer.

But what is the significance of this result? What does this constraint exclude? It excludes factors that are in principle unknowable by human beings; but it is dubious that any of the parties to the discussion are disposed to suggest justifiers that satisfy that description. The putative justifiers that internalists typically wish to exclude are items other than beliefs and experiences of the subject. Bonjour's clairvoyant subject in "Externalist Theories of Empirical Knowledge" is representative of the disputed territory. This person in fact has clairvoyant powers but has neither any understanding of what is going on nor any good reasons for supposing that these powers are reliable. So far as he can tell, the beliefs simply occur to him, and he is, strangely enough, irresistibly constrained to accept them. What shall we fasten on as the

---

[40]We could also attack the direct accessibility form of AI by pointing to the fact that not all commonly recognized justifiers satisfy the constraint. Remember that when we were considering the relations of PI and AI we pointed out that one cannot, in general, retrieve all relevant justified beliefs of oneself just on reflection.

strongest candidate for a justifier here? There are no beliefs or experiences on which the clairvoyant beliefs are based. Let's say that if anything justifies them, it is their resulting from the exercise of reliable clairvoyant powers. The subject knows nothing of such powers. But is it *impossible* that he should discover them and discover that they are reliable? I see no reason to suppose that. He might ascertain this just by discovering that these strange beliefs about distant places that apparently just popped into his mind out of nowhere are invariably true. It appears, then, that the requirement of being knowable somehow is too weak to be of much interest.

Perhaps there is a mean between the extremes that is both of some significance and still not too strong to be supportable. We might try requiring knowability, not just on reflection at the moment, but at least without a great deal of research. Admittedly this is quite vague. The vagueness may be reduced by bringing in the notion of what could reasonably be expected in the way of time and effort devoted to searching out the justifiers. These expectations might differ from case to case, depending on the kind of justifiers that would be required, the capacities and initial position of the subjects, and so on. If a belief is based on experience, we would naturally expect the subject to ascertain that right off the bat. If, on the other hand, a belief is based on a large and complex body of evidence, we would not expect the subject to be able to survey all that in a moment. And so on. We might dub this intermediate conception "reasonably immediate accessibility".[41] Although this may seem a more reasonable requirement than Ginet's, and although it obviously is less restrictive, this increase in modesty has not purchased any greater support by Ginet's line of argument. I can't see that an "ought implies can" principle supports a "reasonably immediate accessibility" any more than it supports a direct recognizability. In the absence of further reasons to the contrary, all that would seem to be required by the principle is knowability in some way or other.

Now let's turn to the question of a higher level extension of AI. It is clear that the AI constraint, like the PI constraint, can be imposed on various levels. We saw that the basic argument for PI equally supported the first and second level constraints. It supported both the claim that a justifier had to be a justified belief, and the claim that one justified belief can justify another only if the subject is justified in the higher

---

[41]Note that all these accessibility requirements, of whatever degree of stringency, can be thought of as related to PI in the same way. Any item that is epistemically accessible to S can be thought of as potentially an item in S's perspective on the world. Hence any sort of AI can be thought of as a broadening of PI to include potential additions to the perspective, as well as its present constituents.

level belief that the first belief does adequately support the second. What about the argument for AI? Ginet does not use his argument to support a higher level extension. As noted earlier, he does impose a higher level PI constraint on mediate justification, but he associates no higher level constraint of any kind with his AI position. He takes AI to require only that *justifiers* be directly recognizable, not that it be directly recognizable that they possess justificatory efficacy. And yet his argument supports a higher level AI requirement just as strongly, or weakly, as the lower level requirement. This can be seen as follows. Suppose that the sorts of things that can count as justifiers are always accessible to me, but that it is not always accessible to me which items of these sorts count as justifications for which beliefs. I have access to the justifiers but not to their justificatory efficacy. This will take away my ability to do what I am said to have an obligation to do just as surely as the lack of access to the justifiers themselves. To illustrate, let's suppose that experiences can function as justifiers, and that they are accessible to us. I can always tell what sensory experiences I am having at a given moment. Even so, if I am unable to tell what belief about the current physical environment is justified by a given sensory experience, I am thereby unable to regulate my perceptual beliefs according as they possess or lack experiential justification. Knowing what the facts are doesn't suffice for enabling me to regulate my behavior accordingly; I also have to know the significance of these facts for what I ought to do. Thus the "ought implies can" argument supports the higher level requirement to just the extent to which it supports the lower level requirement.

Thus AI, too, has higher level troubles. The trouble is not nearly as severe as its PI analogue. For one thing, what is required here is not actual higher level knowledge (justified belief) about justification, but only the capacity to obtain it. Thus we are not required to attribute to all subjects an absurdly inflated body of actual knowledge about the conditions of justification. Second, for the same reason we are not faced with nasty infinite regresses or hierarchies. Since to be justified in believing that *p*, S need not actually justifiably believe that the alleged justifier is fitted to do its job, but only be capable of ascertaining this, we are not committed to an actual infinite hierarchy of such justified beliefs. Nevertheless there are serious questions as to whether even a modest AI higher level requirement is not too severe. The requirement implies that a state of affairs, A, cannot justify me in believing that *p* unless I am capable of determining that A is a genuine justification for a belief that *p*. But how many subjects are capable of this? Indeed, there are substantial grounds for skepticism about the possibility of anyone's having adequate reasons for claims about justification. The grounds I have in mind concern the specter of epistemic circularity, the danger that, for instance, any otherwise promising argument for a principle laying down conditions under which perceptual beliefs are justified will have to use perceptual beliefs among its premises. I have considered this problem elsewhere and have concluded that, despite the pervasive presence of epistemic circularity in such arguments, it is possible to be justified in beliefs about the conditions of justification.[42] But even if that rather optimistic conclusion is justified, it still seems that many subjects are not capable of acquiring adequately justified beliefs concerning what justifies what. To go into this properly we would have to decide what it takes for the justification of such beliefs, and there is no time for this lengthy investigation in this paper. Let me just say that it seems eminently plausible that beliefs about what justifies what would have to be justified by reasons (not directly justified), and it would seem that such reasons are directly accessible to few if any of us.

All this suggests limiting AI to the lower level. Something can function as a justifier only if it is (fairly readily) accessible, but in order to function as a justifier it is not necessary that its justificatory efficacy be likewise accessible. At some point we must rely on things just *being* a certain way, without its also being the case that we do or can assure ourselves that they are that way. And this would seem to be the proper place to draw that line. We shall return to this possibility in the last section. For now, let's sharpen the issue by recalling the fact that a reliability account of justification (S is justified in believing that *p* if and only if S's belief that *p* was reliably produced) is often attacked on the grounds that justification could not be lost by a loss of reliability, so long as the situation is the same, *so far as we can tell*. Consider a possible world that is indistinguishable from the actual world so far as we can tell, but in which a Cartesian demon has rigged things so that our perceptual beliefs concerning external physical objects are all false, since there are no such objects. Since such a world is indistinguishable (by us) from our world, we would have just as much justification for our perceptual beliefs there as we actually do. But *ex hypothesi* those beliefs would not be reliably formed. Hence reliability is not necessary for justification. Here are some snatches of such an argument from an essay by Richard Foley. (The demon world is called 'w'.)

> If we are willing to grant that in our world some of the propositions S perceptually believes are epistemically rational, then these same proposi-

tions would be epistemically rational for S in w as well. After all, world w by hypothesis is one which from S's viewpoint is indistinguishable from this world. So, if given S's situation in this world his perceptual belief p is rational, his belief p would be rational in w as well.

Even if, contrary to what we believe, our world is world w, it still can be epistemically rational for us to believe many of the propositions we do, since the epistemic situation in world w is indistinguishable from the epistemic situation in a world which has the characteristics we take our world to have. The point here is a simple one. In effect, I am asking you: aren't some of the propositions you believe epistemically rational for you to believe? And wouldn't whatever it is that make those propositions epistemically rational for you also be present in a world where these propositions are regularly false, but where a demon hid this from you by making the world from your viewpoint indistinguishable from this world (so that what you believed, and what you would believe on reflection, and what you seemed to remember, and what you experienced were identical to this world)?[43]

In each of these passages the fact that we cannot distinguish w from the actual world is taken to imply that whatever justifies a certain belief in the one world will ipso facto justify that same belief in the other world. This argument presupposes an AI internalist constraint on both levels. For suppose AI put constraints only on what can count as a justifier, not also on what has justificatory efficacy for which beliefs. In that case the reliabilist would remain free to claim that although the same putative justifiers (of perceptual beliefs) are present in the two worlds, they do justify perceptual beliefs in the actual world but not in w, since their production of perceptual beliefs is reliable in the actual world but not in w. If and only if justificatory efficacy were subject to an AI constraint would this be impossible, as Foley claims. If, on the other hand, one follows my suggestion that we adopt an accessibility constraint only on the lower level, we can recognize that a state of affairs, A, can justify a belief that p in one possible world and not in another, even though we can't tell any difference between the two worlds.

IV

The upshot of the essay is that existing forms of internalism are in serious trouble. Both PI and AI run into severe difficulties over their higher level component, but if we try shearing off that component we

[43]Richard Foley, "What's Wrong with Reliabilism?", *The Monist*, 68 (April 1985). See also Carl Ginet, "Contra Reliabilism," ibid.

lose such support as has been provided them. That support is less than impressive in any case. The only arguments of any substance that have been advanced proceed from a deontological conception of justification and inherit any disabilities that attach to that conception. Indeed, PI gains significant support only from the most restrictive form of a direct voluntary control version of that conception, one that is, at best, of limited application to our beliefs. As for AI, the arguments in the literature that are designed to establish a direct recognizability version markedly fail to do so. And it is not clear that a more moderate form of AI can be developed that will be both well supported by these arguments and strong enough to have any cutting edge.

Thus internalism has not emerged in strong shape from this examination. It looks as if no sort of internalist constraint can be justified, and hence that an unrestricted externalism wins the day. I do not believe, however, that so extreme a conclusion is warranted. I am convinced that the considerations advanced in this essay show that existing versions of internalism are untenable, and that such arguments as have been advanced for them fail to establish any form of that position. And yet I am inclined to suppose that a suitably modest form of AI internalism can be supported, though in a very different way from any employed by the internalists we have been discussing. If any readers have persevered this far, I will not further test their patience by embarking on a full dress development and defense of this suggestion, but I will just indicate what I have in mind.

Earlier I indicated that what I called a strong position (SP) conception of justification does not support any sort of internalist restriction. One can believe that *p* in such a way as to be in a strong position to acquire the truth whether or not that belief is supported adequately by other of one's justified beliefs (PI), and whether or not one has strong epistemic access to the grounds for the belief. In my "Concepts of Epistemic Justification" I have argued for the superiority of the SP conception over any kind of deontological conception. Thus, so far as these options for a concept of justification are concerned, pure externalism reigns supreme. Nevertheless I do not take this to be the last word. Even if internalist intuitions cannot be supported by the most basic features of the concept of justification, they may have a certain validity on their own, as an independent contribution to the concept. Let's once more consider "out of the blue" reliable modes of belief formation. Let's say that when I am suddenly seized with apparently irrational convictions concerning the current weather in some distant spot, these convictions always turn out to be correct. If there is nothing to justification other than believing in such a way as to be in a strong position to acquire the truth, then we should say that I am justified in those convictions. And yet we are loath to admit this, at least before I become aware of the reliability of this mode of belief formation. (After I become aware of this, I have an adequate reason for the convictions, and this should satisfy any internalist scruples.) Why this reluctance? What is missing? What is missing, of course, is any basis or ground that S *has, possesses,* for his belief, anything that he can point to or specify as that which gives him *something to go on* in believing this, any *sign* or *indication* he has that the belief is true. Wherever nothing like this is involved, we feel uneasy in taking S's belief to be *justified.* Thus it looks as if there is a basic, irreducible, requirement of *epistemic accessibility of ground for the belief* that attaches to our concept of epistemic justification.[44] For reasons we have rehearsed at some length, let's take the accessibility required to be of the relatively modest sort that we earlier called "reasonably immediate accessibility".

Can this requirement be derived from other features of the concept? It certainly cannot be derived from an SP conception, and we have seen that such support as it gleans from a deontological conception would bring fatal difficulties with it, even if such a conception were viable for epistemology. I am inclined to think that the requirement is a fundamental constituent of our concept of epistemic justification, though I do not take that to imply that there can be no sort of explanation for its presence. I will conclude by briefly adumbrating what I take to be responsible for this internalist feature of the concept.

My suggestion is that the background against which the concept of epistemic justification has developed is the practice of critical reflection on our beliefs, the practice of the epistemic assessment of beliefs (with respect to the likelihood of their being true), the challenging of beliefs and responses to such challenges. To respond successfully to such a challenge one must specify an adequate ground of the belief, a ground that provides a sufficient indication of the truth of the belief. It would, of course, be absurd to suggest that in order to be epistemically respectable, laudatory, or acceptable (justified), a belief must have actually been put to such a test and have emerged victorious. In suggesting that the concept has developed against the background of such a practice the idea is rather that what it is for a belief to be justified is that the belief and its ground be such that it is in a position to pass such a test; that the subject has what it takes to respond successfully to such a

---

[44]Since I do not find any like tendency to withhold the concept of justification when the justificatory efficacy of the ground is not readily accessible to the subject, I am not saddled with the burden of a higher level accessibility constraint.

challenge.[45] A justified belief is one that *could* survive a critical reflection. But then the justifier must be accessible to the subject. Otherwise the subject would be in no position to cite it as what provides a sufficient indication that the belief is true. This, baldly stated, is what I take to be the explanation of the presence of an AI internalist constraint in the concept of epistemic justification. Further development of this suggestion must await another occasion.

[45]One indication that this is the right way to think about justification is the fact that we find it incongruous to apply the concept to beings that are incapable of critical reflection on their beliefs. The question of whether a dog is *justified* in supposing that his master is at the door is one that does not seem to arise. There are, to be sure, problems as to just how this restriction is to be interpreted. It seems clearly all right to apply the concept to human beings that have little skill at the game of challenge and response. The applicability to small children is less clear. But note that in both these cases we are dealing with beings that belong to a species many members of which are capable of critical reflection in a full-blooded form.

An Internalist Externalism

I

In this essay I will explain, and at least begin to defend, the particular blend of internalism and externalism in my view of epistemic justification. So far as I know, this is my own private blend;[1] many, I'm afraid, will not take that as a recommendation. Be that as it may, it's mine, and it's what I will set forth in this paper. I will first have to present the general contours of the position, as a basis for specifying the points at which we have an internalism-externalism issue. I won't have time to defend the general position, or even to present more than a sketch. Such defense as will be offered will be directed to the internalist and externalist features.

In a word, my view is that to be justified in believing that *p* is for that belief *to be based on an adequate ground*. To explain what I mean by this I will have to say something about the correlative terms 'based on' and 'ground' and about the *adequacy* of grounds.

The ground of a belief is what it is based on. The notion of *based on* is a difficult one. I am not aware that anyone has succeeded in giving an

From *Synthese*, 74 (1988), 265–83. © 1988 by Kluwer Academic Publishers. Reprinted by permission of Kluwer Academic Publishers.

An earlier version of this essay was delivered at a conference on epistemic justification, honoring Roderick Chisholm, at Brown University in November 1986. I am grateful to the participants in that conference for many penetrating remarks, and especially to my commentator, Marshall Swain. Those comments have been expanded into his essay "Alston's Internalistic Externalism," *Philosophical Perspectives* 2 (1988).

[1]The position does, however, bear a marked family resemblance to that put forward in Marshall Swain's *Reasons and Knowledge* (Ithaca: Cornell University Press, 1981).

adequate and illuminating general explanation of it. It seems clear that some kind of causal dependence is involved, whether the belief is based on other beliefs or on experience. If my belief that it rained last night is based on my belief that the streets are wet, then I hold the former belief *because* I hold the latter belief; my holding the latter belief *explains* my holding the former. Similarly, if my belief that the streets are wet is based on their looking wet, I believe that they are wet *because* of the way they look, and their looking that way *explains* my believing that they are wet. And presumably these are relations of causal dependence. But, equally clearly, not just any kind of causal dependence will do. My belief that *p* is causally dependent on a certain physiological state of my brain, but the former is not based on the latter. How is *being based on* distinguished from other sorts of causal dependence? We have a clear answer to this question for cases of maximally explicit inference, where I come to believe that *p* because I see (or at least take it) that it is adequately supported by the fact that *q* (which I believe). And where the ground is experiential we can also come to believe that *p* because we take its truth to be adequately indicated by the experience from which it arises. In these cases the belief-forming process is *guided* by our belief in the adequate support relation, and this marks them out as cases of a belief's being based on a ground, rather than just causally depending on something.[2] A belief, however, may be based on other beliefs or on experiences, where no such guiding belief in support relations is in evidence.[3] My belief that you are upset may be based on various aspects of the way you look and act without my consciously believing that these features provide adequate support for that belief; in a typical case of this sort I have no such belief simply because I am not consciously aware of which features these are; I do not consciously discriminate them. And even where I am more explicitly aware of the ground, I may not consciously believe anything at all about support relations. It is very dubious that very small children, for example, ever have such support beliefs; and yet surely a small child's belief that the kitten is sick can be based on her belief that the kitten is not running around as usual. But then what feature is common to all cases of a belief's being *based on* something, and serves to distinguish this kind of causal dependence from other kinds? Here I will have to content myself with making a

[2]For an elaborate development of this idea, along with much else relevant to the notion of believing for a reason, see Robert Audi's "Belief, Reason, and Inference," *Philosophical Topics*, 14, no. 1 (1986), 27–65.

[3]Audi in the article referred to in the previous note alleges that there are such "connecting beliefs", as he calls them, in every case of "believing for a reason" (what I am calling beliefs based on other beliefs). However, I do not find his arguments compelling.

suggestion. Wherever it is clear that a belief is *based on* another belief or on an experience, the belief-forming "process" or "mechanism" is *taking account* of that ground or features thereof, being *guided* by it, even if this does not involve the conscious utilization of a belief in a support relation. To say that my belief that the streets are wet is based on the way they look is to say that in forming a belief about the condition of the streets I (or the belief-forming "mechanism") am differentially sensitive to the way the streets look; the mechanism is so constituted that the belief formed about the streets will be some, possibly very complex, function of the visual experience input. Even where an explicit belief in a support relation is absent, the belief formation is the result of a *taking account* of features of the experience and forming the belief *in the light of* them, rather than just involving some subcognitive transaction.[4] Much more could and should be said about this, but the foregoing will have to suffice for now. In any event, whether or not this suggestion is along the right line, I shall take it that we have an adequate working grasp of the notion of a belief's being based on something, and that this suffices for the concerns of this essay.

In the foregoing I was speaking of the ground of a belief as playing a role in its *formation*. That is not the whole story. It is often pointed out that a belief may acquire a new basis after its initial acquisition. However the role of post-origination bases in justification is a complex matter, one not at all adequately dealt with in the epistemological literature. To keep things manageable for this short conspectus of my view, I shall restrict myself to bases on which a belief is originally formed. That means, in effect, that the discussion will be limited to what it takes for a belief to be justified at the moment of its acquisition.

In taking the justification of a belief to be determined by what it is based on, I am reflecting the subject-relative character of justification. I may be justified in believing that *p* while you are not. Indeed, justification is time as well as subject relative; I may be justified in believing that *p* at one time but not at another.[5] Whether I am justified in believing that *p* is a matter of how I am situated vis-à-vis the content of that belief. In my view, that is cashed out in terms of what the subject was

---

[4] It may be contended that where such "taking account" is involved, this amounts to the subject's having and using a belief in a support relation. And perhaps this is right, for a minimal, low-level grade of belief possession and use. One could "have" and "use" the belief in this way, however, without the belief's being available for conscious entertainment, assertion, or use in inference.

[5] For simplicity of exposition I shall omit temporal qualifiers from my formulations, but they are to be understood. Thus, a tacit 'at *t*' qualifies '*S* is justified in believing that *p*'.

"going on" in supposing the proposition in question to be true, on what basis she supposed p to be the case.[6]

What sort of things do subjects go on in holding beliefs? The examples given above suggest that the prime candidates are the subject's other beliefs and experiences; and I shall consider grounds to be restricted to items of those two categories. Though I will offer no a priori or transcendental argument for this, I will adopt the plausible supposition that where the input to a belief-forming mechanism is properly thought of as *what the belief is based on,* it will be either a belief or an experience. But we must tread carefully here. Where a philosopher or a psychologist would say that S's belief that it rained last night is based on S's *belief* that the streets are wet, S would probably say, if he were aware of the basis of his belief, that his ground, basis, or reason for believing that it rained last night is the *fact* that the streets are wet. The ordinary way of talking about reasons specifies the (putative) fact believed as the reason rather than the belief.[7] I think we can set up the matter either way. I choose to use 'ground' for the psychological input to the belief-forming mechanism, that is, the belief or experience, thus deviating from the most ordinary way of speaking of these matters.[A]

I need to be more explicit about how grounds are specified in my account. I can best approach this by considering a difficulty raised by Marshall Swain in his comments on this essay at the Brown conference. Swain wrote as follows:

> Suppose two subjects, Smith and Jones, who have the same evidence (grounds) for the belief that p, where the evidence consists of the proposition $p \vee (p \& q)$. Both subjects come to believe that p on this basis of the evidence (and no other evidence). In the case of Smith, the mechanism for generating the belief is an inference which instantiates a tendency to invalidly infer p from any sentence of the form '$p \vee q$'. In the case of Jones, the mechanism is an inference which is based on an internalized valid inference schema (of which several are possible). It seems clear to me that only Jones has a justified belief that p, even though they have the same grounds.

[6]Admittedly there are other ways of cashing out this general idea of subject-relativity, e.g., by making justification hang on what the subject "had to go on" by way of support, rather than on what the subject actually went on, but I won't have time to go into those alternatives.

[7]With experiential grounds we do not have the same problem, for, at least as I am thinking of it, an experiential ground is not, qua experiential ground, a propositional attitude, or set thereof, like a belief, so that here there is no propositional or factive object to serve as a ground rather than the experience itself. One who does take experiences to be essentially propositional attitudes will find the same problem as with doxastic grounds.

Such cases can be proliferated indefinitely. For an example involving experiential grounds, consider two persons, A and B, who come to believe that a collie is in the room on the basis of qualitatively identical visual experiences. But A recognizes the dog as a collie on the basis of distinctively collie features, whereas B would take any largish dog to be a collie. Again, it would seem that A is justified in his belief while B is not, even though they have the same grounds for a belief with the same propositional content.[8] Swain takes it that such cases show that characteristics of the subject must be brought into the account in addition to what we have introduced.

However, I believe that unwanted applications like these can be excluded just by giving a sufficiently discriminating specification of grounds. As I am using the term, the "ground" for a belief is not what we might call the total concrete input to the belief-forming mechanism, but rather those features of that input that are actually taken account of in forming the belief, in, so to say, "choosing" a propositional content for a belief. In Swain's case, the only feature of the belief input taken account of by Smith was that its propositional object was of the form '$p \lor q$'. No further features of the input were playing a role in that belief formation; no further features were "guiding" the operation of the belief-forming mechanism. In Jones' case, however, the belief formation was guided by the fact that the input belief had a propositional content of the form '$p \lor (p \& q)$'. In Smith's case any input of the '$p \lor q$' form would have led to the same doxastic output, whereas for Jones many other inputs of that form would *not* have led to the formation of a belief that p. Thus, strictly speaking, the grounds were different. Similarly in the canine identification case, for A the ground was the object's visually presenting certain features that are in fact distinctively collie-like, whereas for B the ground was the object's visually presenting itself as a largish dog.

We may sum this up by saying that the ground of a belief is made up of those features of the input to the formation of that belief that were actually taken account of in the belief formation. (Again, remember that our discussion is restricted to the bases of beliefs when formed.)

Not every grounded belief will be justified, but only one that has an *adequate* ground. To get at the appropriate criterion of adequacy, let's note that a belief's *being justified* is a favorable status vis-à-vis the basic

---

[8]This is similar to problem cases involving perceptual discrimination introduced in Alvin Goldman's "Discrimination and Perceptual Knowledge," *Journal of Philosophy*, 73 (1976), 771–91.

aim of believing or, more generally, of cognition, viz., to believe truly rather than falsely. For a ground to be favorable relative to this aim it must be "truth conducive"; it must be sufficiently indicative of the truth of the belief it grounds. In other terms, the ground must be such that the *probability* of the belief's being true, given that ground, is very high. It is an objective probability that is in question here. The world is such that, at least in the kinds of situations in which we typically find ourselves, the ground is a reliable indication of the fact believed. In this paper I will not attempt to spell out the kind of objective probability being appealed to. So far as I am aware, no adequate conception of this sort of probability (or perhaps of any other sort) has been developed. Suffice it to say that I am thinking in terms of some kind of "tendency" conception of probability, where the lawful structure of the world is such that one state of affairs renders another more or less probable.

The ambiguity noted earlier as to what constitutes a ground has to be dealt with here as well. Suppose that the ground of my belief that p is my belief that q. In order that the former belief be justified, is it required that the belief that q be a reliable indication of the truth of the belief that p, or is it required that the fact that q be a reliable indication? The latter is the ordinary way of thinking about the matter. If my belief that Jones is having a party is based on my belief that there are a lot of cars around his house, then just as I would ordinarily cite the *fact* that there are a lot of cars around his house as my reason for supposing that he is having a party, so I would think that my reason is an adequate one because the former *fact* is a reliable indication of the latter one. The adequacy requirement, however, could be set up in either way. To appreciate this let's first note that in either case the belief that p will be justified only if the grounding belief is justified (a stronger requirement would be that the grounding belief constitute knowledge, but I won't go that far). Even if the fact that q is a highly reliable indication that p, that won't render my belief that p justified by virtue of being based on a belief that q unless I am justified in believing that q. An unjustified belief cannot transfer justification to another belief via the basis relation. But if I am justified in believing that q and if q is a reliable indication of p, then my belief that q will also be a (perhaps slightly less) reliable indication that p, provided a belief cannot be justified unless its ground renders it likely to be true. For in that case my having a justified belief that q renders it likely that q, which in turn renders it likely that p. And so if q is a strong indication of the truth of p, so is my belief that q (assuming that we don't lose too much of the strength of indication in the probabilistic relation between the justified belief that q and q). This being the case, I will simplify matters for purposes of this paper by taking the adequacy of a ground to depend on *its* being a sufficiently strong indication of the truth of the belief grounded.

II

Now we are in a position to say what is internalist and what is externalist about this position, and to make a start, at least, in defending our choices. The view is internalist most basically, and most minimally, by virtue of the requirement that there be a ground of the belief. As we have made explicit, the ground must be a psychological state of the subject and hence "internal" to the subject in an important sense. Facts that obtain independently of the subject's psyche, however favorable to the truth of the belief in question, cannot be *grounds* of the belief in the required sense.

But this is only a weak form of internalism, one that would hardly be deemed worthy of the name by those who flaunt the label. There are, in fact, several constraints on justification that have gone under this title. In Essay 8 I distinguish two main forms: Perspectival Internalism (PI), according to which only what is within the subject's perspective in the sense of being something the subject knows or justifiably believes can serve to justify; and Accessibility Internalism (AI), according to which only that to which the subject has cognitive access in some specially strong form can be a justifier. However, it is now clear to me that I should have added at least one more version, Consciousness Internalism (CI), according to which only those states of affairs of which the subject is actually conscious or aware can serve to justify.[9]

In Essay 8 I argue against PI, partly on the grounds that its only visible means of support is from an unacceptable deontological conception of justification that makes unrealistic assumptions about the voluntary control of belief, and partly on the grounds that it rules out the possibility of immediate justification by experience of such things as introspective and perceptual beliefs. CI has the crushing disability that one can never complete the formulation of a sufficient condition for justification. For suppose that we begin by taking condition C to be sufficient for the justification of S's belief that p. But then we must add that S must be aware of C (i.e., the satisfaction of condition C) in order to be justified. Call this enriched condition C_1. But then C_1 is not enough by itself either; S must be aware of C_1. So that must be added

[9]For an example of CI see Paul Moser, *Empirical Justification* (Dordrecht: D. Reidel, 1985), p. 174.

to yield a still richer condition, C2. And so on ad infinitum. Any thesis that implies that it is in principle impossible to complete a statement of conditions sufficient for justification is surely unacceptable.[10]

I find AI to be much more promising. To be sure, many formulations are, I believe, much too strong to be defensible. Thus Carl Ginet's version is in terms of what he calls being "directly recognizable":

> Every one of every set of facts about S's position that minimally suffices to make S, at a given time, justified in being confident that *p* must be *directly recognizable* to S at that time. By 'directly recognizable' I mean this: if a certain fact obtains, then it is directly recognizable to S at a given time if and only if, provided that S at that time has the concept of that sort of fact, S needs at that time only to reflect clear-headedly on the question of whether or not that fact obtains in order to know that it does.[11]

But there are very plausible conditions for justification that are not directly recognizable in this sense. Consider, for example, the familiar situation in which I recognize something or someone on the basis of subtle perceptual cues I am unable to specify, even on careful reflection. Here it seems correct to say that my belief that the person before me is John Jones is justified, if it is, by virtue of being based on a visual experience with such-and-such features, where the experience's having those features is crucial for its providing justification. But those features are not "directly recognizable" by me. Or again consider the familiar situation of a belief, for example, that Republicans are unlikely to be tough on big business, that is based on a wide diversity of evidence, most of which I cannot specify even after careful reflection. Ginet's form of AI is too stringent to be suited to our condition.[12]

However, I believe that it is possible to support a more moderate version of AI. To determine just what sort of accessibility is required I had better make explicit what I see as the source of the requirement. I find widely shared and strong intuitions in favor of some kind of accessibility requirement for justification. We expect that if there is some-

---

[10]The proponent of CI might seek to avoid this consequence by construing the awareness requirement not as part of the condition for justification but as a constraint on what can be a sufficient condition for justification. Indeed this is the way Moser, ibid., formulates it on p. 174: ". . . we should require that one have some kind of awareness of the justifying conditions of one's given-beliefs". The suggestion is that the awareness does not itself form part of the justifying conditions. But I take this to be a shuffling evasion. If the awareness of condition C is required for justification, then it is an essential part of a sufficient condition for justification, whatever the theorist chooses to call it.

[11]Carl Ginet, *Knowledge, Perception, and Memory* (Dordrecht: D. Reidel, 1975), p. 34.

[12]I might also add that AI is typically supported by inconclusive arguments from an unacceptable deontological conception of justification. For details see Essay 8.

thing that justifies my belief that p, I will be able to determine what it is. We find something incongruous, or conceptually impossible, in the notion of my being justified in believing that p while totally lacking any capacity to determine what is responsible for that justification. Thus when reliability theorists of justification maintain that any reliably formed belief is ipso facto justified, most of us balk. For since it is possible for a belief to be reliably formed without the subject's having any capacity to determine this, and, indeed, without there being anything accessible to the subject on which the belief is based—as when invariable correct beliefs about the future of the stock market seem to pop out of nowhere—it seems clear to many of us that reliable belief formation cannot be sufficient for justification.

Why these intuitions? Why is some kind of accessibility required for justification? Is this just a basic constituent of the concept? Or can it be derived from other more basic components? I myself do not see any way to argue from other "parts" of the concept to this one. Hence I will not attempt to *prove* that accessibility is required for justification. But I believe that we can get some understanding of the presence of this accessibility requirement by considering the larger context out of which the concept of epistemic justification has developed and which gives it its distinctive importance. Thus I will attempt to *explain* the presence of the requirement.

First I want to call attention to a view of justification I do not accept. Suppose, with pragmatists like Peirce and Dewey and other contextualists, we focus on the *activity* of *justifying* beliefs to the exclusion of the *state* of *being justified* in holding a belief. The whole topic of epistemic justification will then be confined to the question of what it takes to successfully carry out the activity of justifying a belief, *showing* it to be something one is entitled to believe, establishing its credentials, responding to challenges to its legitimacy, and so on. But then the only considerations that can have any bearing on justification (i.e., on the successful outcome of such an activity) are those that are cognitively accessible to the subject. For only those can be appealed to in order to justify the belief.

Now I have no temptation to restrict the topic of epistemic justification to the activity of justifying. Surely epistemology is concerned with the epistemic status of beliefs with respect to which no activity of justifying has been carried on. We want to know whether people are justified in holding normal perceptual beliefs, normal memory beliefs, beliefs in generalizations concerning how things generally go in the physical world, beliefs about the attitudes of other people, religious beliefs, and so on, even where, as is usually the case, such beliefs have not been subjected to an attempt to justify. It is quite arbitrary to ban such concerns from epistemology.

But though the activity of responding to challenges is not the whole story, I do believe that in a way it is fundamental to the concept of *being justified*. Why is it that we have this concept of *being justified in holding a belief* and why is it important to us? I suggest that the concept was developed, and got its hold on us, because of the practice of critical reflection on our beliefs, of challenging their credentials and responding to such challenges—in short the practice of attempting to *justify* beliefs. Suppose there were no such practice; suppose that no one ever challenges the credentials of anyone's beliefs; suppose that no one ever critically reflects on the grounds or basis of one's own beliefs. In that case would we be interested in determining whether one or another belief *is* justified? I think not. It is only because we participate in such activities, only because we are alive to their importance, that the question of whether someone is in a state of *being justified* in holding a belief is of live interest to us. I am not suggesting that being justified is a matter of engaging in, or successfully engaging in, the activity of justifying. I am not even affirming the less obviously false thesis that being justified in believing that *p* is a matter of *being able to* successfully justify the belief. Many persons are justified in many beliefs without possessing the intellectual or verbal skills to exhibit what justifies those beliefs. Thus the *fact* of being justified is not dependent on any particular actual or possible activity of justifying. What I am suggesting is that those facts of justification would not have the interest and importance for us that they do have if we were not party to a social practice of demanding justification and responding to such demands.

Now for the bearing of this on AI. I want to further suggest that this social practice has strongly influenced the development of the *concept* of being justified. What has emerged from this development is the concept of *what would have to be specified to carry out a successful justification of the belief*. Our conception of what a belief needs in the way of a basis in order to *be justified* is the conception of that the specification of which in answer to a challenge would suffice to answer that challenge. But then it is quite understandable that the concept should include the requirement that the justifier be accessible to the subject. For only what the subject can ascertain can be cited by that subject in response to a challenge. This, I believe, provides the explanation for the presence of the AI constraint on justification.

Now that we have a rationale for an AI constraint, let's see just what form of the constraint is dictated by that rationale. There are at least two matters to be decided: (a) what is required to be accessible; (b) what degree of accessibility is to be required.

As for (a), the most important distinction is between (1) the "justifier", that is, the ground of the belief, and (2) its adequacy or justificatory efficacy: its "truth-conduciveness". I'm going to save adequacy for the next section and concentrate here on the justifier. But there are still choices. Should we say that in order for S's belief that *p* to be justified by being based on a ground, G, G itself, that very individual ground, must be accessible to S? Or is it enough that G is the sort of thing that is typically accessible to normal human subjects? The latter, weaker requirement would allow a justifying ground in a particular case to be a belief that is not in fact accessible to the subject's consciousness, because of repression, a cognitive overload, or whatever, provided beliefs are in general the sort of thing to which subjects have cognitive access. The rationale offered above for AI would not demand of every justifying ground that it itself be available for citation, but only that it be the *sort* of thing that is, in general, so available. We were not arguing that it is conceptually necessary, or even universally true, that a justifying ground can be cited in response to a challenge. We were only contending that the concept of being justified in believing that *p* (including the concept of a justifying ground for a belief) has been developed against the background of the practice of citing grounds in defense of assertions. This looser sort of relationship of justifying grounds to the activity of justifying supports at most the weaker requirement that a justifying ground is the sort of thing that, in general or when nothing interferes, is available for citation by the subject. And it is just as well that only this weaker requirement is mandated, for, because of the considerations adduced in criticizing Ginet's form of AI, it seems that we must allow cases in which the basis of a belief is blocked from consciousness through some special features of that situation. Thus we are free to recognize cases of justification in which the complexity of the grounds or the rapidity of their appearance and disappearance renders the subject unable to store and retrieve them as she would have to in order to cite them in answer to a challenge.

Now for degree. Just *how* does a kind of state have to be generally accessible to its subject in order to be a candidate for a justifying ground? I have already argued that Ginet's version of AI is too demanding to be realistic. On the other hand, if we simply require that justifiers be the sorts of things that are knowable in principle by the subject, somehow or other, that is too weak. That would allow anything to count as a justifier that it is not *impossible* for the subject to come to know about. That would not even rule out neurophysiological states of the brain about which no one knows anything now. What is needed here is a concept of something like "fairly direct accessibility". In order that justifiers be generally available for presentation as the legitimizers of the belief, they must be fairly readily available to the subject through some mode of access much quicker than lengthy research, observation, or experimentation. It seems reasonable to follow Ginet's lead and suggest that to be a justifier an item must be the sort of thing that, in general, a subject can explicitly note the presence of just by sufficient reflection on his situation. However, the amount and depth of reflection needed for this will vary in different cases. I want to avoid the claim that justifiers can always be spotted right away, just by raising the question. I don't know how to make this notion of "fairly direct accessibility" precise, and I suspect that it may be impossible to do so. Perhaps our concept of justification is not itself precise enough to require a precise degree of ease or rapidity of access. Let's just say that to be a justifier of a belief, its ground must be the sort of thing whose instances are fairly directly accessible to their subject on reflection.

I am going to just mention in passing another internalist feature of this position. Being based on an adequate ground is sufficient only for prima facie justification, justification that can be nullified by sufficient overriding reasons from the subject's stock of knowledge and justified belief.[13] Reasons that override a given justification for a belief that p are of two sorts. First there are sufficient reasons for supposing p to be false; call them *rebutters*. Second, there are reasons such that the combination of them with the initial ground fails to be sufficiently indicative of the truth of p; call them *neutralizers*. Thus even if my current visual experience is, in itself, a strong indication that there is a tree in front of me, I will not be, all things considered, justified in believing that there is a tree in front of me provided I have even stronger reasons for supposing there to be no tree there (rebutter), or provided I have strong reasons for supposing my visual apparatus not to be working properly at the moment (neutralizer). The effect of the requirement (for unqualified justification) of no sufficient overriders is to make unqualified justification sensitive to the totality of what the subject knows and justifiably believes. I am unqualifiedly justified in believing

---

[13]More generally, the points made in this essay specifically concern prima facie justification. For example the accessibility constraint on grounds does not apply to the subject's perspective as a whole, from which overriders emerge. Or, to put the point more modestly, nothing I say in this essay gives any support to the idea that in order for something the subject knows or justifiably believes to override a prima facie justification that something has to be fairly readily accessible to the subject.

that p only if the totality of my knowledge, justified belief, and experience constitutes an adequate ground for that belief. Since the fate of prima facie justification is determined by what is in the subject's perspective on the world, rather than by the way the world is, this is an additional internalist factor, though as the last footnote makes explicit, not of the AI sort.

III

So much for internalism. Now where is the externalism? To see where that comes in we must move from the existence of grounds to their adequacy. An internalist position on this point will make it a condition of justification that the adequacy of the ground be internal to the subject in some way or other. The externalism of my position will consist in the rejection of all such requirements. We can distinguish here between making the internality of adequacy a *necessary* condition of justification and making it sufficient for justification, along with the belief's being based on the ground in question. I shall consider these in turn.

Go back to the distinction between PI and AI. (We may ignore CI in this connection, since we are unlikely to find a plausible way of construing the notion of an "awareness" or "consciousness" of the *adequacy* of a ground.) A PI necessary condition in this area would presumably run as follows.

(I) One is justified in believing that p only if one knows or is justified in believing that the ground of that belief is an adequate one.

Let's focus on the justified belief alternative. This requirement labors under the very considerable disadvantage of requiring an infinite hierarchy of justified beliefs in order to be justified in any belief. For the requirement will also apply to the higher level belief that the ground of the belief that p is adequate. (Call the propositional content of this higher level belief 'q'.) To be justified in the belief that q one must be justified in believing that *its* ground is adequate. Call the propositional object of this still higher level belief 'r'. Then to be justified in believing that r one must be justified in the still higher level belief that the ground of one's belief that r is an adequate one. . . . Since it seems clear that no human being is capable of possessing all at once an infinite hierarchy of beliefs, it is equally clear that this requirement allows no one to have any justified beliefs. And that should be a sufficient basis for rejecting it.

The story with AI is somewhat different. First we have to decide on what is to count as "accessibility to the adequacy of the ground". The most obvious suggestion would be that accessibility consists in the capacity of the subject to come into the state required by the PI requirement, viz., being justified in believing that the ground of the target belief that p is adequate. We can then add the specification of the required degree and mode of accessibility. This will give us the following.

(II) S is justified in believing that p only if S is capable, fairly readily on the basis of reflection, to acquire a justified belief that the ground of S's belief that p is an adequate one.

Clearly (II), unlike (I), does not imply that S has an infinite hierarchy of justified beliefs. For (II) does not require that S actually have a justified higher level belief for each belief in the hierarchy, but only that, for each justified belief she actually has, it is possible for her to acquire, by a certain route, an appropriately related justified higher level belief. To be sure, this does imply that S has, as we might say, an infinite hierarchy of possibilities for the acquisition of justified beliefs. But it is not at all clear that this is impossible, in the way it is clearly impossible for one of us to have an infinite hierarchy of actually justified beliefs. Thus I will have to find some other reason for rejecting (II).

That reason can be found by turning from possibility to actuality. Though it may well be within the limits of human capacity, it is by no means always the case that the subject of a justified belief is capable of determining the adequacy of his ground, just by careful reflection on the matter, or, indeed, in any other way. For one thing, many subjects are not at the level of conceptual sophistication to even raise the question of adequacy of ground, much less determine an answer by reflection. One thinks here of small children and, I fear, many adults as well. The maximally unsophisticated human perceiver is surely often justified in believing that what he sees to be the case is the case, even though he is in no position to even raise a question about the adequacy of his grounds. But even if capable of raising the question, he may not be able to arrive at a justified answer. Our judgment on this will depend both on what we take to be required for adequacy and what we regard as necessary for the justification of a belief that certain grounds are adequate. The two are, of course, intimately connected. I have already made it explicit that I take a ground, G, of belief B to be adequate if and only if it is sufficiently indicative of the truth of B. And this being the case, it seems clear that for me to be justified in believing G to be an adequate basis for belief, B, I must have sufficient *reasons* for supposing that this truth-indication relation does hold. (And, on my view, the belief in adequacy must be based on those reasons.) And many, or most, subjects are just not up to this. Consider, for instance, all the things we believe on authority. If we have been trained properly, we generally recognize the marks of competence in an area, and when we believe the pronouncements of one who exhibits those marks, we are believing on adequate grounds, proceeding aright in our belief formation, and so epistemically justified. But how many of us can, on reflection, come up with adequate evidence on which to base the belief that a given putative authority is to be relied on? Very few of us. (II) would imply that we are rarely justified in believing on authority, even when we are utilizing what we have been trained to recognize as marks of authority, marks that are indeed reliable indications of expertise.

A weaker AI condition on adequacy of grounds would be the following.

(III) S is justified in believing that *p* only if S has adequate grounds for a judgment that the grounds for S's belief that *p* are adequate.

This is weaker than (II) because it does not require that S actually be able to acquire a justified belief about adequacy, whether just on reflection or otherwise. It only requires that she "have" the grounds (evidence, experiences, or whatever) that would serve to justify such a belief if that belief were based on those grounds. A subject could conceivably satisfy (III) even if she lacked the conceptual equipment to formulate the issue of adequacy. Nevertheless, the considerations I have advanced make it dubious that even this condition is met by all or most justified believers. Do I have the evidence it would take to adequately support a belief that my present perceptual grounds for believing that there is a maple tree near my study window are adequate? I very much doubt it. Even if we can overcome problems of circularity (relying on other perceptual beliefs to support the claim that this perceptual ground is adequate), as I believe we can,[14] it seems very dubious that we store enough observational evidence to constitute adequate evidence for the thesis that normal sensory experience is an adequate ground for our beliefs about the physical environment. No doubt our experience reinforces our tendency to believe this, but that is

[14]See Essay 12 for a defense of this view.

another matter. For these and other reasons, I very much doubt that all or most justified believers satisfy (III).

We must, of course, be alive to the point that our AI principle concerning the presence of the ground did not require that the ground be fairly directly accessible to the subject in each case, but only that it be the sort of thing that is typically so accessible. This suggests a weakening of (I)–(III) so that the requirement is not that so-and-so be true in each case, but only that it be generally or normally the case. But if the above contentions are sound, these weaker principles would be excluded also. For I have argued that it is not even generally or typically the case that, taking (II) as our example, one who has a justified belief that p is capable of arriving fairly readily at a justified belief that the ground of his belief that p is an adequate one.

What about an internalist *sufficient* condition of adequacy (sufficient along with the belief's being based on the ground in question)? Here again we will have both PI and AI versions. Let's say that the PI version takes it as sufficient for the justification of S's belief that p that:

> (IV) S's belief that p is based on an accessible ground that S is justified in supposing to be adequate.

The AI version can be construed as taking the condition to consist in the appropriate sort of possibility of S's satisfying (IV). More explicitly:

> (V) S's belief that p is based on an accessible ground such that S can fairly readily come to have a justified belief that this ground is an adequate one.

Since the PI condition is stronger, it will suffice to show that it is not strong enough.[15]

The crucial question here is whether (IV) ensures truth-conducivity, which we saw at the beginning of the paper to be an essential feature of epistemic justification. And this boils down to the question of whether S's being justified in supposing the ground of his belief in p to be adequate guarantees that the belief that p is likely to be true. This depends on both the concept of adequacy and the concept of justification used in (IV). If (IV) employs a non-truth-indicative concept of

[15]Note that if the condition is asserted only as sufficient and not also as necessary, no infinite hierarchy can be shown to follow even from the PI version. Since the claim is compatible with there being other sufficient conditions of justification, it does not imply that one can be justified in believing that p only if one has an infinite hierarchy of justified beliefs. But, of course, if other sufficient conditions are countenanced, the position loses its distinctively internalist clout.

adequacy, the game is up right away. Suppose, for example, that an adequate ground for a belief that p is one on which a confident belief of this sort is customarily based. In that case likelihood of truth is not ensured even by the ground's *being* adequate, much less by S's being justified in supposing it to be adequate. Let's take it, then, that our PI internalist is using our concept of a ground's *being* adequate; his difference from us is simply that where we require for justification that the ground *be* adequate, he takes it sufficient that S be justified in supposing it to be adequate. But then we must ask what concept of justification he is using. If he were using our concept of justification in (IV), the satisfaction of that condition would imply that p is likely to be true. For if S is justified in believing the ground to be adequate, on our concept of justification, then the belief that the ground is adequate is thereby likely to be true; and so, if there is not too much leakage in the double probabilification, the likelihood that the ground of the belief that p is adequate implies in turn that it is likely that p. But this would mean that our internalist opponent avoids our concept of justification (requiring actual adequacy of ground) at the first level only to embrace it at the second and, presumably, at all higher levels. The only effect of this is that the implication of truth-conducivity at the first level is somewhat weaker than on our view; since whereas we flat-out require adequacy at the first level, his view only requires the likelihood of adequacy. But this difference lacks motivation, and in any event it certainly doesn't give his view a distinctively *internalist* cast in contrast to ours, since he uses our concept of justification at all higher levels. Hence if our opponent is to be more than a paper internalist, he will have to be using some non-truth-conducive conception of justification at the higher levels;[16] and in that case the fact that S is justified in believing that the ground of his belief that p is adequate has no tendency to imply that the ground *is* adequate, and hence no tendency to imply that p is (likely to be) true. And therefore (IV) cannot be sufficient for epistemic justification.

Thus it would seem that internalist conditions concerning adequacy are neither necessary nor sufficient for justification. And so the view here being defended is resolutely and uncompromisingly externalist, so far as adequacy of grounds is concerned. In order for my belief that p, which is based on ground G, to be justified, it is quite sufficient, as

[16]We have not ruled out the possibility that our opponent is using, in (IV), some truth-conducive concept of justification other than ours, e.g., a straight reliability concept according to which it is sufficient for the justification of a belief that it have been acquired in some reliable way. But if that's what he's doing, he turns out to be even less internalist than if he had used our concept.

well as necessary, that G be sufficiently indicative of the truth of *p*. It is in no way required that I know anything, or be justified in believing anything, about this relationship. No doubt, we sometimes do have justified beliefs about the adequacy of our grounds, and that is certainly a good thing. But that is icing on the cake.

IV

In this essay I have proposed an account of the prima facie epistemic justification of beliefs according to which that amounts to a belief's having an adequate ground. The justification will be ultima facie provided there are not sufficient overriders from within the subject's knowledge and justified belief. I have given reasons for placing a (rather weak) AI constraint on something's being a ground that could justify a belief, but I have resisted attempts to put any internalist constraint on what constitutes the adequacy of a ground. There I have insisted that it is both necessary and sufficient that the world be such that the ground be "sufficiently indicative of the truth" of the belief, both necessary and sufficient that this actually be the case, and neither necessary nor sufficient that the subject have any cognitive grasp of this fact. Thus my position has definite affinities with reliabilism, especially with that variant thereof sometimes called a "reliable indication" view, as contrasted with a "reliable process" view.[17] But it differs from a pure reliabilism by holding that the justification of a belief requires that the belief be based on a "ground" that satisfies an AI constraint, as well as by letting the subject's perspective on the world determine whether overriding occurs.[18] Beliefs that, so far as the subject can tell, just pop into his head out of nowhere would not be counted as justified on this position. I do hold that mere reliable belief production, suitably construed, is sufficient for knowledge, but that is another story.

[17]To be sure, in explaining early on in the essay the way in which I pick out grounds, I appealed to features of the *process* of belief formation. (I am indebted to Hilary Kornblith and Alvin Goldman for calling this to my attention.) Nevertheless, reliability enters into my formulation of what is necessary and sufficient for justification by way of the truth indicativeness of the ground, rather than by way of the reliability of any belief-forming process.

[18]I would suggest that much of the plausibility of some prominent attacks on externalism in general, and reliabilism in particular, stems from a failure to distinguish externalism with respect to the ground and externalism with respect to the adequacy of the ground. See, e.g., Laurence Bonjour, *The Structure of Empirical Knowledge* (Cambridge: Harvard University Press, 1985), chap. 3; and Richard Foley, "What's Wrong with Reliabilism?", *The Monist*, 68 (1985), 188–202.

Note

A. The position of this essay, that a belief is justified only if it is based on an adequate ground, is obviously in conflict with the position of Essay 11 that beliefs about one's own current conscious states are self-justified, justified just by being the kind of belief they are. See endnote G of Essay 11 for more on this.

PART IV

SELF-KNOWLEDGE

Varieties of
Privileged Access

It is a very common, though by no means uncontested, view that the kind of knowledge a person has of his own mental (psychological) states, such as thoughts and feelings, is in principle not only fundamentally different from but also superior to the knowledge of his thoughts and feelings that is available to anyone else. We may express this view by saying that a person has "privileged access" to his own mental states. It is obvious that this thesis will vary in content with variations in the specific mode of superiority imputed. Nevertheless, discussions of privileged access, both pro and con, have never been sufficiently alive to these variations or to their significance.

The central task of this essay is the exhibition and interrelation of the most important of the ways in which one's access to one's own mental states has been, or might be, thought to be privileged. In addition I shall show, though only sketchily, how failure to be alive to the full range of possibilities has vitiated some prominent discussions of the topic.

I

First, a couple of preliminary points. Privileged access claims vary not only with variations in the mode of epistemic superiority imputed, but also with variations in the category of "mental states" with respect

From *American Philosophical Quarterly*, 8, no. 3 (1971), 223–41. Reprinted by permission of the editor.

to which the claim is made. Many philosophers have advanced privileged access as a *criterion* for the mental or the psychological; they have held that a state of a person is mental (psychological) if and only if that person's knowledge that he has the state is superior, in some specified way, to the knowledge of that fact that is available to anyone else.[1] Others have made distinctions within this class of states and have asserted their favored form of privileged access of some subclass thereof. Thus it is not uncommon to hold that one cannot be mistaken with respect to what may be called "phenomenal states", that is, present contents of consciousness, such as sensations, images, feelings, and thoughts, but not to assert infallibility with respect to what may be called "dispositional states", such as beliefs, desires, and attitudes.[2] However the most common procedure is simply to work with particular examples, for example, sensations or, more specifically, pains, and not even attempt to make clear the several classes of states of which privileged access is being asserted.[3] In this essay I mention this dimension of variation only to set it aside. My sole concern will be to distinguish and compare various types of epistemic superiority; I shall not also be concerned to distinguish and compare various classes of entities with respect to which one or another of these has been asserted. Hence for our purposes we can just work with the rather loose rubric "mental state", remembering that if anyone is to put forward a privileged access thesis, he should be more specific as to the range of states involved.

We can hardly avoid taking note, however briefly, of those philosophers who would make short shrift of our entire problem by dismissing it, on the grounds that it makes no sense to speak of a person *knowing* that he has, for instance, a certain sensation. (See L. Wittgenstein, *Philosophical Investigations*, pt. I, para. 246.) If that is the case, there is no problem as to whether one's own knowledge of his own sensations is in

---

[1]See, e.g., G. E. Moore, "The Subject Matter of Psychology," *Proceedings of the Aristotelian Society*, 10 (1909–1910), 36–62, reprinted in G. N. A. Vesey, ed., *Body and Mind* (London: George Allen & Unwin, 1964); and F. Brentano, selection from *Psychology from an Empirical Standpoint*, in ibid.

[2]See, e.g., J. Shaffer, "Persons and Their Bodies," *Philosophical Review*, 75 (1966), 59–77.

[3]Thus Norman Malcolm, in "Direct Perception" in *Knowledge and Certainty* (Englewood Cliffs, N.J.: Prentice-Hall, 1963) restricts his discussion to after-images; while in "The Privacy of Experience" (in A. Stroll, ed., *Epistemology: New Essays in the Theory of Knowledge* [New York: Harper & Row, 1967]), he specifically discusses pain, and sometimes more generally "sensations". Presumably Malcolm supposes that the things he says about after-images (pains) have a wider scope of application, but he does not make explicit just what he takes this to be. Again, most of A. J. Ayer's discussion in his essay "Privacy" in *The Concept of a Person and Other Essays* (New York: St. Martin's Press, 1963) is in terms of "thoughts and feelings", but he makes no attempt to say exactly how far he means his remarks to extend.

some way necessarily superior to that available to any other person. I cannot really go into the issue in this essay, but it may not be out of place to explain briefly why it seems to me that any argument for this conclusion must be defective in *some* way. Clearly someone else can be in doubt as to whether I am in a given mental state, for example, whether I am thinking about tomorrow's lecture, whether I am worrying about my job prospects, whether I feel elated. That is, he may not know how to answer a certain question, "Does he (Alston) feel elated?". But it seems that normally I *would* be in a position to answer that question, the *same* question to which he does not know the answer. But how can we understand my being in that position without supposing that I know something he doesn't, for example, that I do feel elated? Thus it seems to be as undeniable as anything could be that persons normally do know what mental states they are in at a given moment, and that no argument designed to show that this is false or meaningless can be sound.

II

I shall begin by extracting a number of possible modes of privileged access from a rather wide sampling of the literature. We may begin with the following.

> Am I not that being who now doubts nearly everything, who nevertheless understands certain things, who affirms that one only is true, who denies all the others, who desires to know more, is averse from being deceived, who imagines many things, sometimes indeed despite his will, and who perceives many likewise, as by the intervention of the bodily organs? Is there nothing in all this which is as true as it is certain that I exist, even though I should always sleep and though he who has given me being employed all his ingenuity in deceiving me? . . . Finally, I am the same who feels, that is to say, who perceives certain things, as by the organs of sense since in truth I see light. I hear noise, I feel heat. But it will be said that these phenomena are false and that I am dreaming. Let it be so; still it is at least quite certain that it seems to me that I see light, that I hear noise, and that I feel heat. That cannot be false. . . .—R. Descartes, *Meditations*, II

> . . . for a man cannot conceive himself capable of a greater certainty than to know that any idea in his mind is such as he perceives it to be; and that two ideas, wherein he perceives a difference, are different and are not precisely the same.—J. Locke, *Essay Concerning Human Understanding*, IV, 2

For since all actions and sensations of the mind are known to us by consciousness, they must necessarily appear in every particular what they are, and be what they appear. Everything that enters the mind, being in *reality* as the perception, tis impossible anything should to *feeling* appear different. This were to suppose that even where we are most intimately conscious, we might be mistaken.—D. Hume, *Treatise of Human Nature*, I, iv, 2

The facts of consciousness are to be considered in two points of view; either as evidencing their own ideal or phaenomenal existence, or as evidencing the objective existence of something else beyond them. A belief in the former is not identical with a belief in the latter. The one cannot, the other may possibly be refused. . . . Now the reality of this, as a subjective datum—as an ideal phaenomenon, it is absolutely impossible to doubt without doubting the existence of consciousness, for consciousness is itself this fact; and to doubt the existence of consciousness is absolutely impossible; for as such a doubt could not exist, except in and through consciousness, it would, consequently, annihilate itself.—Sir W. Hamilton, *Lectures on Metaphysics and Logic*[4]

It is a further general characteristic of all mental phenomena that they are perceived only in inner consciousness. . . . One could believe that such a definition says little, since it would seem more natural to take the opposite course, defining the act by reference to its object, and so defining inner perception of mental phenomena. But inner perception has still another characteristic, apart from the special nature of its object, which distinguishes it: namely, that immediate, infallible self-evidence, which pertains to it alone among all the cases in which we know objects of experience. Thus, if we say that mental phenomena are those which are grasped by means of inner perception, we have accordingly said that their perception is immediately evident.—F. Brentano, *Psychology from an Empirical Standpoint*[5]

Subtract in what we say that we see, or hear, or otherwise learn from direct experience, *all that conceivably could be mistaken;* the remainder is the given content of the experience inducing this belief. . . . Apprehensions of the given which such expressive statements formulate, are not judgments, and they are not here classed as knowledge, because they are not subject to any possible error. Statement of such apprehension is, however, true or false; there could be no doubt about the presented context of experience as such at the time when it is given, but it would be possible to tell a lie about it.—C. I. Lewis, *An Analysis of Knowledge and Valuation*[6]

[4]Boston: Gould and Lincoln, 1874, IV, 188.
[5]Selection in Vesey, ed., *Body and Mind*, p. 151.
[6]La Salle, Ill.: Open Court, 1946, pp. 182–83.

Some Philosophers . . . have thought it possible to find a class of statements which would be both genuinely informative and at the same time logically immune from doubt. . . . The statements usually chosen for this role . . . characterize some present state of the speaker, or some present content of his experience. I cannot, so it is maintained, be in any doubt or in any way mistaken about the fact. I cannot be unsure whether I feel a headache, nor can I think that I feel a headache when I do not.—A. J. Ayer, *The Problem of Knowledge*[7]

Besides what is logically certain there are a number of immediately known propositions which we can regard as absolutely certain although there would be no self-contradiction in denying them. In this class I put more specific propositions based on introspection. I cannot see any self-contradiction in supposing that I might make mistakes in introspection; and there is therefore no *logical* absurdity in supposing that I might be mistaken now when I judge that I feel warm or that I have a visual presentation of a table. But I still cannot help being absolutely certain of the truth of these propositions and I do not think that I ought to be otherwise. . . . As we have seen, it is however hardly possible to claim this absolute certainty for judgments about physical objects, and, as we shall see, there are similar difficulties in claiming it for judgments about minds other than one's own.—A. C. Ewing, *The Fundamental Questions of Philosophy*[8]

I think the facts that give rise to the illusion of privacy would be the following: (a) you can be *in doubt* as to whether I am in pain, but I cannot; (b) you can *find out* whether I am in pain, but I cannot; and (c) you can be *mistaken* as to whether I am in pain, but I cannot.—N. Malcolm, "The Privacy of Experience"[9]

But there is also a sense in which a person's report that he sees an after-image *cannot* be mistaken; and it is this sense that I intend when I say that his report is "incorrigible".—N. Malcolm, "Direct Perception"[10]

Among the incorrigible statements are statements about "private" experiences and mental events, e.g., pain statements, statements about mental images, reports of thoughts, and so on. These are incorrigible in the sense that if a person sincerely asserts such a statement it does not make sense to suppose, and nothing could be accepted as showing, that he is mistaken, i.e., that what he says is false.—S. Shoemaker, *Self-Knowledge and Self-Identity*[11]

---

[7]London: Macmillan, 1956, p. 55. It should be noted that this passage sets forth a view that Ayer is examining rather than propounding.
[8]London: Routledge & Kegan Paul, 1951, chap. 5.
[9]In Stroll, ed., *Epistemology*, p. 146.
[10]In *Knowledge and Certainty*, p. 85.
[11]Ithaca: Cornell University Press, 1963, pp. 215–16.

All of these quotations represent one's epistemic position vis-à-vis one's own mental states (or some subclass thereof) as highly favorable in some way or other. In most of the passages quoted there is no contrast explicitly drawn with the epistemic position of other persons, but such a contrast is implicit in what is said. None of these philosophers would suppose that other persons have the kind of cognitive access to my mental states which they impute to me; hence by being in this kind of position one enjoys a kind of special epistemic privilege.

How many distinguishable types of favorable epistemic position are involved in these passages? One type that is clearly imputed in several of the quotations is the impossibility of mistake. Thus one's judgments or beliefs about his own mental states "cannot be false" (Descartes), "are not subject to any possible error" (Lewis), "cannot . . . be . . . in any way mistaken" (Ayer), "it does not make sense to suppose that he is mistaken" (Shoemaker). A great many terms have been used for this kind of epistemic privilege. I prefer "infallibility".

There is also much talk in these passages about immunity from doubt (Descartes, Hamilton, Lewis, Ayer, Ewing, Malcolm). But we can distinguish several different indubitability claims, each of which can be attributed to one or more of our authors. First there is the claim that it is impossible to *have any doubt* as to the truth of a proposition attributing a current mental state to oneself. I am *incapable of being in doubt* as to whether I am now thinking about my lecture for tomorrow, or whether there is now an image of my boyhood home before my mind's eye. This impossibility might be logical, or it might be nomological (based, for example, on psychological laws). Malcolm in the first quotation is clearly asserting the former, for he asserts the three points as facts about the "grammar" of the word "pain"; because of the way we use the word, no sense can be attached to speaking of a person having a doubt as to whether he is in pain. On the other hand Lewis might be plausibly interpreted as claiming that it is a psychological impossibility for one to doubt whether he is currently in some conscious state.

However, we can also discern a quite different concept of indubitability at work in these authors. This is a normative rather than a factual concept—not the impossibility of being, in fact, in a psychological state of doubt, but rather the impossibility of having any grounds for doubt, the impossibility of a rational doubt. In our quoted material this comes out most clearly in the passage from Hamilton. What he is arguing there, in the spirit of Descartes, is not so much that there are psychological bars to the formation of a doubt, but rather that such a doubt would necessarily lack any foundation, since it presupposes that which is called into question, viz., the fact of consciousness.[12] Again, if, as we shall argue later, we can take Ewing to be using "certainty" as equivalent to "indubitability", he clearly distinguishes our two main senses of indubitability and asserts both. "But I still cannot help being absolutely certain of the truth of these propositions and I do not think that I ought to be otherwise." That is, I find it psychologically impossible to have any doubt of their truth, and I am justified in this incapacity, since there could be no grounds for any doubt.

Note that it is only grounds for doubt on the part of the believer himself that is said to be impossible by Hamilton and Ewing. You could certainly doubt that I feel relieved without "doubting the existence of consciousness"; and Ewing's remarks are explicitly so limited. To be sure, there is some basis for the stronger thesis that no one can have grounds for doubting my belief that I now feel serene. Although it is obviously possible for others to have grounds for doubting a *statement* of mine about my current feelings (for there can be grounds for supposing that I am lying or misusing the language), it might be supposed that if I am straight about what *belief* you have about your current conscious states, I can have no basis for doubting that. But this would seem to be too strong a claim. As we shall see shortly, various philosophers have held, plausibly, that no one can have sufficient reasons for *denying* the truth of such a belief (i.e., for affirming its contradictory); but grounds for *doubt* is another matter. If, when I believe that I feel serene, you observe me acting in such a way as to strongly indicate that I feel upset, then those observations constitute some ground for doubt on your part, a doubt that is not negated, as it is on my part, by my feelings themselves. Thus we will restrict normative indubitability to the impossibility of grounds for doubt on the part of the believer.

We have distinguished three forms of indubitability: logical impossibility of entertaining a doubt, psychological impossibility of entertaining a doubt, impossibility of there being any grounds for doubt. Although for any of them it is worth considering whether propositions about one's own current mental states are indubitable in that sense, it is only the third that constitutes a distinctively *epistemic* privilege. If I am so related to a certain group of propositions that whenever I believe one of those propositions to be true I can have no grounds for doubt that it is true, then there can be no epistemic fault in my believing any proposition in that group. Whenever I believe any proposition in that

---

[12]The merits of Hamilton's argument, and any other *substantive* question concerning privileged access, are not within the jurisdiction of this article.

group I am fully justified in so doing; no epistemic fault can be imputed to me. This is to be in a highly favorable epistemic position.^ On the other hand, the mere fact that I find it psychologically impossible to doubt the truth of any such proposition does not in itself confer any cognitive superiority. We can think of many cases where people are unable to entertain doubts about certain matters, and where we regard this as a liability rather than an asset. Very small children are often unable to imagine that what their parents say is mistaken, and religious fanatics are sometimes psychologically unable to doubt the tenets of their sect. We do not take such people to be thereby in a better position for acquiring knowledge; quite the contrary, we suppose this critical incapacity to be hampering them in the cognitive enterprise. To be sure, when the second sort of indubitability is imputed to propositions about one's own mental states, it is supposed that this holds for all men as such, and it may be thought that this renders inappropriate an epithet such as "lack of critical faculty", which one might suppose to be applicable only when the disability in question is peculiar to certain stages of development, types of personality, or kinds of social groups. Nevertheless, if we suppose that a universally shared psychological inability to doubt confers some advantage in the acquisition of knowledge, it is only because we think that this *psychological* inability is conjoined with, and perhaps is a reflection of, indubitability in the normative sense, the impossibility of any *grounds* for doubt. If it *should* be the case that the psychological impossibility of doubting the truth of one's beliefs about one's own current mental states is due to an ingrained weakness in the human critical apparatus, or to an irresistible partiality to one's own case, then this inability would *not* indicate any first person epistemic advantage in these matters.

We shall have to make the same judgment concerning Malcolm's thesis of the logical impossibility of entertaining a doubt. Suppose we grant that the meanings we attach to our conscious state terms are such that it makes no sense to suppose that a given person is in doubt as to whether he is currently in a certain kind of conscious state. That would be a noteworthy feature of our conceptual scheme, but we still have to ask whether or not it is well founded. Unless we accept normative indubitability, or some other principle according to which a person is in a particularly favorable position to discriminate true from false propositions concerning his present conscious states, then we will have to conclude that the features of our "logical grammar" to which Malcolm alludes are ill-advised and that the fact that this "logical grammar" is as it is does nothing to show that persons are in a specially favorable epistemic position vis-à-vis their own current conscious states.

Thus I conclude that only *normative* indubitability clearly constitutes a cognitive advantage. We shall henceforth restrict the term 'indubitability' to that variety.

We might think of indubitability as a weaker version of infallibility. To be infallible vis-à-vis one's present conscious states is to be in such a position that no belief one has to the effect that one is in such a state can *be* mistaken. Whereas an indubitability thesis does not commit one to the impossibility of mistakes, but to the weaker claim that one could have no grounds for questioning the accuracy of one's belief. There is another derivative of infallibility that can be found in the literature, though more rarely. It is set out clearly in the following passage from A. J. Ayer's British Academy lecture on "Privacy."

> If this is correct, it provides us with a satisfactory model for the logic of the statements that a person may make about his present thoughts and feelings. He may not be infallible, but still his word is sovereign. The logic of these statements that a person makes about himself is such that if others were to contradict him we should not be entitled to say that they were right so long as he honestly maintained his stand against them.[13]

What Ayer is saying here is that it is impossible, not that I *am* mistaken, but that anyone else should *show* that I am mistaken in what I say (believe) about my present thoughts and feelings.[14] This is an inherent impossibility, for the "logic of these statements" requires us to give the person in question the last word. We may term this kind of epistemic position "incorrigibility".[15]

"Certainty" is another term that figures prominently in our quotations. A person's judgments concerning his own mental states are said to exhibit the highest degree of certainty; one can be *absolutely* certain about such matters (Descartes, Locke, Ewing). How are we to interpret these claims vis-à-vis the others we have been considering? Here too we may distinguish factual and normative senses. Being certain of something may be construed as a matter of feeling assurance, feeling confident that one is correct; this is presumably the reverse side of the (de

---

[13]Ayer, "Privacy," p. 73.

[14]It may be contended, e.g., by partisans of the "private language argument", that there is no significant difference between an impossibility of anyone else's showing that I am mistaken and an impossibility of my being mistaken. I am unable to go into those issues in this essay.

[15]The use of this term presents the usual chaotic picture. We have seen Malcolm and Shoemaker using it to mean infallibility. Thomas Nagel in his essay "Physicalism" (*The Philosophical Review*, 74 [1965], 344) uses it to mean what I shall next be distinguishing as "omniscience". I believe that the present usage is a more apt one.

facto) absence of doubt. To feel complete confidence that one is correct is to entertain no doubt about the matter. And a psychological (logical) impossibility of the entertaining of any doubt would be the same thing as a psychological (logical) necessity of feeling completely assured that one is correct. Thus this kind of certainty comes under the scope of the arguments just given to dismiss the corresponding forms of indubitability from further consideration.

However there is also a normative concept of certainty, a concept employed by Ewing when after saying "I still cannot help being absolutely certain of the truth of these propositions" he adds, ". . . and I do not think that I ought to be otherwise". To be certain in this sense is to be justified in feeling complete assurance. How is this normative concept related to the modes of epistemic superiority already distinguished? It seems impossible to make a general identification of normative certainty with any of the other modes. To be justified in feeling complete assurance that S is to have a very strong warrant for one's belief that S. But views may differ as to just how strong a warrant is required: the strongest conceivable, the strongest one could reasonably ask for in the subject matter under consideration, and so on. Thus the general concept of normative certainty is really a sort of family or continuum of concepts, differing as to the chosen locus along the dimension of strength of warrants for belief. Our other modes of epistemic superiority, however, are not subject to variations in degree; they are absolute concepts. If one's belief is indubitable, *no* doubt can have any basis: if one is infallible, one's belief must be *wholly* correct; and so on.

But although we cannot make any general identification of the concept of normative certainty with the other modes of epistemic superiority we have distinguished, still I think that the degree of certainty typically ascribed to one's beliefs about one's own mental states amounts either to infallibility or indubitability. Sometimes it is claimed (Descartes, Locke) that such beliefs enjoy the highest conceivable certainty; in that case one is in effect ascribing infallibility, for the highest warrant one could conceive for a belief is one which would render the falsity of the belief *impossible*. In other cases something weaker is being claimed; thus Ewing conjoins his assertion of certainty with the admission that "there is no self-contradiction in supposing that I might make mistakes in introspection". However, in such cases it is plausible to suppose that a warrant strong enough to exclude all grounds for doubt is being imputed, and hence that what is being ascribed is indubitability. Thus I do not feel that we need "certainty" as a separate item in our list.

We have still not exhausted the conceptual riches of our quotations.

Going back to the passage from Hume, we note that he not only says of "actions and sensations of the mind" that they "must necessarily . . . be what they appear", which is infallibility, but that they "must necessarily appear in every particular what they are". In other words, it is not only that every belief or judgment which I form about my present mental states must be correct; it is also necessary that every feature of those states must find representation in those (necessarily correct) beliefs. *Ignorance* as well as *error* is excluded. Let us use the term 'omniscience' for the logical impossibility of ignorance concerning a certain subject matter. Although the Hume quotation contains the only omniscience claim in our original list, we can find other passages in which it is asserted that one is omniscient vis-à-vis one's own mental states.

> It requires only to be stated to be admitted, that when I know, I must know that I know,—when I feel, I must know that I feel,—when I desire, I must know that I desire. The knowledge, the feeling, the desire, are possible only under the condition of being known, and being known by me.[16]

> Thinking and perceiving are essentially conscious processes, which means that they cannot be said to occur unless the person to whom they are ascribed knows that they occur.[17]

We can better represent and interrelate the modes of epistemic privilege we have distinguished, and will be distinguishing, if we have a standard formula for favorable epistemic positions, a formula containing blanks such that when these blanks are filled in differently we get specifications of different modes. One might at first suppose that our formula could simply be: X's knowledge of —— is ——, where the first blank is filled with a specification of the subject matter, and the second blank with a specification of a particular mode of cognitive superiority—infallibility, omniscience, or whatever. This will not work, however, since it is not in general true that the modes we are distinguishing are features of pieces of knowledge, features that a given piece of knowledge might or might not have. This is particularly clear with respect to infallibility and omniscience. We cannot first ascertain that P knows that S, and then go on to ask whether that bit of P's knowledge is or is not infallible or omniscient. The reason is somewhat different in the two cases. Infallibility in the sense of *cannot be mistaken* is a feature necessarily possessed by every piece of *knowledge* in a strong

[16]Hamilton, *Lectures on Metaphysics and Logic*, XI, p. 133.
[17]D. Locke, *Myself and Others* (Oxford: Clarendon Press, 1968), chap. 2, p. 17.

sense of 'knowledge'. That is, it would not be correct to attribute knowledge that S to P unless P's supposition that S were correct. That is part of what we mean by 'know'. If I do not feel elated now, then that is enough to (logically) rule out the possibility that I, or anyone else, know that I am elated now. Thus infallibility does not constitute a feature that distinguishes one kind of *knowledge* from another. With omniscience (in a certain area) on the other hand, the point is that this is a feature of one's position with respect to the possession or nonpossession of knowledge (of certain matters), rather than a feature of any particular instance of such knowledge; it is a matter of what kinds of knowledge one (necessarily) has, rather than a matter of the character of that knowledge once obtained.

But although infallibility and omniscience are not characteristics that (may) attach to some pieces of knowledge and not to others, they clearly have something to do with knowledge. They are, in some way, features of one's epistemic position, powers, or status, vis-à-vis some domain of knowledge. Perhaps we can find an illuminating way of representing these modes of privileged access if we dig into the structure of the concept of knowledge, rather than just using it in an unanalyzed form. For our purposes we can work with the following familiar tripartite analysis of "P knows that S." The analysans consists of a conjunction of the following:

(A) P believes that S.
(B) P is justified in believing that S.
(C) It is the case that S.[18,B]

As for infallibility, although a piece of knowledge is not the sort of thing that may or may not be capable of error, there is, according to the above analysis, a constituent of P's knowledge that S which may or may not be capable of error, viz., P's belief that S.[19] Thus one can be said to be infallible vis-à-vis a certain subject matter provided one cannot be mistaken in any beliefs he forms concerning that subject matter.

[18]Recent criticism has shown that this analysis is not generally adequate without modification or enrichment. See E. L. Gettier, "Is Justified True Belief Knowledge?", *Analysis*, 23 (1962–63), 121–23. It is dubious, however, that Gettier problems arise for one's knowledge of one's current conscious states, and so we may take the above as a sufficient approximation for present purposes.
[19]It will be noted that in the previous discussion we were already presenting infallibility as an impossibility of error for one's *beliefs* or *judgments*.

A person enjoys infallibility[20] vis-à-vis his own mental states = $_{df}$ It is logically impossible that a belief of his about his own mental states should be mistaken.

Now if one is so situated relative to a class of beliefs, he is amply, indeed maximally, *justified* in holding beliefs of that class. For one could hardly have a stronger (epistemic) justification for holding a certain belief than the logical impossibility of the belief's being mistaken.[C] Hence where the mere possession of the belief logically guarantees truth, it equally guarantees the belief's being justified, that is, it guarantees the satisfaction of both the other two conditions for knowledge. Hence we can just as well state our definition as follows (generalizing now over subject matters, so as not to restrict the general concept of infallibility to the topic of one's own mental states):

(D1) P (a person) enjoys infallibility with respect to a type of proposition, R = $_{df}$ For any proposition, S, of type R, it is logically impossible that P should believe that S, without knowing that S. (Condition A for P's knowing that S logically implies conditions B and C.)

Note that by defining infallibility with respect to a *type* of proposition, rather than with respect to individual propositions, we have avoided a well-known difficulty of such definitions. For any necessarily true proposition, it is impossible for me to believe that proposition and my belief be mistaken, *whatever my epistemic situation may be vis-à-vis that proposition.* But, by thinking of infallibility as a position one is in with respect to a type of proposition, for example, mathematical propositions, physical object propositions, or propositions concerning one's own current conscious states, this difficulty is avoided. If it is impossible for me to believe *any* mathematical proposition mistakenly, then I certainly am in a highly favorable epistemic position vis-à-vis that subject matter. To be sure, the types must be chosen properly. If the type is *necessarily true propositions* or *true propositions,* we will still get the result that I can be infallible while being in a poor epistemic position. I have no general recipe for choosing suitable types other than that they be chosen in terms of subject matter.

The philosophers who shy away from speaking of a person's *knowing* that he has certain thoughts and sensations will probably be even more

---

[20]We use this cumbersome locution rather than the more natural "is infallible," so that our standard form will be usable for concepts such as indubitability that are not predicated of persons.

leary of speaking of a person's *believing* that he has a certain thought or sensation. And it must be admitted that one does not ordinarily speak in this vein. But, so far as I can see, this is simply because we ordinarily use the word 'belief' in such a way that it contrasts with knowledge, as in the following dialogue:

What was that noise in the kitchen?
I believe that the tap was leaking.
You *believe* it was leaking! Couldn't you see whether it
was or not?

In this paper, as quite frequently in philosophy, we are using the word in a wider sense. This sense can be indicated by making it explicit that a sufficient condition for P's believing that S is that P would have a tendency to assert that S if he were asked whether it were the case that S, if he understood the question, and if he were disposed to be sincere. In this wider sense one often believes that one has certain thoughts and feelings. At this point the Wittgensteinian will, no doubt, cavil at the idea that one can correctly be said to *assert* that one has a certain feeling, but I cannot pursue the controversy further in this paper.

Omniscience can be given a parallel formulation as follows:

(D2) P enjoys omniscience vis-à-vis a type of proposition R = $_{df}$ For any true proposition, S, of type R, it is logically impossible that P should not know that S. (Condition C for P's knowing that S logically implies conditions A and B.)[21]

Thus this familiar analysis of knowledge permits us to give a neat presentation of the infallibility-omniscience distinction. They differ just as to which of the three conditions for knowledge entails the other two.[22] Indubitability does not fit into the model in quite so neat a fashion, but of course it can be represented there. To say that one's beliefs in a certain area are immune from doubt is just to say that given any such belief, it is impossible for one to have any grounds for doubting that the other two conditions for knowledge hold. In the first

---

[21]I won't try to build up this implication stepwise. I can't see that we get a mirror image here of the infallibility situation, so that by virtue of C's implying A, it would thereby imply B. Even if all facts of a certain sort are necessarily reflected in my beliefs, it would not follow that I do not form numerous false beliefs in such facts. And hence it would not follow that such beliefs are automatically justified. The implication by C of the other conditions will have to be taken as a package.

[22]For a similar presentation, see D. M. Armstrong, *A Materialist Theory of the Mind* (London: Routledge & Kegan Paul, 1968), p. 101.

instance, indubitability entails that one can have no grounds for doubting that one's belief is true (C). But if that is the case, then surely one can have no grounds for doubting that one is justified in holding one's belief, as pointed out above.

(D3) P enjoys indubitability vis-à-vis a type of proposition, R = $_{df}$. For any proposition, S, of type R, it is logically impossible that P should believe that S and that P should have any grounds for doubting that P knows that S. (Condition A for P's knowing that S logically implies that there can be no grounds for doubting that conditions B and C hold.)

Incorrigibility can be given a similar formulation as follows:

(D4) P enjoys incorrigibility vis-à-vis a type of proposition, R = $_{df}$ For any proposition, S, of type R, it is logically impossible that P should believe that S and that someone should show that P is mistaken in this belief. (Condition A for P's knowing that S logically implies that no one else can show that condition C does not hold.)[23]

Having now defined four different favorable epistemic positions in which a person may be vis-à-vis a given range of propositions, we can use these concepts to specify four ways in which a person may be said to have privileged access to his current mental states. To say that a person has *privileged* access to his current mental states is to say that his epistemic position vis-à-vis propositions ascribing current mental states to himself is favorable in a way no one else's position is. The simplest standard formula for a privileged access claim would be:

Each person enjoys ——— vis-à-vis propositions ascribing current mental states to himself, while no one else enjoys ——— vis-à-vis such propositions.

[23]It will be noted that all these definitions have been stated in terms of logical modalities. Later we shall explore the possibility of employing other modalities.
We could, of course, make incorrigibility more parallel with the other modes by construing it to involve also the impossibility of anyone else's showing that P is not justified in believing that S. However, since this goes beyond what is either stated by our sources, or implied by what they say, I have avoided strengthening it in this way. It is clear that an impossibility of anyone else's showing that I am mistaken does not necessarily carry with it an impossibility of showing that my belief is unjustified. And this general possibility of dissociation might conceivably apply to beliefs about one's own mental states. It is conceivable, e.g., that one might show, through psychoanalysis, that I have a general tendency to deceive myself about my attitudes toward my daughter. This might well be taken to show that I am not justified in what I believe about those attitudes, even though no one is able to show (conclusively) that any particular belief I have about those attitudes is mistaken.

By successively filling in the blank with the four terms we have defined, we get four different privileged access theses.

However, it will be useful in our further discussions to have the different versions of a privileged access thesis spelled out more explicitly, with the content of the chosen mode of favorable epistemic position explicitly represented. We can give these more explicit formulations as follows:

(T1) (Infallibility) Each person is so related to propositions ascribing current mental states to himself that it is logically impossible for him to believe that such a proposition is true without knowing it to be true; while no one else is so related to such propositions.

(T2) (Omniscience) Each person is so related to propositions ascribing current mental states to himself that it is logically impossible for such a proposition to be true without his knowing that it is true; while no one else is so related to such propositions.

(T3) (Indubitability) Each person is so related to propositions ascribing current mental states to himself that it is logically impossible both for him to believe that such a proposition is true and for him to have any grounds for doubting that he knows that proposition to be true; while no one else is so related to such propositions.

(T4) (Incorrigibility) Each person is so related to propositions ascribing current mental states to himself that it is logically impossible both for him to believe that such a proposition is true and for someone else to show that that proposition is false; while no one else is so related to such propositions.

III

As I pointed out earlier, it is not my aim in this work to determine in just what way, if any, one does have privileged access to just what kinds of mental states. It may help, however, to motivate our consideration of other modes of privileged access if we briefly allude to some of the considerations that have led many thinkers to reject the modes so far considered. If we think of the range of mental states as including dispositional (belief, desire) as well as phenomenal (sensations, thoughts, feelings) states, there are strong reasons for denying that one enjoys infallibility, omniscience, indubitability, or incorrigibility vis-à-vis all the items within this range. The most dramatic reasons come from the sorts of cases highlighted by psychoanalysis, in which one hides certain of one's desires or beliefs from oneself, and in the process attributes to oneself desires or beliefs that one does not have. Thus consider the classic overprotective mother, who is preventing her daughter from going out in society in order to prevent her from developing into a feared rival. This mother stoutly and sincerely denies wanting to prevent her daughter's development and believing that her policy is likely to lead to any such result. Instead, she says, she is motivated solely by a desire to protect her daughter from harm. It does seem possible that there are cases in which the person both has desires and beliefs without knowing that she has them and attributes to herself desires and beliefs she does not have (at least not the extent she supposes). Moreover, in such cases the person could be brought to the point of having grounds for doubting what she has believed about the desires and beliefs in question, and it even seems possible that she herself or others may sometimes be in a position to *show* that she is mistaken; so that not even indubitability or incorrigibility hold for beliefs and desires.

There is no doubt that proponents of these modes of privileged access are in a stronger position with respect to phenomenal states. I do not feel that this issue is definitely settled by a long way, but still there are substantial negative arguments here.[24] For example, a general argument against infallibility is that knowledge of particular facts essentially involves the application of general concepts to those facts and hence is inherently liable to error. At the very least these negative arguments can move us to consider whether there is not some weaker sense in which a person might be said to be in a necessarily superior epistemic position vis-à-vis his own mental states.

Another candidate that is well represented in the literature is "immediacy" or "directness". The notion that a person is privileged in having *immediate* knowledge of his own mental states is expressed incidentally in several of our original quotations. Thus Brentano says that the perception of mental phenomena is "immediately evident"; Ewing speaks of propositions based on introspection as "immediately known"; Hume speaks of our consciousness of the "actions and sensations of the mind" as that domain of experience where we are "most intimately conscious". Immediacy is closer to the center of the stage in the following quotations.

> It has been suggested, namely, that any entity, which *can be directly known by one mind only* is a mental entity, and is "in the mind" of the person in question, and also, conversely, that all mental entities can be directly known only by a single mind.[25]

---

[24]For some recent presentation of such arguments, see Armstrong, *A Materialist Theory of Mind*, chap. 6, sec. 10; and B. Aune, *Knowledge, Mind, and Nature* (New York: Random House, 1967), chap. 2, sec. I.
[25]Moore, "The Subject Matter of Psychology," p. 241.

It is one such essential feature of what the word "mind" means that minds are private; that one's own mind is something with which one is directly acquainted—nothing more so—but that the mind of another is something which one is unable directly to inspect.[26]

The terms 'immediate' and 'direct' are susceptible of a variety of interpretations. Malcolm in his essay "Direct Perception" maintains that 'impossibility of error' is the main feature of the standard philosophical conception of direct perception". He cites several eminent philosophers in support of this claim, including Berkeley, Moore, and Lewis. He then goes on to construct the following definition: "*A directly* perceives *x* if and only if *A*'s assertion that he perceives *x* could not be mistaken . . . ".[27] Of course if this is what we mean by directness, we have already discussed it under the heading of infallibility. We are therefore led to look for some other interpretation.

Moore, in typical fashion, tries to explain "direct knowledge" by pointing to a certain not further analyzable feature of our conscious experience. Immediately following the passage quoted above he writes:

By "direct knowledge" is here meant the kind of relation we have to a colour, when we actually see it, or to a sound when we actually hear it.

But if we simply leave the matter there, it is not very satisfactory. Presumably *something* can be said about the relation one has to a color when one actually sees it. And if it is not made explicit what the relation(s) in question is, we shall have no basis for resolving controversies over whether something or other is (or can be) directly known, whether, for example, one directly knows that one has a certain belief, or whether it is conceivable that another person could directly know one's own thoughts. Let us try to find something more explicit.

Talk about immediate knowledge has traditionally been powerfully influenced by a spatial-causal model of mediacy. When people deny that perceptual knowledge of physical objects is immediate, it is often on the grounds that there is a spatial and causal gap between my knowledge (or rather the beliefs and/or sense impressions involved) and the object of knowledge—the tree or whatever. There are spatial and causal intermediaries involved, and if these are not aligned properly, things can be thrown off. Similarly there are causal and spatial intermediaries between my desire or feeling and your belief that I have

[26]C. I. Lewis, "Some Logical Considerations Concerning the Mental," in Vesey, ed., *Body and Mind*, p. 332.
[27]In *Knowledge and Certainty*, p. 89.

266

that desire or feeling. Your belief (in the most favorable case) is evoked by some perceptions of yours, which are in turn evoked by some behavior of mine, which is in turn evoked by my desire or feeling. But when it comes to my knowledge of my desires or feelings, no such intermediaries are involved, and here we do not have the same possibilities of distortion. I am "right up next to" my own mental states; I am "directly aware" of them; they give rise to my knowledge without going through a causal chain of any sort. Let us call immediacy so construed "causal immediacy".

The main reason for not using this sense of 'immediacy' here is that we do not know how to determine either spatial or causal directness for knowledge of one's own mental states. We are not able to assign precise spatial locations to mental states.[28] Insofar as such location is possible, it is something rough, like "in the body", or "in the head", or maybe "in the brain". For other cases that is enough for a judgment of mediacy; as long as my belief that there is a tree out there is somewhere in my head, it is clearly not spatially contiguous to the tree; and as long as your desire is in your head and my belief that you have that desire is in my head, then they are not spatially contiguous (even if our heads are touching). But when both the belief and the object of the belief are mental states of the same person, we would need a more precise method of location to determine whether or not they are spatially contiguous. They are both "in the head", but just where in the head? Similar comments can be made concerning judgments of causal immediacy. With no more precise assumption than that the immediate causal antecedents of a belief of mine consist of processes in the brain, I can be sure that no belief of mine has its immediate causal antecedents in a tree. But if I am to determine whether my desire to go to Europe is an immediate causal antecedent of my belief that I have a desire to go to Europe, I need to have a more fine-grained view of the causal processes involved, and unfortunately we do not have any such view. We are in almost total ignorance of the causal processes, if any, involved in the origin of beliefs about our own mental states, and so we simply do not know what intermediaries there may be.

The upshot of this discussion is that although we can have sufficient reasons for terming many cases of knowledge "mediate" in the causal sense, we can have no assurance that any particular kind of knowledge is causally *immediate*, for when we come to the only plausible candidates

[28]I am not maintaining, like some opponents of the identity theory, that such determinations are logically impossible. I am merely pointing out that at present we lack the resources for doing so.

for such immediacy, we do not know enough about the spatial and causal relations involved (if any) to have any basis for the denial of intermediaries. Thus our criterion is quite unworkable if we interpret it in terms of causal immediacy. It will be noted that we have argued for this without casting doubt on the intelligibility of the term 'causal immediacy'. Such a doubt could be raised, but that is another story.

There is a more distinctively epistemic sense of the mediate-immediate contrast, a sense that is suggested by such talk as the following. "You can know what I am thinking and feeling only *through* something (some signs, indications, criteria, or whatever); your knowledge of my thoughts and feelings is *based on* something else you know". But I, by contrast, know directly what I am thinking and feeling. I don't have to "derive" this knowledge from anything else. Let's say that in the sense of the contrast suggested by these remarks, mediate knowledge is, while immediate knowledge is not, *based on* other knowledge.

However, the term 'based on' does not wear a unique interpretation on its face. It is often used in such a way that to say that my knowledge that S is based on my knowledge that T is to say that I arrived at the knowledge that S by inferring S from T. Thus philosophers have often used the presence or absence of inference as the crucial consideration in deciding whether a given piece of knowledge is to be called "direct" or "indirect".

> I affirm, for example, that I hear a man's voice. This would pass, in common language, for a direct perception. All, however, which is really perception, is that I hear a sound. That the sound is a voice, and that voice the voice of a man, are not perceptions but inferences.[29]

However, it is clear that this contrast in terms of inference is not going to make the desired discriminations if we confine ourselves to conscious inference. The perception of speech does not ordinarily involve a conscious inference from the existence of a sound (under some acoustical description) to the existence of a human voice as its source. And more to the present point, it is clear that one's knowledge of the mental states of others is not always mediate if conscious inference is a necessary condition of mediacy. Quite often when I see that my companion feels dejected, I am not aware of performing any inference from specifiable features of his speech, demeanor, and bearing to his dejection. And we certainly want to develop a concept of mediacy which is such that our ordinary knowledge of the mental states of

[29]J. S. Mill, *A System of Logic*, bk. IV, chap. I, sect. 2. Quoted by Malcolm, "Direct Perception," p. 88.

others counts as mediate. Hence if we are going to make the desired discriminations in terms of the presence or absence of inference, we are going to have to rely heavily on the postulation of unconscious inference. I would not wish to subscribe to any general ban on such postulations, and it may be that we are justified in postulating unconscious inferences in just those cases where they are needed to discriminate between mediate and immediate knowledge along the present lines. However, in view of the obscurities surrounding the concept of unconscious inferential processes, and in view of present uncertainties concerning the conditions under which the postulations of such processes is justified, it would seem desirable to search for some other interpretation of 'based on'.

I would suggest that the tripartite analysis of knowledge introduced earlier provides us with the materials for such an interpretation. Using that schema, we can distinguish between mediate and immediate knowledge in terms of what satisfies the second condition. If what justifies P in believing that S is some other knowledge, or justified belief, that P possesses, then his knowledge that S is mediated by (based on) that other knowledge, or justified belief, in a strictly epistemological sense. (Henceforth I shall, in the interest of concision, omit the disjunct "or justified belief" in explaining the mediate-immediate contrast, though it will be tacitly understood.) If, on the other hand, what satisfies condition (B) is something other than P's having some knowledge or other, we can say that his knowledge that S is *im*mediate, not based on other knowledge. Let us call this kind of immediacy "epistemic immediacy". If I know that there was a fire last night at the corner of Huron and 5th because I read it in the *Ann Arbor News,* my knowledge is mediate; since what warrants me in believing that there is such a fire is my knowledge that such a fire was reported in the *Ann Arbor News,* plus my knowledge that it is a reliable source for local news. (The fact that the *Ann Arbor News did* carry this story and the fact that it *is* reliable in such matters will not justify *me* in believing that the fire took place, unless *I* know them to be the case.) Again if I know that my brother is dissatisfied with his job because he has complained to me about it, what warrants me in believing that he is dissatisfied is my knowledge that he has been complaining about it (and means what he says). On the other hand, it seems overwhelmingly plausible to suppose that what warrants me in believing that I feel disturbed, or am thinking about the mind-body problem, is not some other knowledge that I have. There is no bit of knowledge, or disjunction of bits of knowledge, such that if I do not have it (or some of them) my belief is not warranted. What would such bits of knowledge be? This is reflected in the oft-cited, but almost as often misunderstood,[30] fact that it "sounds odd", or even "nonsensical" to respond to a person who has just told us how he feels or what he is thinking, with "What reason do you have for saying that?" or "What is your evidence for that?". One does not know how to answer such a question; there is no answer to give.

This characterization of "immediate" is purely negative. It specifies what sort of thing does *not* satisfy condition B where the knowledge is immediate, but it does not further limit the field of alternative possibilities. Clearly we can have different sorts of immediate knowledge claims depending on what is taken to satisfy condition B. If we consider the most explicit claims to immediate knowledge of one's own mental states in the literature, those of Ayer and Shoemaker, we shall see that in both cases condition C is taken to imply condition B.

> This gives us the clue also to what may be meant by saying that knowledge of this kind is direct. In other cases where knowledge is claimed, it is not sufficient that one be able to give a true report of what one claims to know: it is necessary also that the claim be authorized, and this is done by adducing some other statement which in some way supports the statement for which the claim is made. But in this case no such authority is needed .... Our knowledge of our thoughts and feelings accrues to us automatically in the sense that having them puts us in a position and gives us the authority to report them.[31]

> ... it is characteristic of a certain kind of statements, what I there called "first-person experience statements", that being entitled to assert such a statement does not consist in having established that the statement is true, i.e., in having good evidence that it is true or having observed that it is true, but consists simply in the statement's *being* true.[32]

Let us use the term 'truth-sufficiency' for the sort of epistemic position described by these authors. We can put this notion into our standard format as follows:

(D5) P enjoys truth-sufficiency vis-à-vis a type of proposition, R = $_{df}$ For any true proposition, S, of type R, it is logically impossible that P should not be justified in believing that S. (Condition C for P's knowing that S logically implies condition B.)[33]

---

[30]It is misunderstood when it is taken to show that it makes no sense to speak of a person's knowing that he feels disturbed, rather than taken to show what kind of knowledge this is.

[31]Ayer, "Privacy," in *The Concept of a Person*, p. 64.

[32]Shoemaker, *Self-Knowledge and Self-Identity*, p. 216.

[33]This is the first time we have envisaged an implication of condition B while the

The privileged access thesis that makes use of this concept can be formulated as follows.

(T5) (Truth-sufficiency) Each person is so related to propositions ascribing current mental states to himself that it is logically impossible both for such a proposition to be true and for him not to be justified in believing it to be true; while no one else is so related to such propositions.

Knowledge involving truth-sufficiency is a sort of limiting case of direct knowledge; for here what is taken to justify the belief is something that is independently required for knowledge, viz., the truth of the belief. Thus nothing over and above the other two conditions for knowledge is required for the satisfaction of condition B, and so B becomes, in a way, vacuous. We may call cases of knowledge in which nothing is required to satisfy B over and above the other conditions for knowledge, "autonomous" knowledge.[34]

However, one can hold that a certain kind of knowledge is direct without considering it to be autonomous. Whenever condition B is satisfied by something other than the possession of one or more pieces of other *knowledge* by the person in question, *and* this something goes beyond the other conditions for knowledge, we have knowledge that is direct but not autonomous. Thus a "direct realist", who denies that one's perceptual knowledge of physical objects is based on an epistemically prior knowledge of sense data, will think of perceptual knowledge as direct in the present sense of that term. However, he will certainly not think that nothing but the truth of S (a proposition describing a perceivable state of affairs) is required to justify a perceptual belief in S. The mere fact that it is true that there is now a fire in my living room fireplace does not justify me in believing this, and more specifically does not justify me in accepting it as a perceptual belief. I shall not be so justified if I am out of sensory range of the fire, if, for instance, there is a thick wall between me and the living room, or if my sense organs are not functioning properly. Thus justifiability will at least require the belief that S to have resulted from the normal opera-

---

question of the satisfaction of condition A is left undecided. It may seem that this is impossible, on the grounds that B presupposes that A is satisfied. How can I be justified in having a belief that I do not have? To make the three conditions logically independent, we shall have to interpret B as: "P is in such a position that he will thereby be justified in believing that S if he has such a belief".

[34]Note that where I am infallible or omniscient, my knowledge is "autonomous". For in both those cases one of the other conditions for knowledge entails the justification condition.

tion of one's sense organs and central nervous system, as set into operation by stimuli from S. Perceptual knowledge so construed is direct but not autonomous.

In the light of these distinctions we can see that Ayer and Shoemaker have an inadequate conception of the alternatives to their version of direct knowledge. Let us recall that Ayer says:

> In other cases where knowledge is claimed, it is not sufficient that one be able to give a true report of what one claims to know: it is necessary also that the claim be authorized, and this is done by adducing some other statement which in some way supports the statement for which the claim is made.

Ayer is contrasting (his version of) *autonomous* knowledge with mediate knowledge, ignoring the intermediate category of knowledge that is direct but not autonomous. As our reference to the direct realist view of perception shows, there may be additional "authorizations" required where these "authorizations" do not consist in the putative knower's having some other knowledge that can count as evidence for S. Shoemaker is a bit more inclusive; he gives as alternative modes of "entitlement", "having established that the statement is true, that is, in having good evidence that it is true or having observed that it is true". The latter disjunct could presumably be construed so as to cover perceptual knowledge as viewed by the direct realist, though as stated the condition is uninformatively circular; to say that one has observed that it is true that S is just to say that one has perceptual knowledge that S. However, there are still many other possibilities for direct knowledge. For example, one might hold (with what justice I shall not inquire) that a belief about what makes for successful teaching is justified merely by the fact that one has engaged in a lot of teaching for a long time. More generally one may hold that long experience in an activity puts one in a position to make justified statements (of certain sorts) about that activity, regardless of whether one has any knowledge that could count as sufficient evidence for those statements.[D]

Ayer and Shoemaker have not only overlooked the possibility of direct but nonautonomous knowledge; they have also failed to notice another possibility for autonomous knowledge, viz., taking A instead of C as a sufficient condition for B. To say that this is true of one's epistemic position vis-à-vis a certain range of propositions is to say that *any* belief in such a proposition is necessarily a justified one. We may use the term 'self-warrant' for such a position.

(D6) P enjoys self-warrant vis-à-vis a type of proposition, R = $_{df}$. For any proposition, S, of type R, it is logically impossible that that P should believe that S and not be justified in believing that S. (Condition A for P's knowing that S logically implies condition B.)

The corresponding privileged access thesis may be formulated as follows:

(T6) (Self-warrant) Each person is so related to propositions ascribing current mental states to himself that it is logically impossible both for him to believe that such a proposition is true and not be justified in holding this belief; while no one else is so related to such propositions.

It is clear that self-warrant and truth-sufficiency are weaker analogues of infallibility and omniscience, respectively. In the stronger modes, a given condition for knowledge is held to entail the other two, while in the weaker analogue that condition is held to entail *only* condition B. If one enjoys infallibility, then A entails both B and C, while with self-warrant, A entails only B, leaving open the logical possibility of error. If one enjoys omniscience, C entails both A and B, while with truth-sufficiency C entails only B, leaving open the logical possibility of ignorance.

Let us look more closely at the relations of self-warrant and truth-sufficiency. In a way they are equivalent. Both ensure that conditions A and C, which are required for knowledge in any event, are sufficient for any given piece of knowledge in the appropriate range. Whether I enjoy self-warrant or truth-sufficiency (or both) vis-à-vis my current thoughts and feelings, it will follow in either case that whenever I have a true belief to the effect that I am thinking or feeling *x* at the moment, I can correctly be said to *know* that I am thinking or feeling *x*. And neither privilege implies that anything less will suffice for knowledge. However, they carry different implications as to what can be said short of a full knowledge claim. Enjoying self-warrant in this area guarantees that *any* belief of this sort is justified; it protects one against the possibility of unjustified belief formation. But truth-sufficiency makes no such guarantee; it is compatible with the existence of some unjustified beliefs in the appropriate range. Does truth-sufficiency confer a contrasting partial advantage? Does it put the agent into some favorable position (short of knowledge) that he is not put into by self-warrant? It may seem to. For it guarantees that for any thought or feeling possessed by P at t_1, P is justified in believing that he currently has that thought or feeling. That is, with respect to whatever thought or feeling I have at a given time, the fact that I enjoy truth-sufficiency means that I possess the conditional guarantee that my belief that I currently have that thought or feeling will be justified *if* I have such a belief. But in fact this adds nothing to the guarantee given by self-warrant. For the latter involves the claim that *any* of P's belief in the appropriate range, whether true or not, will (necessarily) be justified, whereas truth-sufficiency guarantees this only for such beliefs as are true. The latter guarantee is a proper part of the former.[35]

Thus, we may conclude that within the range of varieties of privileged access weaker than omniscience, infallibility, indubitability, and incorrigibility, self-warrant is the more interesting and important, since it provides everything in the way of cognitive superiority that is provided by truth-sufficiency, but not vice versa. I would suggest that Ayer and Shoemaker missed the boat when they singled out truth-sufficiency for consideration.

The greater interest of self-warrant is also shown by its greater utility as a principle of cognitive evaluation. We are now taking the standpoint of another person evaluating P's knowledge claims, rather than the standpoint of P and his cognitive capacities. The basic point is that the criteria of justification provided by self-warrant are more accessible than those in terms of which the truth-sufficiency principle is stated. It is generally much easier to determine whether P believes that he has a certain thought, than it is to determine whether in fact he does have that thought. At least that is the case, insofar as a determination of the

---

[35]In fact, if we should interpret truth-sufficiency as involving the claim that C is a necessary as well as a sufficient condition for the justification of the belief (for B), then not only does truth-sufficiency not confer any additional cognitive advantage over self-warrant; it puts one in a less advantageous position. For, contrary to self-warrant, it entails that one cannot be justified in a belief about one's own mental states unless that belief is true. That is, it entails a reduction in the range of cases (intensionally even if not extensionally) in which one's beliefs are justified.

My formulation of truth-sufficiency did not represent C as a necessary condition for B, though Shoemaker could be interpreted in this way. Of course for Shoemaker it is hardly a live issue, since he also commits himself to infallibility without explicitly distinguishing it from truth-sufficiency. If one accepts the infallibility principle, then the question whether C is necessary as well as sufficient for B becomes otiose. For since A entails C, there is not even a logical possibility of a case in which one would justifiably believe that S (A and B) without S's being true (C). However in the case of someone like Ayer, who rejects infallibility, it would seem unjustifiable to make C a necessary condition for B. For this would be to put a person in a worse cognitive position, in a way, with respect to his own mental states than he is in other fields of knowledge. For when it comes to knowledge of the physical world and historical events, it is possible to be justified in believing that S, even though it is not true that S.

latter is a task that goes beyond the determination of the former. And of course where we are employing truth-sufficiency *instead of* self-warrant as a principle for the evaluation of knowledge claims, we must be taking the verification of condition C to be distinguishable from the verification of condition A; otherwise the use of the truth-sufficiency principle could not be distinguished from the use of the self-warrant principle.

IV

I believe that (T6) is the most defensible of the privileged access principles we have considered.[E] It escapes the objections urged against claims of infallibility, omniscience, indubitability, and incorrigibility. It allows for cases in which a person is mistaken about his current mental states (and of course it puts no limit at all on the extent to which a person may be ignorant of his current mental states), and it even allows for cases in which someone else can show that one is mistaken. And at the same time it specifies a very definite respect in which a person is in a superior epistemic position vis-à-vis his own mental states. To be sure, it is not immune from criticism. A thorough examination of such criticism is outside the scope of this paper, but there is one plausible criticism a consideration of which will afford a convenient entrée to still further varieties of privileged access.

The criticism in question is an attack on the logical entailment (and logical impossibility) claim that is imbedded in (T6). It maintains that what the principle holds to be logically impossible, viz., that a first-person-current-mental-state-belief (FPCMSB) should be unwarranted, is in fact consistently conceivable.[36,F] More specifically, it claims that it is just a matter of fact that people are highly reliable in the reports they give us about their feelings, thoughts, and beliefs, that is, that things generally turn out as they could be expected to on the hypothesis that those reports are correct. As things are, if a person tells us that he is feeling depressed or that he is thinking about his income tax, then subsequent events tend to bear this out, insofar as we can form any definite rational expectations, given the complexity of the connections, the undeveloped state of our knowledge of general connections in this area, and the varied possibilities for dissimulation. However, it is quite

---

[36]There are also arguments to the effect that it is logically possible for other persons to enjoy self-warrant (and/or other modes of favorable epistemic position) vis-à-vis one's own mental states, but I will not have time to go into that side of the criticism.

conceivable that the world should be such that a person's reports of his feelings, thoughts, and beliefs would be no better guide to the future than, say, his reports of his immediate physical environment, which are still highly reliable, but by no means so overbearingly so as to be rightly accepted as self-warranted. If the world were like this, it would depend on further factors whether a given FPCMSB were warranted, just as is now the case with perceptual beliefs. Such factors might include how alert the person is at the moment, how good a judge he has proved himself to be in such matters, and so on. Thus in this logically possible world FPCMSBs would be sometimes unwarranted, viz., in those cases in which the requisite additional factors were not present. But then even in our world it cannot be *logically* impossible for a FPCMSB to be unwarranted.[37]

There are various ways in which a defender of self-warrant may try to meet this criticism. First he may roundly deny that what the criticism maintains to be logically possible is indeed so. This denial may take varying forms, but I would suppose that the most plausible is one based on the claim that as we now use mental state terms like "feel ———", "think about ———", etc., it is "part of their meaning" that FPCMSBs are self-warranted. It is impossible, in *our language,* to make sense of the supposition that such a belief should not be warranted. What the critic is doing, in effect, is envisaging a situation in which the meanings of mental state terms would have changed in this respect. But the fact that such a change in meaning is possible leaves untouched the point that, given the present meaning of mental state terms, having a FPCMSB logically guarantees a warrant for the belief.[38]

At the other end of the spectrum would be a capitulation; one might concede, in the face of the criticism, that the epistemic superiority enjoyed by FPCMSBs is only an "empirical" one; it is just a matter of fact that one's own reports of one's current mental states are more reliable in general than the estimates of those states formed by other people.

For present purposes we are interested in replies that lie between these extremes, replies that develop conceptions of self-warrant that lie

---

[37]Such a criticism could, of course, also be brought against the other varieties of privileged access we have distinguished since they all were stated in terms of logical entailment and logical impossibility. However, I have chosen to state the criticism in opposition to self-warrant, since I take this to be the strongest form of privileged access that does not fall victim to other objections.

[38]Just as the criticism in question may be made of stronger forms of a privileged access principle, so this sort of reply may be made in defense of those stronger forms. Malcolm and Shoemaker seem to think that infallibility is guaranteed by the meaning we now attach to mental state terms.

between a *logical* impossibility of unwarranted belief and a mere de facto superior reliability. For this purpose let us imagine that the self-warrant theorist agrees with the critic that the situations adduced by the latter can be consistently described, using terms with their current meanings. Thus he has to give up the claim that FPCMSBs logically entail their own warrant. Nevertheless he still feels inclined to assert a stronger kind of superiority of such beliefs over their third-person counterparts than merely a greater frequency of accuracy.

An obvious move at this point is to consider the possibility of defining self-warrant in terms of modalities other than logical. Two kinds that are familiar from other contexts are nomological modalities and normative modalities. The former is illustrated by such sentences as:

> Water can't run uphill.
> If the cream's been around that long, it has to be sour.
> An airplane *could* go 1200 miles an hour.

Here the modalities are based on laws of nature rather than on logical principles. There is nothing logically impossible about water running uphill, but to do so would be contrary to physical laws. The sourness of the cream in question follows from biochemical laws plus antecedent conditions. And so on.

Normative modalities are employed in sentences like the following:

> Bringing happiness to another person can't be a sin.
> To get a Ph.D. you have to write a thesis.
> You can't win without scoring runs.

Here the necessities and impossibilities are based on normative principles of one sort or another; in these examples they are moral standards, institutional regulations, and rules of games, respectively.

Can we conceive the impossibility of a FPCMSB's being unwarranted in one of these other ways, rather than as logical? It would seem that nomological impossibility is inapplicable here. If it were applicable, the laws involved would presumably be psychological laws, more specifically laws governing the formation of beliefs about one's own mental states. If these laws either asserted or implied a universal connection between a belief's being about one's own mental states and that belief's being warranted, then it would be nomologically impossible for such a belief to be unwarranted. The trouble with this is that warrantedness, being a normative concept, is not of the right sort to figure in a scientific law. To say that a belief is warranted is to say that it comes up to the proper epistemic standards, and to determine what the proper standards are for one or another kind of belief is not within the province of an empirical science, anymore than is any other normative question.[39] Hence it could not be nomologically impossible for a belief to be unwarranted.

But for just the same reasons normative modalities are quite appropriate here. If there is a justifiable epistemic norm to the effect that any FPCMSB is ipso facto warranted just by virtue of its being the belief it is, then it would thereby be normatively impossible for such a belief to be unwarranted. Thus an alternative formulation of the self-warrant principle would be:

> (T6A) Each person is so related to propositions ascribing current mental states to himself that it is normatively impossible both for him to believe that such a proposition is true and not be justified in holding this belief; while no one else is so related to such propositions.

(T6A) presupposes that a defensible epistemic standard would effect a direct connection between being a FPCMSB and being warranted; hence it can be stated in terms of normative modalities alone. A more complicated case can also be envisaged, one in which both nomological and normative modalities are involved. Suppose that there is no such defensible epistemic standard as the one just mentioned; suppose instead that there is a standard to the effect that any belief possessing a certain property, F, is warranted, *and* that it is nomologically necessary that all FPCMSBs have the property F. In that case it would be nomologically-normatively impossible for FPCMSBs to be unwarranted; the impossibility would derive from a combination of epistemic norms and psychological laws. This gives rise to another version of the self-warrant principle:

> (T6B) Each person is so related to propositions ascribing current mental states to himself that it is nomologically impossible for him to believe such a proposition without his belief having property F, and it is normatively impossible for any belief having the property

[39]This conclusion is of course controversial, and it may be contested on the grounds that it presupposes an unwarranted distinction between the scientific (factual) and normative. However, it is not essential to this paper to take a definite stand on this issue. If normative matters are deemed to be within the province of science, it just means that nomological modalities are more widely applicable than I am supposing here, and the varieties of privileged access are even more numerous than I am representing them to be.

F to be unjustified; while no one else is so related to such propositions.

Both of these alternative versions of a self-warrant principle are
immune to the criticisms that launched us on the search for alternative
modalities. Since neither version asserts any logical necessity for the
warrant of FPCMSBs, they allow for the possibility of consistently describing, in our present language, a situation in which (some)
FPCMSBs would not be warranted. According to (T6A) such a situation would involve some difference in epistemic standards, and according to (T6B) it would involve either that or a difference in psychological laws. But there is nothing in these principles to suggest that such
differences cannot be described by the use of current mentalistic
language.

This discussion suggests the possibility of a considerable prolifera-
tion of privileged access theses, through varying the modalities in terms
of which each of our six modes of favorable epistemic position is stated.
We should not suppose, however, that every such mode can be construed in terms of every modality. We have already seen that self-
warrant is not amenable to statement in terms of a purely nomological
modality. The question of just which modalities are combinable with
each mode of favorable epistemic position is a complicated one, and we
shall have time only for a few sketchy and dogmatic remarks. It would
seem that indubitability, incorrigibility, and truth-sufficiency cannot be
stated in terms of nomological modalities alone, for the same reasons
we gave in the case of self-warrant. With truth-sufficiency, which has
the same structure, exactly the same argument applies. Our concept of
indubitability being a normative one, it seems clear that an appeal to
epistemic standards is essentially involved in the claim that there can be
no *grounds* for any doubt. And since incorrigibility involves the impossibility of someone else's showing the person to be mistaken (not just
the impossibility of someone else's being correct while one is mistaken),
again it would seem that standards defining what counts as a demonstration in this area would be involved. By similar arguments I think it
could be shown that these three modes are all construable, like self-
warrant, in terms of both pure normative modalities and a combination
of nomological and normative modalities.

The situation is quite different with respect to infallibility and omniscience. Here what is implied most basically is the correctness of a belief,
and the possession of a belief, respectively. Whether or not a certain
(factual) belief is correct, and whether or not a given person has a given
belief, is sheerly a matter of fact and not within the jurisdiction of

norms or standards. It would not make sense to adopt a standard to the effect that all beliefs of a certain category are correct; that would be as if a city council were to adopt an ordinance according to which all public housing in the city is free of rats. If a certain belief is in fact mistaken, we cannot alter that fact by legislating it away. On the other hand, it might conceivably be *nomologically* necessary that beliefs of a certain category all be correct. The mechanisms of belief formation might be such as to guarantee this. However, since both infallibility and omniscience, as we have formulated them, involve the implication of the warrant condition, B, as well, it would seem, for the reasons given in connection with self-warrant, that they cannot involve nomological modalities alone.[40] Thus a mixed nomological-normative modality would seem to be the only alternative to the logical modalities (at least among the alternatives we are considering). An infallibility principle could be stated in those terms as follows:

(T1A) Each person is so related to propositions ascribing current mental states to himself that it is nomologically impossible for him to believe such a proposition without that proposition's being true, and it is normatively impossible for a belief that satisfies this condition to be unjustified; while no one else is so related to such propositions.

In addition, there is the possibility of nonmodal, de facto universal versions of each of our six basic types. The following is a rough indication of how privileged access principles will look as so construed.

Infallibility—FPCMSBs are, in fact, never mistaken.
Omniscience—A person is, in fact, never ignorant of one of his mental states.
Indubitability—No one, in fact, ever has grounds for doubting one of his FPCMSB.
Incorrigibility—No one ever, in fact, succeeds in showing that an FPCMSB is mistaken.
Self-warrant—FPCMSBs are, as a matter of fact, always warranted.
Truth-sufficiency—True FPCMSBs are, as a matter of fact, always warranted.

---

[40]Of course we could excise this implication from our construal of infallibility and omniscience, in which case infallibility would be defined simply as the impossibility of mistake and omniscience simply as the inevitability of belief formation. (It would still be the case that the beliefs that satisfy these conditions would be warranted and so count as knowledge; it is just that this would not be made explicit in the definition.) As so conceived these modes would be amenable to a formulation in terms of nomological modalities alone.

It is dubious that these formulations in terms of de facto universals are of much use. For it is doubtful that anyone could have solid grounds for supposing that, for example, FPCMSBs are *always* correct, unless his claim were based on some sort of modal consideration to the effect that something in the nature of the case makes it impossible for FPCMSBs to be mistaken; and in that case he would be in a position to formulate the infallibility thesis in modal terms. We can derive a more usable nonmodal formulation by weakening the universals to a "for the most part" status, thus replacing "never" with "rarely", and "always" with "usually". So construed, infallibility and self-warrant, for instance, would become:

Infallibility—FPCMSBs are, in fact, rarely mistaken.[41]
Self-warrant—FPCMSBs are, as a matter of fact, usually warranted.

It does seem *conceivable* that one should acquire solid grounds for, for example, a "for the most part" version of an infallibility principle without thereby putting himself in a position to assert a corresponding modal principle. One might argue, for instance, that we are rarely, if ever, in a position to show that an FPCMSB is incorrect, and that to the extent that we have an independent check on their accuracy, they almost always turn out to be correct. Therefore we have every reason to suppose that they are, in fact, usually correct. This line of argument is not based on any fundamental considerations concerning the concepts, natural laws, or epistemic norms involved, and therefore it does not support any claim as to what is necessary or impossible.

Another way of deviating from unrestricted universality involves a restriction to "normal" conditions. Thus we might construe self-warrant, for example, as follows:

Self-warrant—FPCMSBs are normally warranted (are always warranted in normal conditions).

Certain lines of argument support a "normal conditions" version instead of, or in addition to, a "by and large" version. For example, one may think that he can give an (open-ended) list of "abnormal" factors that are usually absent but which when present would prevent an FPCMSB from having the warrant it usually has. These might include such things as extreme preoccupation with other matters, extreme emotional upset, and derangement of the critical faculties.

[41]Absolutistic terms like 'infallibility' and 'omniscience' are not aptly used for formulations that are weakened to this extent, but that is a merely verbal point.

Our list of varieties of privileged access has now swollen to a staggering thirty-four: sixteen modal principles, six de facto unrestrictedly universal principles, six "by and large" principles, and six "normal conditions" principles. No doubt with sufficient ingenuity one could further expand the list, but perhaps the results already attained will suffice to bring out the main dimensions of variation.

V

Attacks on privileged access invariably fail to take account of the full range of possibilities. The arguments are directed against only some of the possible versions of the position they are attacking; hence at best they fall short of showing that no privileged access principle is acceptable. To illustrate this point I shall take two of the best and most prominent recent attacks on privileged access, those of Bruce Aune in *Knowledge, Mind, and Nature* and those of D. M. Armstrong in *A Materialist Theory of the Mind*.

Aune's arguments occur in chapter 2, "Does Knowledge Have an Indubitable Foundation?", and they form part of his attack on the general idea that our knowledge rests on a foundation that is made up of beliefs, each of which is wholly noninferential and completely infallible. Although at the beginning of the discussion (pp. 32–33) he wobbles a bit between talking of the "reliability of our beliefs concerning immediate experience" (p. 32) and talking about "the alleged infallible character of immediate awareness" (p. 33), it is clear that his actual arguments are directed against an infallibility thesis, and indeed a logical infallibility thesis. The arguments are designed to show that "identifications of even feelings and mental images are not logically incapable of error" (p. 33), and to demonstrate "the possibility of being mistaken about the character of one's momentary experience" (p. 34). But having presented what he claims to be possible cases of mistake about such matters, he then supposes himself to have shown that statements about one's immediate experience are not "intrinsically acceptable", in the sense that their "truth is acceptable independently of any inference" (p. 41). And he seems to suppose that the only alternative to an infallibility claim is the view that there are strong empirical reasons for accepting one's statements about his immediate experience.

> The point seems to be securely established that judgments of phenomenal identification are not, in fact, infallible. We may come to have enormous confidence that, after a protracted period of training, a man's

opinions about the character of his own experiences are never really wrong. But our confidence here is based on empirical considerations. There is no longer any reason to think that such opinions *cannot* be erroneous; rather we have fairly good, though not infallible, reasons to think that they are normally reliable. (p. 37)

In supposing that having disposed of logical infallibility, he has thereby disposed of "intrinsic acceptability" and left a clear field for an acceptability based on empirical evidence, it is clear that Aune has overlooked most of the modes of epistemic superiority we have distinguished, in particular self-warrant and truth-sufficiency. For to say that one enjoys self-warrant vis-à-vis one's own immediate experience is to say that any of the person's beliefs about that experience is justified (acceptable) just by virtue of the fact that it is held, whether or not one possesses anything that has the status of evidence for that belief; and to say that one enjoys truth-sufficiency vis-à-vis one's immediate experience is to say the same thing for one's true beliefs about that experience. These are two forms of "intrinsic acceptability" without infallibility, and Aune will have to mount arguments against these before he can lay claim to having disposed of "intrinsic acceptability". At the most basic level what is overlooked here is the distinction between a belief's guaranteeing its own truth, and a belief's guaranteeing its own justification (acceptability), that is, the difference between the justification (B) and the truth (C) conditions for knowledge.

Moreover, Aune has overlooked the possibility of working, within any of those modes of epistemic superiority, with modalities other than the logical modalities. In the quotation just cited he presents a "normal conditions" variety of infallibility as the only alternative to a logical infallibility thesis. But even within the bounds of infallibility there is also the view that it is *nomologically* impossible that FPCMSBs should be mistaken. And as for self-warrant, even if we should reject the claim that it is logically impossible for FPCMSBs to be unwarranted, there is still the view that their being unwarranted is a normative impossibility, a view that is also distinct from the position that FPCMSBs are "normally reliable".

Armstrong's discussion (in chapter 6, section x of *A Materialist Theory of Mind,* entitled "The alleged indubitability of consciousness") draws more distinctions than Aune. He distinguishes logical infallibility, logical omniscience, and logical incorrigibility (pp. 101–102), in much the same way as I, though he uses for these concepts the terms "indubitability" (alternatively "incorrigibility"), "self-intimation", and "logically privileged access", respectively. He then presents arguments against the claims that FPCMSBs enjoy any of these kinds of privilege. Furthermore he explicitly recognizes nomological infallibility.[42] In chapter 9, section 11, entitled "The nature of non-inferential knowledge", he defines noninferential knowledge as follows: "*A* knows *p* non-inferentially, if, and only if, *A* has no good reasons for *p* but:

(1) *A* believes *p*;
(2) *p* is true;
(3) *A*'s belief-that-*p* is empirically sufficient for the truth of *p*." (p. 189)

He goes on to make it explicit that the "empirical sufficiency" involved here is based on some law of nature (p. 190); hence whenever one has noninferential knowledge of *p*, it is nomologically impossible that his belief should be mistaken. Thus he does not, like Aune, regard some kind of de facto reliability as the only alternative to a logically necessary epistemic privilege. However, like Aune, he fails to note both the possibility of self-warrant (and truth-sufficiency) as distinct modes of epistemic privilege, and the possibility of formulating at least some of the modes in terms of normative modalities. Thus even if he has effectively disposed of logical infallibility, omniscience, and incorrigibility, he cannot yet conclude that nomological infallibility is the only plausible version of a modal privileged access thesis.

Notes

A. Note that this holds only for what is termed in Essays 4 and 5 a "deontological" conception of justification.

B. At this writing I reject the true-justified-belief conception of knowledge for more than Gettier reasons. As made explicit in Essay 7, I reject the view that justification is necessary for knowledge. Though that would not prevent true justified belief from being sufficient for knowledge (though the Gettier considerations do), it strikes another blow against the equivalence of knowledge and true justified belief. However, at worst, the schema developed in this paper depicts the ways in which the various modes of privileged access stand vis-à-vis true justified belief, however that is related to knowledge. For some further discussion of this issue see the end of Part I of Essay 11.

C. It may be objected that infallibility alone will not confer justification; the believer would have to realize that he is infallible with respect to a class of propositions of which this proposition is a member. The objection does hold on a typical *internalist* approach to justification, but not on a typical *externalist*

[42]Where this is construed simply as matter of condition A's nomologically implying C without the further stipulation of an implication of B.

approach. On the latter, the claim made in the text is valid. See Essays 8 and 9 for this distinction.

D. Strangely enough, this paragraph omits mention of the most obvious way in which knowledge of one's own current conscious states might be direct but nonautonomous, viz., that it be based on immediate awareness of the states in question. For some discussion of this see Essay 11, section III.C.2.

E. This conviction is developed and defended at length in Essay 11.

F. This discussion tacitly assumes an identification of logical possibility with consistent conceivability, an identification that I now, along with many other thinkers, reject. I believe, however, that the discussion would still go through on a more adequate account of logical modalities.

Self-Warrant: A Neglected Form of Privileged Access

I. Self-Warrant as a Mode of Privileged Access

It seems obvious (to most of us) that in some way a person has epistemically privileged access to his current sensations, imagings, feelings, and thoughts, to his current *conscious states* (Cs). But in just what way? In seeking to answer that question we must first make the concept of privileged access more explicit.

In the most general terms, to say that someone has *epistemically* privileged access to some subject matter is to say that he is in an unusually favorable position to acquire knowledge concerning that subject matter. The subject matter under discussion here is the state of consciousness of a person at a given time, and the privileged access in question is not just an unusually but a *uniquely* favorable position. Thus we may take the following as an unspecific formulation of the Privileged Access Thesis.

(1) Each person is in a uniquely favorable position to acquire knowledge of his own current conscious states.

The unspecific element in (1) is the term 'favorable position'. Just what is favorable about this position? On this issue, as on so many others, philosophers have taken every logically possible position, and perhaps some that are not. (a) The most common view has been that one's unique position consists in an immunity from one or another of

From *American Philosophical Quarterly*, 13, no. 4 (1976), 257–72. Reprinted by permission of the editors.

the conditions we are concerned to avoid in our quest for knowledge. Those most often alleged are immunity from *ignorance* (omniscience), from *error* (infallibility), from *doubtfulness* (indubitability), and from *refutation* (incorrigibility). (b) Others hold that although one does not enjoy any of these immunities one does have *unique resources* for acquiring knowledge of his own current Cs, for example, a faculty of introspection or "inner perception", that gives him and only him a *direct* awareness of his own Cs. (c) Still others deny that there is any sort of uniquely privileged access. (d) And finally there are those who dismiss the whole problem, on the grounds that it makes no sense to speak of a person *knowing* what he is currently thinking or feeling.

I shall be taking a position that falls somewhere in the middle of this array, thereby exposing myself to fire from all sides. As against (c) and (d) I accept the privileged access thesis. As against (a) I take it that we do not enjoy immunities as strong as those commonly alleged. But as against (b) I suggest that the alternative to those excessive claims is not to be found by making explicit the way in which I *come into possession of* knowledge of my own Cs. In this essay I shall not be defending my rejection of those positions. Instead I shall be presenting and defending my own version of privileged access, *self-warrant*. Self-warrant involves a kind of immunity, immunity from lack of warrant (justification),[1] that is weaker than the more familiar kinds listed above, while at the same time constituting a respect in which one is *in principle and necessarily* in a very strong epistemic position.

Self-warrant attaches to beliefs. To call a belief self-warranted is to say that it warrants (justifies) itself; more soberly:

(2) Belief b is self-warranted = $_{df}$ b is warranted just by virtue of being b (being b is sufficient for b's being warranted).

Thus a self-warranted belief enjoys an immunity from lack of justification; it cannot be the belief it is and fail to be justified.

We can give a more illuminating formulation by making it explicit that a belief will be self-warranted, when it is, by virtue of some of its features rather than others. If my belief that I am now feeling tired is self-warranted, it is not by virtue of its being a belief about a psychological state or even about a C (not all such beliefs are self-warranted), but by virtue of its being a belief of a certain person that *he* is *currently in a certain C*. (Call such beliefs Bs.) Indeed, this point is not restricted to *self-warrant*. Whenever a belief is epistemically justified in any way, it is

---

[1]These terms will be used interchangeably.

by virtue of some of its features rather than others. If my belief that a burglar entered my house during my absence is justified, it is by virtue of its being supported by adequate evidence rather than, for example, by virtue of its being a belief about my house or its being strongly held. When a belief is warranted it is always by its possession of some *general* feature, one shareable by other beliefs. Since epistemic warrant is a position on a dimension of evaluation, we can express this point by saying that the evaluation of a belief as warranted always presupposes some general evaluative principle to the effect that all beliefs with a certain property are warranted.

To return to self-warrant, one can embody the foregoing in the following revised definition.

(3) Belief b is self-warranted = $_{df}$ b belongs to a type of beliefs, K, such that any K is warranted just by virtue of being a K.

Since this paper will be explicitly concerned with a certain *type* of beliefs, we may as well define the term for that application.

(4) Beliefs of type K are self-warranted = $_{df}$ Any belief of type K is warranted just by virtue of being a belief of type K.

To avoid triviality we must observe certain restrictions in our choice of types. Consider the type—beliefs for which the believer possesses adequate evidence. Clearly any belief of this type is justified just by virtue of being of that type. But we should not want to apply the term 'self-warranted' to a belief that is justified in this way. (Similarly the fact that every true belief belongs to a class—true beliefs—such that it is impossible that a member of that class be mistaken, does not imply that every true belief is infallible.) I will not attempt in this essay to formulate criteria that will exclude all unwanted belief-types. Clearly the claim that Bs are self-warranted is not trivial, and the same can be said for other interesting candidates, for example, simple arithmetical beliefs.

As just suggested, beliefs of various types might conceivably be self-warranted, but in this essay we are concerned to defend the claim that:

(5) Bs are self-warranted.

This is the positive part of our version of (1). It says that I am in a favorable epistemic position vis-à-vis my own current Cs in that whenever I believe that I am currently consciously thinking or feeling so-

288

and-so, that belief is ipso facto justified and hence runs no risk of not being justified. But we still need to add the negative clause—that no one else is so situated. We can't do that by adding "and no one else's Bs are self-warranted"; that would contradict (5). It is not in this that my privilege resides. The point rather is that no one else's belief that has the same propositional object as one of my Bs is self-warranted. Hence the complete privileged access thesis (self-warrant version) will read:

(6) For any subject, S, every B of his is self-warranted, and no belief by any one else with the same propositional object as that B is self-warranted.

In taking (5) to spell out a way in which one is in a uniquely favorable position to get *knowledge* of one's current Cs, I am supposing that justifiably believing that p goes at least part way toward knowing that p. If we add the uncontroversial requirement of truth, this means that I am supposing the following familiar conditions to form at least part of a sufficient condition for S's knowing that p.

(Belief) S believes that p.
(Justification) S is justified (warranted) in believing that p.
(Truth) It is true (it is the case) that p.

I am not committed, however, to accepting the True-Justified-Belief (TJB) *conception* of knowledge, according to which S's knowing that p can be defined by the conjunction of these three conditions. Nor am I committed to the claim that these conditions are sufficient by themselves.[A]

Even the more modest claim has been rejected by some epistemologists. Some have maintained that knowledge has nothing to do with belief, and others have denied that it has to do with justification. I believe that an analogue of the concept of self-warrant could be formulated for at least some of these alternative views, but I will not be able to go into that here. Note that one who denies that justification has anything to do with *knowledge* can still consider whether Bs are self-warranted, provided he countenances the concept of epistemic justification at all.

II. Preliminary Elucidations

Before considering the reasons for and against (6), I shall make a few comments designed to clarify the notion of self-warrant and to set it in a wider context.

Self-Knowledge

A. The Concept of Belief

Some readers may feel that, whatever may be the case with other knowledge, one's knowledge of his own Cs does not involve belief. This view may be held in a more or less radical form, on each of which I shall briefly comment.

First, it may be held that it makes no sense to speak of a person's believing that he is aware of a yellow patch or that he is thinking about the election. But even if it is nonsense to say this in the common sense of 'believe' in which it stands in contrast to 'know' ("You *believe* your car is out front! Can't you *see* whether it is or not?"), I am not using 'believe' in any such sense. Without attempting a full-dress analysis, I can indicate the relevant sense by saying that a *sufficient* condition of S's believing that p is that S be prepared to assert that p if the question is raised as to whether p is the case and if he is disposed to give a sincere and candid answer.[2] This condition would normally be satisfied by a person with respect to propositions attributing his current Cs to him.

Second, granting the existence of such beliefs, one may still feel that one's normal knowledge of one's Cs has nothing to do with belief, but simply consists in the state's being "given" or "presented" to his awareness. In Section III, C 2, I suggest that Cs are *not* "presented" to one's awareness. But, even if they are, S will *also* justifiably believe, in the sense just indicated, that he has the C in question. So whether or not there is some nonpropositional sense of 'know' in which his being presented with the C *constitutes* his knowing *it,* he will also have a *true justified belief* that he has the C, and it is with the latter that we are concerned in this essay. Residual resistance at this point may come from the supposition that every belief is consciously entertained for as long as it is possessed. But no such condition is required for a person to have the disposition to assert that p, in terms of which we explained our sense of 'belief.' In this sense each of us at any moment has many, perhaps indefinitely many, beliefs, only a tiny fraction of which "penetrate" into consciousness. Thus in saying that a man not only is aware of a yellow patch but also believes that he is aware of a yellow patch, we are not imputing any extra phenomenological complexity to his current condition.

B. Self-Warrant and Other Epistemic Immunities

In rejecting omniscience, infallibility, indubitability, and incorrigibility, while accepting self-warrant, I was presupposing that the

---

[2]I have termed this *only* a sufficient condition because of the uncertainties of its application to believers without linguistic capacities, like infants and dogs.

latter does not entail any of the former. I shall now do something to support that presupposition.[3]

Omniscience belongs to a different family of concepts from the other immunities. It has to do with what is possible or impossible, given the truth of p, rather than with what is possible or impossible given one's belief that p. More specifically, to say that S is *omniscient* with respect to a range of propositions, L, is to say that for any proposition, p, that belongs to L, it is impossible for p to be true and S not know that p. There should be no temptation to suppose that self-warrant entails omniscience. From the premise that Bs are self-warranted we cannot infer the impossibility of a C's occurring without its possessor's knowing that it is occurring. The latter would obtain if the subject did not form a belief that the C was occurring; and if that should happen it could still be true that whenever such a belief is acquired it is ipso facto warranted.

The other immunities are like self-warrant in attaching to belief; they all have to do with what is rendered impossible, given that a belief of a certain type is acquired. Within this group the TJB condition for knowledge provides a simple scheme for relating infallibility and self-warrant.

> Infallibility—Satisfaction of the belief condition and failure of the truth condition is not a possibility.[B]
> Self-warrant—Satisfaction of the belief condition and failure of the justification condition is not a possibility.

This makes it clear that self-warrant does not entail infallibility. It is fundamental to the concept of epistemic justification that a belief may be justified without being true. Hence from the premise that a belief cannot fail to be justified we cannot infer that it cannot fail to be true.

Indubitability and incorrigibility do not fit so neatly into the scheme, since they have to do not with what conditions must be satisfied given the belief condition, but rather with the epistemic positions that are possible vis-à-vis the truth condition, given the belief condition. Indubitability of a belief (as usually understood) involves the impossibility of *grounds for doubt* that the belief is true, while incorrigibility of a belief consists in the impossibility of anyone's showing that the belief is false. Now if something counts as a ground for doubt that p only if it is a ground (perhaps very weak) for believing that not-p, we can discern a simple whole-part relation between what is declared impossible by in-

---

[3]A much more extensive discussion of these immunities is found in Essay 10. The points made in this section, however, differ somewhat from anything in that essay.

corrigibility and by indubitability. If the belief that p is indubitable, then there can be no grounds, however weak, for not-p; but if the belief is incorrigible and not indubitable, something less inclusive is ruled out, viz., strong enough grounds for accepting not-p. Since what is ruled out by incorrigibility is included, as a limiting case, in what is ruled out by indubitability, if we can show that self-warrant does not rule out the former, we will also have shown that it does not rule out the latter. In other words by showing that self-warrant does not entail incorrigibility we will also have shown that it does not entail indubitability. So let's concentrate on incorrigibility.

The argument again rests on very general epistemic considerations. It is a familiar fact that there can be adequate justification for both sides of a contradiction. Examples are legion. I can be amply justified in perceptually judging that there is a desk in the next room, while someone who knows about the unusual arrangement of mirrors is even more justified in believing that there is no desk there. The detective has adequate reason for believing that the butler did it, until additional evidence turns up. If the self-warrant of a belief that p rules out the possibility of someone's having adequate warrant for not-p, it must be because of special features of *self-warrant*, over and above the features of warrant in general. I can see no features that yield this conclusion: and so I conclude that self-warrant is logically compatible with being shown mistaken.[4]

C. Self-Warrant as a Form of Immediate Justification

Self-warrant is a particular form of immediate (direct) justification. We can throw further light on the concept by exploring its relation to other forms.

Where what justifies S's belief that p includes[5] S's possession of some other knowledge or justified belief that is appropriately related to p (S's having "adequate evidence" or "sufficient reasons" for p), we may say that S's belief that p is *mediately* (indirectly) justified, and, if the other

---

[4]Of course it may be argued that Bs cannot be corrected because no one else can have adequate grounds for a belief about my current Cs, except by taking my word for it. I do not accept this argument, but in any event it is irrelevant to the present issue, which has to do with what is entailed by self-warrant as such, regardless of the content of the self-warranted beliefs.

[5]"Includes" rather than "is" since various other requirements are often imposed, e.g., that S's belief that p be "based on" this other knowledge, and that S realize that the latter constitutes adequate grounds. Whether or not these additional requirements are adopted, it is clear that mediate justification is distinguished by the requirement mentioned.

conditions for knowledge are satisfied, that S *mediately* (indirectly) knows that *p*. Whereas if what justifies S's belief that *p* does not include anything of that sort, we may say that S's belief that *p* is *immediately* (directly) justified, and, if the other conditions are satisfied, that S *immediately* (directly) knows that *p*. On this approach the fundamental distinction is between mediate and immediate *justification*, the distinction between mediate and immediate *knowledge* being derivative from that.

In view of persistent confusion between a belief's *being* justified and someone's *showing* a belief to be justified by *specifying* what it is that justifies it, let me say that it is the former that is under consideration here. As indicated earlier, I am supposing that for a given type of belief, for example, singular perceptual beliefs or empirical generalizations, there are principles that lay down conditions under which a belief of that type is justified. When I speak of "what justifies a belief" I am thinking of what will satisfy such a requirement. It is then a further question whether anyone notes, or shows, that the requirement has been satisfied. Sometimes the principle in question requires, as a condition for justification, that the believer have certain other knowledge or justified beliefs; sometimes not. In the former case satisfaction of the requirement will constitute mediate justification; in the latter case, immediate justification.

We should not confuse what is required for justifying a belief with what is required for possessing it. Thus it has been maintained that one cannot have the concept of red as a property of physical objects, and hence cannot believe that a ball is red, unless he knows in what conditions things that look red *are* red. But even if this is so, it would not prevent a perceptual belief that a certain ball is red from being directly justified. For the distinction between mediate and immediate justification has to do with what is required for a given belief's being justified *rather than unjustified*, not with what is required for one to have the belief in the first place. The latter is a requirement for the existence of a *candidate* for justification; the requirements for justification become relevant only after those requirements have been met.[C]

The above characterization of immediate justification is purely negative; it is justification by something that does not include the possession of reasons or evidence. This leaves room for a considerable diversity. In particular it stretches over both the following:

(a) When a person acquires a perceptual belief (e.g., that there is a tree in front of him), his belief is justified provided it was acquired via the operation of his sense organs in "normal circumstances."

(b) If a person clearly understands what "2 + 2 = 4" means, he is thereby fully justified in accepting that proposition.[6]

The justification of perceptual beliefs as envisaged in (a) is *immediate* because what does the justifying does not include the believer's possession of suitably related *knowledge* or justified belief. The belief is justified provided it has originated in a certain way; it is not also required that the believer know, or even believe, that this is the case. Nevertheless in (a) there are conditions required for justification that go beyond what is otherwise required for knowledge. And in this respect it differs from (b). There it is claimed that I can't lack justification for believing that 2 + 2 = 4, provided I understand what that means, and of course unless I understand what it means, I can't even have the belief. So here nothing is required for justification over and above what is otherwise required for knowledge (in this case the belief condition). Immediate justification like (a), where there are "additional" conditions for justification, we may term "heteronomous"; while immediate justification like (b), where nothing is required for justification over and above the other requirements for knowledge, we may term "autonomous".

Clearly self-warrant is a form of autonomous justification, since only the belief condition is required for justification.[7] There is another form of autonomous justification that has received considerably more attention, that in which it is the satisfaction of the truth condition that does the justifying. Thus in *Theory of Knowledge*[8] R. M. Chisholm writes that whenever "what justifies me in counting it as evident that a is F is simply the fact that a is F . . . we have encountered what is directly evident" (pp. 26–27). Let's call this form of justification "truth-warrant".[9] It is weaker than self-warrant. If *all* beliefs of type K are war-

---

[6]In the interest of avoiding red herrings, let me make it explicit that I am not (in this essay) *asserting* either (a) or (b). I cite them as *examples* of *claims* that count as claims to immediate justification, just in order to illustrate the spread of that category.

[7]The self-evidence of (some) a priori propositions, used above as the paradigm of autonomous justification, differs from the self-warrant of Bs in two ways. First, with self-evidence the requirement for justification is less—only the *understanding* of the proposition is required. This is clearly not sufficient for Bs. I can perfectly well understand the proposition that I am now sensing a purple hexagon, but I have no tendency to believe this proposition and would not be justified in doing so. Second, with self-evidence, whenever a belief is formed with *that* propositional object it is ipso facto justified, whatever the identity of the believer. But with Bs, self-warrant does not follow the proposition across believers. Hence we speak of self-evident *propositions* but self-warranted *beliefs*. However, it is still true that the above claim about 2 + 2 = 4 implies that beliefs with that propositional object are self-warranted, on our definition of "self-warrant".

[8]Englewood Cliffs, N.J.: Prentice-Hall, 1966.

[9]In Essay 10 it is called "truth-sufficiency".

ranted just by belonging to that type, the same will hold for all *true* beliefs of type K, but the latter does not entail the former.

Those who think one's knowledge of his sensations and thoughts derive from one's "awareness" of them are in effect taking Bs to receive *heteronomous* immediate justification.

> We are not only aware of things but we are often aware of being aware of them. When I see the sun, I am often aware of my seeing the sun; thus "my seeing the sun" is an object with which I have acquaintance. . . . Similarly we may be aware of our feeling pleasure or pain, and generally of the events which happen in our minds. This kind of acquaintance which may be called self-consciousness, is the source of all knowledge of mental things.[10]

Russell (and this is typical of partisans of "direct awareness") does not speak of beliefs in this passage. Nevertheless, for reasons analogous to those presented in Section II, A, Russell will have to admit that we do normally believe that we are having a certain feeling when we do have it. And if the question is raised as to what if anything justifies such a belief, Russell would surely have to say that it is justified by the fact that the person is aware of the feeling. Thus Russell is committed to the view that Bs are justified by one's direct awareness of the Cs in question. This will count as immediate justification provided it is not *required* that the subject know or justifiably believe that he is aware of the C, but only that the subject be aware of the C. And the justification will be heteronomous, since this requirement goes beyond the other requirements for knowledge. Even if it is held (and even if it is truly held) that one *cannot* have a B without also being directly aware of the C in question, it will still be the case that the requirement of the latter is distinguishable from the requirement of the former.

III. Are Bs Self-Warranted?

Now for my reasons for accepting (6). Since the negative part of that principle is quite uncontroversial, I shall restrict myself to supporting the positive part (5).

[10]Bertrand Russell, *Problems of Philosophy* (London: Williams & Norgate, 1912), p. 77. See also G. E. Moore, "The Refutation of Idealism" in *Philosophical Studies* (London: Routledge & Kegan Paul, 1922), pp. 24–25; "The Nature and Reality of Objects of Perception" in ibid., pp. 70–71; *Some Main Problems of Philosophy* (London: George Allen & Unwin, 1953), p. 49. C. D. Broad, *The Mind and Its Place in Nature* (London: Routledge & Kegan Paul, 1929), pp. 310–11.

In Section I, I pointed out that when a belief is justified, it is by virtue of satisfying the requirements laid down by some general principle of justification. Thus in accepting (5) I am presupposing the following epistemic principle:

(7) Every B is warranted just by virtue of being a B.

And here the question of whether Bs are self-warranted can be construed as a question about the status of this principle. As with other dimensions of evaluation, we may distinguish a de facto and a de jure version of our question. On the de facto interpretation we are asking whether (7) is in fact accepted in some "epistemic community" (usually our own). On the de jure interpretation we are asking whether (7) is validly or justifiably accepted.

The de jure question is, of course, the one in which we are ultimately interested. If (7) is the principle we should accept, it is of secondary importance how we do ordinarily proceed. I shall be taking the de facto investigation only as a background for the de jure.

As it is neither easy nor profitable to effect a rigid separation between the two questions, I shall proceed as follows. First, I shall present reasons for supposing that (7) is the principle we actually employ for Bs. Then I shall discuss an objection to that argument, viz., that we tacitly presuppose further requirements for justification. I shall consider two putative further requirements: *truth* and *immediate awareness*. But here, rather than discuss the de facto issue head on, I shall sidestep it and argue that (a) immediate awareness cannot justify Bs (whatever we *might* ordinarily suppose), and (b) a truth-warrant principle is not acceptable if (7) is acceptable. Then I shall proceed to argue that (7) is the principle we *should* accept for Bs.

But we will not have a thesis sufficiently determinate to be worth arguing about until we have given a more explicit indication of the boundaries of our B-category. To that task I now turn.

A. What Counts as a B?

'B' was initially explained as a belief of a certain person that he is currently in a certain C. This means that our concept of a B is no more determinate than our concept of a C; and so I must do something to indicate the boundaries of the latter.

First, the intuitive idea of a *conscious state* I mean to be employing is that of a "mode of consciousness" or "way of being conscious". S's being in a certain C simply *consists* in S's being conscious in a certain way; and S is in that C only for so long as he is conscious in that way. This is already sufficient to exclude "dispositional states" like wants, beliefs, and attitudes, which may be possessed during periods when the subject is completely unconscious, and also during periods when nothing relevant to the particular state in question is in his consciousness, whereas a (conscious) thought, sensation, imaging, or feeling is possessed only for so long as the subject is conscious in the appropriate way. I use the term 'state' in a relaxed fashion to cover occurrences, activities, and processes, as well as states more properly so-called.

I should also explain just what is meant by 'conscious' in 'way of being conscious'. However, this being one of the more intractable stretches of the conceptual terrain, I cannot go into the matter properly and still leave room for the epistemological issues that are the central focus of the essay. I can only indicate that my preference would be to explain 'being conscious' in terms of the notion of "immediate awareness" that will be adumbrated in Section III, C, 2; so that a C, a way of being conscious, is a state that involves an immediate awareness of some datum. No doubt much needs to be said as to the kinds of data that are involved in conscious sensations, feelings, thoughts, and so on; but we shall have to forgo that for now. I shall assume that even this much explanation will suffice for a wide area of agreement on particular cases.

But there is still a difficulty. Some beliefs that clearly satisfy the above criterion for B-hood should not be counted as self-warranted. To take an extreme example, suppose I believe that I am currently having a feeling just like the one you had 47 days ago at this time; this is a belief of mine to the effect that I am currently in a certain conscious state, but no one would be tempted to regard it as self-warranted. If warranted at all, part of that warrant comes from whatever reasons I have for thinking your state of feeling at that time was of a certain character.

The general point illustrated by this counterexample is that a C, like anything else, can be identified, or conceptualized, in many different ways; and it depends on which conceptualization we use whether or not we have a strong candidate for self-warrant. Let us survey some modes of conceptualization that prevent a self-attribution of a C from being self-warranted.

i. The type exemplified by the above case can be specified as: similarities between the state in question and others not possessed by the believer at the moment. This includes his own past experiences as well as those of others.
ii. Causal diagnoses, for example, "I have a tooth-ache", where part of

what that means is: "I feel a pain that is due to the stimulation of a pain receptor in one of my teeth".

iii. *De re* conceptualizations of cognitions, for example, my belief that I am thinking of *the mayor* that he wears loud clothes, where the most apt verbalization of the content of my thought is "The man who lives directly across the street from me wears loud clothes", and where I also believe that the man who lives directly across the street is the mayor. Since to be justified in the original belief I would have to be justified in the belief last mentioned, the former is not self-warranted. To avoid these difficulties we shall have to restrict Bs concerning thoughts to de dicto conceptualizations, which characterize referents in the same way as the thought in question.

iv. Descriptions of images in terms of conformity with some external object, for example, a belief that I now have the Rouen Cathedral before the mind's eye. My justification for this would seem to depend on whatever justification I have for my beliefs as to what the Rouen Cathedral looks like. To make the belief a strong candidate for self-warrant the image will have to be described in terms of sensible qualities or, alternatively, in terms of what I take it to be an image of.

The common character of these restrictions may be put by saying that Bs are restricted to conceptualizations of Cs in terms of their "intrinsic content" or "intrinsic character", rather than in terms of external relations in which they or their contents stand, relations of causality, similarity, coincidence, or conformity. In putting the matter in this way we are assuming that we can distinguish the intrinsic features of, for example, a sense-datum or mental image from its similarity to some actual paradigm.

This restriction to intrinsic content will also rule out other candidates for B-hood, where the difference between that candidate and the nearest self-warranted belief is of a somewhat different character. In the above cases it was a matter of different conceptualizations of what it is natural to regard as one and the same state; whereas in those cases to which we now turn the nearest B-correlate concerns a C-component of the original state, rather than that state differently conceptualized. Thus cognitive reports with an external "success implication" like:

(8) I see a beech out there.
(9) I just remembered that Jack said he was coming at 5:00.
(10) I know that you won't like it.

entail that certain states of affairs obtain over and above the present consciousness of the reporter. (8) entails that there is a beech out there,

(9) that Jack did say that he was coming at 5:00, and (10) that you won't like it. Hence a belief that (8), (9), or (10) clearly is not self-warranted. These beliefs are best regarded as beliefs that one is in a certain C, *plus* a further claim as to its correspondence with external fact. To make them bona fide Bs, we simply strip away that latter component, thus transforming our initial reports into:

(11) It appears to me visually that there is a beech out there.
(12) I just had what I take to be a recollection that Jack said he is coming at 5:00.
(13) I feel certain that you will not like it.

A somewhat analogous, though more complicated, reduction will have to be performed on full-blooded emotional state concepts to render them usable in Bs. Thus my belief that I *am* indignant at Nixon will have to be pared down to the belief that I *feel* indignant at Nixon before it can be admitted as a B.[11]

These considerations show that 'B' is to be defined in terms of a kind of concept rather than a kind of state, more specifically, a concept of the intrinsic character of some C. So our chain of definitions should go as follows:

(14) C—a way of being conscious.
(15) I-concept—a concept of the intrinsic nature of some C.
(16) B—a belief of a person that he is currently in a certain C, where that C is conceptualized by an I-concept.

B. Do We Ordinarily Accept a Self-Warrant Principle?

The following remarks may serve as a background to a consideration of the de facto question. I take it that the members of an "epistemic community" judge beliefs to be warranted or unwarranted according as they note certain conditions to be or not to be satisfied, and that there is a considerable consistency among members of the community as to what conditions are (in practice) required. Of course in order to be a "practicing member" of an epistemic community, one need not have explicitly formulated the principles (rules, norms, stan-

---

[11]For some indication of what is involved see my "Emotion and Feeling" in Paul Edwards, ed., *Encyclopedia of Philosophy* (New York: Macmillan and Free Press, 1967), vol. II, pp. 479–86.

dards) that lay down the requirements for a certain kind of belief, any more than a member of a linguistic community has to have formulated phonological rules in order to make judgments of correct or incorrect pronunciation in agreement with other members of the community. By observing the conditions that evoke judgments of "warranted" or "unwarranted" for beliefs of a certain kind, an observer can discover what epistemic rules are being implicitly employed in the community; and a reflective member of the community can disengage the rules by reflecting on the conditions under which he would make one or the other judgment.

My defense of the claim that (7) is accepted in our epistemic community consists of considerations of the sort last mentioned. In reflecting on our epistemic practice, I note that we require nothing for the justification of a B over and above its being a B. If S tells us that he has the image of a snow-capped mountain before his mind's eye, that he feels relieved, or that he is thinking about the election, then, provided we are convinced that his words do straightforwardly express his beliefs, we take it without more ado that he is fully warranted in holding those beliefs. We would unhesitatingly brand as absurd a request for justification such as "Why do you believe that?", "What reason do you have for supposing that?", or "How do you know that?".

C. Do We Assume Other Requirements?

To this argument it may be retorted that although we do customarily proceed in the way just described, that is not because we take Bs to be self-warranted; rather it is because we tacitly take the extra requirements for justification to be so obviously satisfied as not to require mention. Now that *is* a common phenomenon. We often assume without question that a person is justified in a belief (e.g., that he lives in Dubuque) that is *not* regarded as self-warranted. But in those cases we can readily specify what the requirements are that we unhesitatingly assume to be satisfied, for example, that the person has often formed reliable perceptual beliefs concerning his place of dwelling and has not suffered an abnormal loss of memory. While in the present case the common man would be at a loss to answer "How do you know?", except by saying something like "Well, it's my mental image, isn't it?", that is, by simply repeating what is already implied by the original statement. Thus if our unquestioning endorsement of every B is due to the assumption that some further requirement is invariably satisfied, this assumption is beyond the reach of everyday reflection and requires some special digging to bring it to light. Let's consider the more prominent possibilities.

1. Truth as an extra requirement

A partisan of truth-warrant, like Chisholm, will hold that we employ the following principle:

(17) A B is warranted if and only if it is true.

Hence he will take it that we accept all Bs without question only because we take the extra requirement of truth to be invariably satisfied.[12] Is this the case? That is very difficult to determine. First it is difficult to decide whether we do believe that Bs are invariably correct. Of course if Bs are logically infallible or indubitable, then we do believe them all to be true insofar as we are unconfused; but these are dubious claims. Let's suppose, for the sake of argument, that we do suppose Bs to be invariably correct; we still are faced with the question whether we *require* correctness for justification, that is, whether our acceptance of all Bs as warranted is based on that belief of invariable correctness. The most direct way of settling this would be to consider a hypothetical case in which we either became convinced of the incorrectness of a B, or at least came to *doubt* its truth, and then consider whether we would still take it to be justified. But in attempting to construct such a case, we would be led into highly controversial issues. For present purposes I can bypass all this as follows. Even if we do in fact (tacitly) employ a truth-warrant principle, we would not be justified in doing so, if we were justified in accepting (7). For since (17) differs from (7) only in making an extra requirement, if we are justified in taking Bs to be warranted as such, we are not justified in imposing additional conditions. Thus, whatever is to be said about the de facto status of (17), it is not justifiably accepted provided we can justify (7), as I shall go on to argue.

2. Immediate awareness as an extra requirement

The other main candidate for "extra condition" is "immediate awareness". Earlier we saw that many theorists (at least implicitly) advocate a form of heteronomous justification for Bs, according to which a

[12]That is, he will take this position provided he does admit that we unquestioningly accept all Bs as justified, and provided he holds that truth is the criterion of justification we actually employ for Bs, as well as the criterion we should employ. I am not concerned here to determine whether the historical Chisholm holds these views.

B is justified *iff* the believer is "immediately aware" of the C in question. This suggestion does have a certain plausibility. It is natural to think of ourselves as directly aware of our sensations, images, and feelings. And in unquestioningly accepting others' reports of their Cs, are we not tacitly assuming that a similar situation obtains with them? Consider also the distinction between Cs and states of persons with respect to which we do not so unquestioningly accept their reports—for example, the conditions of their organs and muscles. It is tempting to think that the reason for this difference is that whereas Cs are "presented" directly to one's awareness, these physiological conditions are not.

Before yielding to the temptation, let's try to be more explicit about the concept of *immediate awareness*. It is often taken to stand in no need of explanation. But the persistence of debates as to what is and is not an object of direct awareness, and the persistent obscurity as to just how an immediate awareness of *x* supports beliefs about *x*, reveals the danger of taking the concept for granted. The first step toward clarification is to distinguish between awareness of particulars (this color patch or that noise or that visual image) and awareness of facts (that this patch is red or that I am aware of an image of a sunny beach). Clearly the way in which the awareness figures in justification will differ for these types. If my awareness of a certain region of the visual field (first type) is adduced as the justification for my belief that the region is blue, we have to consider the question just how my awareness confers a warrant on some particular belief about that object? Does it confer a like warrant on *every* belief about that object, and if so how? And if not, what gives certain ascriptions their special status? In other words, we have a "gap" between object and conceptualization (or "propositionalization") to be overcome.[D] But this problem cannot arise if it is the awareness of *the fact that this patch is blue* that is said to justify my belief that this patch is blue. Here the object of the awareness fits the belief like a glove. The belief is simply, so to say, the "recording" or "storing" of the object of awareness. But this advantage is purchased at a price, for there are serious questions as to the intelligibility of this later mode of awareness, at least as figuring in justification. Can a fact be *presented* or *given* to a passive apprehension? In order to have a fact as object, is it not necessary to "work it up" through conceptualization, in such a way as to make its apprehension indistinguishable from a judgment or belief? In the latter case, the "immediate awareness" of the fact will turn out to be just a prior true justified belief; so that the problem of what does the justifying, and how, will have broken out afresh. Because of these difficulties I shall restrict myself here to awareness of particulars. I shall take this to be logically independent of any propositional knowledge or belief about the object, and even of any conceptualization of it or capacity to conceptualize it.

There is a circle of terms about which philosophers are wont to move when explaining any one of them. Thus in "Knowledge by Acquaintance and Knowledge by Description,"[13] Russell explains his technical term 'acquaintance' as follows:

> I say that I am *acquainted* with an object when I have a direct cognitive relation to that object, i.e., when I am *directly aware* of the object itself. When I speak of a cognitive relation here, I do not mean the sort of relation which constitutes judgment, but the sort which constitutes presentation. (pp. 209–10)

Other terms brought into the circle by various writers include 'directly (immediately) conscious of', 'directly (immediately) present to mind (consciousness)', 'directly (immediately) apprehend', 'given' 'displayed' 'directly (immediately) experience', and 'intuit.' Unfortunately none of these terms give us more guidance than the others in understanding how direct awareness of *x* justifies beliefs about *x*. Hence by defining one in terms of some of the others we are not making any real progress.

The concept is delimited somewhat by those who stipulate that beliefs justified by immediate awareness are infallible, indubitable, and/or incorrigible. This restriction is often implied by arguing with respect to, for example, physical objects, that they are not "given", since we can be mistaken about them.[14] But even if, as I should deny, Bs enjoy such strong epistemic immunities, this requirement would be at most a peripheral element in the concept. Since it makes sense to attribute infallibility to beliefs that cannot be regarded as resting on immediate awareness of particulars, for example, simple arithmetical beliefs, it can't be that immediate awareness of *x* *consists* of rendering beliefs about *x* infallible.

At this point the wisest of our predecessors in this inquiry have despaired of finding a helpful verbal definition and have resorted instead to an "ostensive" explanation in terms of examples. Thus in *Some Main Problems of Philosophy*, G. E. Moore writes:

> I want you to realize as clearly as possible what sort of thing *this* way of perceiving which I call 'direct apprehension' is. It is . . . that which hap-

---

[13]In *Mysticism and Logic* (London: George Allen & Unwin, 1918).
[14]See, e.g., C. I. Lewis, *An Analysis of Knowledge and Valuation* (La Salle, Ill.: Open Court, 1946), pp. 182–83; H. H. Price, *Perception* (London: Methuen, 1932), p. 3.

pens when you actually see any colour, when you actually hear any sound, when you actually feel the so called 'sensation' of heat, as when you put your hand close to a fire; when you actually smell a smell; when you feel the so-called 'sensation' of hardness, in pressing against a table, or when you feel the pain of toothache, etc., etc. In all these cases you directly apprehend the sense-datum in question. (p. 46)[15]

Quite a variety of examples are given by one or another writer, but the clearest ones, those in which it seems most unexceptionable to think of items being "presented" or "given", are those in which the objects are sense data, like colored shapes and sounds, or mental images. Let's take the concept as fixed by this sort of example.

Now what about the idea that Bs are to be justified by immediate awareness of the relevant Cs? (On this topic I shall, as I indicated earlier, address myself directly to the de jure issue, arguing that "immediate awareness" cannot be what justifies Bs, whatever we might ordinarily suppose.) The trouble with that suggestion is that in the paradigm by which the concept of direct awareness is explained, the object of the awareness was not a psychological state, but rather the *object* of a psychological state. Moore explained "direct apprehension" as that relation which one has to a color or sound, when "actually" seeing or hearing it. In this paradigm the "psychological state" is the awareness rather than the object of the awareness. And this paradigm provides the only explanation of the concept we are able to find. Now of course this by no means *implies* that there cannot be immediate awareness of sensings and imagings, as well as of their objects. Even if a sensing is an immediate awareness, there might also be an awareness of that awareness. Indeed both Russell and Moore insist that this is the case.[16] However, in this they seem to me to be mistaken. I cannot see that the operation of sensing, imagining, thinking, or feeling is "given" or "presented" to us, "spread out" before our awareness, in the way colors, sounds, and mental images are. But even if we should convince ourselves that we are immediately aware of our own sensings and imagings, an analogous question would arise at the next level. One's awareness that he is currently sensing so-an-so is itself a C, and so we have the problem of what justifies one in the B that consists in the belief that one has that C. If that again is an immediate awareness of the C, we are

---

[15]See also G. E. Moore, "The Subject Matter of Psychology," *Proceedings of the Aristotelian Society*, 10 (1909–1910), 36–62; "The Nature and Reality of Objects of Perception," p. 68. C. D. Broad, *The Mind and Its Place in Nature*, p. 145; A. J. Ayer, *The Foundations of Empirical Knowledge* (London: Macmillan, 1940), p. 61.

[16]See the references to Russell and Moore in fn. 10.

faced with the specter of an infinite hierarchy of awarenesses. To avoid that we shall have to recognize at some point a B that is not justified by an immediate awareness of the C in question. Thus even if, as I should deny, first level Cs are presented to our awareness, it cannot be generally true that what justifies a B is immediate awareness of the C involved.

D. Are We Justified in Accepting the Self-Warrant Principle?

The time has come for the de jure question. We have already raised that question with respect to the alternatives to self-warrant. We have seen that Bs cannot be justified by immediate awareness of the Cs involved, and that *if* we are justified in accepting a self-warrant principle, the more restrictive truth-warrant principle is not acceptable. Hence at this stage the de jure question boils down to: "Are we justified in accepting (7)?". That depends, of course, on what it takes to justify a principle of justification. This methodological issue is little explored and bristles with difficulties, but I shall at least have to stick my toes in the water.

Let's begin by considering the role of the justification condition in attribution of knowledge. Why do we need such a condition? Why isn't true belief sufficient? Isn't Truth what we are really after in the believing game? The answer, of course, is that although truth is quite enough along the dimension of the relations of our beliefs to what they are "about", the concept of knowledge is a multidimensional one. The justification condition is there because in recognizing that S *knows* that *p*, we are not only judging his belief that *p* to accurately reflect the way things are (the things he is talking about) but also saying something about *his position* vis-à-vis that range of fact. But what sort of thing about his position? To answer that question we need to complement the above insistence on the distinction between the truth and justification condition, with an equal insistence on their interrelation. Truth is still the object of the believing game, and the "positions" to be applauded in that game are those that are calculated to lead to the truth. That is, to be justified a belief must be reliable, must be at least highly likely to be correct. To spell this out just a bit, there must be relevant facts about the way in which, or the circumstances in which, the belief is acquired and/or held, such that given those facts it is at least highly likely that a belief of that sort will be correct. We may abbreviate this as follows.

(18) A belief is justified *iff* it is reliable.

This formulation cries out for further specification in more than one respect. Do the facts in question have to concern the way the belief was *acquired,* what keeps it from being dropped, both, or either? If other sorts of "circumstances" are relevant, what sorts? Is it enough that given those facts, the belief is *highly likely* to be correct or must there be a logical or nomological *impossibility* of its being mistaken? And if the former, what concept of probability is relevant here? I shall take it that there is some way of answering these questions that renders (18) both specific and adequate. As we shall see, even in this unspecific form the principle will serve in the support of (7).

Considerations of reliability and mode of belief formation have recently been stressed by epistemologists like Alvin Goldman[17] and David Armstrong,[18] who have opposed the idea that knowledge is to be analyzed even in part in terms of justification. They have contended that what has to be added to true belief to make it knowledge is reliability, rather than justification. Now I agree with these thinkers that reliability is required to distinguish knowledge from (mere) true belief, but on my version reliability has this efficacy just because it is what is needed for justification. Thus the opposition between, for instance, Armstrong and myself (apart from the details of the notion of reliability—a major exception!) has to do with the question of whether reliability functions as a straightforward criterion of knowledge, or whether it so functions only because it is a criterion for a certain kind of evaluation, a positive form of which is required for knowledge. This is like the opposition between naturalists who want to identify the criteria and meaning of ethical terms and antinaturalists who want to keep them distinct.[E]

What bearing do these considerations have on the question of how principles of justification are to be evaluated? We might take them to show that (18) is the sole principle of justification. If we took this tack, we would be practicing sharp economy in our general principles, packing all the diversity into applications. However, that is not our only choice. We can, and I shall, opt for an analogue of rule utilitarianism, rather than for an analogue of act utilitarianism. That is, we can take reliability as a criterion for more specific principles governing specific types of beliefs. On such a criterion a principle that lays down a certain set of conditions, I, as sufficient for the justification of beliefs of type A, is acceptable only if the following requirement is met:

[17]"A Causal Theory of Knowing," *The Journal of Philosophy,* 64 (1967), 357–72.
[18]*Belief, Truth and Knowledge* (Cambridge: Cambridge University Press, 1973).

(19) A's that satisfy I are reliable.

Are there other constraints a principle of justification must satisfy? I suggest that there are two. First,

(20) I must be applicable.

What that means is that we can actually use these conditions for determining whether a given A is justified.[19] This does not mean that we can infallibly determine this, nor that we can determine it in every case. But it does mean that by and large we can determine satisfaction with a high degree of reliability and without too much difficulty. After all, evaluation of beliefs is a practical affair (albeit of a theoretical sort), and putative criteria that cannot be applied are thereby disqualified.

A third constraint is suggested by the following consideration. Let's suppose that perceptual beliefs concerning the physical environment are correct in the overwhelming majority of cases; and let's further suppose that this confers a high probability of correctness on every perceptual belief. Should we then adopt a principle that certifies every perceptual belief as such without further requirement? This principle would satisfy the first two requirements. Nevertheless it is not acceptable, and just because we are able to formulate further applicable conditions that increase materially the proportion of true beliefs in the approved class. That is, by adding conditions concerning the state of the perceiver and the environment and concerning the perceiver's orientation vis-à-vis the object, we are able to wash out almost all the false beliefs. Clearly where this is possible we must prefer the enriched set of conditions. We want to increase the proportion of true beliefs as much as possible, without sacrificing applicability. Hence our third requirement:

(21) There is no other applicable set of conditions. I_1 such that the proportion of true beliefs is significantly greater among A's that satisfy I_1 than among A's that satisfy I.

Does (7) satisfy these constraints? As for (19), we have of course very little idea as to how Bs are formed. We have seen that the traditional "immediate awareness" story collapses on inspection, and we have no

---

[19]Cf. R. M. Chisholm's concept of a "mark of evidence" in *Perceiving* (Ithaca: Cornell University Press, 1957), pp. 34–37.

real replacement, apart from some speculative cybernetic models. That, however, does not prevent our being justified in supposing (7) to satisfy (19). If we have adequate reason for taking Bs (without further condition) to be always, or almost always, correct, then we are justified in supposing that Bs are always, or almost always, formed in such a way as to be reliable, even if we have no idea of what that way is.

Are Bs always, or almost always correct? Of course if they are infallible, logically or nomologically, they are all guaranteed to be correct. Even if they are indubitable or incorrigible, no contrary evidence can ever prevail against the subject's sincere belief, and so we will be debarred from having any reason for ever thinking any of them incorrect. But since we are assuming these strong immunities to be inapplicable, how can we justify the claim?

At this point, I would simply allude to the extreme difficulty of finding *actual* cases in which a B is shown wrong. This difficulty is partly due to the absence of independent checks on the accuracy of Bs; to a large extent we have no alternative to taking the believer's word for it. But that is not the whole story. We do have a variety of ways of "getting at" the mental states of others, over and above their direct testimony. The extent and force of these ways vary from one kind of mental state to another. They are greatest with our "dispositional" states that do not fall within our C category. We can, for example, get some purchase on what a person wants and believes by observing his goal-directed behavior. If he walks to his car, gets in the driver's seat, inserts the key in the ignition, starts the engine, and drives away, this surely gives us a considerable basis for supposing that he wanted to transport his car to some other location; that he believed that inserting the key in the ignition was necessary for starting the engine, and so on. With Cs the independent indications are weaker but still not insignificant. We expect a person who feels depressed, relieved, or excited to betray this in a variety of ways in his look, bearing, and behavior. And by listening to a person's conversation we can draw reliable inferences as to the thoughts that are going through his mind, even if he does not explicitly tell us that he is thinking ———. I would suggest that when we do employ these independent checks, we rarely find them at variance with the subject's report; where they are, the rarity of this will justify us in either opting for the self-report or putting its falsity down to insincerity rather than mistake. Thus insofar as we have independent empirical evidence, we have no reason to think that Bs are ever mistaken.[20] I take this to be strong support for the claim that for all Bs

[20]This is a stronger conclusion than we need, and I do not wish to insist on it in this essay. For present purposes it will suffice to show that Bs are, so far as we can tell, rarely

some highly reliable mode of belief formation is operative, even though we are unable to say just what that is. And this means that (7) passes the first test.

As for the other requirements, (20) poses no problem. We are certainly able to determine whether the conditions are satisfied, since they simply consist in the belief in question being a B. If we have a belief before us for evaluation, we can certainly tell whether it is a B or not. As for (21), if, so far as we can tell, Bs are never mistaken, we are quite without motivation for seeking extra conditions. And even if Bs are occasionally mistaken, there would seem to be no applicable conditions that would reduce the proportion of errors. The only remotely plausible candidate I can think of is that the subject, S, be in possession of his faculties, not be too confused, distracted, or whatever, to "know what is going on". But if this condition were violated to such an extent as to engender a significant possibility of S's not being able to tell what he is thinking or seeing, he would not be in a position as much as to form a belief as to what he is thinking or seeing. But in that case there is no belief to be justified or unjustified, and so adding this condition does not rule out any mistaken Bs. I conclude that we are amply justified in accepting (7).

IV. Two Objections to the Self-Warrant Principle

In the remainder of the essay I shall consider two objections to the self-warrant thesis.[21] I discuss these objections not only because they raise difficulties that deserve to be met, but also because in the course of meeting them we are forced to make the thesis more explicit and to uncover various interesting epistemological points.

A. Are Unwarranted Bs Impossible?

The first objection is directed against the modality involved in the concept of self-warrant. (Remember that to say that Bs are self-warranted is to imply that it is impossible for a belief to be a B and not be warranted.) The objection simply is that we can give consistent descriptions of states of affairs (there are possible worlds) in which (some) Bs

---

mistaken. And the extreme difficulty of finding convincing examples of mistake should be evidence enough for *that*.

[21] Arguments of the sort I will be considering have rarely, if ever, been directed against self-warrant as such, since that mode of privileged access has been largely ignored in the literature. Rather, they have been directed against one or another of the stronger forms.

are not warranted; hence even if, as a matter of fact, all such beliefs *are* warranted, it cannot be *impossible* that such beliefs not be warranted; they are not necessarily warranted.

The descriptions most commonly proffered are of the following sort. Let us suppose that physiological psychology has developed to the point at which laws have been firmly established, linking types of conscious states to their neurophysiological correlates. Let us further suppose that the associated technology has been so developed that electronic devices can be used to determine, in fine detail, what is going on in the brain. In that case we might very well use such information to override the subject's sincere testimony as to what he is feeling or thinking. Note that so far we have an argument against incorrigibility but not against self-warrant. Even if it is possible for a person to be shown wrong in a B, it does not follow that Bs are not self-warranting. Our description, however, can be extended so as to involve cases of unwarranted Bs. Suppose we identify enough cases of mistaken Bs to enable us to establish generalizations as to the conditions under which Bs are likely to be mistaken. For example, it might be discovered that people are always correct in their Bs when the overall pattern of brain waves is in the range W_1-W_{49}, while if the pattern is a W_{50}, mistaken Bs occur frequently. After this discovery we would justifiably take a B to warranted only if S were in some state of the range W_1-W_{49}. Now something is required for a B's being warranted other than just being the belief it is; and when a person has a B without meeting those extra conditions, his belief is unwarranted.

We can maintain (5), while admitting the possibility of this kind of development,[22] by making more explicit the order of modality involved in the concept of self-warrant (where "orders" of modality comprise, for example, logical and casual). The objection assumes that our formulation was in terms of logical impossibility: if that were the case, then the exhibition of a consistently describable state of affairs in which one's belief that he feels relieved is not warranted suffices to refute the claim that it is *impossible* for any B to be unwarranted. It is not necessary, however, to employ *logical* modalities in order to have a distinctive concept of self-warrant. What seems to me the most natural way to understand impossibility of nonwarrant, even apart from the necessity for meeting the present objection, is in terms of what we may call "normative" modalities. This is the kind of modality that consists in

[22]Many philosophers would deny that it is possible. Thorny issues are involved, and I do not have time to argue the matter. I shall have to content myself with showing that even if the possibility be admitted the self-warrant thesis can still be saved.

something's being necessary, possible, or impossible, relative to some valid norm, rule, or standard. It is exemplified by such statements as:

(22) It *can't* be right to deliberately take another person's life.
(23) You *must* stand behind the baseline when serving.
(24) You *can't* use a singular form of the verb with a plural subject.

To say something is *normatively impossible,* as in (22) and (24) above, is, of course, to say that it violates some norm, rule, or standard, but that is not the whole of its meaning. Something can be in violation of a standard without being properly termed (normatively) impossible. For example, watching television on a certain occasion might violate some standard, as it would if I had promised to visit someone at the hospital during that time: but we would not say (at least on those grounds) that it cannot be right to watch television. We use the modal formulation when the lack of conformity is due just to the item in question being as described, without any further conditions required. In other words, we use the modal statement when the norm *by itself* implies the lack of conformity of the item in question, without the need for additional premises. In saying "It can't be right to deliberately take the life of another human being", we are claiming that a valid (moral) rule forbids such actions explicitly and categorically, whatever the circumstances. My evening of television watching would be considered wrong, however, not because any moral standard categorically forbids television watching as such, but because the moral rule that one should keep his promise, *plus* the facts that I had promised someone to visit him in the hospital that evening and watching television prevented my doing so, all together implies that it was wrong of me to watch television. This distinction between "isn't right" and "can't be right" is parallel to the distinction between "isn't so" and "can't be so" in casual and logical modalities. Thus a determinist, who holds that every event is causally determined to happen just as it does happen, can still make a distinction between what is causally impossible and what simply *does* not happen though it is causally possible. The causally impossible, for example, my jumping out of a window in still air and moving upward, is that the nonoccurrence of which can be deduced from causal laws alone, without the need of additional premises. The causally possible but in fact nonexistent, for example, my skiing at this moment in Switzerland, is that the nonoccurrence of which can be derived from causal laws only with the aid of additional premises specifying particular matters of fact. Again, the *logically* impossible is that the falsity of which follows from logical truths alone; while the merely de facto false is that the falsity of which follows from logical truths only with the aid of some factually true premises.

Now, as we have pointed out, "warranted" is a normative or evaluative notion. To say that a belief is (epistemically) warranted is to say that the believer has an (epistemic) *right* to his belief, that in accepting it he is proceeding as he *ought* (epistemically), that it is (epistemically) *justifiable* for him to accept it, that the belief (or its acceptance) is in accordance with a valid epistemic *norm*.[F] Hence when we speak of the *impossibility* or *necessity* of a belief's being warranted, it is natural to understand these modalities as being of the normative sort. To say that it is *impossible* for a *B* to be unwarranted is simply to claim that there is in force a valid epistemic norm (7) that categorically declares *every* B to be warranted, with no further conditions required. The warrantedness of any particular B follows from that rule alone without the necessity for additional premises.

On this interpretation can we hold that Bs are self-warranted while recognizing the *logical* possibility of a B's not being warranted? Yes, because it is *logically* possible that we should (justifiably) employ a norm for Bs other than (7), a norm which would require further conditions for warrant. That possibility is, in fact, at the heart of the sort of counterexample adduced by the present objection. *If* such counterexamples are indeed logically possible, then they exhibit a logical possibility of Bs not being warranted *just because* they involve radical changes in those features of our present condition (primarily our inability to be sure that Bs are ever mistaken) that render (7) justifiable. Hence in those circumstances other norms for Bs, requiring additional conditions for warrant, would be justified; and *this* is how unwarranted Bs would occur. But the logical possibility of all this is quite compatible with (7)'s being a valid epistemic norm in our present situation, and hence with its presently being *normatively impossible* for a B to be unwarranted. Thus on the normative modality interpretation (5) survives the objection.

B. Is the Validity of (7) Part of What Justifies a B?

We have been supposing that Bs are warranted only because (7) is a valid principle. But if so, is it not the case that what warrants a B is not just its being a B, but that plus the fact that (7) is valid? In which case the B could hardly be termed *self*-warranted. Of course if the validity of (7) followed from the *concept* of a B, then the "extra" requirement would not really be extra, but since we have supposed this not to be the case, we cannot make use of that defense.

The trouble with this objection is that it involves a fatal confusion of roles. Where *x* justifies *y* (renders it acceptable, desirable, fitting, right, or good), there is always a norm, standard, rule, or principle in the background, which, so to say, empowers *x* to do the justifying; it is essential to justification that there be adequate candidates for *both* these roles—that which justifies, and that norm or principle by virtue of which it is able to do so. These are different roles and they must be kept distinct. Without a valid principle in the background, nothing can do the justifying, and of course the principle by itself is not enough without something to satisfy it. Thus, to return to the case at hand, where a belief is justified just by virtue of being a B, being a B does suffice for justification only by virtue of the fact that (7) is a valid epistemic norm. But if we were to suppose that in this situation what justifies the belief is not just its being a B, but that plus the fact that (7) is valid, we would have confused these roles. To admit that (7) is valid *is* to admit that being a B is all that it takes to justify a B; for that is what (7) lays down as the sole requirement. Admitting the validity of (7) while also insisting that more is required for justification is self-contradictory.

This confusion is interestingly analogous to the confusion of premises with rules of inference exposed by Lewis Carroll in his delightful essay "What the Tortoise Said to Achilles,"[23] and the same unhappy fate awaits it. If we insist on converting any rule of inference we employ into a premise, we are launched, as Carroll showed, onto an infinite regress; for each addition of a new premise defines a new argument, which employs a new rule of inference, which in turn becomes converted into a new premise, which in turn. . . . Similarly, if we suppose that the validity of the presupposed norm is part of what justifies the belief, then the justification by *x* plus the norm presupposes a different, higher level norm, which in turn will be made part of the justification, which then presupposes still a higher level norm, which in turn. . . . Thus on pain of an infinite regress we are forced to distinguish what justifies the belief from the norm by virtue of which it does so, and so are "forbidden" from including the latter in the former.

V

I take the considerations of this paper to have shown that the self-warranted status of *B*'s must find a place in any adequate epistemology.

[23]*Mind*, 4 (1895), 278–80.

Just what that place will be depends on the other features of that epistemology.^G

Notes

A. Nor is there any commitment to justification's being a necessary condition of knowledge. See Essay 7.

B. As I hinted earlier, the impossibility of both believing that p and p's being false will only amount to infallibility provided it is specified for a class or type of proposition rather than a particular proposition, and provided that the type is chosen properly. For further discussion of this point see Essay 10, p. 261.

C. See Essay 3, p. 63.

D. I now feel that this is a pseudo-problem. As James Van Cleve points out in "Epistemic Supervenience and the Rule of Belief", *The Monist*, 68 (January 1985), 90–104, a perfectly good answer to the question "How does S's awareness of X confer justification on some particular belief of S about X, for example, the belief that X is blue?" is the following. "It confers justification on S's belief that X is blue because S is aware of X *as* blue; and it does not confer justification on a belief that S is immaterial because S is not aware of X *as* immaterial." None of this, however, affects the main line of argument in the text, which depends on the claim that, in any event, we lack immediate awareness of conscious states themselves, or at least we lack comprehensive immediate awareness of such states.

E. More recent developments of reliability theories complicate this picture considerably. For example, Goldman now wishes, not to exclude justification from the analysis of knowledge, but to analyze justification in terms of reliability. Moreover, he has developed a form of the view, espoused here, that reliability is a criterion for the evaluation of beliefs as justified. See his *Epistemology and Cognition* (Cambridge: Harvard University Press, 1986).

F. This argument proceeds in terms of what is called a "deontological" conception of epistemic justification in Essays 4 and 5 and is severely criticized there. However, all the argument requires is that justification be an *evaluative* matter of some sort, and that is true on any prominent way of thinking about epistemic justification.

G. This is the point at which, in J. L. Austin's words, "we take it all back". Those who have read Essay 4 or 9 will have noted that this essay is in flat contradiction to those later writings, in which it is maintained that any belief is justified if and only if it is based on an adequate ground. If that is what is required for justification, then no belief is *self-warranted*. In the last paragraph of Section v, Essay 4, I suggest that we can think of the beliefs discussed in this essay as a limiting case in which the ground is not distinguished from the fact that makes the belief true. But this would support a diagnosis of truth-warrant, rather than of self-warrant. In addition to the general considerations in favor of the doctrine of Essays 4 and 9, I now feel that the self-warrant doctrine of this essay is not the best account of the epistemic status of Bs. Consider a case in which a person is abnormal enough to make wild guesses as to what conscious states he currently enjoys. The beliefs so formed would clearly not be justified, while the self-warrant thesis implies that they would be. The doctrine of Essays 4 and 9 explains this; they would not be justified just because they were not formed on a ground that is sufficiently indicative of their truth. And this doctrine also explains the fact that such beliefs are either always or almost always justified. Since states of consciousness are "self-presenting" to their subject, beliefs in their existence are typically formed on the basis of the states themselves, a maximally adequate ground since it guarantees the truth of the belief.

I include this essay despite my rejection of its central thesis, partly for the sake of the general epistemological background sketched here, and partly because I think that the case for the thesis set out here deserves to be kept before the public.

PART V

THE FOUNDATIONS
OF EPISTEMOLOGY

Epistemic Circularity

In this essay I will explore the prospects for justifying, or being justified in accepting, claims that one or another source of belief is *reliable*. I will be particularly concerned with the ways in which these prospects are affected by a certain kind of circularity we often fall into when we try to justify such claims. The results of my investigation will be mixed but mostly, by my lights, on the optimistic side.

I

My first task is to identify the claims the justification of which we will be considering, and to indicate their importance for epistemology.

For Thomas Reid the most basic epistemological issue was whether we are proceeding rationally in trusting as we do our basic sources of belief—perception, introspection, memory, testimony, and reasoning.[1] Less metaphorical terms than 'source of belief' would be *dispositions*, *tendencies,* or *habits* to form beliefs of certain kinds in certain circumstances. A more currently fashionable term is 'belief forming *mechanism*'. Whatever the lingo, the idea is that we are so constituted, whether by nature, experience, or some combination thereof, as to respond to a certain kind of psychological "input" (experiential or doxastic) with a

From *Philosophical and Phenomenological Research*, 47, no. 1 (1986). Reprinted by permission of the editors.

[1]Cf. Nicholas Wolterstorff, "Can Belief in God Be Rational If It Has No Foundations?", in A. Plantinga and N. Wolterstorff, eds., *Faith and Rationality* (Notre Dame, Ind.: University of Notre Dame Press, 1983), pp. 149 ff.

certain correlated kind of belief "output"; and this in accordance with some function of the input. Thus when it appears to me sensorily that there is a tree in front of me, I will normally respond to this by forming the belief that there is a tree in front of me unless I have strong enough reasons to the contrary. Reid noted that we all have a number of such belief-forming habits, and that we ordinarily repose confident trust in their output. We take them to provide us with accurate information about the world; we take them to be reliable sources of such information.

A thorny question for a reliability theory of justification or knowledge concerns the individuation of belief-forming mechanisms. If the justification of a particular perceptual belief of mine to the effect that a tree is before me depends on whether it was produced by a reliable belief-forming process or mechanism, how wide or narrow a mechanism do I examine in order to answer this question? This particular belief formation was a case of forming a belief about a tree being before me upon its looking to me as if there were, a case of forming belief about a close-up tree on the basis of sensory experience, and a case of forming a belief about the immediate physical environment on the basis of sensory experience. And different degrees of reliability may well attach to these three belief-formation types. We need not get involved in all that in this essay. I shall be considering problems about the justification of reliability claims that will arise no matter how belief-forming mechanisms are individuated. For purposes of illustration I shall choose "wide" mechanisms or sources like perception and introspection; but everything I say could be just as well applied to "narrow" sources, like its appearing to me that there is a typewriter in front of me.

What is meant by 'reliability' in this context? I believe that the following will suffice for present purposes. I am not thinking of the reliability of a belief-producing mechanism as a function of its actual track record, but rather of its *tendency* to produce true beliefs in the sorts of situations in which it normally functions. This understanding may be canonically formulated as follows:

(I) We and the world about us are so constituted that beliefs about the immediate physical environment that are based on sense experience in the way such beliefs generally are and that are formed in the kinds of situations in which we typically find ourselves are or would be generally true.

Note that this formulation does not take the reliability of a source to imply that it would yield mostly true beliefs in *any* possible situations, for instance, in a "demon-world" or in artificially gerrymandered situations, but only in the sorts we normally encounter. Nor does the reliability of sense perception imply that it would yield true beliefs no matter how used, but only that we will get mostly true beliefs on the usual input-output function. On this understanding of the matter a track record under normal conditions will be strong evidence for a favorable reliability claim, but more indirect evidence can be used where conditions have been abnormal or where there has been little or no actual use of the mechanism.

I have already noted that Reid took the most fundamental epistemological question to be: Are we justified in trusting our basic sources of belief, that is, in taking them to be reliable? I concur in that judgment. Many contemporary epistemologists would agree that the reliability of belief-forming mechanisms is of central importance epistemologically, and many others will disagree. Let me indicate briefly what I take to be the epistemological importance of the problem of this paper: whether claims to reliability can be justified.

First of all, I take it as obvious that the issue is of intrinsic importance, whatever the relation of reliability to other matters. We certainly do ordinarily suppose perception, introspection, and so on, to be reliable sources of information; and so we will naturally be led to wonder, on reflection, whether we are justified in so supposing, and if so how. But depending on one's general epistemological stance, the question will take on additional importance. If one thinks that reliability is what converts true belief into knowledge, then the question of how we can determine that perception is reliable will be a crucial part of the question of how we can determine that we have perceptual knowledge.[2] There may also be important connections with justification. Those who identify justification and reliability,[3] and those who take the latter as the basic criterion of the former,[4] will suppose that the question of whether sense perception is a reliable source of beliefs about the immediate environment *is* just the question of whether perceptual beliefs are justified. Elsewhere[5] I have argued that the most adequate concept of epistemic justification is one that will put a reliability *constraint* on prin-

[2]See D. M. Armstrong, *Belief, Truth, and Knowledge* (Cambridge: Cambridge University Press, 1973), chaps. 12–15; Fred I. Dretske, *Knowledge and the Flow of Information* (Cambridge: MIT Press, 1981), esp. chap. 4; Robert Nozick, *Philosophical Explanations* (Cambridge: Harvard University Press, 1981), pt. 3.

[3]See Marshall Swain, *Reasons and Knowledge* (Ithaca: Cornell University Press, 1981), chap. 4.

[4]A. I. Goldman, "What Is Justified Belief?", in G. S. Pappas, ed., *Justification and Knowledge* (Dordrecht: D. Reidel, 1979).

[5]Essays 4 and 9.

ciples of justification, even though not all conceivable reliable modes of belief formation will yield justification. By a "reliability constraint" I mean something like this. Take a principle of justification of the form:

If a belief of type B is based on a ground of type G, then the belief is justified.

This principle is acceptable only if forming a B on the basis of a G is a reliable mode of belief formation. On this view, a reliability claim is imbedded in every claim to justification; and so what it takes to justify a reliability claim will be at least part of what it takes to justify a justification claim.

On the other hand, there are theorists who use concepts of justification that are not held subject to a reliability constraint. I think particularly of "deontological" concepts, according to which one is justified in believing that *p iff* one is not subject to reproach in doing so, one has not violated any intellectual obligations in doing so.[6] Using a concept like that, it would seem quite possible that I might be conducting my cognitive activities as well as could be expected of me, doing my best by my lights, even though I am not forming beliefs in a way that is in fact reliable. Just think of a persistent situation in which conditions of observation are quite abnormal, but where I have no way of knowing this.

To summarize. The question of how, if at all, we can be justified in supposing that a common source of belief is a reliable one is, of course, a question of great intrinsic interest. And, depending on one's further epistemological commitments, it may be a large part of the question of how we can be justified in supposing that we know this or that, or that we are justified in believing this or that.

For the sake of concreteness I shall focus much of the discussion on the reliability of sense perception, understood in terms of (I). We may abbreviate (I) as:

(II) Sense experience is a reliable source of perceptual beliefs.

When I speak in unspecific terms of the reliability of sense perception, or of sense experience as a reliable source of belief, that is to be understood in the way spelled out in (I).

What does it take to be justified in accepting (I)? It seems very plausible to hold that one rationally accepts (I) only if one has adequate reasons for that thesis, either in the form of a favorable track record or

[6]See Essays 4 and 5.

in the form of more indirect evidence, for example, evolutionary or theological considerations to the effect that we would not be here with these belief-forming mechanisms unless they mostly gave us true beliefs. What alternatives are there to justification by adequate reasons? Even if we are justified in accepting propositions that seem self-evident to us, that would not seem to apply here. Any tendency to suppose (I) to be self-evident can be put down to a confusion between self-evidence and being strongly inclined to accept the proposition without question. It does not seem at all plausible to take it to be the sort of proposition that one cannot believe without its being true, or justified. Moreover, whereas propositions about one's own current conscious states, for example, are plausibly regarded as "self-warranted", (I) is not plausibly so taken. Nor does it appear to enjoy any of the other forms of "direct" justification. Thus I shall take it without more ado that we are justified in accepting (I) only if we have adequate *reasons* for supposing (I) to be correct. What are the prospects of acquiring such reasons, for (I) and for analogous principles concerning other common sources of belief?

The rest of this essay will be devoted to considering what I take to be the chief source of pessimism concerning these prospects. This is a certain kind of circularity, "epistemic circularity", into which we frequently fall when we set out to adduce reasons for the reliability of a belief source. I shall first illustrate and describe this mode of circularity. Then I shall consider its extent and the deleterious effects it does and does not have on the epistemic status of reliability claims and, more generally, on the epistemic status of our beliefs generally.

II

The simplest way of supporting a reliability thesis like (I) is to point to a record of success. Many beliefs have been formed in accordance with the principle, and they have mostly been correct. But how do we tell that this is the case? You form the perceptual belief that there is a goldfinch just outside the kitchen window, basing your belief on your sense experience in the usual way; and the situation is quite normal. Your belief is correct. But how do I tell that your belief is correct?[7] The most obvious way is to take a look myself to see whether there really is a goldfinch there. But then I am relying on the reliability of sense percep-

[7]There is also the question of how I tell whether your belief was based on sense experience in the usual way, and how I tell that the situation was of the sort we typically find ourselves in. But we will find problems enough with the initial question, and the further questions would simply give rise to more difficulties of the same sort.

tion in order to amass my evidence. In supposing that I have ascertained in each case that the perceptual belief under examination is correct, I have assumed that my sense experience is yielding true beliefs. Thus I am assuming (I) in adducing evidence for it, and so it would appear that my argument is circular.[8] Of course I could determine the accuracy of your report without taking a look myself. For one thing, I could get someone else to take a look; but that hardly changes the logic of the situation. More relevantly, I could have arranged to have a continuous photographic record of the scene outside the window. But even in this case I, or someone, must look at the photographs to determine what they show. Or if we have the photograph read by still another instrument, and the output of the instrument recorded by still another. . . , at some point someone must use his or her senses to determine the reading of some instrument. No matter how much sophisticated technology we employ, we must rely on someone's sense perception at one or more points. Any track record argument that depends on ascertaining the truth value of particular perceptual beliefs will involve a reliance on sense perception to obtain some of its premises.

This would not be the case if we had some way of finding out about the physical environment that did not essentially involve the use of sense perception, but it seems that we do not and cannot. Consider something much more roundabout that the use of cameras. Suppose that we had a science of ecology comparable to the Newtonian mechanics of the solar system that enabled astronomers to determine the existence and location of Neptune without having seen it. We might then be in a position to infer that there must have been a goldfinch just outside my kitchen window at that time. But this will not alleviate the circularity. We are still assuming the reliability of sense perception at two points. First, we rely on observed facts as evidence in developing our super-ecology. Second, the inference to the goldfinch in that spot at that time must make use of particular facts about the environment as well as general ecological principles. And in the ascertainment of those facts sense perception must have played a role at some stage(s).

[8]To be sure, (I) is only one of many ways of spelling out the idea that sense experience is a reliable source of belief. Other formulations might be in terms of probability rather than in terms of a lawlike tendency, or they may restrict the relevant class of situations in some other fashion. And I might protest that in trusting my senses I am assuming one of these other formulations rather than (I). Thus a more precise statement of the circularity claim would be that in putting forward the evidence one is assuming some member of a family of theses, each of which constitutes a particular version of the view that sense experience is a reliable source of beliefs about the physical environment. For purposes of exposition I shall take (I) as paradigmatic of this family of theses and speak, loosely, of one's assuming (I), whenever one supposes oneself to have acquired accurate information about the physical environment through sense experience.

So far we have just been considering the most direct way of arguing for the reliability of sense perception, viz., the comparison of its deliverances, one by one, with the facts. But there are more indirect strategies. "Pragmatic" arguments have been popular. It has been pointed out that reliance on sense perception enables us (1) to successfully predict and thereby (2) to exercise considerable control over the course of events. Furthermore (3) when several independent investigators use sense perception to explore the physical environment, they generally come up with the same answer. It has been felt that these facts testify to the reliability of sense perception. For if its deliverances were not accurate, why should the general principles supported by those deliverances give us a basis for successful prediction and control? And if perceptual beliefs were not under the effective control of the facts, why should these beliefs agree to the extent they do? In short, the practice of forming beliefs about the immediate physical environment on the basis of sensory experience *works*. It is a *successful* practice and not just successful in some irrelevant respect; it is cognitively successful. It makes a powerful contribution to the attainment of intellectual goals. And is this not an indication that it is a reliable source?

Well, yes; except for the recurrence of circularity. How do we know that predictions formed on the basis of observationally based principles are often correct? By looking to see whether things came out as predicted, or by using instruments to determine this, which in turn. . . . How do we know that different observers generally agree on what is before them? By listening to what they say. Once more we have to rely on sense perception to gather the data that are being used in the argument for its reliability.

We find less obvious forms of the same circularity in other lines of argument. Consider, for example, the Wittgensteinian argument that if sense perception were not reliable, we would not have a common public language, which, for Wittgenstein, implies that we would not have any language at all.[9] In that case we would not be able to raise the question of the reliability of sense perception. Thus if we can raise the question, the only possible answer is that sense experience is a reliable source. But, apart from other difficulties with this line of argument, there is the question as to why we should suppose that unless sense perception were reliable we would not have a common language. We certainly cannot establish this thesis just by sitting at our desks and thinking about the matter. For all we can tell by this method, we might

[9]My primary source for this particular argument is some unpublished writings of, and conversation with, Peter van Inwagen.

be born with a common language and not have to acquire it at all. It is only by relying on what we have learned about human beings and the world in which they live, through sense perception and reasoning based on that, that we have reason to suppose that this is the only way we could acquire a common language. And so once more the argument is vitiated by circularity.

These considerations strongly suggest that it is impossible to present an (otherwise) effective argument for the reliability of sense perception without assuming that reliability in asserting the premises. I certainly have not established this. I have not considered all the lines of argument that have been used, much less all possible lines of argument. For all I have shown, some argument that uses only a priori premises, like that of Descartes in the *Meditations,* might be successful. But it is no part of my purpose here to *show* that sense perception, or any other source of belief, cannot receive a noncircular proof of reliability. One aim has been to use some familiar arguments for the reliability of sense perception to illustrate the kind of circularity with which I am concerned. Another aim has been to suggest the strong possibility that the reliability of sense perception cannot be established in a noncircular fashion, in order to introduce the concept of a source of belief for which this is true. Let us call such a source "basic", defining the term as follows:

(III) O is an (epistemologically) basic source of belief = $_{df}$ Any (otherwise) cogent argument for the reliability of O will use premises drawn from O.

It is plausible to take not only sense perception but also memory, introspection, and deductive and inductive reasoning as basic sources. The reasons for these judgments are familiar in the literature, though they are widely dispersed in discussions of one or another source.

III

Before proceeding to investigate the extent and consequences of the kind of circularity just illustrated, we will need to characterize it and distinguish it from its kindred. First of all, the concept of circularity that is involved here applies primarily to arguments. The most general notion could be stated this way. An argument is circular when the conclusion is being assumed in the attempt to prove the conclusion. The simplest and most crippling form of circularity is that in which the conclusion actually figures among the premises. In setting forth the premises we are, in effect, already claiming to know the conclusion. While this will not render the argument invalid (what can be more obviously valid than 'p, therefore p'?), it will vitiate the argument as a way of establishing the conclusion. If we were entitled to assert that p before going through the argument, the whole procedure is pointless as a way of showing that p. Any proposition can be logically deduced if it itself is included in the premises. Let us call this simplest form of circularity "logical circularity".

This is *not* what is involved in the attempt to establish the reliability of basic sources. Suppose I give a simple inductive argument for the reliability of sense perception. I lay out a large, carefully chosen sample of perceptual beliefs and report in each case that the belief is true. Thus the argument looks like this.

(IV) 1. At t_1, S_1 formed the perceptual belief that p_1, and p_1.
      2. At t_2, S_2 formed the perceptual belief that p_2, and p_2.

. . . . . .

Therefore, sense experience is a reliable source of belief.

Let us say it turns out that 97 percent of the perceptual beliefs were true. The conclusion "Sense experience is a reliable source of belief" does not appear anywhere in the premises, which consist solely of reports of perceptual beliefs and reports of perceived states of affairs. Then in what way is the argument circular? We can get at this by bringing out several ways in which it is unsatisfactory.

(1) If I were to ask myself why I should suppose that my premises are true, or why I should consider myself entitled to assert them, I would have to reply that it is because of the reliability of sense perception. It is only by taking sense perception to be reliable that I can regard it as reasonable to believe that there is a tree in front of me when there visually appears to me to be a tree in front of me. In reposing confidence in the practice of forming beliefs on the basis of sense perception in the ordinary way, I am presupposing the truth of (I). That is not to say that I use (I) as a premise to arrive at a perceptual belief as a conclusion each time I form such a belief. I may never have performed such an inference. Indeed I may never have formulated (I), or (II), even in thought. I may just unself-consciously form perceptual beliefs in a way that accords with (I). Therefore in putting forward an argument like (IV), I need not be explicitly presupposing (I). What this paragraph reveals is rather that when I form perceptual beliefs I "practically" assume something like (I), assume it "in practice". In confidently forming perceptual beliefs in accordance with (I), I proceed as if (I) is true. I manifest an acceptance of it in my practice.

(2) This is reflected in the dialectical point that if my premises were challenged I would have to appeal to the reliability of sense perception to answer the challenge, at least if it were pushed far enough. At the first stage I could simply point out that I had heard S_1 testify that he had formed the belief that p_1 on the basis of sense experience, and that I had seen that p_1 for myself. But if the challenger persists by asking why anyone should suppose *that* is any basis for that first premise, I would have to appeal to (I).

(3) An allied point is this. If one wholeheartedly denied or doubted (I), he could not, rationally, be convinced by the argument, if he kept his wits about him. Being disposed not to accept the reliability of sense perception, he would not accept the premises. Again, one need not have explicitly accepted (I) in order to be able, rationally, to accept or use this argument. But a person who truly rejects (I) does not accept it even practically, and hence cannot accept the premises.

What all this comes down to is that in using or taking this argument to establish (I), one is already, implicitly or explicitly, taking (I) to be true.[10] In this way we might say that the argument "presupposes" the truth of the conclusion, although the conclusion does not itself appear among the premises. Note that the necessity of this presupposition does not stem from the logical form of the argument, or from the meaning of the premises. It is not a syntactical or a semantic presupposition. It stems rather from our epistemic situation as human beings. Beings of another sort might have some nonsensory way of ascertaining these premises, but we do not.[11] Thus the presupposition falls into

[10]I have been supposing that when one takes oneself to know, or be justified in believing, something on the basis of sense experience, one is assuming the *general* reliability of sense experience as a source of knowledge. This may be contested. It may be suggested that when I take myself to possess perceptual knowledge that there is a typewriter in front of me, I need only be making some more restricted assumption, e.g., that *visual* sense experience is a reliable source of belief concerning the existence and position of *artefacts* (or, even more restrictedly, *typewriters*) in the vicinity. This must be conceded. If an opponent were to make this move, we should have to point out that an adequate inductive argument for (I) would have to cover the whole range of sense modalities and the whole range of perceivable objects, situations, and features thereof. Thus the complete argument would involve a conjunction of assumptions that would amount to the general assumption of the reliability of sense experience. To simplify the discussion I shall make the natural assumption that it is always the general assumption that is being made.

[11]I can imagine someone maintaining that this presupposition is necessitated by the very meaning of 'There is a tree in front of me'. But such a person would be taking on the very considerable burden of arguing that just by virtue of the meaning of this sentence, no epistemic subject could know, or be justified in believing, this otherwise than by sense perception. A position like this is taken by John Pollock in *Knowledge and Justification* (Princeton: Princeton University Press, 1974). There he holds that the meaning of (many) sentences is given by what he calls "justification conditions". See especially chap. 1.

the large basket called "pragmatic". More specifically, we might call it an "epistemic" presupposition, since it depends on our epistemic situation vis-à-vis singular propositions concerning middle-sized physical objects in one's immediate environment. In parallel fashion we might term the kind of circularity involved "epistemic circularity".

IV

Next I want to consider the bearing of epistemic circularity on the epistemic status of reliability claims. To focus the issue, let us assume sense experience to be a basic source of belief, one for which no otherwise cogent, non-epistemically circular argument for reliability can be given; and let us ask how this basicality affects the epistemic status of (I). Since we are assuming that *any* otherwise acceptable argument for (I) will be infected with epistemic circularity, we may as well work with the simplest argument that is otherwise cogent, viz., the track record argument, (IV). Given that this argument is epistemically circular, can it in any way render it reasonable or justifiable for us to accept (I)?

First, let us consider whether I could use an argument like (IV) to *justify* my belief that (I).[12] That, of course, depends on what it takes for S to justify his belief that p by an argument. So far as I can see, the requirements are as follows.

(A) S is justified in believing the premises, q.

If I validly derive a conclusion from premises I have no basis for accepting, how does that make it reasonable for me to believe the conclusion?

(B) q and p are logically related in such a way that if q is true, that is a good reason for supposing that p is at least likely to be true.

These support relations are studied by deductive and inductive logic, and I will say no more about them here.

(C) Many theorists also require that S know, or be justified in believing, that the logical relation between q and p is as specified in (B).

[12]If the reader is puzzled as to what might come second, under the rubric specified by the last sentence of the previous paragraph, the answer is: *being* justified in accepting (I) by the reasons specified in (IV), even though one has not engaged in the *activity of justifying* (I) by presenting the argument.

I do not accept this requirement,[13] but I will adopt it here for the sake of argument.

> (D) by virtue of S's inferring p from q, justification is conferred on S's belief that p.

We cannot absolutely require that as a result of the inference this belief comes to be justified for the first time, for there are overdetermination cases. But we are requiring that the inference is sufficient to produce justification, that if S's belief that p were not already justified, this argument would ensure that it is. Thus this requirement cannot be satisfied if the situation is such that the argument can do its work (the other requirements can be satisfied) only if S's belief that p is already justified. If the argument cannot produce any justification of the belief that p over and above what it already possesses, then that belief cannot be justified *by virtue of* its inferential relation to the belief that q.

If the epistemic circularity of (IV) interferes with the satisfaction of any of these requirements, it would seem to be (D), in the first instance.[14] For if I have to presuppose the conclusion, (II),[15] in order to be entitled to assert the premises, it would seem that I have to be justified in accepting (II) as a precondition of being justified in accepting the premises. But then the derivation of (II) from the premises could not confer justification on it. It will already have been justified for that subject, else that subject would not have been justified in accepting the premises and so would not have satisfied requirement (A). And if, as we are supposing, all arguments for (II) are infected with epistemic circularity, (II) cannot be justified at all. But then, by the above considerations, no perceptual belief can be justified, and so condition (A) cannot be satisfied either.

There is a way out of this quandary provided something like the following principle of justification for perceptual beliefs is acceptable.

---

[13]See Essay 6 and "Higher-Level Requirements," forthcoming.

[14](B) seems clearly unaffected. Surely the appropriateness of the inferential pattern is unaffected by the circularity. As for (C), there could be trouble only on the assumption that one's justification for supposing an inductive argument to be valid involved the use of perceptual premises. But in that case the difficulty would be the same as the one we are about to explore with (A) and (D).

[15]If the reader is puzzled by the flip-flop between (I) and (II), he should remember that (II) is simply a shortened form of (I) and that they are the same thesis, differently expressed. Since (IV) used (II) as the formulation of the conclusion, we shall often refer to (II) when discussing that argument.

(V) If one believes that p on the basis of its sensorily appearing to one that p, and one has no overriding reasons to the contrary, one is justified in believing that p.

According to (V), all that it takes to be justified in a perceptual belief about one's immediate environment is that the belief stem from one's sensory experience in a certain way, given the *absence* of sufficient overriding reasons. It is *not* required that one also be *justified* in accepting (V), or some correlated reliability principle like (II). Thus I do *not* already have to be justified in believing (II) in order to be justified in accepting the premises of the argument. Hence the epistemic circularity of (IV) poses no obstacle to my being justified in the perceptual premises of the argument. The circularity certainly does not prevent my having a treelike visual appearance and my basing my belief that *there is a tree in front of me* on this appearance. Moreover, since I do not have to be *justified* in believing (II) in order to be justified in the premises, it is not impossible that my belief that (II) should *acquire* justification from this argument. To be sure, we have seen that in coming to believe the premises on the basis of sense experience I am "practically" assuming (II). But that by no means implies that I am *justified* in making this presupposition. Hence as far as the epistemic circularity of (IV) is concerned, my belief in (II) might remain unjustified until I bring it into inferential connection with the premises of this argument. I conclude that, assuming the truth of (V), the epistemic circularity of (IV) does *not* prevent its being successfully used to justify one's belief that (II).[16]

Nor do we have to assume (V) in particular to secure this result. We get the same verdict on any principle that lays down sufficient conditions for the justification of perceptual beliefs that do not include the subject's being *justified* in the correlated reliability claim that perceptual beliefs formed under those conditions are or would be generally true. Most contemporary epistemological theories of perception adopt prin-

---

[16]For another presentation of this kind of position, with application to the Cartesian circle, see James van Cleve, "Foundationalism, Epistemic Principles, and the Cartesian Circle," *Philosophical Review*, 88, no. 1 (1979), 55–91. It must be remembered that we are not seeking to prove that (II) can be justified by (IV). To show that we would have to show that (V) is true and satisfied in many cases, and that reasonable principles of inductive inference are satisfied by (IV). We are only seeking to show that justification is not precluded by epistemic circularity, that if all other factors are favorable the epistemic circularity will not throw things off.

ciples that satisfy this negative condition,[17] though they differ among themselves in various ways.[18] To be sure, it has been argued by some that one can be justified in a perceptual belief only if one is justified in accepting the correlated reliability claim.[19] But there are fatal objections to the imposition of this additional requirement. Such a position escapes an infinite regress only at the price of arbitrariness. If the mere holding of condition C cannot justify one in believing that *p* unless one is also justified in accepting the general principle that beliefs like *p*, in conditions C, are generally true, would it not be sheerly arbitrary to refuse to take the same attitude to this new enriched condition, consisting of C and a justified acceptance of the reliability principle? Call this enriched condition, D. By the same reasoning, the mere holding of D cannot justify belief that *p* unless conjoined with justified belief in a new reliability principle linking D and the belief that *p*. Call this still more enriched set of conditions E. But by the same reasoning, E is not enough. . . . And so on ad infinitum. At some point we must rest content with the mere holding of a condition, and not also require that S be justified in believing *that* that condition confer reliability. But if at some point, why not at the outset?[20]

In arguing that S can justify his belief that (II) by a simple inductive argument that uses perceptual premises, we have been thinking of S as *merely* implicitly assuming (II) in the accepting of those premises. But what if S comes to realize that he is making this assumption? What if he becomes conscious that in supposing himself entitled to believe that there is a tree in front of him he is thereby assuming (II)? In this more sophisticated condition can he still use (IV) to justify his belief that (II)?

[17]See Roderick M. Chisholm, *Theory of Knowledge*, 2d ed. (Englewood Cliffs, N.J.: Prentice-Hall, 1977), chap. 4; Carl Ginet, *Knowledge, Perception, and Memory* (Dordrecht: D. Reidel, 1975), chap. 6; Pollock, *Knowledge and Justification*, chaps. 2, 3.

[18]For example, some drop the 'on the basis of' clause and merely require that the appropriate experience occur when the belief is formed. There are also different ways of specifying how the content of the experience has to be related to the content of the belief. And there are various conceptions of what it takes to override.

[19]For an explicit presentation of this kind of position see Laurence Bonjour, "Can Empirical Knowledge Have a Foundation?", *American Philosophical Quarterly*, 15, no. 1 (January 1978), esp. 5–7. I discuss Bonjour's argument, as well as a similar argument of Wilfrid Sellars' in Essay 3. Some rather similar positions are discussed in Essay 6.

[20]It may be objected that I am inconsistent in allowing on p. 329 that S cannot be justified by reasons R in believing that *p* without being justified in supposing that R adequately supports *p*, while rejecting out of hand the view that S cannot be justified by sensory experience in believing that *p* without being justified in believing that this is a reliable mode of belief formation. Indeed, I would be inconsistent, or incoherent, if I were to *affirm* the former and deny the latter. But, as I made explicit at the time, I deny the former as well. I was only pointing out that even if the former were granted, S could still justify (II) by inductive reasons.

Will he not realize that it is a meaningless charade to first assume a principle in order to get some premises, and then use those premises to justify the principle? And if, when thus enlightened, he realizes that the argument has no justificatory force, does that not show that the argument was deficient all along? How can an argument lose evidential force by its character being seen more clearly?

I think the answer will have to be that while S may lose confidence in the argument, the epistemic situation is unchanged. If (V) is true, and satisfied by the premises of (IV), then the fact remains that by inferring (II) from the premises of (IV) S *has* justified that belief, has provided adequate reasons for supposing it to be (at least probably) true, however shaky he may feel about it. The shakiness may inhibit him from carrying out the inference and therefore from reaping its epistemic rewards. But if he does carry through the reasoning, he will succeed in justifying his belief that (II), whatever his doubts about the operation. He may not believe that he has justified his belief that (II), and even if he holds that higher level belief he may not be justified in holding *it;* but it will be true all the same.

Does the epistemic circularity of (IV) prevent its being used to *show* or *establish* that (II)? That, of course, depends on what is required for showing or establishing. Insofar as the conditions for justifying one's belief that (II) are required for showing that (II), we have already taken care of that. What additional requirements are there? I will not try to determine exactly what is necessary for showing that *p* or establishing the fact that *p*. I shall simply list all the plausible requirements I can think of and consider whether any of them are knocked out by epistemic circularity.

(A) Both the premises and the conclusion of the argument are *true.*
(B) The subject knows the premises to be true.
(C) If *show* is an audience-relative concept, the audience must:
   (1) Accept the premises.
   (2) Be justified in accepting the premises.
   (3) Accept the premises without already having accepted the conclusion.

As for (C1), it is clear that the circularity will not prevent someone from accepting certain perceptual propositions; and we have already dealt with the problems posed by (C2). (C3) looks stickier, but it is a plausible requirement only if 'accept' is understood as 'explicitly accept'; and we have seen that epistemic circularity may involve only an implicit prior acceptance of the conclusion. As for (A), surely the defects of an argument can have no bearing on the possibility of the premises being true. And as for (B), since we have already shown that the epistemic circularity of (IV) does not interfere with one's being justified in accepting the premises, or with the truth of the premises, there would seem to be little ground for supposing it to interfere with any further conditions for knowledge, for example, one's belief being reliably formed or the absence of defeaters. I conclude, then, that the epistemic circularity of (IV) does not render it useless for showing or establishing that (II).

But then how does epistemic circularity reduce an argument's power? Why did it seem a crippling disability when first introduced? Was that just a misleading appearance? No, epistemic circularity really does render an argument useless for some purposes. As noted earlier, an epistemically circular argument cannot be used to rationally produce conviction. At least it cannot be used to rationally move a person from a condition of not accepting the conclusion *in any way*, to a condition of doing so. For if the person does not already, at least practically, accept the conclusion, he cannot be justified in accepting the premises. Note that this does not prevent (IV) from being used to rationally bring a person from the state of only practically accepting (II) to the state of explicitly accepting it.

These distinctions have interesting implications for the possibility of using (IV) against skepticism. (IV) cannot be used against a skeptic, if there be such, who totally doubts or denies (II), even practically. But epistemic circularity does not render the argument ineffective in the following situation. Suppose that, while continuing to rely on (II) in practice, I cannot see any adequate reasons for accepting it and am in a state of perplexity about whether I am rational in accepting it. (This is, of course, the situation of Descartes in the *Meditations*.) I can quite legitimately use (IV) to assure myself that I do have adequate reasons for supposing (II) to be correct. Or at least epistemic circularity has no tendency to show that this is not the case.

The fact that epistemic circularity renders an argument useless for producing conviction de novo is hardly of great moment epistemologically. So far we have not seen any way in which the *epistemic status* of a principle of reliability is seriously affected by the fact that it has to do with a basic source of belief. In Sections VI–VIII we will explore one arguably serious epistemic consequence of epistemic circularity.

We are interested not only in the prospects of an argument like (IV) being used to *justify* belief in (II), but also in the prospects of one's *being justified* in believing (II) by virtue of the reasons embodied in the premises of (IV). The distinction being invoked here is that between the *activity* of *justifying* a belief that *p* by producing some argument for *p*, and the *state* of *being justified* in believing that *p*. Of course one way to get into that state is to *justify* one's belief by an argument. We have already seen that this is possible with (IV). However, it is a truism in epistemology that one may be justified in believing that *p*, even on the basis of reasons, without having argued from those reasons to *p*, and thus without having engaged in the activity of justifying the belief. Since we do not often engage in such activities, we would have precious few justified beliefs if this were not the case. Indeed, we have exploited this possibility in claiming that one may *be justified* in accepting the premises of (IV) without having justified them by argument. If the latter were required, one would have to appeal to (II) as a premise, and the enterprise of justifying (II) would run into logical circularity. It even seems possible to be justified on the basis of reasons in believing that *p* without so much as being able to produce an argument from those reasons to *p*. It may be that the reasons are too complex, too subtle, or otherwise too deeply hidden (or the subject too inarticulate), for the subject to recover and wield those reasons. Consider beliefs based on perceptual cues one is unable to specify. The way my colleague looks, talks, and acts may give me adequate reasons for supposing that he is angry, and thus justify me in that belief, without my being able to articulate what those ways are, and hence without my being able to mount an adequate justifying argument.

Where no argument for (II) has been given, can the epistemic circularity of (IV) prevent S from being justified in believing (II) by virtue of having the reasons embodied in the premises of (IV)? A thorough discussion of the issue would require us to specify the conditions under which a set of reasons can render S justified in believing that *p*, where S has not argued from those reasons to *p*. And we have no time for that here.[21] However, we can see that, whatever the details of the conditions, the epistemic circularity of (IV) cannot prevent S's being justified by those reasons. For, just as with the argument, the crucial requirement for S's being justified by those reasons in accepting (II) is that justificatory status be transferred from the belief in the reasons to the belief in (II), that otherwise absent justification can be conferred on the belief in (II) by virtue of its appropriate relation (whatever that is) to the reasons. And, just as with the argument, the only way epistemic circularity can interfere with that is either by preventing S from being justified in the reasons or by preventing that justification from obtaining antecedently to the justification of the belief in (II). But in consider-

---

[21]One thorny issue we are bypassing is the interpretation of 'based on', in speaking of a belief's being *based on* certain reasons.

ing the argument we saw that the epistemic circularity of (IV) has neither of those effects. Therefore it cannot prevent those reasons from rendering S justified in accepting (II).

V

If what I have been saying is correct, we can justify (II), and be justified in accepting it, even if any otherwise cogent argument for it is infected with epistemic circularity. But what about knowing, or being justified in believing, that I have justified (II) or that I am justified in believing it? Does epistemic circularity rule out these higher level cognitive achievements? No, we get the same story on the higher level. To see this, let us consider the prospects for justifying the belief that one has justified one's belief that (II). If we can see that the epistemic circularity of (IV) does not throw that off, this result can be transferred to being justified in supposing that one is justified in believing (II), in the way indicated at the end of the preceding section.

In the light of the conditions we earlier suggested for S's justifying S's belief that *p*, the strongest, most explicit argument for S *has justified S's belief that (II) by presenting argument (IV)* would go something like this.

(VI) (A) S has presented (IV).
    (B) S is justified in believing the premises of (IV).
    (C) The premises of (IV) imply (deductively or inductively) the conclusion.
    (D) S is justified in believing C.
    (E) by virtue of S's deriving the conclusion of (IV) from the premises, the conclusion, (II), could thereby acquire previously unpossessed justification.
∴   (F) S has justified S's belief that (II).

Let us suppose that S has presented this argument. Does the epistemic circularity of (IV) imply that S has not justified his belief that (F)?

Now we saw that the lower level argument, (IV), could be used to justify (II), despite epistemic circularity, just because the justification of the premises only presupposed the practical acceptance of (II), not its justification. This left the premises of (IV) free to confer justification on (II). But that out may not be available to us here. If we adopt the previously mentioned "reliability constraint" on justification,[22] then I can be justified in supposing that my belief that *p* is justified by arising

[22]See Section 1 and Essays 4 and 5.

from source O in a certain way only if I am justified in supposing that O is a reliable source. But then I can be justified in the higher level belief that *I am justified in accepting the premises of (IV)* only if I base that supposition on justified beliefs about the reliability of perception. And this means that I can be justified in accepting (VI) (B) only if I am justified in accepting (II). Does this not commit us to supposing that S cannot be justified in believing (VI) (B) without antecedently being justified in believing the conclusion of the argument?

No. This argument too comes through unsullied even if there is a reliability constraint on justification. The reason is that just as premise (B), as well as the requirements for its justification, has moved up a level from the analogue in (IV), so has the conclusion. If the conclusion of (IV) were still (II), then it would indeed be the case that one could not be justified in accepting (B) without already being justified in accepting the conclusion. But the conclusion of (IV) is the higher level proposition "S has justified S's belief that (II)". It would be a level confusion to suppose that since S cannot be justified in accepting (B) without being justified in accepting (II), S cannot be justified in accepting (B), without being justified in accepting (F). Thus the epistemic circularity of (IV) poses no bar to S's being justified in supposing that he has justified (II) by the use of (IV).

What about *knowing* that one has justified (II)? Well, if knowledge requires justification, that will be the only requirement of knowledge that might fall victim to epistemic circularity. Surely the epistemic circularity of arguments for (II) cannot prevent (II) from being true, or from being believed; nor does it have any bearing on whether there are states of affairs that defeat a claim to know (II). And we have seen that epistemic circularity does not interfere with justification. Whereas if what converts true belief into knowledge is not justification but rather something like reliability, it seems clear that the circularity of an argument cannot prevent it from being the case that beliefs of a certain type are reliably formed under certain conditions.

An essential tool for drawing the fangs of epistemic circularity has been the distinction between *being justified* and *justifying*. It is because only the former is required for the premises of a justifying argument that one can use (IV) to justify (II). For if that required *justifying* those premises by argument, one would have to appeal to (II) to do so, and the original enterprise would run aground on logical circularity. And because of this same distinction one can *be justified* in accepting (II) without arguing for it at all. I conjecture that the neglect of this distinction is largely responsible for the widespread impression that epistemic circularity is more potent than is the case.

VI

The epistemically deleterious consequences of epistemic circularity are proving most elusive. This mode of circularity is a veritable Jekyll and Hyde. Whenever we are about to apprehend it in an act of destruction, it metamorphoses before our very eyes into a benign, law-abiding citizen. But surely it interferes with justification or knowledge in some way. Surely it does not leave us totally unimpaired in our capacity to reach our cognitive goals. Surely it is not just a matter of the forensic effectiveness of arguments.

Well, yes and no. Epistemic circularity does leave our capacities for justified belief and knowledge just where they were. We have seen that, with respect to any given belief, it does not render us less capable of justification or knowledge than we would be without it. And it is really true, so far as I can see, that it affects only the status of *arguments*. But it does not follow that the only significant consequences of the circularity have to do with the conditions under which I can mount an *effective* argument against someone else. There is one respect in which the basicality of a belief source does affect the epistemic status of the belief in the reliability of that source and, as we shall see, the epistemic status of many other beliefs as well.

To bring this out, let us consider once more someone, S, who is concerned with whether he is justified in believing (II). To settle the matter he seeks to show that his belief in (II) is based on adequate reasons; or else he seeks adequate reasons on which to base it. Since, as we are assuming, sense perception is a basic source, some of these reasons will be perceptual beliefs, in accepting which S is relying on (II). Since we will run into epistemic circularity whatever the otherwise adequate reasons, we may as well continue to work with the simplest kind of argument for (II), viz. (IV). Thus S's argument for supposing that:

(VII) S is justified in believing that (II)

will run something like this.

(VIII) (A) S's belief that (II) is based on a number of pieces of inductive evidence of the form, 'At t A formed the perceptual belief that p and p'.
  (B) This evidence constitutes adequate support for (II).
  (C) S is justified in accepting each of the pieces of evidence.
  (D) S is justified in accepting (B).
  (E) S is justified in accepting (II).

It may be that this argument suffers from epistemic circularity in a way similar to its lower level analogue, (IV). But if so, there will be analogous reasons for denying that this renders it unfit for being used to justify or establish its conclusion. In any event, that is not my present concern. I am interested now in the way the story continues. S is in too reflective and critical a mood to rest content with the mere possibility that (VIII) has shown that he is justified in accepting (VII), or with the negative point that epistemic circularity does not preclude this. He wants to determine whether the argument *has* shown this. An essential component of that will be determining whether the premises of this argument are true. Let us focus on premise (C), since this is where epistemic circularity is most germane. Consider a particular premise of the sort referred to in (C).

(IX) At t_1 A formed the perceptual belief that there was a tree in front of him, and at t_1 there was a tree in front of him.

Let us further focus on the second conjunct:

(X) At t_1 there was a tree in front of A.

Let us make the simplifying assumption that S has checked out all the perceptual premises of (IV) himself, so that his belief in (X) is a perceptual belief. Now let us go back to S's attempt to determine whether he is justified in believing that (X), an attempt to which he was driven in trying to do an ideally thorough job of determining whether he is justified in accepting (II). How can he show that he is justified in accepting (X)? It seems overwhelmingly plausible to suppose that I can only show that a particular belief is justified by showing that it satisfies a sufficient condition for justification.[23] This means that my argument will have to contain a general principle of justification as one premise, and a claim that this belief satisfies the requirements laid down in that principle, as the other premise. Let us suppose that the principle S picks for this purpose is (V). Then the argument he uses to show that he is justified in believing (X) will go as follows.

(XI) (A) If one believes that p on the basis of its sensorily appearing to one that p, and one has no overriding reasons to the contrary, one is justified in believing that p.

[23]To be sure, (VIII) does not cite a principle of justification and seek to show that S's belief that (II) satisfies it. The principle was merely implicit in the argument as stated. If I had made it explicit, that would not have affected my present line of argument, which is based on other features of (VIII).

    (B) S believes that (X) on the basis of its sensorily appearing to him
    that (X), and S has no overriding reasons to the contrary.

∴   (C) S is justified in believing that (X).

This argument would appear to be in good order. If S is justified in accepting its premises, he can use it to show that he is justified in believing (X). But, still driven by the thirst for reflective assurance, S is not content with this conditional. He wants to know whether he is justified in accepting those premises. Just as at earlier stages, S cannot shirk the challenge of looking into this. Let us focus on his attempt to show that he is justified in accepting (XI) (A)—that is, (V)—the principle of the justification of perceptual beliefs. What does it take to be justified in accepting a principle that lays down sufficient conditions for the justification of beliefs of a certain kind? Recall once more the "reliability constraint" on justification. This is the assumption that the satisfaction of conditions C can suffice to justify beliefs of type B, only if Bs are reliably formed when C holds, and that this latter, reliability claim is part of what is asserted when one asserts the former, justification claim. As indicated earlier, I argue for this assumption in Essay 4, but it is controversial. However, I am going to conduct the rest of this discussion on that assumption. This will enable me to show that when S attempts to carry his enterprise beyond the present point, it will soon bog down in logical circularity. If my reliability constraint is unjustified, it will only follow that epistemic circularity is even more benign than I am claiming, by no means an unwelcome result.

Assuming, then, the reliability constraint, (V) can be true only if beliefs that arise from sense experience in that way are, or would be, generally true. That is, (V) can be true only if sense experience is a reliable source of belief.[24] Indeed, (II) is part of what is asserted by (V). But then one is justified in believing (V) only if one is justified in believing (II). And so any argument that is designed to show that S is justified in believing (V) will have to include as a premise the proposition that S is justified in believing (II). But that is precisely what S set out to establish.

Thus when the attempt to show that one is justified in supposing a basic belief source to be reliable is pressed in the way S has been doing,

[24]Of course (II) is much less explicit than (V) as to how beliefs must arise from sense experience if they are to be justified or reliably formed. But remember that (II) is to be taken as an abbreviation of (I); and (I), though still much less explicit than (V), does restrict the class of beliefs in question to those that are based on sense experience *in the way such beliefs generally are*. I am taking it that (V) makes that usual way explicit; and so I take it that (I) and (II) is precisely the assumption that beliefs that satisfy (V) are reliably formed.

the attempt will founder on *logical* circularity. At some point back along the way, and not so very far back at that, one will be appealing to the very reliability thesis one is seeking to justify. So this extended argument for the reliability of the source goes, in part, like this.

(XII)　(A)　J(Reliability of source).
∴　　　(B)　J(Principle of justification of beliefs from that source).
∴　　　(C)　J(Beliefs from that source).
∴　　　(D)　J(Reliability of that source).

(The 'J' operator indicates that what we are concerned with in each case is the proposition that the subject is justified in accepting the proposition in parentheses.) So long as we keep pushing the problem back in this way, the attempt to show that one is justified in the reliability claim will inevitably run into logical circularity; and this for the very same reason that made arguments like (IV) epistemically circular, viz., the fact that any adequate reasons for the reliability claim will include beliefs from that very source. And whatever may be the case with epistemic circularity, logical circularity obviously renders an argument useless for showing, establishing, or justifying its conclusion. It is clearly impossible that justification should be conferred de novo on the conclusion by virtue of its being inferred from justified premises, when the conclusion is one of the premises. The conclusion is justified just by *being* one of the premises; bringing it into an inferential relation with the premises comes too late.

We run into this logical circularity "so long as we keep pushing things back the way S is doing". But why should we insist on pushing things back in this way? What importance, if any, does it have? As a preliminary to considering these questions, let us get a clearer idea of the character of S's procedure.

S was taking what we might call the attitude of "critical reflection" toward his beliefs. He was seeking what we might call "full reflective assurance" with respect to his beliefs. The belief under initial scrutiny was (II). S produced argument (VIII) to show that it was rational for him to accept (II). But, of course, he made use of various other beliefs to show this; and what about them? If they have not already been shown to be justified, why should they be exempted from the demand for rational credentials? What sort of critical reflection would this be if one were to make a fuss over the status of (II), while accepting uncritically the premises of (VIII)? If we are to accept those premises without showing ourselves to be rational in doing so, why did we boggle at (II)? Once the enterprise of critical reflection has been launched, its momentum carries it forward as long as new beliefs come into the picture. For every premise that is adduced in the attempt to show any given belief to be justified, there is a question as to *its* epistemic credentials, and it would be arbitrary to cut this off at any particular point.

Thus in seeking "full reflective assurance" with respect to his belief that (II), S has committed himself to seeking the same for any belief employed in showing (II) to be justified, any belief employed in showing any of those beliefs to be justified, ...[25] Let us say that when this enterprise has been completed, the belief with which we started has been "fully reflectively justified" (FRJ).[26] When a belief has been FRJ, no questions are left over as to whether the subject is justified in accepting some premise that is used at some stage of the justification. Clearly, every premise that is used in a procedure of fully rationally justifying a belief will, when that procedure is completely followed out, itself be FRJ.

Let us recur to the point that it is by appreciating the distinction between *justifying* and *being justified* that we can see the (relative) innocuousness of epistemic circularity. We have finally found some negative consequences thereof, but *only by washing out that distinction*. The quest of FRJ is undertaken just when we ignore, or lose interest in, merely being justified. To demand FRJ is to demand that any premise we use in justifying a belief itself be justified by argument. Hence it is not at all surprising that an enterprise that depends on ignoring our basic distinction should be scuttled by epistemic circularity.

So far we have seen that beliefs in the reliability of a basic source are not susceptible of FRJ. This disability attaches as well to all the beliefs that stem from such a source. For to show that it is rational to accept such beliefs one would have to appeal to the reliability of the source. And since a given belief can be FRJ only if any premise used to show it to be justified can itself be FRJ, the unavailability of FRJ for the reliability claim extends to the particular beliefs that depend for their justification on that reliability. Moreover since a principle of justification like (V) can be justified only if the corresponding principle of reliability, (II), is also, the latter will have to be appealed to in any attempt to show that the principle of justification is justified. And so the unavailability of FRJ for (II) will extend to (V) as well. Where basic sources are

---

[25]Obviously an infinite regress looms. We shall turn our attention to that side of the matter in the next section. For now we are exploring the way in which epistemic circularity queers things far short of infinity.

[26]Here 'justified' is used in the *upshot of a successful activity of justifying* sense, rather than in the *in a desirable position vis-à-vis the belief* sense. That is, 'B is justified' means here that someone has *succeeded in justifying* it, rather than that someone *is justified in believing* it.

concerned, it will be in principle impossible to attain full reflective assurance with respect either to the principles of justification or reliability, or to the particular beliefs that fall under those principles. So the consequences of basicality for FRJ are not insignificant.

Thus the situation with respect to basic sources of belief is this. So far as epistemic circularity is concerned, I can justify, and *be* justified in, taking the source to be reliable and to be a source of justification. But as soon as I direct a critical scrutiny on this happy state of affairs, it disappears before my eyes; it eludes my reflective grasp. When I try to be fully critical about my justification, I very soon run into logical circularity. I can justify, or be justified in, accepting either particular perceptual propositions or a general principle of perceptual justification or reliability, only by practically accepting that principle of reliability. But in the enterprise of seeking to answer critical questions whenever they arise, one is driven to convert that practical acceptance into theoretical justification. And that is where we run into logical circularity. All is well so long as we rely on justification that obtains in fact and do not insist on demonstrating it. But as soon as we look back with a critical eye, we meet the fate of Orpheus.

VII

Thus far the consequences of epistemic circularity for FRJ have been restricted to basic sources of belief. How extensive is that domain? We have not provided a conclusive answer to this question. I have indicated the plausibility of supposing that sense perception and various other sources are basic, but I have not established this. I have not even shown that there are any basic sources. It *may* be that for any reliable source of belief a cogent argument for its reliability could be constructed that would exclusively use premises obtained from other sources. What I want to do now is to explore the prospects for fully reflective justification without assuming either that there are or that there are not basic sources of belief.

Let us consider a randomly selected principle of reliability, Q_1. Q_1 states that beliefs of type P are justified when based on source R_1. Now R_1 is a basic source or it is not. If it is, the previous argument has shown that because of epistemic circularity, we cannot attain a fully reflective justification of Q_1. If it is not, then to attain an FRJ of Q_1 we must be FRJ in accepting the reliability of the other sources(s) of the reasons we have for accepting Q_1. For simplicity, let us suppose that there is only one such source, R_2, and that the principle of reliability making reference to it is Q_2. Now R_2 is either a basic source or not. If it is, then the project grinds to a halt at this point. If not, then if Q_2 is justified, there is another source for the reasons that provide this justification. This other source is either R_1 or some other. If the former, then the enterprise bogs down by reason of a slightly larger epistemic circle. If some other, then the same question arises with respect to the principle of reliability for beliefs that stem from that source. It is clear that either this quest for FRJ generates an infinite regress and cannot succeed for that reason, or at some point it is vitiated by circularity, either because we encounter a basic source or because our reasons for a given source are obtained from a source we were relying on at an earlier stage. Whichever of these possibilities is realized, we get the same conclusion that FRJ of any principle of reliability is impossible, and hence that FRJ of any belief is impossible.[27]

Let me say a little more about the infinite regress horn of the argument. First, since this regress concerns an actual process of demonstration, it is more unquestionably vicious than the infinite regress of justification invoked in the standard argument for foundationalism. It is not obvious that we are incapable of an infinitely complex structure of

---

[27]This argument, with its alternatives of circularity and infinite regress, is very similar to the standard argument for foundationalism. Those who are disenchanted with that position may seize on this as an indication that my argument has force only if one has antecedently made a commitment to foundationalism. But this would be a mistake. So far as I can see, the argument is neutral between foundationalism and coherentism, and holds on any view that allows for principles that lay down sufficient conditions of epistemic justification. Consider how the quest for FRJ would look from a coherentist perspective. There are, of course, various forms of coherentism. On one extreme version the one and only principle of justification is that a belief is justified *iff* it is a member of a coherent system of beliefs. Here the relevant reliability principle is that a member of a coherent system of beliefs is thereby likely to be true. To justify this principle we would have to show *it* to be a member of a coherent system, since, according to the theory, that is the only thing relevant to justification. But then, by the line of argument we have been using, in order to fully reflectively justify the principle we would have to show that what we are appealing to in attempting to justify it (membership in a coherent system) yields beliefs that are mostly true. But that is precisely what we set out to justify. And so once more the quest for FRJ bogs down in logical circularity.

On a more moderate form of coherentism one would allow secondary principles of justification in terms of sources of belief, of the sort we have been considering, but one would regard any such principle as valid only if it passes the basic coherence test of being a member of a coherent system of beliefs. When we seek FRJ of one of these lower level principles of justification, we will seek to show that it is a member of a coherent system. But then in seeking to show that one is justified in accepting this higher level principle of justification, in terms of a coherent system, we will be led into the circularity described in the previous paragraph.

There are many other forms of coherence theory that put various additional restrictions on the system in question and that differ in other ways. I cannot go into all that in this essay. Let me just say that I cannot see that these variations help us to avoid the above conclusion.

mediate justification, for it may be possible for a human being to have an infinite number of beliefs. But it does seem quite obvious that one cannot carry out a demonstration that involves an infinite number of steps. And this is what it would take to actualize *this* infinite regress. Second, I do not think that this infinite regress horn need be taken seriously. For it seems clear that there is not an infinite variety of sources of human belief, at least on any natural way of dividing such sources into types. Therefore, what would actually happen in any such regress is that either we will run into a basic source of belief or we will come back to sources that had already made an appearance; thus we will encounter circularity fairly quickly.

Even if one accepts the foregoing, one may doubt that it throws any new light on the prospects for FRJ. For, it may be said, if we countenance infinite regress arguments, there is a much simpler way of establishing the impossibility of FRJ, a way that makes no appeal to epistemic circularity. Start with any belief and give reasons for supposing it to be justified. The original belief is not justified until we have shown the beliefs in those reasons to be justified. And, in turn, we must show the reasons involved in this second showing to be justified. It seems clear that this process must either go on infinitely or bog down in circularity. So what new light does a consideration of epistemic circularity throw on the matter?

I agree that the above argument demonstrates the impossibility of FRJ for any belief. But I still feel that a consideration of epistemic circularity adds to our understanding of the matter. More specifically, it shows that an attempt at FRJ runs into logical circularity rather quickly, so that, as pointed out above, the infinite regress horn of the dilemma can, in practice, be ignored. The very general, abstract infinite regress argument of the last paragraph may leave us feeling that we can keep up the regress indefinitely; so long as there is never a day of reckoning we are in no way a loser. This may be an irrational reaction, but to show the justificatory inefficacy of an infinite regress has proved to be a singularly difficult task. The argument of this section shows, or at least makes it plausible, that in the quest for FRJ we run into logical circularity fairly quickly. If we begin with a basic source, or outputs thereof, we encounter logical circularity in a few steps. If we begin with a nonbasic source, it is reasonable to suppose our epistemic situation to be such that we will be thrown back on a basic source fairly quickly.

But even if the epistemic circularity argument added nothing to the more general infinite regress argument, as far as demonstrating the impossibility of FRJ is concerned, the main point of this section would remain. That point is that the impossibility of FRJ is the only significant implication epistemic circularity has for the epistemic status of principles of reliability and of our beliefs generally.

VIII

Thus no epistemic principle can be FRJ, and hence no belief can be FRJ.[28] How shocking a result is this? Into what depths of despair would it be appropriate to fall? Does it leave us a prey to the ravages of skepticism?

To start with the last question, our result certainly does not support any of the most dreaded forms of skepticism. Not only does it not imply that we cannot know or be justified in believing *anything*. It places no limits whatsoever on what we can know or be justified in believing. Any skeptic emboldened by the absence of FRJ would be but a paper skeptic. It is true that some classical skeptical arguments have appealed to the impossibility of establishing, in a noncircular fashion, all the epistemic principles presupposed in a putative case of justification by reasons.[29] But, as we have pointed out, this establishes the nonexistence of justification or knowledge only if we make the gratuitous assumption that justification by reasons requires the *justification* of the epistemic principles presupposed.[30]

Nevertheless I think that this result has fatal implications for certain traditional philosophical aspirations. Philosophers are wont to inculcate the ideals of "critical reflection", of converting the implicit into the explicit, of letting nothing pass without critical examination, of subjecting all our beliefs, assumptions, and presuppositions to critical scrutiny, determining which of them are based on adequate reasons and jettisoning the rest. "The unexamined principle is not worth accepting." When we engage in these lofty flights of rhetoric, these solemn exhortations, we are likely to treat all this as too self-evident to itself require scrutiny or critical examination. What I have shown in these last sections is that

[28]We have been conducting our discussion in this essay on the assumption, defended in Section III, that I can be justified in a belief about reliability only if I have adequate reasons for it. But this last argument for the impossibility of FRJ for any belief will go through without that assumption. Suppose that I can be immediately justified in accepting (II) because it is self-evident. Still the goal of FRJ requires me to show this, i.e., to show that it is self-evident and that this suffices for justification. In order to do this I will have to use premises that are either themselves self-evident or come from some other source. Whichever alternative is chosen, we will be launched on the argument just given and so impaled on the dilemma of infinite regress or circularity.

[29]See, e.g., Sextus Empiricus, *Outline of Pyrrhonism*, bk. 2, chap. 4.

[30]See Essay 6, Section III.

there are definite limits to the realization of these ideals. Not every-thing can be subjected to the test of critical examination, or else we shall be bereft of all belief. We can establish some conclusions only by assum-ing other propositions, not all of which can themselves be established. There is, perhaps, no particular assumption that cannot be disengaged and successfully argued for, but we cannot turn the trick with the whole lot all at once. We can make some justifications explicit only at the cost of leaving others implicit. We can *show* that some sources of belief are reliable only by dint of an implicit reliance on others. We can justify our theoretical acceptance of some principles only by exploiting our merely practical acceptance of others. Or, to give the point a more Wittgensteinian flavor, we can set out our reasons for certain particular beliefs only by engaging in "language games" (I prefer the term "dox-astic practices") our mastery of which must remain largely implicit. This may be a severe blow to philosophical pride, but by the same token it is a salutary lesson in intellectual humility.

Let us not overreact on the *significance* side of the ledger either. It is only the *total* explicit rationalization of belief that is ruled out. It is the finishing of the job *once and for all* that is beyond our powers. This does not imply that we cannot make fully explicit what justifies a particular belief. For any belief we are justified in holding it is possible, in princi-ple, to show that we are justified. At least nothing in this essay goes against that possibility. It is not that each individual piece of justified belief crumbles into dust once we scrutinize it, as my earlier Orpheus analogy might suggest. We can tie down any particular belief as se-curely as we like. It is just that we cannot also tie down the rope with which the former is tied down, and the rope with which that is tied down, and. . . . A closer Orpheus analogy would be one in which the legendary bard had an infinitely large harem that has been lost to Hades. And now the point is that although he can *have* the whole harem as his possession, he has lost his power to survey the whole lot in one glance. I must admit that this is a poor second to the original Orpheus legend in dramatic force, but it is a close analogue of our epistemic situation.

The last two paragraphs are reminiscent of the position known as "contextualism", classically expounded by C. S. Peirce and John Dew-ey. According to contextualism, all justification must take place in a context defined by the assumption of certain beliefs that are, in that context, fixed, not subject to question. These beliefs can be questioned in turn, but only in some other context that is defined by some other (temporarily) fixed assumption. For contextualism the attempt to justi-fy our belief system as a whole is quixotic. All justification is relative to some context. Contextualism meshes with the pragmatist insistence that the need for justification arises only when there is some special reason to question a belief. Those beliefs there is no special reason to question can serve as the context within which the questionable belief can be examined. The main difference between contextualism and the position of this essay is as follows. Contextualists, like many other epistemologists, concentrate on the activity of justifying to the neglect of the state of being justified. Hence they miss the point that one can *be justified* in believing that *p* (without having engaged in the activity of justifying that belief) absolutely, not just relative to some context. Since no activity of justifying has taken place, there is no question of identifying a context relative to which it has taken place. And hence they miss the point that even where one does justify a belief by argument, one may simply *be justified,* absolutely, in the premises of that argument, rather than simply assuming those premises for the purposes of that demonstration. This paper agrees with contextualism only in finding fully reflective justification to be impossible. From the present standpoint, contextualism has erred in taking this result to be the whole story about epistemology, just because it has been unaware of the other dimensions of justification we have distinguished.

IX

Since this paper has been dealing with the epistemic status of reliability claims, I should say a word about its bearing on reliability theories of knowledge or justification. Such theories have been taxed with making it impossible for us to determine when we have knowledge or justification. The strongest reasons for this charge have to do with what in this essay we have called epistemic circularity. If I have to know that sense perception is reliable in order to know that my perceptual beliefs are justified, and if I have to be justified in perceptual beliefs in order to gain that knowledge about reliability, then I am in a pretty pickle. In this essay resources have been provided for answering this charge. We have seen that, despite appearances, epistemic circularity will not prevent one's using what is learned from perception as a basis for knowledge or justified belief that perception is reliable. Hence a reliability theory of knowledge or justification does not make it impossible, at least for this reason, to know (be justified in believing) that we know (are justified in believing). Hence the effect of this essay on reliability theories is to remove one objection thereto.

X

Let us pull together the threads of this essay. We have been primarily concerned to explore the bearing of epistemic circularity on the epistemic status of claims to the reliability of sources of belief. We have seen that even where an argument for reliability involves epistemic circularity, as it does with basic sources, one may still justify, and *be justified* in, the reliability claim by virtue of basing it on the reasons embodied in the epistemically circular argument. On the other hand, assuming the "reliability constraint" on justification, epistemic circularity does prevent "fully reflective justification" of a reliability claim and, hence, of the corresponding principle of justification. Furthermore, when it is FRJ we are pursuing, we inevitably fall into logical circularity sooner or later, whatever source of belief we start with. This implies that no reliability principle can be fully reflectively justified; and since the FRJ of any belief requires the FRJ of one or more reliability principles, we arrive at the result that no belief whatever can be fully reflectively justified; FRJ is a pipe dream. But though this result runs counter to much philosophical ideology, it puts no limits whatever on the beliefs that can be justified, nor does it limit what can be known. Hence it lends no aid or comfort to any of the more familiar forms of skepticism. Though reflection on epistemic circularity serves as a check on overweening philosophical ambition, unsuited to our condition, it by no means reveals that condition to be a hopeless one. It leave us free to pursue knowledge and rationality with good cheer and lively hopes, albeit without a cosmic guarantee of success.[31]

[31]An earlier version of this essay was presented at the State University of New York at Albany. I am grateful for the comments provided by Kenneth Stern and the other participants in that discussion. I am especially grateful to Robert Audi, Jonathan Bennett, George Mavrodes, Alvin Plantinga, and Nicholas Wolterstorff for many helpful comments and suggestions.

Index

Index

Critical reflection, 71, 173, 226, 240, 341–47

Danto, Arthur, 28, 56
Defeaters, 61. *See also* Overriding
Deontological (normative) conception of epistemic justification, 3, 7, 74–77, 84–96, 115–52, 173–75, 199–209, 214–16, 224, 255–56, 312, 322; involuntaristic form of, 92–96, 174–75, 206–8; voluntaristic form of, 91–92, 173–74, 205–9, 116–36. *See also* Blame; Intellectual (cognitive, epistemic) obligations; Permission; Prohibition; Requirement; Violation of intellectual obligations
Descartes, René, 19, 35–36, 42, 119, 166–67, 251, 254, 257–58
Dewey, John, 51, 235
Dicker, Georges, 61
Direct apprehension, 303–4. *See also* Acquaintance; Presentation
Direct (immediate) awareness, 49, 61, 297, 301–5, 307; of conscious states, 304–5; explanation of, 302–4; of facts, 302; of particulars, 302; as source of immediate justification, 49, 61, 295, 301–2, 304–5. *See also* Acquaintance; Presentation
Direct recognizability, 213–20. *See also* Accessibility (form of internalism)
Dretske, Fred, 171–72, 181, 321

Epistemic beliefs, 24, 28–30, 37; immediate justification of, 24, 28–30; mediate justification of, 24, 222. *See also* Epistemic principles; Level confusions; Levels
Epistemic community, 299–300
Epistemic justification: autonomous, 294; concept of, 7–11, 81–153, 172–77, 200–202; development of concept of state of, 2, 236–37; distinction between state and activity of, 7, 27, 43–45, 47, 50, 55, 70–71, 73–74, 166, 182–83, 197–98, 235–36, 293, 329, 334–35, 337, 342, 348; evaluative conception of, 7, 97–113; fully reflective, 15, 342–46, 349; heteronomous, 294–95; higher level requirements for, 9–10, 24, 31, 112–13, 155–66, 180–81, 195–96, 202–3, 209–11, 220–22, 239–44, 312–13, 329–30, 332; immediate (direct), 3, 11–13, 20–32, 34–38, 42–43, 45–46, 48–55, 58, 68–70, 72–73, 101, 154, 158–63, 176, 189,

222, 292–95, 323; inferential, 22–25, 68–69, 162; mediate (indirect), 11, 20, 24, 37, 42, 58, 68–70, 73–76, 101, 154, 163–66, 189, 192–94, 198–99, 201–7, 211, 292–93; mixed, 60; nature of, 2–11, 305–6; as necessary condition of knowledge, 172–82; pretheoretic concept of, 2–6, 83–84; requirements for mediate, 163–66; requires proper source of belief, 10, 102–5, 117, 176–77, 229–30; "strong position" conception of, 7, 144, 175–76, 200, 224; truth conducivity of, 72–74, 111, 115, 144–47, 149–50, 201, 232, 242–44, 305. *See also* Deontological (normative) conception of epistemic justification; Ethical justification; Grounds (of belief); Reliability
Epistemic point of view, 3, 83, 85, 97–98, 101, 104–5, 111–12, 116. *See also* Cognitive goal
Epistemic principles, 299–300, 312–13, 343–44, 346; basis of, 48–51; evaluation of, 305–9, 322–23. *See also* Circularity: epistemic; Epistemology: epistemology of
Epistemization, 58–64, 66, 192; immediate, 59–64; mediate, 59, 62–64
Epistemology: epistemology of, 15; meta-, 2; nature of, 1; substantive, 2. *See also* Epistemic principles
Ethical justification, analogy with epistemic justification, 217
Evident, 155–60, 294; directly, 155–57, 159–60, 294
Ewing, A. C., 253–55, 257–58, 265
Externalism, 8, 108, 117, 143–50, 185, 224, 227, 243–44, 263. *See also* Internalism

Firth, Roderick, 24, 60, 64–65, 103
Foley, Richard, 103, 150, 196, 222–23, 244
Foundationalism, 11–14, 19–56, 60–61, 66, 218–19; argument for, 26–32, 53–56; definition of, 19–21, 41–43, 61; impure forms of, 13–14; iterative, 25, 28, 32–36, 50–51; minimal, 41–44, 46–53, 55–56; simple, 25, 28, 31, 33, 36–38. *See also* Epistemic justification: immediate; Knowledge: immediate
Foundations, 21, 48; extent of, 61–62

Gettier, Edmund, 4–5, 172, 260

Library of Congress Cataloging-in-Publication Data

Alston, William P.
    Epistemic justification : essays in the theory of knowledge / William P. Alston.
        p.   cm.
    Includes index.
    ISBN 0-8014-2257-4 (alk. paper). — ISBN 0-8014-9544-X (pbk. : alk. paper)
    1. Justification (Theory of knowledge) I. Title.
BD212.A47   1989   121—dc20   89-42865

Printed in the United States
133781LV00001B/240/P